"Here is the definitive book on John D. Spreckels, a titan who came [to San Diego] and ended up seeming to own or control everything in town. To read Sandra Bonura's biography of John D. Spreckels is to understand how many of the very foundations of America's finest city came to be."

—Ken Kramer, creator and host of *Ken Kramer's About San Diego* on KPBS-TV

"This book will not only guide you to a world of business and wealth but will tell you the fascinating story, private until now, behind John D. Spreckels's success."

—Uwe Spiekermann, author, historian, and expert on immigrant entrepreneurship

"A sweetly told story of not only an important figure in San Diego and California history but a fractious family that helped give America its sweet tooth."

—Roland De Wolk, award-winning investigative journalist and author

"Sandra Bonura breaks new ground exploring John Spreckels's escapades and incredible accomplishments across the Pacific. Bonura has a penchant for finding history's obscured truths and retelling them vividly and honestly. *Empire Builder*'s story does not disappoint."

—Edgy Lee, award-winning documentary film writer and director

"Bonura takes a deep and satisfying dive into the history of one of the leading families of the West's Gilded Age. The narrative is accompanied by fascinating narrative tangents."

—Leon Fink, distinguished author, historian, editor, and recognized expert on labor unions and immigration

"Through masterful research and clear writing, Sandra Bonura allows readers to more fully understand the motives and genius of J. D. Spreckels."

—Iris Engstrand, recognized authority on San Diego's history

"Bonura expertly conveys the passion and drive of a man who invested his fortune and energy in building San Diego, a sometimes herculean task that earned him praise but also the enmity of those who resented his dominance."

—Theodore "Andy" Strathman, coeditor of the *Journal of San Diego History*

"Although best remembered as a transportation magnate, John D. Spreckels led in almost every aspect of a developing Southwest region, including water and agriculture. This work is long overdue and should be a must-read for anyone with an interest in our history."

—Bruce Semelsberger, archivist and historian at the Pacific Southwest Railway Museum

D1501254

EMPIRE BUILDER

Claus Spreckels
7-9-1828   12-26-1908

Anna Christina Mangels
9-4-1830   2-15-1910

John Dietrich
8-16-1853   6-17-1926
Lillie Siebein
9-8-1855   1-8-1924

Adolph Bernard
1-5-1857   6-28-1924
Alma de Bretteville
3-24-1881   8-7-1968

Claus Agustus
12-18-1858   11-11-1946
Oroville Dore
12-29-1863   8-22-1933

Emma Claudine
1-23-1870   5-2-1924
Thomas Watson
John W. Ferris
Arthur Hutton

Rudolph
1-1-1872   10-4-1958
Eleanor Jolliffe
3-21-1868   2-22-1949

EMPIRE BUILDER

*John D. Spreckels and the
Making of San Diego*

SANDRA E. BONURA

Foreword by Uwe Spiekermann

University of Nebraska Press
LINCOLN

The University of Nebraska Press is part of a land-grant institution with campuses and programs on the past, present, and future homelands of the Pawnee, Ponca, Otoe-Missouria, Omaha, Dakota, Lakota, Kaw, Cheyenne, and Arapaho Peoples, as well as those of the relocated Ho-Chunk, Sac and Fox, and Iowa Peoples.

First Nebraska paperback printing: 2022

Library of Congress Cataloging-in-Publication Data
Names: Bonura, Sandra E., author. |
Spieckermann, Uwe, other.
Title: Empire builder: John D. Spreckels
and the making of San Diego / Sandra E.
Bonura; foreword by Uwe Spieckermann.
Description: Lincoln: University of Nebraska Press,
2020. | Includes bibliographical references and index.
Identifiers: LCCN 2020010779
ISBN 9781496222916 (hardback)
ISBN 9781496233417 (paperback)
ISBN 9781496223784 (epub)
ISBN 9781496223791 (mobi)
ISBN 9781496223807 (pdf)
Subjects: LCSH: Spreckels, John Diedrich,
1853– | Businesspeople—United States—
Biography. | San Diego (Calif.)—History.
Classification: LCC HC102.5.S6 A633
2020 | DDC 338.092 [B]—dc23
LC record available at https://
lccn.loc.gov/2020010779

Set in New Baskerville by Laura Buis.
Designed by N. Putens.

Frontispiece: The descendants of Claus Spreckels and Anna Mangels. Courtesy of Adolph Rosekrans.

To my formidable German-born grandmother, Ida Groh Hollinger, who was left a widow in this strange new land with a toddler, my mother, to raise. She struggled to learn English and to make a living here, all while enduring persecution during two world wars because of her German heritage. She was a natural storyteller, especially after a few late-evening sips of cherry schnapps from a hidden stash in her closet. From Nana I developed my love for storytelling.

Gentlemen, I love San Diego.

—JOHN D. SPRECKELS

CONTENTS

List of Illustrations   *ix*

Foreword by Uwe Spiekermann   *xi*

Acknowledgments   *xv*

Prologue: "It's Hell for the 'One Man' in the
One-Man Town"   *xix*

1. Chasing the Sweet American Dream   *1*

2. Taking Hawai'i by Storm   *17*

3. Crazed Land Boom and Bust   *41*

4. Sugar and Strife   *55*

5. Aloha Hawai'i   *69*

6. Raising the Spreckels Clan   *77*

7. Roots in San Francisco 97

8. Building San Diego's Infrastructure 121

9. Earthquake, Death, and Legal (and Romantic) Chaos ... 141

10. Influencing San Diego Politics 169

11. Coronado's Uncle John 179

12. The So-Called Impossible Railroad 215

13. Building Up Broadway 225

14. John and the Wobblies 245

15. Gifting the Panama–California Exposition and the Zoo ... 253

16. Standing Up to the U.S. Government 273

17. The Cruel 1920s 287

18. The Departed Skipper 315

    Epilogue: Breaking Up the Empire 323

    Notes on Sources and Research 345

    Notes 349

    Bibliography 381

    Index 391

ILLUSTRATIONS

The descendants of Claus Spreckels and Anna Mangels   *frontispiece*

1. John D. Spreckels (1853–1926), the empire builder   *xxi*

2. John Spreckels with his father, and brother Adolph Bernard   *8*

3. The impressive Spreckels California Sugar Refinery   *11*

4. John Spreckels, a dashing twenty-two-year-old in 1875   *18*

5. Lillian Caroline Siebein (1854–1924)   *19*

6. John and Lillian's four children   *25*

7. Oceanic Steamship Company, dominating Pacific transport   *35*

8. Elisha Spurr Babcock Jr. (1848–1922)   *46*

9. The resplendent Hotel del Coronado   *49*

10. John and Lillian's opulent mansion in Pacific Heights   *80*

11. John and his girls at sea   *83*

12. Jack Spreckels, handsome and tragic heir to Spreckels fortune   *90*

13. The Call Building, iconic the moment it was finished   *98*

14. Being a "club man," a symbol of power, prestige, and privilege   *106*

15. Republican senator Samuel Morgan Shortridge (1861–1952)   *113*

16. The San Diego Electric Railway Company   *124*

17. Edward Willis Scripps (1854–1926), the eccentric
owner of the *San Diego Sun*   *132*

18. Praise in Hawai'i for Claus Spreckels   *143*

19. Earthquake rubble   *147*

20. The Spreckels mansion on Glorietta Bay, ca. 1909   *150*

21. Rudolph and Eleanor Jolliffe Spreckels, with their children   *153*

22. Anna Christina Mangels Spreckels (1830–1910)   *159*

23. Claus Jr. (1888–1935) as a young man   *164*

24. Coronado, founded in the 1880s, incorporated in 1891   *182*

25. Opa Spreckels in Coronado with his beloved grandchildren   *193*

26. Harriet Holbrook (1911–1997) with her mother, Lillie   *195*

27. John and Lillian's grandchildren from son Claus Jr.   *196*

28. Ellis Ethel Moon Spreckels (1888–1967)   *199*

29. John and Lillian's children in the Del's courtyard   *207*

30. Spreckels declared the inaugural run of the
SD&A "the happiest day of my life"   *222*

31. The south side of Broadway, ca. 1915   *229*

32. Interior of the opulent Spreckels Theatre   *232*

33. The world's largest outside organ!   *262*

34. The 227-foot steam yacht *Venetia*   *274*

35. Coronado's shallow channel, the Spanish Bight   *276*

36. Claus A. Spreckels Jr. (1888–1935)   *293*

37. Grace Alexandria with her two daughters   *305*

38. Lillian Caroline Siebein Spreckels   *307*

39. One of the last photos of Skipper Spreckels   *314*

FOREWORD
Uwe Spiekermann

Spreckels—this is a name suggestive of sauerkraut and pickles! Claus Spreckels, the uncrowned "Sugar King" of the West, was born in northern Germany as a poor farm boy. He migrated to the United States as a young man, aiming for a better life, and there he lived the American dream. He became a grocer and, like a typical German with an opportunity, started a brewery but providentially switched to sugar refining. In that business, he was instrumental in turning Hawai'i into a cane sugar land, and he started a large-scale beet sugar operation on the mainland. Claus Spreckels and his sons were pioneers who made California what it would become.

Spreckels—when I heard this name for the first time a decade ago, it was simply a name belonging to one of the many successful German American businessmen who were part of America's transition into the world's economic superpower. As a German scholar, I was fascinated by such careers, impossible in Claus's fatherland, at that time a monarchy, the kingdom of Hanover. From poverty to being named as one of the "richest men in the world," his is a compelling immigrant story of immense proportions. Claus Spreckels, rich but still humble, was always thankful to the United States in general, California in particular: "I am not a native of California, but there is no other place for me than California."

But Spreckels was also the name of a family. The dream continued; Claus's four sons each became a multimillionaire in his own right. John D., Adolph B., Claus A. ("Gus"), and Rudolph Spreckels all started in the sugar business, but when they got older, they all switched to other pursuits: to finance and real estate, horse breeding and utilities, streetcars and water infrastructure, and more. The Spreckels family shaped California, shaped America.

This book is about the most important protagonist in this family saga: John D. Spreckels, the man who built up San Diego. Though he was born in Charleston, South Carolina, John maintained close ties to Germany and its culture—he studied in Hanover, for example, the city where I'm currently residing—and throughout his career, he employed the typically German characteristics of discipline and efficiency as well as a strong German work ethic. Following his father's orders, he not only managed the Hawaiian property, he became engaged in the transportation business: His steamships connected American shores with the Hawaiian Islands, New Zealand, and Australia. Sandra Bonura, the author of this book, is a renowned expert in Hawaiian history, and already in her earlier books, she explored the role of the Spreckels family during the final decade of the Hawaiian kingdom. She discovered, however, that the Spreckels story was broader and even more fascinating. In this book, Bonura, a descendent of German immigrants and a citizen of San Diego, will not only guide you to a world of business and wealth but will tell you the story, private until now, behind their success.

Along with other historians in Germany, I am happy that *Empire Builder* is now available. Happy because, up to now, the Spreckels family hasn't received the historical attention it deserves as one of the most important upbuilders of the American West. Like other powerful pioneers of California, the Spreckels family lost countless private and business papers in the disastrous fire following the San Francisco earthquake of 1906. Fortunately, Bonura, with great tenacity, researched collections across both the Atlantic and Pacific to restore the record. She has been able to find a striking number of new sources and photos, heretofore fiercely protected in private family archives. You will love the human touch of this book—but this is not fiction; it is solid history.

This biography of John D. Spreckels is an important contribution to understanding the rise of San Diego as one of California's leading cities. But it is also the story of finding and building a home for John D., for his family, and for tens of thousands of employees and newcomers to southern California. This is a book about settling, of creating and finding *Heimat* (homeland) for a second-generation German American immigrant. Bonura skillfully documents the chances that this land of opportunities has always offered to immigrants from remote lands who chased the American dream.

ACKNOWLEDGMENTS

I began the daunting task of tracking down the living descendants of John Spreckels with my fingers crossed and with prayers that I would find interesting people with even more interesting stories to tell. All of my expectations were exceeded. It is with heartfelt gratitude that I begin my acknowledgments with a proper "thank you" to the various genealogical lines of John's family. They trusted me with their family artifacts, diaries, correspondence, and priceless photographs, which made this biography all the richer. Here are just a few who attended special reunion events at great effort and/or embraced me as though I were a long-lost relative: Frank "Mike" Belcher, the late John "Garry" Belcher Sr., Carrie Berger, Brian Brey, Curtis Brey, Rick Brey, Torry Brey, Jessica Burch, Cathy Lloyd Butler-Hickey, Gretchen de Limur's family, Christine Donald, Judi Fleener Griffith, Lisa Fleener Grey, Laurie Fletcher Guidry, Camille Harrison, Drucy Walsh Illanes, Nancy Jakobsen, David Lewis, Suzy Lewis, Paula Fleener Lynch, Chelsea Micek, Victoria Norton Nelson, Barbara Northcutt, Jonde Northcutt, Claus Russell, Erin Bright Russell, Harriet Russell, David Holbrook Wilson, Silvie Wilder Wilson, Virginia Wilson, Lily Wilson-Browne, and Codey Wuthrich. The collective enthusiasm from all the foregoing kept *me* going, and I am humbly grateful for their input.

I am grateful to Allan Edmands, who not only had to deal with the rules of grammar, punctuation, and style, he had to deal with *me*. Having his seasoned eyes on my work, step by step, over the entire length of the project, sailed John Spreckels into publication.

A big shout-out to author/researcher Vincent J. Dicks, whose thoughtful and critical responses to my nagging queries regarding the Spreckels influence in nineteenth- and twentieth-century politics were offered with extraordinary patience and kindness.

A special thanks to author Molly McClain, who, for two of my books, has consistently shared attention-grabbing excerpts from her "stash" on Ellen Browning Scripps.

I thank the staff of the Coronado Historical Association, who inadvertently inspired me to write this book after I curated their 2018 exhibit *John D. Spreckels: The Man*. Also, my research proceeded smoothly and provided consistent excitement and pleasure due to the help of some very capable people from other library and research institutions. Out on top is the delightful Patricia Keats, director of Library and Archives with the Society of California Pioneers in San Francisco. Many thanks to Beth Auten, from the San Diego Zoo Archives; Kathy Connor, legacy curator at George Eastman Museum; Samantha Ely, City of San Diego, Office of the City Clerk; Hampton Flannigan, who shared parts of Hampton Story's life; John Hibble, from the Aptos Chamber of Commerce and the Aptos History Museum; Molly Haigh, Library Special Collections, UCLA; Ross Porter, executive director of the Spreckels Organ Society; Renato Rodriquez, from the San Diego History Center; Randolph Ruiz, for sharing his wonderful trolley map; and the staff at the Coronado Public Library.

I thank Claudia Ludlow, general manager of the Glorietta Bay Inn (the former home of John and Lillian Spreckels) and the many volunteers of the Pacific Southwest Railway Museum Association, who give of their time and energy to preserve the legacy of John D. Spreckels's San Diego & Arizona Railway. Special thanks to Gina Petrone, the historian for the Hotel del Coronado, who shares my love for the "Lady by the Sea."

My warm thanks go to Bridget Barry, acquisitions editor at University of Nebraska Press, and the entire publication staff who brought this book into publication. Their respectful, friendly, and steady guidance was much appreciated. I am also grateful for the time UNP's selected reviewers, Iris Engstrom and Theodore "Andy" Strathman, spent reading the manuscript and providing thoughtful and critical evaluation.

Dankeschön to Uwe Spiekermann, who provided this book's foreword. His scholarly work on the many Spreckels family branches in and out of Germany was foundational reading for me, right from the beginning. My discussions with him were invaluable, as he helped me to see the Spreckels family from a German's perspective. When we finally met, we had an instant and, I hope, lasting connection over our shared fascination with the extraordinary Spreckels family. Uwe, *ich werde dich nie vergessen!*

This biography could not have been finished without the selfless contribution of all these people and more—archivists, librarians, historians, editors, and families. I heartily thank them and hope they see how much life they helped breathe into this book.

PROLOGUE

"It's Hell for the 'One Man' in the One-Man Town"

A little girl was with her father at breakfast one morning at the Hotel del Coronado. The "Spreckels" sugar packet he used to sweeten his coffee aroused her curiosity. She was then told that the profits from that sugar had purchased both the hotel and the island they were presently enjoying.

Watching her father reading the *San Diego Union*, she asked, "Papa, whose newspaper is that?"

"This newspaper is published by Mr. Spreckels, my dear."

"Papa, I am thirsty. May I have a glass of water?"

"Of course. By the way, Mr. Spreckels owns the drinking water."

After breakfast, touring the city on the streetcar, the little girl asked, "Papa, whose streetcar is this?"

"Mr. Spreckels's."

"Who owns this ferryboat, Papa?"

"Mr. Spreckels."

"Papa! Whose gigantic ship is that?"

"That's from the Spreckels steamship line."

"Papa, what theater is that?"

"That's the Spreckels Theatre."

"Papa, whose skyscraper is that?"

"It's the John D. Spreckels Building."

"Papa, where is that loud whistle coming from?"

"That's Mr. Spreckels's train, my dear."

"Papa, whose huge outdoor organ is that in Balboa Park?"

"Mr. Spreckels had it built."

Upon returning to Coronado, the little girl looked at the ocean and said, "Papa, who owns the ocean?"

"My dear, *God* owns the ocean."

"Papa, tell me: *How* did God *ever* get it away from Mr. Spreckels?"

I smiled when I discovered this witty tale, an earlier, shorter version of which had begun circulating around the country in 1916. I then found a 1954 version published in J. Harold Peterson's *The Coronado Story*.[1] It was lengthier due to the expanding enterprises of Mr. Spreckels. I amused myself by bringing it into the twenty-first century with my own amendments. When I stepped back from the little tale, however, it dawned on me that the enlarged story didn't even begin to describe the empires this man built.

I am a native San Diegan who thrives on research, and the sight of the name of our city's "foster father," John D. Spreckels, in *any* historical document captures my attention. It's a familiar name to most baby boomers who grew up here. During my childhood, the John D. Spreckels skyscraper rose high above San Diego's modest skyline, even though that "skyscraper" is today dwarfed among the twenty-first-century glass and steel buildings. I often stayed weekends with my German immigrant grandmother in her boarding house, Hotel Metropole, on Broadway, a downtown street actually named by Spreckels. Directly across the street from her lobby window, seared in my memory, was the flashy marquee identifying the Spreckels Theatre. I could press my face to that second-floor glass window and look south, east, and west along Broadway and see one or another Spreckels building. I remember the two Spreckels sugar cubes Nana stirred in her coffee every morning. (In her thick German accent, the name was "Shpreckels.") On Sunday afternoons, she took me on the bus to the Spreckels Organ Pavilion in beautiful Balboa Park for the free concert at two o'clock, and I remember disliking the

1. John Diedrich Spreckels (1853–1926), the empire builder. Permission granted from the Terrence and Virginia Wilson Private Family Collection.

"loud noise." In other words, I could easily have been the little girl in the tale I told above, and "Papa" could have been my "Nana."

My journey to writing John Spreckels's biography began when an old house in Berkeley, California, passed from one generation to the next. Tattered steamship trunks that had voyaged on a Spreckels steamer were discovered in the attic. Forgotten for more than a century, the trunks contained valuable scientific papers, rare artifacts, correspondence, photographs, old newspapers, and more.

Charles Atwood Kofoid (1865–1947), the late professor who had owned the home, had been a famous marine biologist, so the Scripps Institution of Oceanography at the University of California, San Diego, was delighted to receive the donated contents of the trunks. Kofoid and colleague William Emerson Ritter had established a marine biological laboratory in 1903, when John Spreckels, farseeing, provided his Hotel del Coronado's boathouse to become a laboratory for the new field of "oceanography." From this early biological station in the Spreckels boathouse grew the world-renowned Scripps Institution.

The Scripps archivist cataloging the scientific research records determined that the contents of one of the steamer trunks was out of place in an institution that deals with all things ocean. Being my friend, she allowed me privileged access to that trunk's contents in 2008. As she had predicted, my heart, mind, and imagination were instantly captured by the hundreds of love letters written in charming nineteenth-century vernacular by a homesick young teacher and journalist, Carrie Winter, who was on a three-year assignment in Honolulu, to her fiancé, "Charlie" Kofoid.

Winter had embarked from San Francisco Harbor in late August 1890 on the Spreckels steamship *Zealandia*, and due to her incredible talent as a writer, she vividly took me with her on her journey. Some of her correspondences, as well as newspaper articles she had written for the *Hartford Courant* and various other documents, richly describe the Spreckels sugar and shipping empires of those years in the Pacific region. Winter was an important eyewitness to the greatest political turmoil the Hawaiians had ever experienced, and her written accounts are rare. Recognizing their historical significance, the archivist and I transcribed, edited, and researched her letters and articles, and in 2012, we published *An American Girl in the Hawaiian Islands: Letters of Carrie Prudence Winter, 1890–1893.*

During the editing of *American Girl*, another name, Ida May Pope, jumped out from Carrie's letters into my heart. As my research continued, I was puzzled by one question: How had history ignored this bold social activist, from a small town in Ohio, who had inspired, elevated, and ultimately sacrificed her life for an entire generation of Hawaiian women? Both Ida Pope and John Spreckels partnered with Hawai'i's Queen Lili'uokalani in the same turbulent era. I was honored to write her story, *Light in the Queen's Garden: Ida May Pope, Pioneer for Hawai'i's Daughters, 1862–1914*, published in 2017, awarded top honors in 2019.

Those forgotten steamer trunks gave me one more story to tell: that of the forgotten empire of John Diedrich Spreckels. During my research, I became curious about why J. D. Spreckels had earned the privileged mention as a "friend" in the queen's autobiography, *Hawai'i's Story by Hawai'i's Queen Lili'uokalani*. While reading the queen's correspondence in the Hawai'i State Archives, I learned the depth of their friendship. When the United States seized her funds in the summer of 1898, she found herself stranded in Washington DC, in "financial embarrassment." With great relief, the queen reported to her business manager that "Mr. J. D. Spreckels" had wired her $2,000 (more than $60,000 today) to bail her out of an awkward situation, and *that* was neither the first time nor the last time.

This book looks behind the scenes at the pioneer who almost singlehandedly built San Diego after building empires in sugar, shipping, transportation, and building development up and down the coast of California and across the Pacific.

I know that many marvel at San Diego's beauty and bustling activity and that they have wondered about its history. Our beautiful bay is impressive, and some thirty-five million people who annually visit our city might assume that it was the natural place for a city to emerge, but they might not appreciate why a single name, John Diedrich Spreckels, stands out here and there on both San Diego's and Coronado's buildings and parks.

Despite the fact that John created and/or owned much of the city's early twentieth-century infrastructure *and* superstructure, his name is unknown to many contemporary San Diegans. Considering that he put an astonishing amount of his energy and money into the city and its resort suburb Coronado, it's unfortunate that most residents know little about his pioneering legacy beyond a few structures that still bear his name and some salacious bits of gossip about the Spreckels family.

John Spreckels was a skillful entrepreneur in his own right, but his accomplishments were ever-threatened to be eclipsed by the looming shadow of his father, the German-born "Sugar King," Claus Spreckels, who was one of the wealthiest men of the nineteenth century. John fulfilled the role of a dutiful heir, navigating the family's sugar empire to further success well into the twentieth century. In his twenties, he branched out into shipping, a venture that took him around the world, turning his Oceanic Steamship Company into a global concern.

When he first dropped anchor in San Diego Bay on a warm June day in 1887, his immediate desire set into motion a series of events that later defined the city. His moves were so decisive and sweeping that, within just a few years, he owned and controlled the majority of San Diego industry. He was always oriented toward the future, and this orientation thrust him to the forefront of innovation, demanding advanced techniques of building construction, water supply, and improvements in transportation—particularly by ship, rail, electric traction for streetcars, and automobile.

Still, his accomplishments incurred a heavy personal toll. His high points were offset by prolonged periods of pain and contention. For decades, he had been harshly criticized for what others perceived to be his ruthless business tactics. As John's grip on San Diego and Coronado tightened, he came to control almost every aspect of the city's business, and his monopolistic behavior was not kindly regarded. His business rivals said his business interests were the epitome of a company grown too big and too dominant for the public good—even though the general public disagreed. To the strenuous charge from his rivals that all of San Diego's troubles were derived from the city being a "one-man town," John responded, "If being a one-man town is bad for the town, take it from me, it's hell for the 'one man'!"[2]

Never compelled to justify his actions, John simply walled himself off from his critics, remaining silent until his seventh decade of life. How long might he have rehearsed his fiery address rebuking those critics and thereby stunning one hundred of San Diego's city leaders—a speech he delivered on May 19, 1923, with an impassioned voice, shaking hands, and watery eyes? That day, for the first time, his opponents realized the full depth of his passion for the city he had been instrumental in building. He had had his say at last, and the room's applause would still be practically ringing in his ears at the end of his life.

Apart from that one emotionally charged public address, though, John, reserved and pensive, was as silent as one of the many pioneering, earthquake-resistant buildings he left behind. It's been a challenge for me to gain insight about the inner man, whose preference was for isolation and solitude. Historical accounts that chronicle his life have come primarily from archived articles in the three main newspapers he carefully controlled to ensure his privacy. The most widely cited source on his life is a single book, *The Man, John D. Spreckels,* penned by preacher-turned-playwright Henry Austin Adams and published in 1924. Racing against the "clock" of his life, John employed Adams to write his biography. The result is a fanciful and fawning recount of selected incidents and achievements, full of errors of chronology and omitting any references to his family life. In contrast, my deeply researched biography pulls together newly discovered primary source documents, including diaries, oral histories, interviews, scrapbooks, photos, and other family documents.

John Spreckels conducted his business affairs on a global scale. He rubbed shoulders with world leaders, he bailed out royalty, and he even successfully sued the U.S. government twice, all while contributing to numerous educational, charitable, and cultural institutions in Hawai'i, San Francisco, and San Diego. When people lauded his generosity, he rejected the philanthropic label; he allowed his hard exterior to conceal a well-known soft heart. It is only from more distant sources, such as a biography of Baseball Hall of Famer Ted Williams, that you learn in these pages that John had quietly paid off the mortgage on the house owned by Williams's impoverished mother when Williams himself was still a child.[3]

When the public pointed to his underwriting of the San Diego Zoo as well as his sponsoring of the very first zoo animal exchange with Australia using his luxurious steamships, leading to a dramatic and harrowing story that gave Americans their very first koala encounter, John was nonchalant. After creating Balboa Park, donating the world's largest outdoor municipal organ, and building hospitals, libraries, and more, he rebuffed the label of a Good Samaritan. He never wanted to be publicly associated with promoting charity: "I am a business man, and not a Santa Claus—nor a fool."[4] He believed that the "best charity you can give a man is work," and since, at the end of his life, one in fifteen city residents worked for a Spreckels-owned company, he had fulfilled his own mission of charity, in his own way.[5]

One observer, a newspaper editor from Coronado, was both bemused and puzzled by the fact that someone would put so much of his heart, soul, and wallet into one city and get nothing but criticism for it. The editor humorously questioned Spreckels's sanity, suggesting, to John's delight, that his middle initial, *D*, stood for "demented," for who could understand why he

> kept on dumping one million after another on our devoted (and thank-less) hole-in-a-corner—when he might have invested all his wealth in government bonds, lived in any one of the world's most delightful spots, cruised over the seven seas in his palatial yacht, and let us scrub along the best way we could. . . . Thank Heaven that Mr. Spreckels isn't entirely sane. I live in terror lest he may have a lucid interval one of these days, suddenly realize what he has been doing all these years, and then clear out, bag and baggage! Let us pray that his dementia has now become incurable. Amen![6]

John's grit in the face of challenges and setbacks helped him triumph in an environment rife with cronyism and corruption. He did not mind being referred to as an empire builder, and he knew there was a universal expectation in his era that the San Diego public would one day erect a monument to him, for he had almost single-handedly transformed a bankrupt village into a thriving city. Nobody, especially not John himself, could then have foreseen that his various empires would be all but forgotten in too short a time.

EMPIRE BUILDER

1

Chasing the Sweet American Dream

Charleston, 1848–1854

Our story begins with a young man who had big dreams. Trudging behind a plow in Lamstedt, a small village in the kingdom of Hanover, held little promise for such a dreamer. Adolph "Claus" Johann Spreckels had seen many farmers, including his own father, left impoverished by the revolutionary wars that had spread from France. When he turned eighteen, Claus knew he had little time to deliberate about his future, for Hanover, then a province of the kingdom of Prussia, had a law stipulating that men be conscripted into the army at the age of twenty.[1] In any case, Claus appears to have had other ideas that he was determined to pursue. The young man had been fed dreams of prosperity via pamphlets that had appeared in Hanover and Prussia, promoting emigration to South Carolina.[2]

German immigrants had a good reputation in the American South, where they were often said to be industrious, thrifty, and proficient at farming—characteristics that Claus Spreckels possessed in good measure. Thus, confronted with the certainty of conscription in his near future, Claus made the heart-wrenching decision to leave his ancestral homeland for the United States, as did many desperate but hopeful Hanoverians. His parents pleaded with him to stay; however, even though their protests were seconded by their minister and friends, Claus was not to be convinced. His family must have realized that it was pointless to argue once his mind was made up.[3] In 1848, then, with very little in his pocket, he left the farm and a childhood sweetheart, Anna Christina Mangels, in their small village and sailed in pursuit of his dreams.[4]

Though South Carolina's agricultural Lowcountry region would have been a logical choice for a young farmer such as Claus, he chose instead to settle in the vibrant city of Charleston, a seaport central to the important cotton and rice trades. Charleston also had an active German Friendly Society, which offered practical assistance to newly arrived immigrants such as Claus. Through the society, he found his first job as a clerk in a German-owned grocery store that included room and board.

Claus quickly recognized that his options would be limited if he didn't try to prepare himself to get beyond his émigré roots, learn what he could from the business end of things, and move on. He also realized he could not hope to achieve the American dream without learning English, and so he began to acquire the language.[5] He later attributed his success to his attentiveness to the minute details of running a business.[6] His impressive work ethic soon led to his promotion to manager. When the store's owners retired a year and a half after his arrival, they sold the store to him on credit. They also recommended him to their vendors, who likewise agreed to extend credit to Claus, thus assisting his prospects for success. Their faith was not misplaced. True to his word, Claus repaid the entire amount, about $1,200, within the year.[7] Indebtedness did not appeal to him, for, as he would later say, "I make a strict rule of cash purchasing."[8]

After his departure from Hanover, Claus had remained in close communication with his beloved, Anna Mangels. She immigrated to New York in 1849 with her younger brother, Claus Mangels. They had all been childhood classmates and now shared the new status of émigré. Anna soon found domestic work in a sugar refiner's home, and there she waited for her beau. Once Claus Spreckels had become settled with a business of his own, he traveled to New York to propose marriage.

The couple wed on August 11, 1852, and they returned to Charleston to begin married life as shopkeepers.

Anna, like her husband, detested idleness, and she soon put her baking talents to use in the shop. Claus partitioned off a small area of the store as a bakery, but he soon needed to expand the space as Anna's delectable German sweets and baked goods far outsold the other products.[9] This success kept her busy, but it was not long before Anna had a more important occupation: On August 16, 1853, she gave birth to John Diedrich Spreckels.[10]

Although the Spreckelses' home was free of strife in those early days, the same could not be said of the world outside their windows. The issue of slavery had begun to divide the nation in the 1830s, and South Carolina was a stronghold of proslavery opinion. By midcentury, tensions with the Northern states were high and soon to become worse. German immigrants in the slaveholding states had earned a reputation for tolerance and liberalism with regard to race, which sometimes put them at odds with the established white communities there. In fact, Claus's opinions about individual liberty did not allow him to accept the popular racial ideologies of others. In Charleston, his attitude drew sharp criticism from his neighbors, many of whom resented Germans who did business with African Americans. Historians now suggest that in Charleston, "German grocers undermined the slave system to a significant degree" by acting as "bold breakers of the law against selling liquor to the blacks."[11] This commerce had been illegal in South Carolina since 1831, and, by flouting this law, they had undermined an institution of racial division.

It was now South Carolina, rather than Hanover, that was imposing personal restrictions and sanctions on Claus, which he likely found unbearable. Thus, according to Spreckels family lore, when Claus and Anna were found to have blatantly broken the law by selling goods to African Americans, Charlestonians forced them to give up their grocery store and flee town.[12] In fact, they probably moved quickly rather than face severe penalties: fines and perhaps imprisonment. Their success could protect them no longer, and it was time to find new fields to plow.

New York and Then San Francisco, 1854–1856

In 1854, the Spreckels family relocated to New York. Claus joined forces with Anna's brother and continued in the grocery business. The store they opened prospered beyond expectations, but neither the work nor the climate contented Claus and Anna.

After the move, they welcomed their second son, Henry, into the family. They were able to save enough to make a return visit to Lamstedt and introduce one-year-old John and the baby to their grandparents, who must have been overjoyed at their children's achievements in America.

After six months in Germany, they returned to New York and there met with Claus's younger brother Peter Spreckels, who had immigrated to California sometime after his older brother left. It was Peter's turn to visit his parents, and on his way back to Germany, he stopped over in New York to visit Claus and Anna. Peter reported that the grocery store where he worked in San Francisco was doing well, and he also told of numerous lucrative opportunities in that city, still feverish from the Gold Rush. Claus, restless and bored in New York, was intrigued by his brother's stories, and he began to make plans to join him there. He appears to have paid no attention to the newspaper stories, common at the time, that told of sickly and disillusioned adventurers who had returned home after failing to strike it rich in the West. Any misgivings that Anna, who was now pregnant with their third child, might have had did not stop Claus. He sold the New York store to his brother-in-law, who would later follow him, and then packed up his family once again; in June of 1856, they began the long trek to northern California. It is difficult to know if John, then three years old, grasped that his father had always been, and would always be, renowned for his autocracy, authority, and obstinacy.

The pursuit of Claus's grand schemes was arduous. The family journeyed two thousand miles by ship down the East Coast and then across the Caribbean Sea. Then, rather than following most travelers who undertook the thirteen-thousand-mile voyage around Cape Horn at the southern tip of South America, they took a grueling "short cut." Using an array of transportation methods, they crossed forty-seven miles of malaria-laden wetlands in Panama to connect with the Pacific Mail vessel waiting at the other side of the isthmus. Although arduous and full of peril, shaving off eight thousand miles was worth the hardship for the ever-efficient Claus, who was undoubtedly grateful that his family had avoided tropical fever. The subsequent three-week ocean voyage on the SS *John L. Stephens* from Panama to San Francisco was quite the coincidence for little John, who one day would own the shipping route of the line (Pacific Mail Steamship Company) that carried his family to the West Coast.

Claus Spreckels, Grocer to Brewer

When the Spreckels family arrived in San Francisco on July 1, 1856, the city was still feeling the impact of the Gold Rush; San Francisco was rapidly transforming itself from a sleepy hamlet to a thriving town. Just six years earlier, California had become a state, and a large portion of San Francisco's population were young males under the age of twenty-four who were "bold, enterprising, and a speculative set of men, who were engaged in every sort of game to make money."[13] It was the wild, Wild West in every way.

Many young men, out of money, gave up the search for gold but stayed in California to become farmers, businessmen, or workhands. Claus joined the fray, but he had the advantage of being flush, having $8,000 after selling his grocery business in New York. His third grocery venture on Post Street in downtown San Francisco proved unrewarding and brief, however. It wasn't long before he discovered a more familiar opportunity for a German: the prospect of becoming a beer brewer. The opportunity was more lucrative too: At the time, though breweries owned by German settlers were common throughout most of the country, that was not the case in San Francisco, so Claus faced little competition.

Claus, the persuasive entrepreneur, convinced his brother-in-law, Claus Mangels, and his brother Peter Spreckels to pool their money and enter the brewery business together. In the spring of 1857, they opened the Albany Brewery, downtown on Everett Street, advertising "superior cream ale to supply the increasing demands of the pub-lic."[14] The brewery soon expanded across the road to include a saloon, which the partners named the Albany Malt House. "Albany Cream Ale," brewed from pale hops in Albany, New York, was famous at that time for its smoothness and high alcohol content. It's likely that Claus was reproducing and publicizing this popular type of beer to win over the West Coast the same way that Easterners had been won over. But, he later recollected, he realized that the only way to become successful would be not to rely on others to share his work ethic:

> You know in brewing great attention has to be paid to the thermometer. If the mercury goes too high the beer will turn sour and spoil. The men would all knock off at a certain hour and think no more of business, but I have frequently gone into the brewery after all hands have left and found the thermometer making unpleasant records, and I have slipped on my overalls and worked all night by myself. Why at one time I only took four hours sleep in the twenty-four for months.[15]

Claus was on his way to becoming a beer baron when providence struck. The brewery and saloon were located near the city's sole sugar manufacturer, San Francisco Sugar Refinery, and most of its workers, like Claus, were German. As he listened to the complaints of the refinery workers as they nursed their beers after work, he learned that a significant quantity of the sugar liquor that was produced in the refining process was overflowing and going to waste. John later related his father's exact words as to why he went into the sugar refin-ery business: "If men can run liquor into the sewers day after day and night after night, and the firm can still make a good profit, those profits must be enormous!"[16]

White Gold

As grocers, the Spreckels family had already discovered that the price of sugar was extraordinarily high in California. The Civil War was cutting off the transport of sugar across the United States, rendering it a household luxury. Realizing that there was a fortune to be made in the sugar-refining business on the West Coast (but knowing little about the actual process of sugar refinement), Claus informed Anna that he would be taking young John to New York to study, firsthand, the technique of refining sugar from a more progressive operation than the one neighboring his San Francisco brewery.[17] At that time, the sugar-refining industry was central to New York City commerce and industry, and there were more than fifteen refineries that might employ them.

Despite the fact that the Civil War was raging at the time and that John was only ten years old, he was pulled from his schooling and his newfound passion, the piano, to accompany his father on this hands-on learning expedition. His younger brothers—Henry, eight years old, and Adolph, six years old—remained behind in San Francisco with their mother, and the brewery was left in the hands of Claus's partners.

While his father continued to work into the moonlight hours, John was often left alone at night. He remembered this "lonesome" time in New York as cementing his love for California.[18] Once his father had assimilated the technical methods of sugar refining and felt confident that he could successfully make the refining process more economical, he purchased machinery from the bankrupt United States Refinery in New York at a bargain and shipped it to San Francisco. He established the refinery at the foot of that city's Telegraph Hill and proclaimed that father and son were now sugar refiners.

Claus convinced his family business partners to sell the Albany brewery enterprise and join in his new venture. Thanks to the hefty profit of $75,000 from closing that sale (still in 1863), the partners were able to found the Bay Sugar Refinery Company in downtown San Francisco. By many accounts, the Bay Sugar Refinery was a success from its incorporation in January of 1864.[19]

The "College" of California

Throughout his youth, John worked as his father's apprentice in the sugar refinery business, and, as a result, his formal schooling was

2. John Spreckels posing with his arm over his father's shoulder alongside his younger brother Adolph Bernard. Permission granted from the Terrence and Virginia Wilson Private Family Collection.

inconsistent. When the Bay Sugar Refinery began to prosper, however, it was time for John to get a formal education; Claus would see to it that his son would become well equipped for the new technologies and changing economic environment that were to follow the Civil War.

As a young adolescent, John was sent across San Francisco Bay to the newly created College of California, a boy's academy in Oakland designed to prepare secondary students for higher education.[20] Though nonsectarian in its mission statement, the academy was run by ultra-conservative ministers of the Congregational and Presbyterian faiths, unlike the more liberal Lutherans, who would have been the Spreckels family's preference.

Although it was well intentioned, the Oakland academy struggled from the beginning and was always short of money. As the 1864–65 school year commenced, John was among the group of 207 pupils that had grown too large for twelve teachers (many working only part time) to manage.[21] The meager endowments discouraged the faculty, who could not obtain the resources necessary to achieve the level of distinction they envisioned for their college. (The problem would not be solved until 1867, when the academy decided to merge its assets, both buildings and land, to form the University of California, in the newly named college town of Berkeley.[22])

Claus Selling His Shares in a Huff

Whereas some accounts described Claus Spreckels as outgoing and jovial, others characterized him as driven, ruthless, and impatient. Both at home and at work, he was accustomed to getting what he wanted, and he had little patience for business partners, family or otherwise, who were foolhardy enough to question his decisions or priorities. Consequently, his personal and business relationships suffered. When his cautious business partners rebuffed his expansion plans, which they felt were too grandiose after only two years since founding the Bay Sugar Refinery, Claus was furious. As a result, he sold them his shares of the company at a considerable profit in 1865, and John left the Oakland academy.

Sugar Beets

The Spreckels family left for Europe in 1865, with John's father harboring new ambitions. Claus was immensely satisfied at having founded the Bay Sugar Refinery, and now he was deeply committed to building not only another refinery but also a sugar empire. In his native Germany, the entire population consumed sugar derived from beets.[23] Claus realized that by refining sugar from beets instead of from the more expensive sugarcane, he would be able to realize greater profits, but he first needed to explore the viability of reproducing the European method in California.

Jacob Hennige owned and operated a highly successful beet sugar refinery in the medieval town of Magdeburg in north central Germany. He hired Claus as a common laborer in the factory, likely unaware that his new hire was investigating trade secrets in the refining of beet sugar.[24]

After eight months in Europe, the family returned to San Francisco with seeds in their pockets; Claus was fired up to meet the nation's ever-increasing demand for sugar. Unfortunately, once back in California, Claus had to postpone his ambition to turn sugar beets into white sugar when he realized that labor costs would outweigh profits.

But Claus Spreckels never started anything he couldn't finish, so he had to employ something he didn't have a reputation for being abundant in: patience. It wasn't until 1888—more than two decades later, and only after he had induced local farmers to grow sugar beets by guaranteeing to buy their crops—that he was able to establish the Western Beet Sugar Factory in Watsonville, California.[25]

The Spreckels California Sugar Refinery

John's father had rejoined the family sugar refinery business in 1866, moving at breakneck speed; in fact, he took over that business. Back in his favor were his brother Peter and brother-in-law, Claus Mangels, but by now, they knew their place under President Claus Spreckels. The company, renamed the Spreckels California Sugar Refinery and

3. The Spreckels California Sugar Refinery, established in 1867. Notice who is vice-president! Permission granted from the Terrence and Virginia Wilson Private Family Collection.

relocated at Eighth and Brannan Streets, not far from San Francisco's Mission Bay, was now in full operation. The company grew fast, expanding to an enormous factory. By 1880, they were employing three hundred men and were refining fifty million pounds of sugar yearly.[26]

Harnessing centrifugal force, Claus invented new machines to speed up the refining process from three weeks to, astonishingly, only twenty-four hours. Before the Spreckels operation arrived on the scene, sugar had been sold in blocks, or loaves, which required the user to crush them to obtain loose sugar. Claus's invention provided customers with either sugar cubes or crushed sugar, ready in a single day. After other innovative patents, the Spreckels name became a force to be reckoned with among other sugar refiners; "Spreckels Sugar" was now a recognized contender in the refining business. The partners' thriftiness enabled them to lower prices, ultimately squeezing competitors' profits and forcing them out of business.

On the company letterhead, John Diedrich Spreckels was listed as vice-president. Little did the business world know that John, the "Sugar Prince," as he began to be called, was only thirteen years old.

The Polytechnic Institute in Hanover

Claus must have been frustrated with the American education system; when John became fourteen, his father decided that he should pack his trunk for Germany to continue his education at the Polytechnic Institute in Hanover. Claus likely intended to give John not only a broader intellectual perspective but focused scientific training, with the bonus of his getting in touch with his German ancestry.

Newspaper articles of the time described Claus as either an "amiable German" or a "greedy Prussian." When criticized for being ruthless in business, Claus repeatedly defined himself as an American businessman fighting for American values. He was often quoted in the press as being grateful to the American democratic society for providing the liberty he had been denied in Hanover. He publicly thanked America for giving him economic opportunities, even funded a Fourth of July parade for San Francisco, but he unabashedly and exclusively attributed his success to his personal stamina, to his fighting for American values.

Being an American did not mean forgetting his German heritage, however. He maintained very close ties with his homeland. He sent money back regularly, even buying a bell for the Lutheran church in the village of Lamstedt. There is no doubt that Claus and Anna transferred their homeland's values and worldviews to John, as did their household helpers, who were mainly German immigrants. John was fluent in German, and he worked closely with the skilled workers from Germany his father preferred to hire for his refineries, quite possibly recruits from the Magdeburg refinery.

Because Claus believed that German science was more infallible, he wanted John to gain the technological know-how that would benefit the family business. Whether or not John wanted to leave San Francisco did not matter. He was being groomed to be his father's successor, and his father's wishes were always commands. On the journey by ship to Germany, John, despondent at being uprooted from the familiarity of home, spent hours exploring the vessel and watching the sea. He recollected later that this long and lonely voyage to Europe was the true beginning of his "magical allurement" for the sea.[27]

John arrived at the Polytechnic Institute in 1867. It had been founded three and a half decades earlier to deal with the need for technical expertise generated by the nineteenth-century Industrial Revolution. In fact, many of the early graduates from Europe's polytechnic schools were renowned for having designed and built America's early highways, bridges, canals, and railroads. The Polytechnic Institute's progressive curriculum for young men distinguished itself by shifting its pedagogical focus from the podium to the laboratory. It differed from vocational training because of its advanced level, and it prepared students for specialization in occupations that required skills more demanding than manual labor.

Claus realized that his operation's modernization might be outpaced without the benefit of John's training, so he enrolled his son in the field of mechanical engineering, a field that was emerging in the nineteenth century as a result of discoveries in physics. In Germany, the development of machine tools caused mechanical engineering to advance as a separate field within engineering, providing manufacturing machines and the engines to power them. Mechanical engineering was a field divided into three areas of discipline: marine, locomotive, and mill. John's lifelong passion for engines was likely ignited here and would inform his future career choices.

By all accounts, he was enjoying the intellectual stimulation of school and his freedom. But if John thought he could independently maneuver his life at this point, he was sorely mistaken. As far as his eldest son was concerned, out of sight never meant out of mind for Claus. John was boarding with a family close to the campus. On one visit, Claus discovered that the landlady's lovely and well-endowed daughter had been regularly visiting his son's room with refreshments. Surmising that John's mind might be on matters outside of school, Claus took decisive action: He quickly moved John that very evening to another location. John knew there was no point in arguing with his inflexible father and thus reluctantly complied.[28]

Breakdown

In the late summer of 1869, just when the Spreckels family company was in the middle of even greater expansion, Claus, unable to withstand the depression and exhaustion brought on by the quick succession of dying children that befell his family, had a nervous breakdown. John's parents had lost seven children—six sons and one daughter, some in infancy and others in early childhood—to conditions or incidents lost to history: Henry, age nine, in December 1863; Louis Peter, sixteen months old, in January 1864; the family's first girl, Anna Gesina, age three, in February 1864; Louis, five months, in December 1866; and Edward H., age five, in 1869. Records indicate that two more infant brothers also died, one in 1868 and the other in 1876.[29] Between those losses survived Emma Claudine, born in 1870, and, later, Rudolph, born in 1872.

It is difficult to imagine the grief and devastation the family must have collectively experienced, even though infant mortality was high in that era. With little societal structure in place to manage multiple tragedies, one after the other, likely too many for one family to endure, Claus broke down. So, in 1870, at doctor's orders, they packed up for Europe to recuperate. It was a heavy burden for sixteen-year-old John, who needed to assist both parents in handling his siblings—twelve-year-old Adolph Bernard, eleven-year-old Claus Augustus "Gus," and soon his baby sister born in Germany, Emma Claudine—while also dealing with his own grief and fear of losing so many of his other siblings.

After eighteen months of convalescing among the top health resorts in Germany, Claus's "disorder of the brain" was seemingly cured.[30] John had left the Polytechnic Institute in 1869, and Adolph immediately took his place. When the highly educated brothers returned to San Francisco along with their family in 1871, they found that not only had the California Sugar Refinery thrived in their absence, but it now held a stranglehold on the San Francisco sugar business.[31] With his nervous breakdown behind him, Claus returned to work, along with his sons. Eighteen-year-old John began earning a salary of $50 a month while he was learning the business from the bottom up, working his way through all the departments of the refinery. In 1874, he was made superintendent, managing men twice his age, and his monthly salary increased to $250. In today's market that would be more than $5,000. Not bad for a twenty-one-year-old!

The Aptos Resort

The nervous breakdown had given Claus a fresh perspective, so he decided to build himself and his family a summer retreat. Flush with money in 1872, he purchased almost 2,600 acres in Aptos, sixty miles south of San Francisco, to build a ranch to raise racehorses. Horses had always been his passion, and given his competitive nature, he loved the idea of breeding and raising champions under his name.

Not only did Claus build a beautiful summer mansion in Aptos, but rather than relaxing, he began building a resort hotel there. He saw the tourism potential of the estuary land where Aptos Creek entered Monterey Bay, so he created what the *Santa Cruz Sentinel* dubbed the "Newport of the Pacific": a hotel with scenic views of the bay that had all the latest improvements, including indoor plumbing and gaslights, a bowling alley, a billiards room, a promenade, and riding stables.[32] The Aptos resort was soon known as the finest hotel on the California coast, and this is where guests of the Spreckels family were lavishly entertained—including Hawai'i's King David Kalākaua in 1881.

In 1874, while Claus busied himself expanding his property in Aptos, he sent John to Hawai'i to clerk at a sugar company under another German immigrant, Heinrich Hackfeld. H. Hackfeld and Company had been founded in 1849, and, at this time, it dominated the sugar and shipping industries in Hawai'i. In 1857, Hackfeld had also established a fleet of ships connecting Bremen, Germany, to Honolulu. As an agent for various steamship lines, John providentially got to learn firsthand how a shipping company was run from the inside out. Unfortunately, the relationship with the Hawaiian government had broken down, and in 1872, H. Hackfeld and Company suffered from the repercussions of that breakdown. As a result, Pacific Mail Steamship Company had acquired Hackfeld's routes in 1873, and Hackfeld's role was reduced to acting as an agent for Pacific Mail. Soon, there would be feelings of both respect and betrayal when Heinrich Hackfeld's former apprentice, John Spreckels, took over Pacific Mail and created a monopoly of the freight and passenger traffic between Honolulu and San Francisco.

When John returned to California in 1877, he found his father busy developing the area around Aptos. Claus helped finance the Santa Cruz Railroad (which had opened in 1876), expanded the Aptos resort with a racetrack, and installed a large area surrounding the hotel with a twelve-foot-high fence to hold the deer and elk he had stocked for the guests to hunt. Guests were picked up at the Aptos train station in a carriage and were taken to the hotel by a team of four horses and liveried coachmen. Although the resort's success was short-lived, the experience would prove instrumental to John when, in the following decade, another noted California hotel came up for sale on a beautiful island named Coronado.

2

Taking Hawai'i by Storm

Lillian Caroline Siebein

Brimming with enthusiasm and energy after his Hawai'i apprenticeship, twenty-four-year-old John Spreckels was then sent to New York in 1877 by his father to study the advanced techniques in sugar refining. John had heard that hired hands were being employed by the burgeoning industry in that city, so he signed on as one. In the aftermath of the Civil War, sugar refining became New York City's most profitable industry, a distinction it maintained until World War I. Exactly which refinery John went to work in is unknown, but he'd purposefully chosen lodgings in Hoboken, New Jersey. With its waterfront location opposite New York, Hoboken had established itself as a water transportation center and a major port for transatlantic shipping lines. It also had ferries, which left the harbor for New York throughout the day, and that is how John made his daily commute across the Hudson River. He found that a shuttle across water soothed his soul.[1]

It was during one of these commutes that John met and fell in love with a local girl from Hoboken. Lillian Caroline Siebein was twenty-three years old, spunky, blue-eyed, and petite (only five feet two), and she instantly appealed to John. They surely found common ground: Both of them were offspring of parents from Hanover, both spoke German, both had suffered the loss of siblings, and both were musically proficient. Lillian's father, also named John, had been a ship chandler

4. John Spreckels, blond and blue-eyed, a dashing twenty-two-year-old in 1875. Permission granted by the Society of California Pioneers.

5. Lillian Caroline Siebein (1854–1924), spunky, blue-eyed, and petite. Permission granted from the Terrence and Virginia Wilson Private Family Collection.

for years. His "supermarket for ships" was popular in Hoboken, and it's likely that when he met John, he shared with him harrowing trans-oceanic accounts heard and seen from the crew as they replenished their ship's stock. He would have had an enraptured listener in Lillian's suitor because John loved all shipping sagas and likely had a few to share from his own oceanic ventures.

We can imagine that John and Caroline Siebein were pleased when Lillian informed them she would be marrying this young and bright entrepreneur. Even though Lillian obtained permission from her parents to marry, John Spreckels did not, as he later recounted: "I didn't ask anyone when I picked out a girl I liked and that was all there was to it."[2] Perhaps John's reluctance to involve his father in his decision had something to do with what had happened when his father suspected an unsuitable relationship with the Hanover landlady's daughter. Anyway, after only a few months of courtship, Lillian and John married in New Jersey on October 29, 1877.

Shortly after the wedding, Lillian informed her family that she would be moving to the Hawaiian Islands with her new husband. It's unknown how Lillian's parents reacted to this news, but most Americans in the nineteenth century considered Honolulu to be utterly wild and rough. American schoolchildren had read mythical stories about Captain Cook's violent murder in 1779 at the hands of Hawaiians, and of cannibals living in the Pacific islands not very far away. But Lillian Spreckels was in love, and she would go wherever John would take her. She knew she would be supporting her new husband in the family's sugar ventures, but she must have known that this was only until he could fulfill his real desire: to be in shipping.

The Treaty

Sugar had been an important export business in the tiny kingdom of Hawai'i for decades before the Spreckels contingency arrived. Although Canada, Australia, and New Zealand were customers for Hawaiian sugar, two-thirds of the crop had been going to the West Coast of the United States. Until the American Civil War cut off the transportation of sugar from Louisiana, sugarcane had been grown on a relatively small scale in Hawai'i. The outbreak of that war, however, triggered a surge in sugar exports from the Hawaiian Islands.

After the war, the Reciprocity Treaty of 1875 granted duty-free entry into the United States of Hawaiian sugarcane in exchange for a naval coaling station at what is known today as Pearl Harbor.[3] The treaty promised huge profits for *haole* (white) sugar planters, who could count on increased dividends. John later reported that his father "bitterly opposed" the treaty because he feared it would threaten to ruin a beet refiner, as he was working to become. Claus "did not think he could operate the beet factories successfully with free sugar coming in [from Hawai'i]."[4] Both father and son had studied the nuances of the treaty and fought it, but in the end, Claus said, "they beat me."[5]

But it didn't take long for Claus and John to see an opportunity in this defeat. "If we lost in one direction," John later stated, "we could make it up somewhere else."[6] If they could *own* the sugarcane that was being refined at their California Sugar Refinery, the Reciprocity Treaty could actually *increase* their wealth. As soon as the treaty passed, and before the competition realized what was happening, Claus and John rushed to Hawai'i to begin investing. Had they not acted so quickly, the Spreckels name would have become nothing more than a minor footnote in American and Hawaiian history. Their quick and astute action, however, would soon make theirs a name to contend with in the business circles of the late nineteenth and early twentieth centuries.

When the Spreckels retinue arrived in Honolulu, the place was no longer an "overgrown village" but a thriving business community with a population of fifteen thousand, a good fifth of them foreigners from all over the globe.[7] By then, the city had well-defined streets dotted with wooden houses, which had recently replaced the "little grass shacks" later made famous in song, along with a post office, churches, a hospital, a jail, lodges, a forty-two-room hotel, and a brass band that performed every weekend.[8] The village was working hard to becoming a cosmopolitan city. Much of the arable land outside the city was covered with sugar plantations that had become exceedingly profitable to the white businessmen who owned them, and that is where the Spreckels family directed their attention.

The family's goal was to purchase sugar crops cheaply and quickly, before their U.S. competitors or the island plantation owners could fully grasp the implications of the new treaty. With plenty of cash in hand, Claus and John aggressively bought up any and all crops that could be quickly acquired. The languid islanders didn't know what hit them, and, within days, sugarcane farmers were already grumbling about the "poor deals" they had made, which had rendered Claus Spreckels and sons the majority holder of all the Hawaiian sugar crops. Newspapers of the day showed John right by his father's side, the two working together on the shrewd negotiations.

The Spreckels Family Detested

Upon their arrival in Hawai'i, the Spreckels family discovered that the reign of the five lines of Hawai'i's royal Kamehamehas had come to an end in 1872. David Kalākaua, of the succeeding dynasty, had been ruling the kingdom for only a short time. Claus and Anna, who had been born in the kingdom of Hanover, understood the nuances of living in a monarchy better than most other American transplants.

King Kalākaua had been raised, educated, and "Christianized" by American Congregationalist missionaries in a strict, austere boarding school along with other heirs to the Hawaiian throne. In an unparalleled partnership between the monarchy and these missionaries, the royal children were isolated from their future subjects during their education in order to be taught English and groomed for future leadership. This schooling had been led by a mentally unstable and inexperienced teacher from Connecticut, Amos Starr Cooke, and it is unsurprising that it failed to yield what either side had anticipated when the Chief's Children's School, soon to be renamed the Royal School, was founded some four decades earlier.[9] After an advanced education under Cooke but a childhood of deprivation in all areas, many of the "little royals," including David Kalākaua, were instead prone as adults to excessive and indulgent habits.

After deciding that the Islands' natives were successfully educated and, more importantly, evangelized, the American Board of Commissioners for Foreign Missions withdrew its missionary support. By the time the Spreckels clan arrived, the missionaries and their descendants who remained in Hawai'i were virtually running the Islands' economy and politics, as well as influencing their cultural framework.[10] Indeed, the leading businessmen, still aligned with the Congregationalist denomination, looked upon the Spreckels family—which had no connection to the missionaries—as interlopers, and they treated them with undisguised hostility. Businessmen in Hawai'i described Claus rather unkindly as "short, squat, and pudgy," with a penchant for "crusty, arrogant and demanding" behavior.[11] They abhorred his lack of social graces and his "boorishness," and they refused him entry into their social circles.[12]

Wooing the King

One wonders, however, if the snobbish behavior of the Congregationalist businessmen really bothered the "crusty" patriarch. In the dark and smoke-filled saloons of Honolulu, Claus, the former saloon owner, might have easily found influential friends. Perhaps it was there that he first met the connections that would lead him to the hard-drinking King Kalākaua. It's easy to imagine the boisterous Claus picking up countless bar tabs in a showy effort to display his wealth. Historians, have much to say about his shrewdness in lending money to the king and his government at a time when such loans were desperately needed. The loans would eventually enable Claus to obtain a stranglehold on king and kingdom both.

While Claus and John were procuring available sugar plantations across the Islands, Kalākaua, flush with new money, was busy building an ornate palace named 'Iolani, or "Bird of Heaven." With its neoclassical facade, the stately palace, finished in 1882, verified the legitimacy of the Hawaiian monarchy for many, but Claus Spreckels, who had seen monarchies rise and fall in his native country, was unlikely to have been as impressed as others were. The lavish parties, extravagant luau, and royal balls at 'Iolani Palace were legendary, and John and Lillian often found themselves on the royal guest list. David Kalākaua became known in his reign as the "Merrie Monarch," due to the pomp and splendor of those events.

The House That Sugar Built

Claus and Anna had never been thrilled with the chilling fog and extremes of temperature in San Francisco. The tropical warmth and humidity of Hawaiʻi was a welcome climate for body and soul, and they decided to build a second home there. Perhaps in competition with the king, Claus built a beautiful mansion in the Punahou neighborhood of Honolulu, which the press called the "grandest habitation barring those of royalty."[13] The Spreckels estate was built to impress, with its wide verandas and staircases, its garish towers and battlements. Only a select few ever entered the property because it was fully enclosed with a padlocked iron picket fence to ensure privacy.

The German Henry Berger, leader of the Royal Hawaiian Orchestra, was the king's personal bandmaster, but he was frequently found at lavish dinner parties in the Spreckelses' ornate ballroom, conducting his cotillion string orchestra under soft candlelight. It was beginning to look to others as if the king had a social rival. The power of Claus's celebrity is plain, given the sheer number of newspaper stories that referenced his every move.

John's wife, Lillian, was also prominent on the social scene. Her vocal talent had been recognized locally, and she performed in the Honolulu Music Hall. One such concert under the patronage of King Kalākaua and Queen Kapiʻolani featured two of Lillian's vocal solos. Her impressive range is notable from the two completely diverse selections: the operatic "Heaven Hath Shed a Tear," composed by the German Friedrich Wilhelm Kücken, and the fast-tempo "Carnival of Venice," by the German Julius Benedict. Both selections reveal not only her exceptional talent but also her allegiance to her German culture.[14]

Behind the scenes, John's family was growing: Lillian gave birth to their first child, Grace Alexandria, on September 16, 1878. By the time John and Lillian's second daughter, Lillian "Lillie" Caroline, entered

6. John and Lillian's four children. (From left) Lillie (1880–1965), Claus Jr. (1888–1935), John "Jack" Jr. (1882–1921), and Grace (1878–1937). Permission granted from the Terrence and Virginia Wilson Private Family Collection.

the world in November 1880, the family business was headed toward a virtual monopoly on Hawaiian sugar crops. And, by 1882, when John Diedrich Jr. ("Jack") was born, Opa (Grandfather) Spreckels had become the "Sugar King." And when the younger Claus Jr. was born in 1888, Spreckels had become a household name. .

Backdoor Purchase of Hawaiian Lands

On July 1, 1878, in what some historians call an unscrupulous "midnight deal," Claus Spreckels acquired the lease on as much as forty thousand acres of royal land, primarily on Maui, as well as the right to redirect the water from the slopes of the large volcano Haleakalā to his farm.[15] Because redirecting this water would harm locals, their livestock, and their own farms, the deal was brought up as an emergency situation to the Hawaiian legislature. An investigation followed, but the Spreckels money prevailed, and the natives lost. Claus was quick to buy the *Pacific Commercial Advertiser* in 1880 in order to control criticism and garner support for his business interests.[16]

To safeguard his vast financial investments, Claus looked for a way to buy the royal land he was leasing. Though crown lands were ostensibly and officially not for sale, and this obstacle may have seemed insurmountable to other investors, he was not deterred. He found a "backdoor" way by approaching and convincing Princess Ruth Keʻelikōlani, heir to the vast Kamehameha estate, to sell him land. The princess, who stood six feet tall and weighed more than four hundred pounds, intimidated Hawaiians and non-Hawaiians alike with her rigid stance and formidable appearance. Claus, however, was not daunted, and he somehow convinced her to privately sell him a parcel of land in what was clearly an illicit real estate deal.

As Queen Liliʻuokalani later wrote, the princess had no actual legal right to sell lands intended "to descend to the heirs and successors of the Hawaiian crown."[17] Furthermore, "Mr. Spreckels paid the Princess Ruth $10,000 to release her claim to a small tract of these lands, although she had never ascended the throne."[18] When the act was legally questioned, Claus threatened a lawsuit. The Hawaiian legislature ultimately reached a compromise with him that gave him outright title to his leased land in return for a quitclaim deed on the remaining crown lands. Princess Ruth might be considered shrewder than Claus because she knew her claims to the lands were worthless: Previous court cases had already decided that crown lands belonged only to the ruling monarch. She pocketed $10,000 from the deal and it seems they both got what they wanted.

Spreckelsville

Claus and his three eldest sons—John, Adolph Bernard, and Claus Augustus ("Gus")—worked alongside hired hands to cultivate Maui's arid land into a highly productive sugarcane plantation, though locals laughed because his chosen tract of land was at the foot of Haleakalā. They viewed the soil as poor due to the volcanic dust that covered the surface. Undaunted, Claus hired an irrigation engineer from Germany and remedied the situation by breaking up the crust that had formed over the soil, mixing it with a "small quantity of vegetable mold."[19] The laughter ceased when "Spreckelsville" became the largest sugar plantation in the world. When the family's Hawaiian Commercial & Sugar Company was incorporated with $10 million of capital in 1884, it included four sugar mills, thirty-five miles of railroad, a water reservoir, and the most advanced canal system in the Pacific region.[20]

Between California and Hawai'i, the Spreckels family had created a veritable sugar empire. Rival planters in Hawai'i criticized the absentee sugar baron, who they believed had become the Sugar King because he had corrupted Hawai'i's king.

In 1881, the Spreckels family expanded even more by building a second refinery outside of San Francisco on Potrero Point, naming it the Western Sugar Refinery. Having two massive refineries required intensive oversight. Claus spent a great deal of time traveling back and forth between Hawai'i and San Francisco to oversee the expansion. While in Hawai'i, John was in complete charge when his father was away, and he became a force to be reckoned with among his fellow planters. He even talked them into selling their entire sugar crops at a low fixed price, having convinced them that they would certainly benefit if prices later plummeted below that price. Many planters were justifiably furious when sugarcane prices climbed instead. The planters were mourning the money they had lost due to John Spreckels's aggressive business tactics, which they viewed as underhanded.

One plantation on the island of Kaua'i traditionally held back part of its sugar crop for the local retail market, so area residents could enjoy it without paying a premium. But John Spreckels soon stopped that tradition. Uncompromising, he forced men such as William Allen, president of the Princeville Plantation Company, to sell their entire sugar harvest to him, as described in this letter from Allen to his father:

> *Honolulu, September 29, 1879*
>
> John Spreckels returns this trip having bought all the crop. We were completely in his hands. He would have all or none, and as Spreckels controlled all the refineries, we could not send our sugar to an open market with but one purchaser and that him, so we have sold.[21]

The Islands were virtually covered in sugarcane, but refined sugar was considered "white gold" and was a very expensive commodity in Hawai'i. In 1891, an American boarding school teacher in Honolulu revealed that, for many native girls, stealing sugar was worth the resulting punishment:

> This last week we ran across the fact that the girls were stealing sugar. Eight or nine girls acknowledged to crawling into the pantry window after dark and carrying off pockets-full of sugar and I should say ¾ of the girls had feasted on the stolen sweet knowing how it was obtained. Some of our oldest and best girls sent the younger ones in for them. They are now going without sugar in their morning tea and with their bread Wednesday night.[22]

"John Sugarcane"

Emma Kalanikaumaka'amano Rooke, queen consort of King Kamehameha IV, was very much beloved among Hawaiians. After her husband's death in 1863, she had run for the title and office of queen of Hawai'i against the charismatic David Kalākaua. She was defeated in a hotly contested 1874 election, and the result was mutual animosity between them.

Queen Dowager Emma also took an instant dislike toward the young Spreckels, whom she nicknamed "John Sugarcane." In her biography, one incident with John illustrates how monarchs, who were used to absolute submission from their subjects, were appalled at the aggressive nature of foreign businessmen.[23]

It seems as if John may have chosen one particular day in March of 1882 to invite the royal Emma to tour the new Spreckels mansion in Honolulu so she could view the latest and best inventions that money could buy. She had previously toured the Spreckelsville plantation in Maui and had expressed a great interest in the only electrically lit building in Hawai'i. As they rode to the Punahou neighborhood, John, no doubt purposely, trotted past the government building on King Street, where he knew a big event was underway. At the event, King Kalākaua was hosting a business dinner for all the Islands' planters, which John had refused to attend. Apparently, he was upset because his father had been offended by some royal edict that was not in the Spreckels family's best interest. Upon seeing the large number of men gathered, Emma covered her face with a veil. John "firmly demanded" that she remove it because he wanted to make sure that the dinner attendees saw them together, but she flatly refused.[24] The public viewed Emma as an enemy of the king, which is precisely why John had been so eager to be seen keeping company with the king's adversary.

When the queen dowager asked John why he was not attending the very important business meeting, he replied that he "did not want to socialize with liars or those who break their promises to friends[,] as David Kalākaua [had done] to his father." (To both John and his father, an agreement, even by a handshake, should never be broken.) Emma scolded him about speaking badly about his friends, whereupon John snapped that they were not his friends. After touring his new home, she told a confidante that John Sugarcane was ostentatious and a "pretentious show-off."[25]

Adolph Spreckels on Trial

The Spreckels sugar operations in Hawai'i were well known back in California, especially among the business enemies of the family. The *San Francisco Chronicle* was always eager to publish criticisms of Claus and his sons.

In the tumultuous early days of San Francisco's newspapers, slander, libel, distortion, defamation, scandal, and corruption were commonplace—and so was a fierce rivalry for circulation and advertising. The founders of the *Chronicle* were the feisty de Young brothers, Michael and Charles, who were unafraid to publish personal insults against various powerful men and their families in order to influence political decisions. Claus Spreckels was certainly not the only target of the de Youngs. For example, an 1879 spiteful editorial in the *Chronicle* criticizing Isaac Smith Kalloch, a local preacher running for mayor, resulted in Charles de Young's death. Kalloch responded to the editorial from the pulpit by calling the de Youngs' mother a prostitute. This enraged Charles enough to shoot Reverend Kalloch, who survived. But, the reverend's son, Isaac Milton Kalloch, sought revenge for the assault; he shot and killed Charles.[26]

In an unrelated but uncannily similar situation, Adolph Spreckels shot and wounded the surviving de Young brother, Michael, in 1884 for what was stated to be retaliation for unfavorable press. De Young had published accusations that the Spreckels family's Hawaiian sugar business was defrauding stockholders, that the plantations were little more than slave camps, and that Claus was a pimp for King Kalākaua. Later in life, John revealed that the real reason for shooting Michael de Young was to avenge their mother's honor, which had been tarnished like that of de Young's mother.[27] John, the amateur boxer, had planned to avenge the family name with "clenched fists," and he always regretted that his timing had been off and his brother had gotten to Michael de Young first.

Adolph Spreckels, like Isaac M. Kalloch, was arrested after the shooting, but both were fully acquitted: Adolph on account of a neuralgic headache, or temporary insanity, and Isaac by reason of "justifiable homicide." The acquittal of Adolph after six weeks of trial was followed by an ostentatious celebration at the Spreckels mansion. This sensational trial was covered nationwide, and its aftermath was condemned by many observers who denounced the Spreckels family for its lack of decency. But the family rallied in full mutual support of one another, and the Spreckels Hawaiian operations that the *Chronicle* had targeted continued as before, with Claus enjoying strong influence over the king.

In and Out of Favor

King Kalākaua was a profligate gambler. According to popular lore, one night during a card game of euchre, when the king demanded to know where a missing king card was, Claus carelessly remarked that *he* was the other king. This was purportedly the last straw for Kalākaua, who had grown tired of Claus's increasing demands, and he immediately left the card game. Prior to the game, Claus and John had been negotiating with the king for many things, including control of Honolulu's wharves. In exchange for those favors, Claus had offered to extend the $600,000 loan he had made to Kalākaua and even suggested the possibility of a new loan.

The king wanted out from under Claus Spreckels, and he was feeling great pressure to do so from the prominent Charles Reed Bishop, a Bostonian who had married into the Hawaiian royal family. No other non-Hawaiian name outside of royalty evoked more respect in the community than that of Charles Bishop. His name was associated with the Bishop Bank, Bishop Estate, Bishop Hall, Bishop Museum, Bishop Street, and Bishop Trust, but, sentimentally, he was the tragic widower of Princess Bernice Pauahi Pākī Bishop, the last of the Kamehameha line. The turning point in the Spreckels influence over the king occurred in 1885, when Bishop began to vocalize his distaste for Claus. In disgust he wrote that "it was strange that the King does not see that he and his family are being made tools of by Claus Spreckels."[28]

The king was also under great pressure from the Hawaiian people. His parties, gambling activities, trips, and the building of ʻIolani Palace generated a lot of criticism from those who felt he was using public money for personal pleasure. Their cries that he free himself from the "bribes" of Claus Spreckels finally spurred him to action. In 1886, Kalākaua was able to secure a loan from a London creditor and paid off his debt to Claus, freeing himself and his government of the Spreckels influence and the businessman's ever-increasing demands.[29] After having exerted a clenched fist over the economy of the Islands for nearly two decades, Claus, it seemed, had permanently fallen out of Kalākaua's favor.

But everything was forgiven when politics went haywire and the king needed all the friends he could get. In addition to the stress the king had been suffering with Claus, his political situation was in deep turmoil. In 1887, a group of descendants of the early missionaries who were now the principal industrial leaders of the Islands, along with their sympathizers, formed a secret organization called the Hawaiian League. They soon pressed King Kalākaua to sign a new, more liberal constitution. It became known as the Bayonet Constitution because it was purportedly signed under the threat of force. It benefited the businessmen's financial interests and eliminated every vestige of the king's monarchical powers, leaving him to reign but not to rule. It's not known what Claus's reaction was, but John's lack of sympathy was recorded in the *Hawaiian Gazette*: "The king is a good enough sort of fellow in his way, but he is more like an overgrown schoolboy than a statesman, and his authority under the new constitution has been reduced to an amusing shadow of a regal power."[30]

It's also unknown if the king read John's sentiments in the newspaper, but he seemed to be full of forgiveness and renewed admiration for the Spreckels family. On September 1, 1890, the king; his wife, Queen Kapiʻolani; and his sister, Princess Liliʻuokalani; as well as every other high-ranking official in the Hawaiian government attended a "royal dinner party" at the palace in Claus Spreckels's honor. Sitting at the table alongside the three majesties was John's eldest daughter, twelve-year-old Grace Spreckels.[31] Newspapers put Grace alongside her father at many events such as this, perhaps making the case that he was mentoring his firstborn in the same way that he had been mentored.

J. D. Spreckels and Brothers

As his family's sugar enterprises expanded, John sought a way to fulfill his own dreams. While still supporting the family's business ventures in sugar, he needed a solution that would let him branch out from the career his dominant father had chosen for him. At the age of twenty-six, he found that solution: He convinced Claus to let him begin his own shipping line. Up to then, the Spreckels family had not owned the ships that hauled raw Hawaiian sugarcane to their California refinery, and John's transportation plan would give the family a virtual monopoly on all aspects of sugar production. Such industry dominance appealed to Claus. He financed his son's dream with $2 million in capital with the stipulation that John would be president while Claus—along with his other sons, Adolph and Gus—would be equal financial partners.

John embraced the opportunity and launched J. D. Spreckels and Brothers in 1879. Even though "Brothers" was part of the name, it was clear that the designation was in name only. Adolph was one of the brothers referred to in the company name, but his father kept him busy as "secretary," managing the books for both the California Sugar Refinery and the Hawaiian Commercial & Sugar Company. Adolph did not have the same energetic physical stamina as John had and was content to work on the books, or so it seemed. Gus, a year younger, was elevated to director, theoretically his elder brother Adolph's supervisor. John was not concerned, however; the shipping business was to be *his* sole focus. It was up to his brothers to support their father in the majority of the other aspects of the sugar business.

The transport company began with a single ship, the schooner *Rosario*. John commissioned a 247-ton brigantine named *Claus Spreckels* in 1879 (possibly to stroke his father's ego), and another brigantine of 300 tons, named after himself, in 1880. In short time, John added a fleet of several other vessels and named them after family and friends. These ships were fast. They sailed between San Francisco and the Spreckelsville plantation on Maui in nine and a half days, breaking all previous records.[32]

The Oceanic Steamship Company

By 1880, it was clear to anyone in the shipping industry that sails were giving way to steam. Ships powered by sail simply could not perform as well. When John began to face competition from the new steamships, he jumped into action. He recognized that steamships would not only be more versatile and reliable than the line's schooners but quicker, too. To the amazement of all on the sidelines, he incorporated the Oceanic Steamship Company in 1881. Quickly, the brothers began buying and chartering nearly a dozen freight ships, hauling raw sugar from Hawai'i to the Spreckels refinery in San Francisco and returning with merchandise back to the Islands.

In 1882, John commissioned two elegant steamers, the *Alameda* and the *Mariposa*, to be built in Philadelphia. These ships would carry passengers in comfort, along with the freight. Leaving nothing to chance, he went to Philadelphia himself to supervise the details. The ships soon became known as the "finest and fastest ships" flying the American flag.[33] Newspapers covered the launch of additional ships acquired by the fleet, with the christening ceremonies presided over by John's eldest child, Grace.[34]

The Oceanic Steamship Company became the first shipping line to offer regular service between Honolulu and San Francisco. With his new fleet, John Spreckels managed to reduce travel time by nearly half. On July 31, 1883, with John's parents, his sister Emma, and his brother Rudolph on board, the *Mariposa* completed a run from San Francisco to Honolulu in a record speed of five days and twenty-one hours.[35] It's easy to imagine the pride on both sides of his family.

It was a red-letter day for Hawaiians, who would now have regular service to and from California. King Kalākaua ordered a twelve-gun salute when the *Mariposa* glided into port. His private carriage met the Spreckels family when they disembarked. These gestures established John D. Spreckels as a celebrity in the eyes of Hawaiians and, more importantly to John, as a formidable competitor in the Pacific maritime trade.[36]

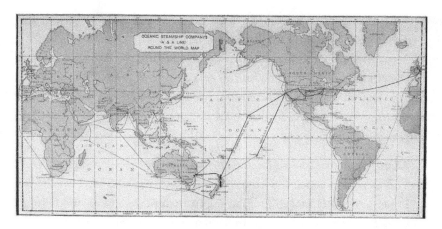

7. Oceanic Steamship Company, dominating Pacific transport. The Spreckels vessels were the only ones flying the American flag in the South Pacific during this era. Courtesy Huntington Library, San Marino, California.

Transporting the Mail

When an opportunity to deliver the mail arose in 1885, John's reputation as a man who met deadlines became vitally important. The Pacific Mail Steamship Company had withdrawn from its monthly sailings between San Francisco, New Zealand, and Australia. John wasted no time in pursuing the business. He won the contract and added "an additional $150,000 a year to the Oceanic Steamship's coffers."[37] He had journeyed aboard a Pacific Mail ship from Panama to California at the age of three; now, as president of this major shipping company, he was taking over that same company's routes and ships. He was doing more than transporting cargo, passengers, and mail to and from the Southern Hemisphere; he was living his dream and doing it in style.

When John added the *Zealandia* and *Australia* to his line in 1886, the Hawaiian flag flew from the masts because, as John explained, the ships had been built in England, and this fact "forbade the use of the stars and stripes."[38] One year later, he strategically hired American shipbuilders to heavily alter the *Australia*. He then petitioned Congress to acknowledge his newly modified "American" ship, and, by a special act of Congress, the *Australia* was granted her American registry. The British ship now flew Old Glory from her mast.[39]

Soon the Spreckels line was the only one flying the American flag in the South Pacific. With the addition of a contract to deliver U.S. mail to Tahiti, New Zealand, and Australia, the Oceanic Steamship Company soon dominated transport in the Pacific. A passenger described John's industry dominance and succinctly outlined the schedule:

> All the regular steamers that stop at Honolulu are owned by one company. There is one steamer, the Australia, that makes only the trip between San Francisco and Honolulu, remaining in each place a week and taking a week for each voyage, thus requiring a month for the round trip. Then there are three steamers that make the trip to Australia, stopping at Honolulu and Auckland, with time so arranged that one from the colonies and one from San Francisco meet, or rather just miss each other at Honolulu once every month. It was one of these through steamers that we were to take. The rates of travel are higher than on the Atlantic, as there is no competition. The fare to Honolulu is seventy-five dollars.[40]

The *Oceanic* became highly respected for meeting schedules without incident. As more business came John Spreckels's way, keeping to a schedule was paramount for him. The U.S. government learned this the hard way when, on July 29, 1887, the overland mail-carrying train was running one hour behind from the East Coast. On board the train were time-sensitive U.S. government dispatches from Washington regarding the political upset then brewing in Hawai'i, dispatches that were meant to reach government officials in Honolulu. The transatlantic telegraph cable had not yet reached Hawai'i, so important government intelligence, along with personal letters for those living in the Islands, would now sit in mailbags at the dock for a month until the next steamer arrived. John justified his decision not to wait the extra hour and have the *Mariposa* carry the dispatches and letters to Hawai'i but rather to stick to his schedule and send the ship to New Zealand because, at that point, his allegiance was to that country, which could initiate a fine for lateness.[41]

John's insistence on maintaining the schedule was enforced for not only the mail. *Southern Magazine* reported comments in 1890 from a passenger on the *Zealandia* that illustrate how nobody would be given latitude when it came to keeping to a Spreckels ship schedule:

> A funny thing happened. A German Professor had been aboard to bid his friends farewell and they had become so engrossed in conversation that they did not hear or heed the warning gong. When he came to himself, he went to the captain and besought him to turn back. His friends did not know where he was, [he said,] they would be dragging the harbor for him. He had to lecture at three that afternoon. The captain would not at all consent to turn back, but told him he might go off with the pilot. So, when we had reached the rough water outside the Bay and the little row boat came along side for the pilot, he had the pleasure of climbing down the rope ladder and dropping into the rocking and tumbling boat. We were told that he would be taken to the pilot boat and there was no knowing when he would reach land as these pilot boats frequently stayed out for a week or ten days.[42]

Catering to the Elite (and Runaways)

John's vision grew larger still. Despite his known dislike of mingling with the high-society crowd where pomp and circumstance were required, John set his sights on catering to clientele who craved luxury. Voyaging on big steamships was a relatively new mark of high status, and John's ships were among the first to provide an extravagance on par with fine hotels and restaurants. The luxuries of the Spreckels ships became newsworthy, with travel journals across the country lauding the ships: "To say that this fine fleet is furnished with all the modern improvements does not fully convey the extreme comfort, which is enjoyed in the voyage. The state rooms are furnished with . . . electric lights, the table is up to the standard of the best first-class hotels ashore, and good order and cleanliness everywhere prevail."[43]

John was frequently on board his ships, not to lounge on the deck or entertain guests as a rich shipping magnate but to assist in all aspects of navigation. He was more comfortable swapping yarns of navigational challenges with the captain or with some rough-and-ready shipmates in the pilothouse.[44] Yet, it became known among his passengers that his most prized possession was a shipmaster certificate that authorized him to oversee all aspects of any large ship's operation, at sea or in port. Fiercely proud of what it had taken to achieve this, he stated more than once, "I know what manual labor means. I have earned a pilots and a Masters license at sea."[45]

His pride was well deserved, considering that at that time ships did not have the highly accurate navigational equipment used today. In John's era, marine navigation was based on a nineteenth-century maxim known as "the three L's, '*log, lead,* and *look out*': *log* for determining ship speed, the *lead* in line for sounding or sampling the bottom, and *look out* for the crucial attention required at all times."[46]

By 1890, the Spreckels line was carrying a staggering one hundred first-class passengers per month to Hawai'i, up from thirty in 1885. Part of John's success was linked to the first-ever all-inclusive package deals to the Islands, which included hotel and volcano excursions. Passengers were directed to his co-owned Honolulu Music Hall, across from the 'Iolani Palace, where they might rub shoulders with Hawaiian royalty.

John wrote one of the earliest tourist articles encouraging voyages to the Hawaiian Islands. He urged "timid" Americans to get off their couches and look toward the "Isles of the West." He told them to "flee from the great extremes of heat and cold of the rest of the country" and discover "La Dolce Far Niente," or the sweetness of doing nothing (something he could only visualize and promote to others, not something he could personally actualize during this time in his own life).[47] He wrote, "There is but one Pacific Ocean, but one Hawaiian group, [and] to sail for a week over the clear and calm waters of the one and to luxuriate in the tropical beauty of the other are pleasures not to be duplicated the world over."[48]

Not all who heeded the call were born sailors like John Spreckels. For some, it was difficult in the extreme to appreciate a transoceanic voyage. Carrie Winter was one passenger who found the journey less appealing after suffering debilitating seasickness. On her voyage to Hawai'i aboard one of the Spreckels ships, she wrote to her fiancé, Charles Kofoid, with a vivid description of her experience. It's clear that the romance of the handkerchief-waving departure at the wharf disappeared along with the coastline as the steamer departed San Francisco's harbor.

SS. ZEALANDIA
August 27, 1890

Dear Charlie:

When we reached the ocean the ship began to rock and roll. Oh Charlie, the misery of what followed. I did not leave my state-room till Monday morning. Saturday night was the worst though. We were on the storm side and every crack was stuffed tight. Not a bit of fresh air till Monday. The waves pounded, way above us on the hurricane deck, the boat rocked so that I had to hold on all the time to keep in my berth the awful sounds, and smells!!! The sickness was bad enough but then there was that indescribable feeling of being poised in the midst of the air and sky and water and swaying there with nothing to grasp.[49]

However, her narrative changed soon enough during the latter part of the seven-day cruise. Once she discovered the romance of moonlit nights on deck, she could feel what had constantly lured John Spreckels to the sea: "For us every day dawned clear and beautiful and every evening saw the sun sink into the ocean in a blaze of glory, leaving its glow in the sky long afterwards, while every night the stars and moon seemed brighter."[50]

Others were lured to the sea as well—including runaways, who constantly attempted to stow away on Spreckels ships. Charles Burnett Wilson, an important dignitary under King Kalākaua, had a son, Johnny, who would later become mayor of Honolulu. Johnny's mother, Eveline "Kitty" Townsend, was a protégée and intimate friend of Lili'uokalani.

With so many ships leaving Honolulu Harbor, stowing away for adventure was enticing to a young man, and Johnny was caught a few times on ships before they left for sea. One time, he actually got away by hiding on a whaling boat. When John received notice from Charles Wilson to be on the lookout for Johnny, he took it seriously. He himself was now a father of four and fully empathized with the dignitary.

After several months, John learned that the young runaway was in a San Francisco boarding house on Bush Street. He broke into Johnny's room while he was gone and took all his possessions. When the young man returned, he found a policeman ready to escort him to the thief. To Johnny's surprise, the "thief" was none other than the well-known millionaire John D. Spreckels. Young Johnny Wilson never forgot that Spreckels quietly slipped a twenty-dollar gold piece in his pocket before sending him home to Honolulu on the *Alameda* the next morning.[51]

Satisfaction That Comes with Success

As John surveyed the accomplishments of the previous decade, he likely felt deep satisfaction. Not only had he refused the career his father had in mind for him and set a course of his own, he had set it with his father's blessings and financial backing. He had long since made back that initial $2 million from his father. He had accomplished far more than any of his family could have imagined. His steamship line served the entire Pacific, he had created a demand for travel to the Hawaiian Islands among the rich and pampered, and by trusting his business acumen during turbulent times in the shipping industry, he'd become a millionaire before he turned thirty. By trusting his own instincts, he'd built a recognized shipping empire. Another opportunity would soon become apparent.

3

Crazed Land Boom and Bust

Southern California's Boom

Whereas northern California had been settled in the wake of the Gold Rush, the settling of southern California was a consequence of a crazed land boom. With most of northern California now spoken for, and with a westward and southward railway expansion underway, thousands of real estate speculators from across the country rushed in 1886 and 1887 to southern California, looking for land to buy cheap and sell dear. The Southern Pacific Railroad (whose nickname was Espee, for "SP") and the Atchison, Topeka and Santa Fe Railway owned most of the land where the frenzied hubs were: Los Angeles and San Diego, respectively. Eager to sell their lands and develop southern California for future profits, they started a rate war, undercutting each other's rates and thereby enabling thousands of newcomers to travel to California, which in turn triggered a massive buying of land for astronomical prices.

Bordered by the shimmering Pacific Ocean, southern California was marketed across the country by the railroads' promotional brochures as a subtropical paradise. For example, though San Diego had no industry, no factories, no farms, and no lumber, it did have an appealing climate that promised health and longevity. Southern California, the land of sunshine, became a destination in the late 1800s for tuberculosis patients seeking a climate cure for their incurable disease. Lots that had initially sold for $10 to $30 an acre were now going for as high as $10,000 an acre! Hordes of hungry buyers would pay just about anything to live long and healthy lives beneath the California sunshine.

The boom stimulated growth far beyond the wildest dreams of San Diego's early settlers. Alonzo Horton, the acknowledged founder of San Diego, had initially given away lots to encourage settlement. He watched in amazement as lots previously valued at $5,000 now sold for $50,000.[1] So many people migrated to the area that in order to capitalize on the incoming flux, speculators quickly had to spread out from central San Diego.

Stoking San Diego's Boom

John Spreckels met his destiny, and San Diego met hers, in July of 1887. John, now vice-commodore of the San Francisco Yacht Club, was an expert racer of yachts, and his schooner *Lurline* was the victor of many competitions. This particular summer, at the victorious end of a race from San Francisco, he stopped at San Diego Bay to restock the *Lurline*. It was there that he saw the boom in full swing and, in his later words, "discovered" his future and likened himself to Christopher Columbus, who "stumbled" upon a new land by "accident."[2] The arrival of the "Sugar Prince" was a newsworthy event for the small town. A delegation of prominent local businessmen rushed to greet him and offer him a grand tour of their growing community, hoping to entice John somewhere with an opportunity to invest.

One of them, Elisha Spurr Babcock Jr., had visited John in San Francisco in the middle of the previous month, to encourage him to reroute his South Pacific steamer line to include San Diego.[3] As a developer, Babcock needed large amounts of bulk commodities such as cement and iron that were proving hard to obtain. Since no facilities existed in San Diego's sleepy harbor, the hull of a large ship, such as those operated by the Spreckels line, could save the day and bring huge financial returns for an interested shipping mogul.[4] John was impressed with the pitch made by the persuasive entrepreneur only five years older than himself but was unable to redirect his steamship routes to accommodate San Diego's needs.

Babcock had arrived in 1883 from Indiana with his wife, Isabella Graham, and their two sons, Arnold Edgar, age ten, and Graham Elisha, age nine (first son Elisha Spurr died at age one). Like John, he was energetically in pursuit of new opportunities and profit. After serving in the army, Babcock became a railroad agent and then a president of both a telegraph and a telephone company.[5]

This fact that Babcock had already pitched San Diego as a place of financial opportunity to John makes one wonder how much of an accidental discovery the port town actually was on John's part. Regardless, the mariner in John immediately saw that San Diego's natural harbor was superior to that of the man-made Los Angeles Harbor and would be much more of a logical distribution point of merchandise for the Southwest. He saw with his own eyes, as Babcock had described, the lack of harbor facilities to accommodate the great sailing ships that came around the infamous Cape Horn. He immediately knew this was a sound opportunity for investment. Already, the J. D. Spreckels and Brothers company had been transporting building materials and merchandise to different ports all around the Pacific and had made him and his brother Adolph a fortune since its incorporation in 1879.

During the tour of the town by the leading businessmen, John was made aware of a particular looming threat to future development: The Santa Fe Railway, indispensable to San Diego's growth, was on the verge of abandoning the town due to the lack of a local coal supply to keep the locomotives running. The delegation would eliminate any red tape if only John would consider building a coal wharf. John perceived that an outlay of $90,000 for a new wharf and coal bunker near the train station would bring immense returns; since the railway line was having financial difficulties, he promised to advance them all the coal they needed on credit if they would agree to keep the line running, which they did.[6]

Because John lived and worked out of San Francisco, he needed to hire some local businessmen to oversee San Diego's new branch of the Spreckels Brothers Commercial Company as well as spur San Diego's economy. John was impressed enough with Babcock's skills and entrepreneurial spirit to engage him part-time along with retired riverboat captain Charles T. Hinde, full-time, with whom he instantly felt a connection. The fifty-five-year-old captain and his wife of thirty-nine years, Eliza Halliday, were newcomers to San Diego and had been invited to relocate from Indiana and partake in San Diego's prosperity by close friends Elisha and Isabella Babcock. They were financially well off but had lost their only child, thirteen-year-old daughter Camilla, and were ready for a fresh start out West. After meeting Captain Hinde, John instantly hired this veteran shipmaster to be in charge of the comings and goings of the Spreckels Wharf. He instantly knew that his wharf would be in good hands with someone who understood the life of a ship captain.[7] John's instincts were good, because Hinde's "efforts to increase the efficiency" of the Spreckels Commercial Company quickly earned him the title of "most valued member."[8]

The fact that the Santa Fe's line to Los Angeles represented the only land transportation out of San Diego made many San Diegans applaud John's investment and regard him as somewhat of a saint, but not every resident of the city felt the same way. There were several small piers already in existence that belonged to merchants, many of whom were reluctant to face competition from the proposed modern wharf. They grouped together and—through a series of injunctions in which they claimed not only that the new pier would cause devaluation in their businesses but that the city's beautiful waterfront would be ruined by the silting up of the harbor—blocked construction of the Spreckels Wharf.[9] John was undeterred, however. The first pile for the new pier was driven on January 10, 1888, and John ordered the work to proceed despite the legal injunctions.[10] So determined was he to see his contract fulfilled with the Santa Fe Railway, he organized two full crews to work for a handsome wage to build the pier at the foot of G Street. As soon as the first crew was hauled off to jail for violating the injunction, the second crew picked up where the first one had left off. When the second crew was arrested and jailed, the first crew, already bailed out with Spreckels money, returned to the job.[11] Gus Larson, one of the pile drivers on the job, recalled that this strategy ultimately "wore down the opposition."[12]

Despite court injunctions and harassment, John successfully established the largest coal depot, warehouses, and coal wharf (15,000 tons!) anywhere along the Pacific Coast. By the end of 1888, six hundred longshoremen were employed on the waterfront—the largest number in the history of San Diego.[13] Just as he had imagined, he was earning large financial rewards from the very beginning while connecting San Diego to the trade routes of the West.[14] Almost from the beginning of building the wharf in San Diego, the Spreckels Brothers Commercial Company became the largest supplier of coal, oil, cement, wood, fertilizers, and more for the struggling town desperate to grow.[15]

The Coronado Beach Company

On that warm summer day when John had dropped anchor in San Diego's bay, Babcock had given John a tour of the four thousand acres of the barren peninsula just south of San Diego that would later be named Coronado, but which was then under development by him and his partners. The Coronado Beach Company, with $1 million in capital, had been formed on April 7, 1886, with high hopes.

Babcock introduced John to his "older" Beach Company business partners, Hampton Lovegrove Story and Jacob Gruendike. The three of them had pooled $110,000 in November 1885 to begin development. It's likely that Babcock, who admired John's skill as a developer, hoped that he would easily grasp their enthusiasm for the peninsula's great potential due to its close proximity to the developing town of San Diego. Even though none of them had any hotel experience, they intended to turn the empty land into a superlative resort anchored by a grand hotel. They also wanted to live there, so they decided to surround the resort with a master-planned community. Story named the island "Coronado" after Mexico's Coronado Islands, less than twenty miles away.[16]

Story had relocated from Chicago to begin a new life after his wife, Marion Lydia Fuller Story, divorced him in 1875 for adultery with his secretary, Adella B. Ellis, an employee of the Story and Clark Piano Company he cofounded.[17] He was forty when he married Adella, twenty-eight, in 1876. He moved to San Diego in 1885 with Adella, leaving

8. Elisha Spurr Babcock Jr. (1848–1922), who came to San Diego from Indiana in search of a healthy retreat. When he sensed opportunity, he engaged in massive real estate developments, which he ultimately lost to John Spreckels when the economy collapsed. Courtesy of Hotel del Coronado Records.

behind a disgruntled business partner and three sons, Edward, Robert, and Frank. When he shook hands with John for the first time, he was fifty-two and the father of two more children, Addie and James. It became well known that John was not charmed by Story's personality.[18]

Babcock's other partner was sixty-two-year-old bank president Jacob Gruendike, a California pioneer and lifelong bachelor. Gruendike was at that time "the richest man in San Diego County," and since Babcock and Story had a good amount of "vision and enthusiasm," but not a lot of money, the banker's involvement gave the venture much-needed credibility.[19]

Babcock, the youngest and most energetic of the three investors, became president of the Coronado Beach Company. Story was named vice-president, and Gruendike (who, as a bank president, would not be as engaged as his partners) was made secretary-treasurer. Two other capitalists, also from Babcock's home state of Indiana, Josephus Collett, a railroad man, and Heber Ingle, sensing the excitement and opportunities, later each bought a one-eighth interest.[20]

With astonishing speed, the Coronado Beach Company established a number of additional and supporting ventures during the following months: The Coronado Ferry Company built wharves and storage facilities and developed ferryboat service between Coronado and San Diego; the Coronado Water Company piped fresh water under the bay from the San Diego River; and the Coronado Railroad Company provided rail lines in Coronado, eventually connecting Coronado to downtown San Diego via the sandy isthmus, the Silver Strand, that effectively rendered Coronado a peninsula rather than an island.[21]

Selling the Coronado Dream

When they were ready to show off, the Coronado Beach Company entrepreneurs notified selected newspapers of an extravagant but free community celebration for the Fourth of July weekend. Although they billed it as a patriotic festival, they intended to promote the forthcoming beachfront hotel and demonstrate to visitors what it would be like to live in "paradise." Pamphlets endorsing the virtues of Coronado were handed out to the 3,500 in attendance.

Immediately after the summer event, Babcock financed a nationwide advertising campaign to emblazon the Coronado name across the timetables of transcontinental railways, featuring a sketch of the fabulous proposed hotel. Those who had attended the Independence Day celebration were invited back on November 13, 1886, for Coronado's first public land auction. The vast improvements that had been made in just a few months, especially the fountains and lush landscaping, impressed the 6,600 guests who crossed San Diego Bay "by skiff, power launch, and overburdened ferry."[22] Auctioneer Robert Pennell's persuasive techniques were so effective that 350 lots sold on the first day, immediately recouping the visionary trio's entire initial investment.[23] The first parcel sold that morning went to real estate attorney Levi Chase for $1,600. By the afternoon, the enthusiasm mounted to such a feverish pitch that Chase was offered $3,500 for the very same lot. By January 1887, there were thirty completed dwellings inhabited by "a population of highly intelligent character."[24]

Finally, on March 19, 1887, to the delight of the growing community—and of the founding visionaries, whose dreams were finally being realized—Babcock's wife, Isabella, and Story's wife, Adella, performed the groundbreaking ceremony for the Hotel del Coronado. Babcock, who had selected architects James, Merritt, and Watson Reid, brothers he knew from his home state of Indiana, described his expectations for the huge turreted complex, stating that it

> would be built around a court—a garden of tropical trees, shrubs and flowers with pleasant paths—balconies should look down on the open court from every story. From the south end, the foyer would open to Glorietta Bay with verandas for rest and promenade. On the ocean corner there would be a pavilion tower and northward along the ocean a colonnade terraced in grass to the beach. The dining wing would project at an angle from the southeast corner of the court and be almost detached to give full value to the view of the ocean, bay and city.[25]

Building the Hotel del Coronado

Building this vision was no small task. All construction materials for the hotel had to be ferried to San Diego and then transported three miles

9. The resplendent Hotel del Coronado, with its sweeping silhouette and whimsy of red turrets and towers. It opened on February 14, 1888. Courtesy of Hotel del Coronado Records.

by train to the thirty-five-acre building site in Coronado. Approximately 250 construction workers were employed, and, in spite of the island's enforced temperance, the promise of a cold beer daily after work kept the men on the job.[26] San Diego was short on skilled carpenters, so the company brought in a Chinese workforce from San Francisco who received training on the job. These workers proved to be talented, but they could not read architectural blueprints. Astonishingly enough, however, using only general sketches, they built the hotel in just eleven months.[27] The resplendent hotel, with its sweeping silhouette and whimsy of turrets and towers, rose swiftly and stood out amid the growing charm of the planned neighborhood. This was the fantastic dream—still under construction then but displaying from the Reid brothers' architectural blueprints its promised splendid completion—that inspired John Spreckels's imagination during his July 1887 visit.

The hotel was nearing completion when its newly appointed manager, John B. Seghers from the Chicago Union Club, arrived at the end of the year. Before the public opening, famed chef Frederick Compagnon created a succulent Christmas dinner for the small group of founders and supporters who gathered to celebrate their accomplishment. With toasts all around, the hotel's success seemed promising during the 1887 Christmas season.

On February 14, 1888, the "Queen of the Beach" opened its doors, attracting dignitaries from across the country. Because it had yet to be furnished, however, its opening was without a full fanfare—a nonobservance that foreshadowed the hotel's immediate future. Unfortunately, by now the entire country had begun to feel the effects of a spreading depression, and savvy financial insiders suspected that the Hotel del Coronado was in trouble. Investors and purchasers of Coronado lots found themselves unable to meet their financial obligations, and a domino effect of debt plunged the Coronado Beach Company into a financial predicament that would directly provide John Spreckels with another opportunity.

Bust and Despair

What goes up must come down. This axiom was never truer than when southern California's great land boom collapsed in the early months of 1888. Eastern newspapers had been warning citizens who were packing up for California to use caution in their financial investments. Those who did not listen ended up being sorry, as thousands of "paper millionaires" were now suddenly penniless. Banks in San Diego and Los Angeles recognized that the inflated values placed on southern California real estate were ridiculous and unsustainable, and for their economic survival, they rallied together to restrict credit to speculators and refuse to lend more than the pre-boom cost of real estate. After the banks called a halt to loans, Babcock and Story's optimism turned to despair.[28] Without the financial support of local banks, or of the wary bankers on the East Coast, an economic slump abruptly crippled the entire San Diego region. Thousands of new residents fled, and the population plummeted from a robust fifty thousand to an anemic eight thousand.[29]

As John recollected, "Everybody who could get out, got out." He retrospectively scoffed at the "thousands scurrying off like rats from a sinking ship. . . . Only the brave men full of grit had the nerve to hang on, hoping against hope, determined to weather the storm."[30] The California exodus made headlines across the country, and those outside the state who had bought lots in Coronado were anxious. With false bravado, hoping what he said would prove true, Babcock promised concerned investors that the general depression would be temporary.[31]

All this was happening just as the new community of Coronado was beginning to generate its collective identity and just as the Hotel del Coronado was nearing completion. The hotel lost $60,000 in the first three months it was open, and many employees had to be laid off. The laborers in charge of putting the final touches on the hotel began packing up when they could not be paid. Babcock pleaded unsuccessfully with them to finish. Those who had bought stock in the Coronado Beach Company sold or exchanged their shares as soon as possible.[32] In this uncertain economic environment, the problems seemed insurmountable. The event that seemed to mark the end of the dream was when twenty boxcars, loaded with furnishings for the hotel, were "consumed by fire" in a tragic railroad accident that also took the life of the engineer.[33]

Babcock wrote to a friend in a confidential letter on May 19, 1888, "Mr. Story's health has not been good, and he has endeavored to drop business."[34] It was up to Babcock to address the numerous logistical problems regarding the completion of the hotel and the development of the surrounding community. He informed his investors on August 10, 1888, that he had assumed complete management of the hotel and would be presiding over the Coronado Beach Company.[35] He alone would supervise the company's enterprises, including Coronado's electrical plant, ferry system, water company, and railroad.[36]

When it became clear that Story's condition would not allow him to continue in the partnership, Babcock searched desperately for someone to buy out his interests.[37] Unfortunately, many other hotels in the region could no longer attract prospective buyers and either were being torn down for salvage materials or were left to rot and ruin. The Hotel del Coronado was at high risk and was threatened with foreclosure. But

Babcock would never let his dream fade into history; he needed a loan, and he knew just whom to ask.

The Bailout

Without hesitation, John Spreckels lent Babcock $100,000 to help complete the hotel. Implored by Babcock, he also bought out Story's investment. Story's one-third interest in all of the Coronado Beach Company's ventures cost John $511,050.[38] John chose to remember himself as somewhat of a savior: "He turned to me for help when the inflated balloon collapsed, and I completed the building of Hotel Coronado. So you see, circumstances forced me to get deeper and deeper into the big game of helping to develop San Diego. So I took off my coat and pitched in for all I was worth!"[39]

John was certain that he and his brother Adolph could supervise, in addition to their other holdings, the hotel, the extensive Coronado Beach holdings, and their San Diego wharf and coal bunker ventures from their desks in San Francisco. Nevertheless, John vividly remembered his 1887 tour that attracted him to Southern California; in his words, "The San Diego bug got me!"[40]

Babcock's correspondence to an attorney in San Francisco on July 28, 1889, reveals that Story did not sell his shares as easily as one would have thought given the circumstances, and the differences were settled by arbitration after Story stopped communicating with Babcock. The following day, Babcock wrote to an investor to assure him that "the general feeling in San Diego is much better than it was. The purchase by John D. Spreckels of Mr. Story's interest in all our companies has strengthened confidence greatly."[41] He boasted that "San Francisco and vicinity think a great deal more of San Diego than they did before Spreckels invested."[42]

It seems as if Babcock was not the only grateful beneficiary of John's bailout. The San Diego Land and Town Company, created by the Santa Fe Railway in 1888 to develop the city of Chula Vista, had an immediate upturn when the news was broadcast that millionaire John D. Spreckels had invested in Coronado.[43] Babcock elatedly wrote to John that due to his reputation as a shipping and sugar magnate, the company's stock rose from 23 to 28 points.[44] At this point, Babcock must have been congratulating himself for his partnership with John, which had bailed out his dream and helped him retain his 50 percent partnership.

Babcock's joy soon turned to despair, however, when the nationwide financial depression continued and he was unable to repay the initial loan he had acquired from John, who did not seem affected by the economic slump. Babcock was forced to stand by and watch John buy out every venture he had dedicated years of effort to. By 1890, John assumed complete ownership of the Coronado Beach Company and, in addition, purchased Babcock's Coronado's Belt Line as well as the San Diego and Coronado Ferry Company. Moving swiftly, he bought all unsold lots in Coronado, as well as the Silver Strand and North Island. By 1903, he was the owner of the hotel and had relegated Babcock to the position of hotel manager.

The southern California bust had been timely for John, who by now had millions upon millions of dollars from both his shipping and the family's sugar enterprises. San Diego was evidently the opportunity he had been looking for to break free from the family wars that were on the horizon as well as his father's ventures; he wanted to create his own legacy. He recalled, "I was not a retired capitalist looking merely for safe investments. I was not in the market for coupon bearing securities of enterprises already established. No! I was a young man, a young American businessman, looking for opportunities. I was out to find a big opportunity to do big constructive work on a big scale, and in San Diego I thought I foresaw just such a chance."[45]

John's father did not approve of his southern California investments. He viewed those side ventures as "impulsive and rash." Claus believed that John was leading with his heart over his head after "an accidental episode of a summer yachting cruise."[46] Claus also believed that his son's starry-eyed business venture into an unknown island called Coronado, adjacent to insignificant San Diego, was impractical and absurd. But John was resolute and rebuffed him, reminding his father and any other critics that this was his opportunity to do "big things on a big scale."[47]

4

Sugar and Strife

The Battle of the Two Sugar Kings

The beginning of the end of the Spreckels family solidarity stemmed from a business decision involving expansion in the late 1880s. The family's California-based company was the top sugar refiner, as well as the leading grower and importer of Hawaiian sugar, on the Pacific Coast. Indeed, their output of sugar was more than could be consumed on that coast. Never afraid of competition, Claus decided to ship sugar across the country and compete with the East Coast sugar refineries. He did not anticipate the hardships that lay ahead, however.

New York had its own millionaire "Sugar King," a third-generation German American entrepreneur named Henry Osborne "H. O." Havemeyer. Havemeyer owned the American Sugar Refining Company and was the leader of a "Sugar Trust," which had been founded in 1887. The economic muscle of the trust can be gauged from the fact that it was one of the twelve companies setting the Dow Jones Average at that time. He was as aggressive and outspoken as Claus was, and like Claus, he was simultaneously celebrated and reviled by the public. With more notoriety on the East Coast, Havemeyer was widely considered to be the second-most significant trust organizer after John D. Rockefeller, and the newspapers frequently villainized him as a robber baron. But Claus as well as Havemeyer had been called out for ruthless business tactics that focused on eliminating competition.

Upon learning that the West Coast Sugar King was encroaching on his territory, Havemeyer was straightforward about his monopolistic intentions; in 1887, he invited Claus to join the Sugar Trust, asserting that cooperation was far better than competition. If Havemeyer thought that the two sugar kingdoms could merge, however, he was sorely mistaken. The zealously independent Claus flatly refused a partnership, despite the fact that the collaboration would have augmented the family's wealth. He revered independence much more than he valued profit, declaring at one point, "I never yet have gone into anything unless I could have it all my own way."[1]

Outraged by the rebuff, Havemeyer instigated an aggressive price war in an attempt to completely eradicate the Spreckels family's sugar-refining business. He swiftly purchased a San Francisco refinery to compete with Spreckels on his home turf, and he slashed sugar prices in the California market. Incensed at this bold move, Claus declared to anyone within earshot, "This trust has trampled on my toes and I won't stand it."[2]

Claus retaliated in 1888 by aggressively undercutting Havemeyer's Sugar Trust business in the East, a campaign that would not come cheap. He went to Philadelphia and purchased a site fronting the Delaware River, spending nearly $5 million to construct the most modern and highly efficient refinery of its time. By 1889, the new enterprise refined an astonishing two million pounds of sugar daily.

Claus's revenge efforts against his rival would add strain to his sons' lives. John, consumed with running the Oceanic Steamship Company, his new San Diego and Coronado investments, and more, was now also tasked with managing the California refinery so that Claus could battle on his competitor's turf in the East. Claus put Claus Junior, aka "Gus"—who was very popular in the San Francisco social scene and was considered "the most jovial of the Spreckels boys"—in charge of the Philadelphia refinery.[3] Gus and his wife, Susan Oroville "Orey" Dore, whom he had married in 1883, were enthusiastic at the prospect of a new adventure as well as the news that Gus would be receiving a hefty yearly salary of $24,000.[4]

Seventeen-year-old Rudolph Spreckels was the only brother with no clear direction in life. Likely owing to his childhood struggles with asthma, which kept him from straying too far from home and his mother, he was known in the family as a mama's boy. After Anna had lost eight children, she became overly cautious, keeping such a careful watch on her youngest that Rudolph missed plenty of school. When Claus unexpectedly dropped by the house one afternoon, he found his youngest lounging with a novel, with servants and his mother attending to his needs. Rudolph later recalled that his father, displeased, looked him straight in the eye and gave him exactly one minute to choose which direction his life would take: school, a trip around the world with a tutor, or life in the family business. Without hesitation, Rudolph chose business. His father ordered him to pack immediately and sent him to Philadelphia so that his brother Gus could induct him into the family business.[5] Thus began a lifelong partnership between John's two youngest brothers as they presided over the Philadelphia refinery, a decision Claus later deeply regretted, as did John.

The East Coast public found the West Coast Spreckels family's competition with the Sugar Trust intriguing and entertaining. The press frequently cartooned the portly Havemeyer, in a black frock coat and silk hat, as a capitalist class enemy. To Easterners, Claus was David confronting the Goliath of the Sugar Trust, and standing alone without being forced to join the trust, he was venerated as a prominent symbol for private entrepreneurship. Faced with aggressive competition from the Spreckels family, the Sugar Trust began to lose money. Worried, Havemeyer's organization persisted in trying to partner with the Spreckelses, but Claus stubbornly and proudly refused; he was more inclined to bolster his public status and the success of his own Philadelphia plant, saying, "I came here to fight the trust, and I have fought it, and I intend to keep on fighting it."[6]

If the Spreckels men wanted to embrace competition, Havemeyer and the Sugar Trust were up to the task, but they would fight dirty. Gus and Rudolph loathed the Sugar Trust's underhanded methods, which were typical of hostile takeovers in those years. Some of the scurrilous tactics and sabotaging operations at the Philadelphia plant that they accused the Sugar Trust of resorting to included breaking equipment and depositing dead rats in vats of sugar liquor. Any mention of a settlement with the trust enraged Gus, so disgusted was he by Havemeyer's unethical tactics, which kept him and his brother working overtime to monitor every plant operation vulnerable to potential sabotage.

The fierce price war continued for two long years, until Claus realized he lacked the emotional stamina to "keep on fighting it" in the face of heavy financial losses. So, in 1891, he and the Sugar Trust came to an agreement: Each would stay out of the other's territory permanently, and Claus would walk away with a hefty profit. The Philadelphia refinery was sold to Havemeyer's Sugar Trust for $7 million, despite the strenuous objections by Gus. Both kings went back to their respective kingdoms, each proclaiming victory, but in terms of profit ($2 million), Claus was the clear victor.

The Family Breakup

The "Sugar Trust War" may have ended, but it was only the beginning of a family war. This war had many causes, but the primary one was the family atmosphere that Claus himself had established. He had created the sugar business for the benefit of his family. Each of the Spreckels sons had started learning that business from an early age, working in every capacity, including managing the finances, because it was expected that they would eventually inherit it. But because of Claus's uncompromising stubbornness, an environment of cooperation, loyalty, and trust never took hold.

Time after time, Gus had seen his father go into competition with an adversary, inevitably forcing that adversary to submit, and obliging him to purchase the Spreckels's assets at twice the cost of the original investment. But Gus was personally offended and unconcerned with the Spreckels company's profits after his father had left him, the vice-president and general manager of the Philadelphia operation, out of the negotiations with Havemeyer and had dismissed Gus's objections to the sale of "his" refinery. He was so aggrieved that he informed his father that, after an agreed-upon transition period, he would be leaving the family sugar business altogether. In an attempt to stave off another nervous breakdown, Claus went to Europe to recuperate, thereby avoiding any more confrontations and leaving John in charge of the sugar company at a time when that son was already overcommitted with his side ventures.

Yet the worst was yet to come. The originally well-timed transition period of Gus's resignation abruptly ended when Adolph, going through the financial records, "found" that $250,000 from the proceeds of the sale of the Philadelphia factory had gone missing on paper. He accused Gus of stealing it. When Claus returned from Europe, he and Adolph met with Gus at the Philadelphia refinery, and the three of them pored over the figures. Gus reported of this meeting that, as far as he could tell, his father "was satisfied with my account."[7] Yet back in San Francisco, Adolph soon convinced his father of Gus's role in the missing funds, and Gus was denied access to the financial records by which he might prove his innocence. Intending to humiliate his brother, Adolph demanded an extensive written statement detailing Gus's accounting. Gus, insulted and furious, quit on the spot. When his father published statements calling him an embezzler, Gus published a letter of his own to his father.[8]

Philadelphia, November 24, 1891

Dear father:

The other day you said that my explanation as to what became of the money paid by the Havemeyers was perfectly clear to you. This afternoon Adolph informed me that the matter was not clear to you, and that you had instructed him to investigate further into the matter. He insinuates that I have stolen the money, and says that for my own justification it was necessary to make a detailed statement. All that I can say is that every cent that has ever passed through my hands is still there. It was my earnest desire to settle everything as amicably as possible and to resign my position only after you had become familiar with many of the details of the company; but I can no longer remain in an office to be thrown in contact with him, who is evidently determined to put me under a cloud, and bent on blackening me in your eyes, in order that we might part with an unfriendly feeling. He is not satisfied with the breach he has caused in our business and family relations, but now stoops to this base and cowardly accusation. I therefore enclose herewith my resignation.

I have always worked in your interest as faithfully, honestly and conscientiously as any man could do, and no one deplores more than I do the way things have turned. In conclusion, I want to say that I part with the best of feelings toward you knowing full well that you are being wrongfully influenced against me, and that in time you will see things in a different light.

Your loving son,
Gus

It's unknown whether or not John had doubts about Gus's misappropriating funds, but he was resolute in his loyalty to Adolph. As brothers and business partners, their personalities meshed well. Adolph seemed content to manage assets and let John expand them; he knew that everything his brother touched seemed to turn to gold.

John must have been frustrated with the family turbulence that took him away from his real passions, the Oceanic Steamship Company and the growth of his budding passion, his San Diego investments. He was forced to spread himself thin, taking the reins of the family business while his father and brothers battled in Philadelphia during the Sugar Trust War. In his father's absence, he had developed a very high profile on the West Coast, and the press took notice: "The sugar king's colossal fortune has been amassed by his own indefatigable industry, [but] the ability of his son, John D. Spreckels, in guarding those millions, proves him a worthy second to his father."[9]

The family warfare must have seemed permanent by this time, and John and Adolph removed Gus from the "Brothers," buying out his interest in John D. Spreckels and Brothers in 1892. At the inception of the company, Claus had insisted that all the brothers would be partners, but he now agreed it could never be the same.

At this point, Rudolph, in a brotherly emotional alliance with Gus, kept out of the disputes. Claus, hoping to keep his youngest son's loyalty, gave him a piece of the Spreckels Hawaiian holdings, five thousand shares of Pa'auhau Plantation stock, in July 1893.

Lawsuits and Countersuits: Taking the Gloves Off

Back home in San Francisco, Claus, bone weary from the Philadelphia battle, announced that he wanted to narrow his holdings and sell most of those in Hawai'i because they were losing money. John, never enamored with any part of the sugar industry, agreed with his father, and Adolph went along with his older brother, establishing a pattern that endured for the rest of their lives. As the family disputes continued over the next decade, these three would stay on the same side.

Rudolph, however, disagreed with selling off holdings that had made the family a fortune, and he sailed to Hawai'i for a firsthand look at the "losing business." What he saw was "neglect, mismanagement, extravagance and stealing," which he attributed to the absence of family oversight.[10] He insisted that the family's detached management practice was the only reason the holdings were losing money. Gus and Rudolph teamed up and asked for control of the property, vowing to turn it around. They firmly believed that if only their father would entrust its management to them, they could make it prosper. Claus categorically denied the request and ordered the property sold.

Gus and Rudolph informed their father that they were undeterred in their resolve to acquire control over the family's Hawaiian Commercial & Sugar Company, Hawai'i's largest sugar operation. In a fit of rage, Claus publically disowned his two youngest sons, and to prevent any of their machinations to prevail, he blackballed their credit at every bank on the West Coast.

In November 1893, Claus, John, and Adolph began quietly looking for a way to remove Gus and his financial interest in the Hawaiian Commercial & Sugar Company. Gus caught wind of it, however, and took quick legal action—but on the sly, hoping to keep it away from the public. When he filed suit, he collaborated with another stockholder, H. M. Wooley, using Wooley's name as plaintiff. The case settled in just six weeks, and Gus became the new owner of the company, worth $2 million.[11] Escalating the family feud, Gus appointed Rudolph director of the company.

In 1894, Claus raged against both of his sons and sought vengeance for their disloyalty. He attempted to legally regain control of the five thousand shares of Pa'auhau Plantation stock he had previously gifted Rudolph after discovering that it had been used in the settlement to purchase Hawaiian Commercial. His legal action failed, and though it further alienated him from Gus and Rudolph, it strengthened the bond between the two youngest brothers.

Emboldened and bitter, Gus sought his revenge in another area of the family business: the Oceanic Steamship Company, John's turf. Gus appeared at the annual stockholders meeting in January 1895 with some aggressive demands that were rebuffed by the company's president, John. Upset by the rebuff, Gus filed a legal action three months later, a writ of mandamus, which would have enabled him to inspect the Oceanic records in a forced stockholders meeting, had the judge not ruled in John's favor. John was thoroughly outraged at Gus's attempts to "vex and harass the other stockholders."[12]

Probably to protect their father's emotional state of mind, John and Adolph did not tell Claus about Gus's provocative actions within the inner sanctums of the Oceanic Steamship Company. But a newspaper reporter inadvertently dropped the bombshell during a casual interview with Claus on the streets of San Francisco. Caught unawares, the family patriarch could not contain his anger toward the "family villain": "I never whipped him in my life, but I feel like going out and cowhiding him now. This is a piece of blackmail—that is what it is. He is trying to force himself upon us in that company when he knows we do not want him there. That boy cannot bulldoze me that way. He and his younger brother are trying to beat me out of two millions of dollars, but they will never do it."[13] He then barked at the reporter for the *Examiner*. "I will show the people how those boys will die in the gutter and why they ought to."[14] Nobody could have foreseen that Gus would then sue his father on April 5, 1895, for slander, regarding his accusations of embezzlement of the Sugar Trust settlement.

The family's dissension was blazoned through the public courts, and family members aligned themselves on opposite sides. John and Adolph sided with their father, while Gus and Rudolph sided with each other. The trials and tribulations of the wealthy Spreckels family were a veritable soap opera, and the press followed their every legal move with great fervor: "The Spreckels family is not popular. The Spreckelses fight. They fight hard. But they don't fight together. They are not a unit. The family fights inside as well as out, and not all the members speak to one another. They differ among themselves in character, tastes, methods, purposes and, apparently, morals. All they all seem to have in common is a certain aggressive independence."[15]

When Claus's deposition took place, he and John were seated across the table from Gus and Rudolph. The tense scene was vividly described in the *San Francisco Chronicle* under the headline "Claus Spreckels Declined to Answer." It was noted that the "uncooperative" Claus literally created a smokescreen; whether it was sabotage or nerves or both, he lit up cigar after cigar, creating billowing "clouds of smoke" while refusing to answer "hundreds of questions" from Gus's attorney, Henry Ach.[16]

During the questioning, that attorney was able to produce the startling evidence that $150,000 of the "missing" $250,000 allegedly embezzled by Gus had actually been "used to pay a draft drawn by Adolph Spreckels."[17] The revelation that Adolph had apparently created a smokescreen of his own might have influenced the next surprising move: Instead of showing up for a second hearing, Claus accepted the judgment of slander, paid Gus the $300 in damages, and left for Europe. He had a lot to think about on that trip, particularly about how Adolph, by accusing Gus of embezzlement, might have deflected attention from his own misappropriation of funds.

After the slander lawsuit was settled, Claus, still bitter, left instructions with his attorneys to retaliate against Rudolph for having humiliated him; his single-minded purpose with these instructions was to get the Pa'auhau Plantation stocks returned. In 1891, California had passed the first of its laws that would give a wife some control in the disposition of a couple's community property. Prior to this, the husband was considered the legal owner of the marital property. Claus and his lawyers appealed to the 1891 statute, using his wife's legal rights as a guise. His lawyers argued that the value of the stocks gifted to Rudolph must be returned because Anna had not consented to the action back in 1893. Everyone who knew Claus knew Anna was never consulted on anything of this nature, but they considered this was a legal wrangling that might work. That argument failed in court, however, because the written-consent statute could not be applied retroactively to community property.[18] The court ruled that the gift was valid because Anna Spreckels, still married to her husband, had never been financially harmed by the decision. In any case, it is unlikely that Anna went along with her husband's court case, because it was well known that Rudolph, her youngest, the one who had spent the most time with her, was her favored child.

John, who owned the *San Francisco Call*, used the paper to denounce the California Supreme Court the day after the decision with the following headline: "Wives Declared to Have No Right in Community Property."[19] The family's archenemy, the *San Francisco Chronicle*, spun the story differently: "Rudolph Spreckels Defeats His Father."[20] Claus then gave almost $26 million to John and Adolph, publicly proclaiming that he was deliberately omitting his three youngest children, Gus, Rudolph, and Emma from sharing in his wealth.

Much of the Spreckels litigation between 1893 and 1895 involved untangling the children's interests in the family businesses. By 1897,

John and Adolph handled most of the family's business interests. True to their word, Gus and Rudolph improved the Hawaiian sugar holdings' efficiency and sold the company for a profit of $2 million in 1898 to the Hawaiian company Alexander & Baldwin.[21]

It seemed the feuding would never die. When Claus organized an independent gas, light, and power company in San Francisco, Gus and Rudolph funded rival gas and electric companies. Many said that wealth itself was stoking the family's highly publicized feuds, but pride more than money was evidently the real motivation. Slander suits often followed court cases, triggering hard feelings on both sides that John, for the rest of his life, never felt the need to mend.

In the course of this turmoil, Rudolph and Gus did their best to carry on with their lives while maintaining a distance from their brothers and father. Rudolph made a fortune in business before turning to politics, where he sought to reform city government. He married socialite Eleanor "Nellie" Jolliffe in 1895, well known for her beauty. The couple moved into a San Francisco mansion on prestigious Pacific Avenue, just two blocks down from John and Lillian, but there might as well have been hundreds of miles between them. Rudolph and John never spoke a word to each other after the Sugar Trust War.

Gus used his capital from the sale of the Hawaiian Commercial & Sugar Company to establish a new refinery in the industrial town of Yonkers, New York, far away from the San Francisco hostilities. Thanks to new sugar-refining technologies, a strong German workforce, plus a location adjacent to both railroad and shipping facilities on the Hudson River, Gus's Federal Sugar Refining was a major competitor of his father's by 1902, and, by 1905, Gus was the owner of the largest independent refinery in the nation. After his son's success, Claus's bitterness sounded like pride in an interview: "I was never beaten but once in my life, and it was by my own boy."[22] Even though Gus was the principal owner, public face, and the main decision maker for the Yonkers company, he spent half of his time in his mansion on the French Riviera, enjoying a European lifestyle of more relaxation than work. He and his family thrived far away from his family of origin and their relentless search for business and political opportunities.

Defying Her Father: Emma Claudine Spreckels

Amid all the family strife, John's only sister, Emma Claudine Spreckels, was left sitting quietly in the background. Iretta Hight, who was teaching in Hawai'i, went on a volcano excursion with Emma. She wrote in her diary in 1890 that she felt sorry for the twenty-year-old Spreckels daughter, for, despite her wealth, Emma seemed depressed and lacking of self-esteem: "Miss Emma impressed me as being a girl of good sense and kind heart lacking only some strong and true friend to lead her out. It sounds egotistical to say that I pitied her but such was the fact. She has so little within herself that she is wholly dependent upon others for her happiness."[23]

Emma had never done anything sufficiently imprudent to incur the wrath of her father. She was reportedly as reserved as her mother and stayed out of San Francisco society, and this undoubtedly pleased Claus. As she was the only daughter, nothing was too good for Emma, and he reserved all his fatherly affection for her. Among the prime parcels of real estate the family owned on Market Street in downtown San Francisco, he built an office structure in 1895 that he named the "Emma Spreckels Building."

But then, at the very end of 1896, Emma unexpectedly defied her father by eloping with Yorkshire-born Thomas Palmer Watson, a widower twice her age. John was as furious as their father. It was well known that John had tried to play matchmaker between his sister and good friend Sam Shortridge a few years earlier, but it had gone nowhere despite the rumors of an engagement. The press congratulated Watson, Claus's former card-playing friend, on his marriage and good fortune because by then Emma, not quite twenty-seven years old, was worth millions and would be an heiress to even more upon the death of her father.[24] To prove that Watson had married her only for love, she quitclaimed expensive Honolulu real estate and an endowment worth $2 million that had been given to her by her once-doting father, and the newlyweds fled to Lower Kingsford, England.

Emma was relieved that she had retained possession of the Emma Spreckels office building on Market Street, however, because she soon renounced her vow of poverty and unsuccessfully sued her father to recover the prime parcels of real estate in Hawai'i. After that legal action, the heartbroken Claus felt further betrayed and refused to see his daughter and the son-in-law he considered an elderly fortune hunter. After Thomas Watson died in 1904, Emma reconciled with her father and moved back to a San Francisco mansion that Claus built for her on Van Ness Avenue (but she soon returned to England to spend the rest of her life in subsequent marriages).[25]

5

Aloha Hawai'i

King Kalākaua in California

Not long after John had purchased Coronado, Hawai'i's king, David Kalākaua, in poor health, arrived in San Francisco. It was big news that a king had arrived at the wharf, and his December 4, 1890, arrival was greeted with great pomp and ceremony.

John embraced the king and took him sailing for the day aboard the *Lurline* on San Francisco Bay.[1] The following day, Adolph hosted the king in Sausalito. The king also visited Claus and Anna at their San Francisco mansion. But during all these visits and celebrations in Kalākaua's honor, it was clear to the Spreckels family that the king's health situation was dire.

John invited Kalākaua to stay at his Hotel del Coronado in San Diego, where many went specifically to improve their health. After a couple of weeks in frigid San Francisco, the king was undoubtedly anxious to go south by rail to that warm port city. He arrived on December 28, 1890, to find another "immense crowd" of prominent citizens waiting to greet him. Even though it was after ten p.m., a "company of troops snapped to attention," and the City Guard Band played, followed by the state militia and its brass band, to signify the importance of the royal presence.[2] The *San Diego Union* newspaper, now owned by John, in a reversal of his earlier opinion toward the king, reported favorably the following day that Kalākaua was "one of the most enlightened and thoroughly able monarchs of modern times, a patron of art, science and literature, a friend of liberal government and a wise and sagacious ruler."[3]

On New Year's Eve, the king was entertained lavishly in the Hotel del Coronado's beautiful Crown Room, but it is doubtful that he enjoyed any of it. He left for San Francisco the following day, not realizing that he had just had his last royal gala. On the way, he had a bilious attack; he died of Bright's disease on January 20, 1891, in the Palace Hotel.[4] It was a painful death, and Claus "hovered in the room" with his old friend until the bitter end.[5] The king of Hawai'i, who had made him the king of sugar, was no more.

The Overthrow of the Hawaiian Kingdom

When Lili'uokalani succeeded her brother and began her reign as queen, she was determined to negate the Bayonet Constitution that King Kalākaua had been forced to sign in 1887, which authorized the monarch only to reign but not to rule. She firmly believed in the divine right of absolute monarchy, so she privately drafted a replacement constitution and waited for an opportunity to proclaim it publicly and thereby reclaim her sovereignty. The date she chose for the proclamation was Saturday, January 14, 1893, and when that day was over, the lives of the Hawaiian people would be changed irrevocably.

Queen Lili'uokalani's intentions in making her proclamation—and the turmoil that followed it—have been well covered by historians. American businessmen, protecting the power they had wrested from the monarchy in 1887, labeled the queen's move revolutionary and three days later staged a coup. Backed by an American naval force, they seized the government from her.

The saga of the Hawaiian overthrow reveals a history full of paradoxes. After the benevolent works the missionaries had accomplished during the first part of the nineteenth century, the schism between their descendants and the Hawaiian rulers had grown progressively wider and increasingly contentious. There is a well-known saying, with an unknown origin, in Hawai'i today regarding those early missionaries:

"They came to do good, and they did right well." In fact, however, historical documents reveal that most came poor, lived poor, and died poor. Their children, on the other hand, did much better. By the time the Spreckels family arrived in Hawai'i to make their fortune, many of the male descendants of those early missionaries had become the Islands' principal industrial leaders. Having been born in Hawai'i, they were bilingual and bicultural. Many of them had been sent to the United States for their education, had returned as doctors, lawyers, merchants, and planters, and had amassed great wealth. And as a group, they despised interloper Claus Spreckels as much as, or more than, they had King Kalākaua. It is therefore no surprise that when Claus attempted to gather support for the queen from plantation owners and convince them that such support would be in their best financial interest, he was rebuffed.[6] In fact, the plantation owners and the provisional government they had installed were now appealing to Washington for Hawai'i to be annexed by the United States.

Ousting the Spreckels Family

The Spreckels bank in Honolulu, founded eight years before the queen's overthrow, had been making extensive loans to members of the "new" Hawaiian government, the one installed with the Bayonet Constitution. Claus told the queen on May 29, 1893, that he would embarrass her enemies, demand immediate and full repayment, and thereby put an end to their government. To Claus's surprise and disgust, though, the usurpers somehow raised $95,000 to satisfy the loans. Members of the Spreckels family then vigorously used every method of public communication at their disposal—chiefly Claus's *Pacific Advertiser* in Honolulu and John's *San Francisco Call*—to struggle against the usurpers' provisional government and to support the restoration of Queen Lili'uokalani and the royalist party who supported her.

Officials in the provisional government began spreading a rumor that Claus was determined to financially ruin any planters who did not share his views against annexation. Another rumor appeared in the form of a direct threat: "If Spreckels does not stop meddling with

Hawaiian politics the Provisional Government might cause his arrest, confiscate his property and send him out of the country."[7]

Soon, the general feeling among the annexationists was that the Spreckels family "should be put out of the way."[8] An explicit threat of assassination discovered on the morning of June 22, 1893, ultimately convinced Claus to abandon his Honolulu home: An anonymous supporter of annexation had written the warning in simulated blood and left it on the gate of the Spreckelses' Honolulu mansion. Above the sketched crossbones was a scrawled message: "Gold and Silver will not stop lead!!!" This was frightening enough for Claus to demand police protection while his family planned their exit. Ten days later, they uprooted and moved back to San Francisco. After having occupied a position of unrivaled power and political influence in the Islands since 1876, the Spreckels family was forced to leave its beautiful mansion in Hawai'i in 1893.[9] With the overthrow of the queen came disillusionment and uncertainty in the Islands. A January 1895 attempt to restore Lili'uokalani to her throne ended horribly with the mass arrests of royalists, including the queen herself. Lili'uokalani was charged with treason and imprisoned in a wing on the second floor of 'Iolani Palace.

Supporting the Dethroned Queen from San Francisco

After eight months of lonely imprisonment, Queen Lili'uokalani, "with a long breath of freedom" (her words), left for Washington DC, the first of seven such voyages to continue pleading the "Kingdom's case."[10] As part of her efforts to stave off annexation and give journalists her own views, the queen published *Hawai'i's Story by Hawai'i's Queen Lili'uokalani* in early 1898. She memorialized a significant show of support from the wealthy and influential Spreckels family. She recounted that when she arrived in San Francisco, "many friends had hastened to call upon me; amongst these were Mr. and Mrs. Claus Spreckels, Mrs. J. D. Spreckels and her lovely daughter, Miss Emma Spreckels, Mr. and Mrs. C. A. [Gus] Spreckels."[11]

The entire Spreckels family told Lili'uokalani to "fight it" to the end and assured her of their financial assistance.[12] For example, it had been whispered that John had looked the other way when the queen's supporters surreptitiously transported guns and ammunition on one of his ships to support the royalists in Hawai'i.[13] The Spreckels family was publicly implicated by Hawai'i's former minister of foreign affairs (under King Kalākaua), John Adams Cummins. After he was arrested for conspiracy, Cummins confessed that he had "a letter from the Queen telling his aide to go to San Francisco, where he would be furnished funds by Rudolph Spreckels with which to purchase '248 Winchester carbines, 80 revolvers and thousands of rounds of ammunition.'"[14] The press implied that Rudolph should be arrested for conspiracy, but in the end, nothing happened.

The Spanish-American War of 1898: A Point of No Return for Hawaiians

On February 15, 1898, Spain's alleged sinking of the USS *Maine* in Havana Harbor set in motion a series of explosive events that led to the United States declaring war on Spain. In the spring of 1898, young patriotic Americans gathered at Fisherman's Wharf in San Francisco, ready to fight for their country. The U.S. Navy needed ships and support vessels of all kinds. Three of John's tugs were conscripted at the outbreak of the war in April 1898. On June 22, Lili'uokalani reported that she was "disappointed to find that [John's steamer] *Alameda* has been taken by the government" to transport troops that month.[15] It was no longer available for civilian transport between California and Hawai'i, and the war began to cost John dearly.

It was said that almost all of the volunteer sailors and soldiers headed toward the western Pacific, many as young as sixteen years old, were seeing the ocean for the first time and were ill prepared for the misery that followed their departure from San Francisco. The crowded conditions, the seasickness that kept them hanging over the railing, and the lack of fresh water and food even took lives. Every volunteer highly anticipated the moment when he could put his boots down on dry land in the tropical paradise of Honolulu, in the newly proclaimed republic of Hawai'i, en route to expected combat in the Philippines and Guam. On July 7, 1898, President William McKinley signed the resolution annexing Hawai'i, and it caught the volunteers off guard. What they had not expected upon arrival at the dock that summer was the jingoistic atmosphere among the throngs of cheering Americans residing in Hawai'i who welcomed each shipload ashore to the sounds of "The Star-Spangled Banner."

John Sends the Queen Home

While all this American mayhem was going on in her homeland, Queen Lili'uokalani was thousands of miles away, experiencing her own private turmoil. She was "stuck" in Washington DC. She wanted to return home from America's capital, but she found herself in a predicament. In a letter dated July 1, 1898, to her business manager in Honolulu, John Oliver Carter, the queen anxiously reported that due to the conscription of the Spreckels ships, she was stranded in "financial embarrassment" because regular service to Hawai'i was heavily curtailed. Without transportation to Honolulu from San Francisco (which she reached by train), she was left with one option, that of going home via Vancouver, Canada, at a cost she could not afford, since her funds had been seized. Lili'uoka- lani clearly viewed John Spreckels as both protector and supporter.[16] With great relief, the queen reported on July 8, "Mr. J. D. Spreckels" had sent her $2,000 (more than $60,000 today) to enable her to go home the alternate way.[17]

Despite Queen Lili'uokalani's best efforts, the colorful but troubled kingdom of Hawai'i would be no more. Among native Hawaiians, there was nothing but despondency. Passionate speeches had been given, debates held, articles written, and petitions signed so that the native Hawaiians could show their opposition to the American takeover, and now all appeared to be lost. In the place of their beloved kingdom arose (from 1893) the new republic of Hawai'i, and within five more years, that white, American-run "republic" had been annexed as a subject territory of the United States. The speedy annexation of Hawai'i in 1898—ostensibly a defense measure taken by the United States in the interest of its own national security—dashed all hopes for Lili'uokalani's restoration to her throne.

Admiration for the Queen

Lili'uokalani was a standout in her era. She was a highly educated and talented woman. Both John and Lillian deeply admired her musical abilities, and Lili'uokalani admired theirs. It is likely that John played the piano for her on more than one occasion, and she had heard Lillian perform locally. The queen was a proficient musician who composed more than one hundred songs, including the famous 1878 "Aloha 'Oe," which means "Farewell to Thee," or "Until We Meet Again," and which was one of John's all-time favorite compositions.[18]

It is obvious from his published comments that John generally liked David Kalākaua but did not respect him as a ruler. Kalākaua's sister, Lili'uokalani, had earned his deep respect, however. She had been one of the kingdom's most progressive royals even before she took the throne. She had worked tirelessly to improve the native Hawaiians' health, education, and overall welfare. She spoke many languages, including some German. On Sundays in Kawaiaha'o Church, she often played the organ, John's favored instrument.

In 1908, the Spreckels bank in Honolulu lent Lili'uokalani $70,000 in order to pay off her remaining property mortgages and, more importantly, to fight the U.S. Congress to win compensation for the crown lands it had taken.[19]

6

Raising the Spreckels Clan

Living in the Mission District

As much as the entire Spreckels family tried to use their influence, they had not been able to prevent the U.S. annexation of the beautiful islands they loved. During the years that the provisional government had ruled Hawai'i—and even after his parents had abandoned the elegant Victorian mansion in Honolulu—John used the home for vacations with his family and on business stopovers as he crisscrossed the Pacific. But apart from a few visits, the windows were woefully shuttered and the iron gates slammed shut and tightly locked. The Spreckels mansion, like the 'Iolani Palace, remained for years only as an ornamental symbol of a bygone era. The foliage grew high around the home, rendering it invisible. The one-block-long Spreckels Street, where the mansion once stood, is today a small reminder of a very colorful time of Honolulu's history.

Prior to developing their sugar empire in Hawai'i, the Spreckels family had already established their homes and business in San Francisco's "South of Market" neighborhood (newspapers of those days simultaneously referred to it as the Mission District). John and Lillian had lived in various houses on Howard Street until 1880, when they had a massive Italianate mansion built for them at number 2504 on that street. Many Spreckels family members, as well as extended family members, lived up and down busy Howard Street.

The Mission District made good sense for the Spreckels family logistically. San Francisco is a hilly city, hard to traverse, but the horse-car line in the neighborhood was an efficient way to travel; it was easily accessible from both their Howard Street homes and their Brannan Street factory.

Claus had been instrumental in transforming the unappealing South of Market area into a vibrant neighborhood of skilled laborers, mainly recruited from northern Germany.[1] In the 1860s and 1870s, he had invested heavily in real estate in the neighborhood. As a result, hundreds of Spreckels sugar factory employees moved to the area and lived in apartments and houses owned by Claus. The streets became lined with German grocery stores, churches, and restaurants. Within those establishments, a familiar language and culture created a sort of home away from home for German immigrants, including Claus and Anna, and they were, by most accounts, content. The neighborhood became a primary site of integration for first-generation German immigrants and their children. Its proximity to the piers and wharves of the waterfront, through which passed virtually all of John's shipping empire, was equally important.

Moving Out and Up

The invention of the cable car enabled those with the means to move up and away from the congestion of the city's working-class neighborhoods. By the 1880s, Pacific Heights, a previously inaccessible hilly area with magnificent vistas of San Francisco Bay, had become the city's premier residential district. A move up to the Heights meant for Claus and Anna a move away from the familiar comforts of a German way of life. But, as a prominent multimillionaire, Claus decided in the 1890s that it was their time to "leave an ethnically defined neighborhood in favor of a socially defined district."[2] They kept their Howard Street home in the family for sentimental reasons, a decision that would prove providential when a natural disaster of immense proportions would later strike San Francisco.

Claus and Anna acquired a choice lot on Van Ness Avenue to build conspicuously. The avenue had been named after San Francisco's seventh mayor, James Van Ness, and was one of the widest in its day. The rows of eucalyptus trees on either side of the avenue completed the picture of wealth and beauty.

At John's urging, Claus hired the Hotel del Coronado's architects, the Reid brothers, to build their three-story mansion, which became one of the most expensive private California homes of its time. Its architecture resembled the German hunting lodges and summer residences that were in fashion during the era of Kaiser Wilhelm II. Unheard-of luxuries were found in the stone mansion, including forced-air heating and cooling as well as indoor plumbing for the fourteen bathrooms. In a nod to his love for Hawai'i, Claus had the library walls paneled in rare Hawaiian koa wood. The mansion rivaled in its opulence those of J. P. Morgan, John D. Rockefeller, and Andrew Carnegie. In 1897, the *San Francisco Call* gushed over the magnificence of the new mansion for a public that would likely never see the interior:

> Floored with mosaic, wainscoted with Algerian marble, whose decorated panels show the luxury of the art of the Renaissance; the walls covered with priceless tapestries from the looms of France, and divided by columns of polished marble; surrounded at the second floor by a balcony railed by red marble and paved with mosaic, curving on each side into projecting alcoves overlooking the floor below; the noble hall rises through two floors to the height of thirty-four feet, and is roofed with art glass through which the light streams soft and mellow as the beams of a summer moon when all the sky is cloudless.[3]

Both Claus and Anna were, by all accounts, ultra-private and uncomfortable in high society, so they did not entertain as lavishly as society dictated. Those guests whom they did invite were predominantly family and in-laws who were also employees, which meant business and leisure always went together. Claus never settled easily into the beautiful, art-filled Van Ness mansion, which was more museum than home, and he always regretted having left the old neighborhood. He pined for the days he had walked through the commotion of the Mission District, smoking his cigar and bantering with fellow immigrants in his native tongue.[4]

10. John and Lillian's opulent mansion in Pacific Heights. It was filled with treasures from around the globe. Permission granted from the Terrence and Virginia Wilson Private Family Collection.

John and his family soon followed the migration to the Heights. Evidently, according to the local press, the old neighborhood had also enjoyed the liveliness of John and Lillian's brood in their "large old-fashioned residence in the warm belt of the Mission." The article noted further that "it was a serious loss to that locality when they deserted it for the more pretentious neighborhood of Pacific Heights."[5] With the words "more pretentious," the newspaper did little to hide its opinion of the family's destination.

John chose a prime location for his family residence at the northeast corner of Pacific and Laguna, which had unobstructed views of the sparkling bay. The Reid brothers were again retained in 1900 to draw up the plans for John's Italian Renaissance mansion, making sure, however, that the grandeur did not exceed that of his parents' house. But, as with John's parents' home, every inch was decorated with European ostentation and treasures that John and Lillian had brought back from their European tours. Their mansion was noted as a "must see" on a tourist guide map of the day.[6]

John and Lillian's Progeny

John and Lillian lived in their opulent mansion in Pacific Heights with their four children: Grace, Lillie (Lillian Caroline, the spelling of whose nickname was a deliberate way to distinguish her from her mother), John "Jack" Diedrich Jr., and young Claus Jr. Grace and Lillie, newly adults, were second mothers to little Claus Jr., who was only a toddler when they moved to Pacific Heights. Jack, then eighteen years old, had been marked from birth for high achievement; John wanted his dynasty perpetuated, and he was grooming his older son, just as his father had groomed him. Jack believed wholeheartedly in his own value (some said this excess was a Spreckels trait) to take over the business.

After being estranged from his own siblings, John stressed to his children the importance of family unity and the need to support one another. Each child was required to learn an instrument, and they made music together at home. There is no record of any church membership or religious training during their upbringing, but when they did attend, it was at St. Markus Kirche, the Lutheran church that Claus and Anna attended and financially supported. Even though the family lived in luxury and traveled the world, John and Lillian encouraged the children to be frugal and self-disciplined. At the same time, John stressed the need for them to be competitive, even with one another. The result was a cohesive though argumentative family, with each member looking to one another for friendship rather than looking outside the family circle.

Class and Culture

Neither socialite nor clubwoman, Lillian found enjoyment in domesticity. Creating a beautiful home in which to raise her family was her chief occupation. Like her mother-in-law, she disliked hosting frivolous and fussy society events; thus, the visitors who enjoyed her opulent mansion were predominantly family members. One by one, beginning in 1881, the following kin made their way to San Francisco to join in Lillian's prosperity and to make new lives: her widowed mother, Caroline (1833–1920); brother, Louis J. Siebein (ca. 1862–1908); and younger sisters, Minnie Siebein (1863–1926), Adele Siebein Consmiller (1864–1925), Emily Augusta Siebein Gibson (1866–1941), and Etta Elise Siebein Dilworth (1870–1922). Minnie, the only one of her five sisters who never married, lived on and off with John and Lillian over the years, providing a much needed helping hand with the children. But Lillian had been well trained during her husband's long absences to engage in the ceremonial tasks required of a mother of four children. Events surrounding their development, health, or education held her sole attention when John was traveling, which was way too often for her liking.

Like others in their class, John and Lillian took their children to Europe as an extension of their education, to broaden their perspectives on geography, architecture, culture, and language. They shopped fine galleries to procure for their home a collection of rare and highly prized works of art. John, in particular, had a keen eye for art; painted landscapes of German villages, signed by him at age twelve, reveal an extraordinary artistic talent.

John also had a genuine concern for preserving German history and culture. The children remembered being heavily inculcated into that culture. They had a rotation of strong nannies recruited from Germany. John and Lillian also acquainted their children with their German ancestors by keeping scrapbooks and photo albums that remain today. Family stories told and retold both by their parents and by grandparents made the children appreciate the hardships their elders had courageously faced in order to bring them the comforts they now enjoyed two generations later.

The children were well read. In 1903, John purchased six thousand rare books from a private collector's estate in Germany. Professor Karl Weinhold, recognizably the greatest of German folklorists, had amassed the world's largest Germanic collection. John saw the value of both his culture and research, and he later gifted the collection, valued at

11. John and his girls at sea. When he was at the helm of his yacht, the children experienced their father at his best. The ocean became a classroom, and the children often served as crew, learning every aspect of sailing. Permission granted from the Terrence and Virginia Wilson Private Family Collection.

$7,000, to form the Karl Weinhold Library at the University of California, Berkeley.

The family loved Paris in particular, and it was said that Grace spoke French "like a Parisian." In 1900, the entire family attended the Paris Exposition to celebrate the technical advances of the nineteenth century. This world's fair put Paris, the Spreckels family's favorite destination, at the center of the world stage. What John experienced there surely sparked his imagination later for his own leadership in an exposition.

Memories at Sea

A family pastime enjoyed by all was leaving the cold, foggy, and damp city of San Francisco and sailing to Hawai'i, where the winds were soft, fragrant, and warm. John and Lillian had started their married life together in the Islands, and it was always their preferred sailing destination.

They could have easily boarded one of the Oceanic's luxurious steamers and been treated like royalty for seven days. But taking the long two-week stretch on the Pacific Ocean in his beloved eighty-four-foot schooner yacht *Lurline* enabled John to reenter active parenting while experiencing the pure and simple pleasure of sailing. With his family, he was not the competitive commodore at the helm of a racing machine, relentlessly scrutinizing the ocean, exploiting the slightest of chances to wring success from every gust of wind. On the contrary, with his family, the long stretches of quality time with them were undoubtedly restorative.

When he was at the helm of the *Lurline*, the children experienced their father at his best. The ocean became a classroom, and the children often served as crew; they learned every aspect of sailing, including celestial navigation. After seeing their mother, an adept sailor herself, take on the same roles aboard the *Lurline* as their father, they would never consider women to be the weaker gender.

All aboard were infected with John's passion for piloting his yacht across the varied conditions of the Pacific and into the beautiful harbor of Honolulu. However, Lillie recounted one "catastrophe" encountered on the *Lurline* when she was a child that forever invaded her dreams. John had brought a live cow on board to provide the children with fresh milk during the two-week voyage. It seemed a good idea at the time, but when a storm came up, to the horror of all, the poor "animal was washed overboard into shark-infested waters."[7] It was noted that there was a dampening of enthusiasm on that particular trip.

Competition Good for Boys

Jack graduated in 1900 from the San Francisco Polytechnic High School, a coeducational public school; he was one of sixty-two in his graduating class. His choice of college, Stanford, had probably been dictated by its prestige and location. And, perhaps, because Claus had given $25,000 to Stanford in 1894 toward the building of its hospital, his grandson might be treated with deference. John no doubt remembered the lonely years away from home during his own schooling and realized that he could mentor his son better if he went to college close by.

That nearness also enabled father and son to share a passion for show dogs. Dogs were always important family members in the Spreckels household, but the family valued competition; the thrill of competing fueled them, and this thrill extended to their dogs. The canine breed of choice for the girls was Pomeranians, but for Jack and John, it was the relatively unknown bull terrier. The bull terrier breed had been designed for fighting contests in the "pit," but the Spreckels family had an aversion to professional dog fighting. They chose the breed because bull terriers were faithful and courageous watchdogs that would guard their home.

Jack was intent on winning at the big turn-of-the-century dog shows, so, after high school, he began frequenting the shows with his dog Banjo, who won many awards. Starting in 1905, Banjo's son Titus followed in his father's footsteps. John's love for the breed was well known; the following was published a decade later in association with his personality: "There are not many who ever heard John D. Spreckels' voice raised or his speech hot in wrath. His sternest rebuke is put in level tones and tempered words. He fights hard, bitterly, but serenely. You do not wonder, knowing the man, that his favorite dog is the bull-terrier."[8]

The Girls and the Cars

In John's era, the popular culture still considered a woman's place to be in the home, with marriage and children a woman's ultimate goal. However, the reformer Mary Livermore traveled around the country presenting a popular speech that urged parents to "train their daughters for self-support because their chances of getting a good husband were dwindling."[9] One clear reason: The four-year Civil War, which John had observed up close as a boy of ten, had cost an estimated 620,000 men their lives, creating more "spinsters" in his generation than any other in American history. His daughters, Grace and Lillie, did not have to worry, however, because their wealth and social standing alone assured marriage.

Even though his daughters never held jobs or attended college, John was a thoroughgoing progressive when it came to preparing Grace and Lillie to be self-reliant in the real world. This was especially with his firstborn, Grace, who was his "buddy," accompanied him on hunting trips, and was known as a "crack shot" with a gun.[10]

John looked disdainfully at San Francisco's socialites who, in a display of untrammeled wealth, strolled through the city's streets with nowhere to go but just to be seen. In 1890, one middle-class tourist, a passenger on one of John's ships, Carrie Winter, was shocked at seeing furs worn in summer and had "a few impressions" of the city's gilded ladies in their social whirl: "The ladies seem to be good-looking and are loaded with diamonds and wear bright colors and wear heavy furs. I am told that is the custom the year around."[11]

John's sister, Emma Claudine Spreckels, who (before her surprise elopement with Thomas Watson) was living an unremarkable life as a lonely heiress, exemplified privileged females who suffered from a lack of mentally stimulating activities. A popular resort published this "Routine for a Lady" advertisement as an enticement to draw young ladies of this generation. It underscores the lack of engaging things to do in a rich woman's day:

> Rise and dress; go down to the spring; drink to the music of the band; walk around the park—bow to gentlemen; chat a little; drink again; breakfast; see who comes in on the train; take a siesta; walk in the parlor; bow to gentlemen; have a little small talk with gentlemen; have some gossip with ladies; dress for dinner; take dinner an hour and a half; sit in the grounds and hear the music of the band; ride to the lake; see who comes by the evening train; dress for tea; get tea; dress for the hop; attend the hop; chat awhile in the parlors, go to bed.[12]

Even though they lived very luxuriously, John and Lillian's daughters were not going to be indulged princesses. Grace and Lillie had watched their mother contentedly stay outside the charmed circle of

San Francisco's elite feminine society. Very few socialites really knew Lillian Spreckels, and there are very few mentions of her in the society pages. In 1902, she was described in the society section as a "small woman with refined, quiet style, and most agreeable manners."[13] She avoided as many dinner invitations to balls or receptions as etiquette would allow. A European excursion, a yachting trip with John, a season in Coronado—all were excellent excuses for not being seen among San Francisco's fashionable socialites.

John's daughters faced hurdles regarding the rigidly defined roles and restrictions of the era, and there was nothing he could do about that. But he purposefully gave Grace and Lillie a broader perspective than most females of their time had. John encouraged them to do everything their brothers did, including driving cars, something virtually unheard of in their day. (Their wealth alone required a chauffeured car.) For example, one early nineteenth-century orator bellowed that "no license should be granted to a woman [because] the natural training of a woman is not in the direction to allow her to properly manipulate an automobile in case of emergencies."[14] But, because John was an early automobile enthusiast, he bought his daughters their own autos and taught them to be expert drivers, despite the tongue clicking from "proper ladies" and the overall disapproval they undoubtedly faced.

Owning cars at the beginning of the twentieth century was rare; they were considered mere toys for rich men, and they were virtually unheard of for women. In 1903, John purchased two ornate White steamers for himself, named for the manufacturer, the White Motor Company. Within a few years, his "Whites" became the preferred presidential cars. He kept one in San Francisco and one at the Hotel del Coronado.

A steam-powered car was okay for his father, but electric vehicles had just become wildly popular, and when Jack was twenty, his father bought him the "handsomest electric auto in the city—an Exide battery and capable of high speed."[15] Because of the rarity of seeing females driving, a *Town Talk* reporter found it noteworthy to follow the two Spreckels daughters' auto adventures in cars sportier than what their brother drove: "Misses Grace and Lillie Spreckels enjoyed a spin in their Autocar Runabouts last Sunday and both can handle the chug-wagon with proficiency."[16] (Autocar's history had begun at the end of the nineteenth century, when Louis Semple Clarke built a tricycle powered by a one-cylinder gasoline engine, which is now in the Smithsonian Museum.)

In 1904, John became the director of the Automobile Club of America. In 1905, California issued automobile operation regulations, and the registration of autos began. In 1909, the *Blue Book* of California listed the names of all 18,328 registered owners, and "John D. Spreckels" undoubtedly used his political clout to be listed first. He enjoyed boasting about his favored status of being number 1 among fellow pioneering automobilists. Number 2 went to his daughter Grace; numbers 3 and 4 went to John Jr. and Claus Jr.[17] Gossip sheets in San Francisco stated that Lillie became "bored" with driving, and preferred being chauffeured, which is likely why there was no registration attributed to her name.

Leaving the Nest

When John and Lillian's daughters were presented to hundreds of San Francisco's elite, the debutante ball in 1899 was described in newspapers as the social event of the season. The "coming out" of Grace, twenty-one, and Lillie, nineteen, represented a change in their status from girl to woman. Their "introduction" to society was required by their social standing, and their parents rose to the occasion. As one society page noted, several years after the fact, "The Spreckels, though exceedingly rich people, paid little attention to fashionable society before the debut of the two daughters. The transformation of young and bashful debutantes into ladies of fashion does not take long, and by the time the palatial home of the Spreckels on Pacific Avenue was completed, there were no smarter debutantes in town than Miss Grace and Miss Lillie."[18]

At the time of the ball the Pacific Heights home was not yet finished, so the opulent Native Sons of the Golden West Building provided a good choice of location. At ten p.m., John and Lillian, dressed to the hilt, stood by the entrance to greet a continuous stream of carriages that brought 550 "beautifully gowned women and well-dressed men" to celebrate their daughters' double debut.[19] At eleven p.m., guests waltzed to the strains of Rosner's Hungarian Orchestra, heard but not seen due to a bank of tropical foliage shipped in from Hawai'i.

Following nineteenth-century custom, society expected Grace and Lillie, once they had been formally introduced, to attract suitable husbands in the social seasons that followed. With each of John's daughters, her admirers would need to demonstrate the same enterprising, energetic, and winner-take-all spirit that their father had. Unlike her reserved and petite mother, Grace was an outgoing, tall, athletic girl. Lillie, while also sporty, was more diminutive in stature and more reserved in personality.

The San Francisco society pages followed each of the daughters everywhere, speculating about who might be worthy enough to become John D. Spreckels's son-in-law. While the gossiping wags chewed on this question, however, debutantes' college-student brother was able to keep a budding romance secret. Society was stunned when it was neither Grace nor Lillie who married first; it would be their younger brother, John Jr. ("Jack"), not quite twenty-one.

Jack at the Altar

Jack Spreckels—handsome, tall, fair-haired, blue-eyed Jack—had arrived at Stanford as a millionaire's son with a hefty allowance. He had been easily rushed into Stanford's chapter of the Sigma Alpha Epsilon fraternity. When President William McKinley arrived in San Francisco in May 1901 to ceremonially launch the battleship USS *Ohio*, young Jack was selected by a fraternity brother's father, General Richard Henry Warfield, to take a place of honor on the welcoming platform. The general's son, Richard, remembered the confidence and boldness that Jack had exhibited as he firmly grasped President McKinley's hand, in a handshake that only a former fellow Sigma Alpha Epsilon fraternity member would recognize, and spent "five or six minutes" in "straightforward conversation with the president of the United States."[20] (No one could have predicted that in just a few months' time, William McKinley, the twenty-fifth president of the United States, would be assassinated.)

12. Jack Spreckels, the handsome and tragic heir to the Spreckels fortune, standing between his father and his uncle Adolph. Note the Royal Hawaiian Band, shipped in for the occasion, with their ukuleles in the background. Permission granted from the Terrence and Virginia Wilson Private Family Collection.

The Wasp, a widely read satirical weekly on the West Coast, noted that the popular college boy did not have "the heavy Spreckels beauty of his sisters, but rather the delicate beauty of his mother [and] if he were a girl he would be decidedly pretty."[21] Whether he was "handsome" or "pretty," girls were quite impressed with the heir to the Spreckels fortune. But the one who captured his heart was Edith Marie Huntington, the grandniece of the wealthy and famous Collis P. Huntington, one of the "Big Four" who had invested in the Central Pacific Railroad as part of the first U.S. transcontinental line.[22]

During his second year at Stanford, Jack, not yet twenty-one, told his parents that he wanted to marry eighteen-year-old Edith, the "beautiful brunette with expressive brown eyes with girlish graciousness and simplicity of manner."[23] When the public announcement was made, society pages pointed out that even though all the sons of Claus Spreckels married poor girls, "Mr. John D. has a fear that his children will be married for money, and so he demands that those allying themselves with them have some of their own." The public was reminded that in 1899, John had been so serious in this matter that he had taken Grace with him far away on business to Australia "because she had an attachment for a poor young man."[24] The press speculated that Edith, heir to the vast Huntington fortune, earned the full approval of Jack's father on this fact alone.

Jack and Edith were wed in a spectacular Catholic ceremony officiated by Archbishop Patrick Riordan on December 13, 1902, in the Marble Room of the luxurious Palace Hotel in downtown San Francisco. Due to the renown of both families, the Spreckels-Huntington nuptials were displayed in many papers across America.

After a honeymoon in Coronado, Jack and Edith returned to San Francisco and set up housekeeping in a beautiful Pacific Heights mansion provided by John, who wanted his children and future grandchildren nearby. Edith gave birth to the couple's first child just one day short of nine months later. Marie Spreckels came into this world on September 12, 1903, followed by Adolph Bernard Spreckels II in 1906 and John Diedrich Spreckels III in 1910.

Putting Jack to Work: From the Bottom Up

A new daughter-in-law and granddaughter convinced John that it was time to begin inducting Jack into the family business. Jack's induction began literally on the ground floor, as had John's in the sugar refinery. Apparently, it was newsworthy that a well-known millionaire's son was working his way to the top from the very bottom. The *St. Louis Republic* found the "twenty-one-year-old son of a tycoon" selling tickets in a ground-floor office instead of working in the lavish Spreckels offices on the top floor of the Call Building.[25] Asked to describe his duties at the Oceanic Steamship Company, Jack justified his lowly position:

I am selling tickets here because this is a department I did not know anything about. Lots of people come in here with complaints—they have something to kick about. Now, I hear all these complaints and I learn what action should be taken in regard to them. I hope some day to follow in my father's footsteps. Supposing I was down in the lower office, I could not be looking after my father's interests properly unless when a person comes in with a complaint. I should be in a position to know whether he or the company was in the wrong. I am fond of pleasure the same as everybody else, yet I know of no reason why I should not work because I happen to be a rich man's son. I want to be in such a position that my father shall have the utmost confidence in my ability. I think that the only way to be successful in any business is to learn it from the groundwork up.[26]

By all accounts, Jack was living up to what was expected of him, even graduating on time from Stanford in 1904. Later, after their last child, John Diedrich III, was born, John built Jack and Edith a beautiful country home in San Rafael, where the children could run free. *The Wasp* noted that, at first, "papa Spreckels was like a Spartan father with the young people, giving them very little money, but now they have everything they want."[27]

Lillie at the Altar

In 1905, Lillie beat her older sister, Grace, to the altar when she married the wealthy and popular Henry "Harry" Morgan Holbrook. Harry's father, Charles Holbrook, a noted California pioneer and founder of the mercantile firm Holbrook, Merrill & Stetson (specializing in hardware, stoves, and plumbing), had become one of the wealthiest men in San Francisco and then lived in a spectacular mansion near the Spreckels families in Pacific Heights. After his graduation from the University of California, Harry worked as treasurer on a trajectory to become president in his father's firm. Harry was highly sought out by dinner hostesses to liven up their parties. He was not only exceedingly rich but extremely merry and entertaining. It seemed that Harry had been happy in his role as a confirmed bachelor until his sister intervened. Olive, who had been Lillie's schoolmate, encouraged her brother to consider wooing Lillie, which he did. When it was clear that a romance had sparked between the two, gossips wondered what Lillie saw in a man fourteen years older, a known hard drinker and pleasure seeker.[28] But Harry Holbrook, the only son of a wealthy and prominent family, was good enough for John, and the proposed marriage was viewed as a financial merger rather than as a love match.

Their elaborate wedding, with more than four hundred friends and Spreckels employees assembled in the grand hall of Lillie's parents' home, was covered extensively in the society pages across the country. Papers noted the presence of many "common people" at the wedding, who were without "social ambition," praising the Spreckels family "for their loyalty to old friends and faithful employees."[29]

It seemed as though all eyes were on the seventy-seven-year-old Claus, and a touching scene was recounted: Lillie, at the close of the ceremony, ran over to her grandfather and threw her arms around him. Guests witnessed "the old gentleman [become] much affected by the tenderness of his grandchild."[30]

As a wedding gift, John presented Lillie and Harry with "one of the handsomest homes on Pacific avenue, commanding a beautiful marine view."[31] Even so, Harry preferred life in society more than the home, and the mansion became lonely for Lillie until their one and only child, Harriet, named for her father, was born six years after the wedding. By then, the drinking lifestyle had caught up with Harry, who became sick, and Lillie became his miserable caretaker.

Grace at the Altar

Grace Alexandria, John and Lillian's firstborn, had become more than a girl to be treasured and protected until the right man came along. More than "Daddy's little girl," she was Daddy's buddy. She enjoyed being outdoors, and she traveled with her father all over the world on his ships and up and down the coast in his cars. But "tomboy" was never applied to the feminine Grace; as mentioned in the San Francisco society pages,

"She is a typical daughter of the golden west, good-looking, majestically tall, blue-eyed, and golden haired. She is very popular, speaks French like a Parisian, and dresses like one. Her exquisite frocks have been the envy of her fair townswomen. One of her favorite walking suits this summer was a green silk with which she wore a rose trimmed hat."[32] Newspapers put Grace by John's side at most major events. *The Wasp* went so far as to say what many were thinking: "Grace is regarded as his favorite child, and naturally anybody aspiring to win her would find the X-ray of parental scrutiny more than usually penetrating."[33]

Apparently, one young man withstood John's scrutiny and was able to secure his approval: Alexander "Alec" Hamilton. Grace fell hard for Alec, an outdoorsman, on a fishing excursion in the summer of 1905. Her engagement was like a "thunderbolt from a clear sky" and "could not have surprised society's 'smart set' more."[34] But society pages did not gush over Grace's choice of a man sixteen years older, especially when she could have had her pick among any of a number of suitors: "He is a handsome man of fine physique, though in recent years he has taken on a trifle too much flesh for perfect symmetry. Some 10 or 12 years ago he was as trim and attractive a chap as one can see anywhere."[35]

The "smart set" also predicted that they would not be seeing the rich young couple among their inner circle, because "Alec Hamilton is not cut off the bolt of cloth that makes a typical society man."[36] Alec's family owned the prosperous Baker & Hamilton hardware store in San Francisco, and Alec was busy running it. His father, Robert M. Hamilton, and Livingston Baker had come to California in 1849 to mine for gold, but they'd given it up to open a hardware store.[37] Since his father's death in 1893, Alec had been running the company, which employed more than a hundred people. He would have been much too busy for social events.

That was fine for Grace Spreckels, who was becoming more and more like her father; she declared that she would not be "goaded" into having an extravagant wedding like her younger sister had. Society papers noted her "aversion" to fussy events and reported that her "plans are to have a very quiet affair."[38] And, if that were not enough, she refused all the preliminary festivities her contemporaries planned, including the supposedly requisite engagement party. The couple had an intimate and simple ceremony on November 27, 1905, in the white-and-gold drawing room of Grace's parents' home on Pacific Avenue. It was a happy marriage, which resulted in two daughters, Grace Alexandria, born in 1907, and Mary Leila, who always went by "Happy," born in 1909.

Mischievous Claus Jr.

It seemed as if every year, someone could say about young Claus Jr. that he had reached a difficult age. Photos show a tousled-haired youth with a mischievous smile, always standing apart from the group and clowning for the camera. As the baby of the family, Claus Jr. was coddled by his older sisters, especially by Grace, who was ten years older.

As he grew, Claus Jr. was considered a headstrong child, which might have been why his parents enrolled him in a semi-military preparatory boarding school. The Belmont School for Boys was situated on thirty-six isolated acres south of San Francisco. Because of its expensive tuition, Belmont was patronized only by the very wealthy. Belmont boys wore heavy blue uniforms, and both saber training and rifle drills were part of the required curriculum. Though Belmont was touted as strictly nonsectarian, boys were required to have daily Bible studies and mandatory Sunday services. Jack London, at that time an aspiring but starving young novelist, worked in the school's steam laundry for a paltry $30 a month. London made it well known that he thoroughly hated working for the privileged sons of the rich, such as Claus Jr., as much as he hated the "clouds of steam, the dirty suds, the heaps of soiled linen" that "dulled his mind and aching muscles."[39] With so many of the entitled rich boys that London despised and so few teachers to keep them in line, discipline was a real problem, and teachers used severe methods to turn rambunctious boys into men. Whatever the reason—likely the structure he loathed—Claus Jr. hated Belmont as much as Jack London did.

Where father and son met on equal ground was tinkering on cars. John had become a very capable mechanic, and he allowed no one to touch his White steamer except himself and, later, Claus Jr., who of all the children acquired his "father's talent for mechanics." The two of them were the happiest when "they had aprons on and [were] working in their garages with oil can and monkey wrench."[40]

It is unlikely that John and Lillian desired to raise spoiled offspring, but for children such as Grace, Lillie, Jack, and Claus Jr., who faced relatively few material limits, some spoiling was inevitable. After years of inspiration at prominent schools, Jack and Claus Jr. in particular did not need to wonder where their talents might take them; they had but one choice, one direction—to be businessmen in a Spreckels-owned company.

7

Roots in San Francisco

Claus Builds Out

John's father showed no signs of slowing down during the last decade of his life. By 1895, Claus's seven-year-old Western Beet Sugar Factory in Watsonville was so successful he decided to expand. Two years later, he bought six thousand acres in California's Salinas Valley in order to surround his sugar refinery, the world's largest, with a company town.

For Claus, the ultimate statement of his power was to name his notable projects after himself. In Maui, he had built a town around his factories and fields and named it Spreckelsville. Now, near this new giant beet sugar factory in California, he built the company town of Spreckels. Claus shrugged off criticism for naming a city after himself; he said that he was doing it not for notoriety but rather to "show California [that] Claus Spreckels has done something for this state when his bones are at rest."[1]

Adjacent to workers' housing in the new town of Spreckels, Claus added parks, baseball fields, grocery stores, churches, a library, and a modern theater. The utilities and all real estate were owned by Spreckels business interests. Upon the town's completion in 1899, its daily water consumption equaled that of San Francisco. A railroad depot was constructed, and the thriving little town of Spreckels became a railroad stop.

Lincoln Steffens described Claus Spreckels as a man who "must dominate whatever he took part in, impatient, implacable, ruthless."[2]

13. The imposing Call Building, iconic the moment it was finished. Courtesy of Adolph Rosekrans.

But it was well known that Claus paternally loved the town of Spreckels and took an active interest in the lifestyles of his employees, who in turn became very loyal. Both the town and the factory were important sources of income as well as inculcation with American ideals for immigrants, in the same way as San Francisco's Mission District. The town of Spreckels was predominantly made up of German and Danish immigrants who worked and lived there year-round. In German tradition, a pint of beer was served to the hardworking laborers at noon. Spreckels was also important in the early life of John Steinbeck, who lived in nearby Salinas and worked as a farmhand during summers on the Spreckels farm. Steinbeck's imagination was captured by the tough lives of his fellow workers—either "sugar tramps" or other seasonal migrant laborers who roamed California in the summers, willing to work hard for little pay. Those immigrants later found their travails and struggles famously chronicled in Steinbeck's fiction.

The town of Spreckels became the crown jewel of the Spreckels family's beet sugar operations, which had spread out in northern California as a result of numerous mergers and buyouts.[3] The town's fame continues today; in 1991 it was designated a Monterey County historic district.

John Builds Up

While his father moved south of the city to spread *out* in the Salinas Valley, John, back in San Francisco, decided to build *up*. The Reid brothers, now known unofficially as the Spreckels family architects, were hired to build a skyscraper on Market Street as the new headquarters for the *San Francisco Call*.

The conservative *Call*, a rival to the liberal *San Francisco Chronicle*, had a rich history. It had been founded in 1856 with the literal "shoot-to-kill" attitude that then pervaded San Francisco's free-for-all journalism. Mark Twain had provided the *Call* (originally known as the *Morning Call*) a bit of fame in his day for his high-spirited reporting before he was fired for fear he would incite riots.[4] Claus bought the *Morning Call* from the publisher of the *San Jose Daily Mercury*, Charles Morris Shortridge, who had only recently purchased it when it went on the auction block in 1895. Many believed that Shortridge, in a secret handshake, had bid on the paper using Spreckels money in order to keep the price in check. Once the purchase was complete, the paper was then "sold" to John Spreckels two years later. The paper was well used to promote the family's business investments and real estate holdings as well as to promote the progressive wing of the Republican Party. Although Claus owned a newspaper in Hawai'i, he never cared much for journalism for the sake of journalism. John did care, however; he was an excellent writer who valued editorials of the highest quality. John officially took over the *Morning Call* in 1897 and renamed it the *San Francisco Call*. It then became known as a "feisty, in-your-face newspaper."[5]

Henry James, a former columnist, described his years working under John as a "pleasing memory." He recalled that the news staff became fiercely loyal to the man who paid them well and greeted everyone by name with a "hearty handclasp." When he first took over the *Call*, John had wanted to move the printing process over to the newest innovation, the typesetting machine, but he discovered that the printers were old men who had been with the *Call* for decades and would not be able to convert to the new method. He did not have the heart to sack the "aged compositors" and carried on with the old methods, even though that was to his financial disadvantage. This act, in James's recollections, made John's employees fiercely devoted to him.[6]

The new Call Building, set on a 70-by-75-foot plot, stood at the intersection of the city's two main traffic arteries, Market and Third. The 315-foot-high steel-frame structure was, when completed in 1897, the tallest building west of Chicago, and it became *the* most recognizable San Francisco landmark. With its nineteen stories, it towered "majestically" over the neighboring ten-story building that housed its newspaper rival, a fact the *Call* repeatedly reported, to the chagrin of the *Chronicle*'s publisher, Michael de Young.

The *Call* extensively informed the public on every aspect of the building's progress, a type of reporting (self-marketing) unprecedented in the city's history. Finally, on a day that readers thought would never come, the *Call* asked San Franciscans to step outside their homes at dusk on December 17, 1897, to witness and celebrate a new Spreckels accomplishment, a "spectacular light show":

> As darkness fell the crowd outside grew quiet until, as if by magic, all the lights in the building were turned on simultaneously—from the basement to the lantern on the dome—and "the whole vast pile suddenly shone forth in a blaze of glory." Hundreds of people stood along Market Street or on the hills and rooftops of San Francisco to witness the spectacle. Hundreds, possibly thousands more lined the shores of the East Bay from San Pablo to what was then Hayward.[7]

Because electricity was still a novelty, the show was the most talked-about spectacle for some time and was considered to be "one of the sights of a lifetime."[8]

The most prominent men of the time pulled out of existing leases to secure office space at the Call Building and did not mind paying a premium just so their business cards could display that prestigious address. It was interchangeably known as the Claus Spreckels Building, and it was an instant sensation with the public, who often ascended to the fifteenth-floor café, the Spreckels Rotisserie, known for elegant French cuisine "in the clouds." This restaurant was one of the first of its kind, and San Franciscans reveled in the panoramic view of their burgeoning city. The skyscraper became iconic the moment it was finished and was prominently featured in many postcards of the day.

John and Adolph: Business Partners

At the top of the tower were the luxurious offices of the J. D. Spreckels and Brothers company. John Spreckels was becoming so well known across the country that he had the distinction of being profiled at the time of the building's construction as one of "America's successful men of affairs." The editor of the New York Tribune, Henry Hall, noted his reporter's astonishment after naming a long list of John's various business interests: "Such diversified interests would crush a man of ordinary talents, but Mr. Spreckels manages them all with admirable ease, coolness, skill and judgment."[9]

The business partnership of John as president and Adolph as vice-president of J. D. and A. B. Spreckels Securities Company was a successful one. With their combined assets, the two owned and operated their own companies at the same time that they began to manage their father's business interests as he aged. Adolph did not mind sitting at a desk, managing their joint partnership, and operating in his brother's shadow, while John, out in front, invested deeply and widely. Whether or not Adolph had full confidence or apathy is unknown, but there is no record of any tension or of Adolph questioning or challenging any business decisions by John. John recounted that financial discussions between the two brothers approximated the following: "'Oh, by the way, A.B. [Adolph] I'm thinking of putting a few millions into so and so.' The response was always, 'Sure! Go ahead, J.D. [John], fifty–fifty, of course.'"[10]

At the end of the nineteenth century, as John invested deeply in San Diego, he supported Adolph's investment in a large parcel of land in Napa—a gateway to the lush agricultural valley north of San Francisco. With no expense spared, the five-hundred-acre Napa Stock Farm became a horseman's paradise. John, in a unique position, remained the silent partner in the horse breeding and racing operation that Adolph initiated there, leaving the development and management of the thoroughbred breeding operation to his brother. Adolph, once he had discovered his passion in the horse business, demonstrated the same entrepreneurial and managerial acumen that his father and brothers had demonstrated in their own successful enterprises.

One way that John supported Adolph was to report on all the successes of the Napa Stock Farm in the *Call*. Soon, Eastern stables could not help but take notice, and Adolph, demonstrating his earnestness—in producing not only fine racing stock but also horses that won races—sent his horses to the country's major tracks. Adolph bred and sold a crippled colt named Morvich, who would later heal enough to become the first California-bred Kentucky Derby winner.

Once he was recognized for his equestrian accomplishments, Adolph was asked to serve as San Francisco park commissioner. The city leaders were happy that he stayed on through three terms because he energetically developed Golden Gate Park to be the masterpiece it is today.

The ownership of magnificent champion horses provided a step up in the social strata for Adolph, apart from his brother or the rest of his family. Due to his willingness to pick up the check and his amiable personality, he was highly sought out by socialites and soon became known around the town as a ladies' man. While John's family grew and his children gave him grandchildren, Adolph resisted marriage. Due to their closeness, John was well aware of Adolph's dark secret: He was living with an incurable sexually transmitted disease—syphilis.[11]

Tugboats

In the late 1880s, John added six enormous tugboats to his fleet of vessels in California: the *Fearless, Relief, Vigilant, Active, Reliance,* and *Alert.* His steam-powered 157-foot vessels, with their 1,400-horsepower engines, were unlike any other hardworking tugs on the Pacific Coast; they earned quite the reputation for pulling massive ships in and out of harm's way. Operating a tugboat took unique skills that John apparently possessed. A frantic tugboat captain once approached him to report the absence of a chief engineer that threatened their timely departure. Without blinking, John took off his coat, jumped below, and sailed off as the chief engineer.[12]

People close to John believed that his fleet of tugs held a special place in his heart. It was well known that he avoided big parties in favor of small, intimate affairs, mainly aboard his favorite luxurious tug, *Fearless.*[13] John and Lillian's "Tug Boat Parties" were legendary in San Francisco. As the boat glided away from the wharf, the sounds of a lively Hungarian instrumental ensemble wafted behind.[14] This is where John was at his best, smoking cigars and swapping sea stories.

John, known as a fastidious man, was particular about his six tugboats. He prohibited their use for towing any coal barge for fear of their decks getting soiled.[15] The *Fearless* had electric lights, unusual in that era. The tug was also in demand for her twenty-thousand-candlepower searchlight, a tool rivaled only by what the U.S. Navy had. The *Fearless* was an especially luxurious vessel; its crew's staterooms were finished in rich mahogany and were luxuriously appointed, and its officers "lived high on the hog."[16] John had a private stateroom aboard the *Fearless*, and it was spectacularly adorned with leather, velvet, and silk.[17]

When the newly sworn-in vice president of the United States, Adlai Stevenson, steamed into San Francisco on July 17, 1893, the city went all out. On the deck of the steamer *Corona*, Stevenson was welcomed by a salute of nineteen guns from the Presidio. Making their way to the *Corona* was a parade of fourteen decorated tugs. At the front of the line was the *Fearless*, the "official tug" carrying John D. Spreckels, the "Commodore of the naval escort."[18] By this particular summer, the unemployment rate had risen to 20 percent, and the nation was in a depression. John disliked President Grover Cleveland's Democratic administration, including Stevenson, but likely he would have drawn deeply from his cigar, taken a gulp of gin, and guffawed how bipartisan he could be for the right occasion.

The most popular tugboat account reported in the papers was about the "hero tug," the *Santa Fe*, from John's San Diego fleet. He would have boasted proudly as he recounted his tug's key role in saving lives. On July 21, 1905, the U.S. Navy suffered the worst peacetime catastrophe of its history up to that time when the visiting gunboat *Bennington*'s boilers exploded in San Diego Harbor, killing sixty-six sailors and injuring even more. The Spreckels Brothers tug *Santa Fe* raced to rescue the surviving sailors, who dove overboard in an attempt to escape the scalding spray. Eyewitnesses were traumatized by the vision of young sailors "penned between decks and cooked by steam."[19] John's tug was the only vessel strong and quick enough to push the *Bennington* onto the shore to save her from sinking, thereby preventing further loss of life. It has been said that the tragedy bonded San Diego to the navy in a powerful and enduring way. Scores of San Diegans attended the burial services of the young sailors, and a granite obelisk was dedicated at the Fort Rosecrans cemetery in honor of the *Bennington* dead.

Another story John might have told was about the time he was asked by the Union Iron Works to accompany a trial tour out of San Francisco

Bay on a newly completed battleship. Because it was a cause for great celebration, the wine flowed freely. When it was time to return to San Francisco, everyone was drunk. John boasted that since he was the only one "sufficiently sober to tell port from starboard," he piloted the battleship home to the harbor.[20]

Aboard his boats, after a drink or two, when women were absent, John was well remembered for his mischievous pranks and bawdy, if not downright racy, humor. According to his biographer friend Austin Adams, some of his pranks were "not for publication," nor for the "prudish and puritanical." One cringeworthy story Adams recounted concerns the time John served an "inedible" but seemingly "tempting dish" to his pals. Scattered on top were "facts of nature," leaving no doubt that they were feces. One wonders if John's guests considered this as funny as he did.[21]

The Club Man

When the celebrated English writer Rudyard Kipling visited San Francisco at the end of the nineteenth century, he found it a "mad city—inhabited for the most part by perfectly insane people."[22] In particular, Kipling found the exclusive social clubs for men to be full of brash and spirited people. Indeed, San Francisco was known for its clubs—some social, some altruistic, and some political. To be a "club man" was a symbol of power, prestige, and privilege for men such as John; even more to the point, the clubs were places of brotherhood, places where he and other men could escape from the feminine sphere of domesticity. Club memberships were expensive, but John valued the camaraderie he found there, which, moreover, served as compensation for the rigors of the business world.

For the most part, John was bored by the formal customs of "society," often avoiding large parties in favor of the smaller and informal gatherings that took place in these private clubs.[23] All the clubs he joined were bastions of masculinity. On the other hand, they were not wild halls reeking of stale cigar smoke and alcohol; rather, they consisted of luxurious and well-appointed rooms, many in mansions, with servants

14. Being a "club man" was considered a symbol of power, prestige, and privilege. John is seated on the far right. Permission granted from the Terrence and Virginia Wilson Private Family Collection.

to wait on the needs of their members. More importantly, such places as the Bohemian Club, the Pacific-Union Club, and the yacht clubs were important meeting places; they helped John foster connections with like-minded individuals, most of them from the conservative side of the political spectrum. While constructing his own commercial buildings, he reserved the top floors for these "businessmen's clubs."

THE BOHEMIAN CLUB

The club that most captured the heart and imagination of John was the Bohemian Club, which had been founded by journalists, artists, and musicians in 1872. Members met in an ostentatious clubhouse near Union Square, a venue that included a theater, where they produced their own highly secretive performances. Early attendees included such literary talents as Ambrose Bierce, Jack London, Robert Louis Stevenson, Mark Twain, and Oscar Wilde.

The artistic criterion for membership changed when wealthy capitalists such as John were granted admission in the 1880s to help fund their elaborate productions. Those who knew John knew that he was a very artistic soul who was both an accomplished painter and pianist. The Bohemian Club answered this side of his interests, and the financial resources of men like him would help to fund such events as the two-week encampment known as the "greatest men's party on earth," held every summer at Bohemian Grove, a heavily secured site situated on a private piece of land on the banks of the Russian River in Sonoma County, about ninety miles north of San Francisco. Attendees referred to one another as "Bohos" or "Grovers."[24] In the summer, under the majestic redwoods, alongside the lazy river, and among the picturesque, rolling hills, the men of the club relived the carefree days of their youth. For John, who had little chance to be a carefree child, having grown up under his strict father's work ethic, it was likely therapeutic.

The club had a tradition of presenting musical and theatrical performances at individual camps within the grove as well as a polished and expensive production for a grovewide audience at the end of the two weeks. John and his sons had trunks full of costumes kept in their attics for just this very purpose. The club motto "Weaving spiders come not here" was taken from Shakespeare's *Midsummer Night's Dream,* and it expressed the desire to ward away everyday affairs.

Within the club, there was a strict understanding that what goes on at the Bohemian stayed at the Bohemian; therefore, members and their guests were rigorously screened. Through John, many male members of his family were able to join, including his brother-in-law, Walter D. K. Gibson, and his sons, Jack and Claus Jr.[25] The old boys' network continues to this day, attracting not only descendants of the Spreckels family but also presidents, politicians, business leaders, artists, and musicians.

THE PACIFIC-UNION CLUB

Among the oldest social clubs in the city, the extremely exclusive Pacific-Union Club (PUC) was the foremost representative of wealth and civic prestige. It had been formed in 1889 through the merger of two older clubs, the Pacific Club (founded in 1852) and the Union Club (founded in 1854). John and Adolph must have made many a deal while sitting in front of the club's roaring fireplace and enjoying expensive cognac and fine cigars. The PUC was the place where club members would bring visiting dignitaries and host sumptuous dinners. When King Kalākaua visited San Francisco in 1890, John hosted him and his retinue at the club. When the California Republican Thomas Bard was elected to the Senate in 1900, John honored him with an elegant lunch there as well. It is said today that this iconic club, housed since 1907 in James Clair Flood's enormous brownstone mansion on Nob Hill, has a membership waiting list of up to twenty years.

THE OLYMPIC CLUB

At the end of the nineteenth century, there was a heightened enthusiasm for competitive sports and physical fitness. Athletic clubs were formed to support the upper classes as they engaged in this new pastime. John's preferred sport was boxing. The Olympic Club, founded in San Francisco in 1860, was where he trained as an amateur boxer. There he once sparred with James John Corbett, a world heavyweight champion and best known as the man who defeated the great John L. Sullivan. The outcome of his encounter with John Spreckels led Corbett to also become known as the man who broke the young Sugar Prince's nose. During this friendly match, in which Corbett was also a paid coach, the heavyweight unintentionally caused a nosebleed. He wanted to stop the fight out of deference to his "lightweight" client, but John was so livid that he flew at Corbett, who then raised his mitt and broke John's nose. The press, with some admiration, compared John to his favorite dog, a bull terrier charging an "approaching locomotive."[26]

When the club was in financial trouble, John donated half a million dollars to build a "bath house." He is still remembered today for his support of the club, as an inscription on a silver art object given to him by the club attests: "Presented to John D. Spreckels in recognition of his loyal and unselfish service in providing for the club its splendid salt water system. 1901."[27] John's written response to this gift was unusually humble: "What I have done would have been done by any other one of you. I have always been fond of athletics and what little I have done was from my own desire and my best conviction to establish something permanent for the Olympic Club. We are all here as friends devoted to manly efforts and clean sports. To me this gift will represent many a pleasant hour of good fellowship which I have known in the Olympic Club."[28]

YACHT CLUBS

The yacht clubs to which John belonged were much less formal than either the PUC or the Bohemian; they were places where his family could also be comfortable. Compared with the glitz and glitter of the male social clubs, the yacht clubs had more ordinary comforts and were primarily devoted to building camaraderie among men who shared a passion for boats and the sea. The clubs in both San Francisco and Coronado offered safe anchorage, a network of mutual assistance in emergencies, and useful technical information. They also administered racing events, and members flew special flags from their yachts that identified them to other club members.

Despite the relative informality, there was some affiliation with the navy. Thus, dress codes for private captains and crews were modeled after naval uniforms. The sheer number of photographs left behind of John wearing his well-tailored sailing jackets and gold-braided sailing caps reveal that he found it an honor. The titles used in the club, such as commodore and vice-commodore, were also derived from the naval hierarchies. Over the years, John held both titles.

The Spreckels Republican Club

No club was more important to John's stepping out from his father's long shadow than San Francisco's Republican Club. By the 1890s, John wanted to stand as his own man, and his rise in the Republican Party was his chance to carve his own identity.

In 1893, with the onset of a national economic depression and the resultant repeal of the 1890 Sherman Silver Purchase Act, whose unintended consequence had been a severe depletion of the nation's gold reserves, currency issues became even more intensely divisive than they had been in the preceding decades. As the 1896 presidential election approached, Republicans geared up to retake the White House. The contest largely came down to economic conditions and monetary policy. The Republican candidate from Ohio, William McKinley, with the support of the rich Eastern establishment, was in favor of a strict gold standard; he believed the "free coinage of silver" (the unlimited coinage of silver on demand) would bring financial ruin to the country. The Democratic candidate, William Jennings Bryan, developed a reputation as a defender of the working class, especially farmers; he believed that bimetallism, allowing both gold and silver as legal tender (with silver dollars produced at a fixed weight ratio of sixteen to one against dollar coins made of gold), was necessary for the nation's economic health.

Western Republican industrialists such as John Spreckels, from a state where silver mining was prolific, favored the gold standard but wanted the coinage of silver to also be considered, which was necessary, in their view, for a more equitable economy. John's newspaper declared his intentions: "We propose to have one final standard, gold, and on that standard we will circulate the two metals, gold and silver, besides paper money. Could anything be plainer?"[29]

John's foray into politics at age forty-two was pitched as a charitable endeavor, but economic issues were the catalyst to a western industrialist such as himself. Anti-corruption was also a major issue—by the end of the nineteenth century, corruption between San Francisco's prominent businessmen and politicians was widespread. In fact, the moral incentive to oppose corruption was probably the only issue John and his estranged brother Rudolph agreed on.

On May 7, 1896, a headline in the *Call* proclaimed, "John D. Spreckels Is Doubly Honored." The Republican Party's state central committee secured his services as vice-chairman, and, on May 9, he was also elected delegate at large to the national convention and member of the national committee from California, receiving 565 out of 635 votes cast.[30] By promoting the powerful John D. Spreckels, who openly railed against the city's graft problem, his western supporters hoped their views would find their way onto the national stage. After all, presidents visiting the West had sought his and his father's support over the years, and by this time, John controlled a significant part of California's economy. His ascension to the party leadership in California was celebrated by those who hoped for change, and he naively thought he was invincible.

But things didn't go as planned. The Republican National Convention in St. Louis, Missouri, in the summer of 1896 would prove to be an embarrassment for John for the rest of his life. He was not welcomed with open arms to the national stage, and his views were not heartily embraced. Established Republicans had already settled behind the scenes among themselves that a monetary system based on gold alone would be the campaign focus and that any other ideas, especially from a California upstart, would be quickly squelched. Specifically, the wealthy industrialist Marcus "Mark" Alonzo Hanna, McKinley's campaign manager, had promised to uphold the gold standard to the Wall Street crowd on the East Coast, and he was determined to protect that standard at all costs.[31] John's platform of "free silver" was in direct conflict with Hanna's strategy.

After being formally introduced to Hanna, John brought up his concerns about corruption and patronage in California, believing that he would have full sympathy. Hanna, however, was not interested in California's problems; he was prepared to meet the "great nerve of the California's leaders" and "force them into line."[32] Anticipating the topic of silver next, Hanna brusquely silenced John and told him in no uncertain terms to forget about silver because McKinley would be promoting a strict gold standard. When the word got out that John had been publicly silenced, the *San Francisco Examiner* was delighted to illustrate his humiliation by showing a contented cigar-smoking tiger (Hanna) after eating canaries (John D. Spreckels and the *San Francisco Call*) at the convention.[33]

Once he returned home, John might have retreated from supporting the party, but the record shows that he increased his efforts to deliver

California for McKinley. The California Republican League was demoralized, and the push to elect McKinley had sputtered. M. J. Dowling, secretary of the National Republican League, took steps to remedy this situation; he established Republican clubs throughout the state in order to "organize and educate" their districts. John responded to this plea, and he later became so admired among district Republicans for not quitting on them that the Republican Club of San Francisco was renamed the "Spreckels Republican Club."[34]

Even though John was proclaimed the "the local leader of the great Republican Party," he looked for a front man with more time on his hands than he had.[35] After all, he was very busy with building up San Diego, running a shipping company, and raising a family. The man he chose was the younger brother of Charles Shortridge, the previous owner of the *Morning Call*. Samuel Morgan Shortridge, a schoolteacher turned lawyer, staunch Republican, and Masonic brother, became John's closest friend and then his personal attorney. They became too close, in the opinion of John's father, who disliked both of the Shortridge brothers. Despite Claus's strong objections, John proclaimed he was backing Samuel Shortridge for senator during the 1896 campaign. Claus was backing incumbent George Clement Perkins for the same senate seat, and he told anyone who would listen to him, including the press, that he would "call down hard" on his son and demand that he fall in line.[36] John flagrantly disregarded his father's concerns, however, and continued to use his money and newspaper to promote his friend Sam, whom he believed would fight graft and reform "the wild west of his father's generation."[37] Claus insisted that his son was attempting to buy himself a senator and that "these Shortridges must have hypnotized him [John]" and would harm his son's reputation while "feathering their own nests."[38]

Claus had thrived in an age where one man could capitalize on the triumphs of industrial progress and bend the politics of a city or state. After all, that is what he had done in the small kingdom of Hawai'i. In the 1880s, he had been the most powerful man in California, and he was looking to pass that baton on to his firstborn son. Unfortunately,

15. Republican senator Samuel Morgan Shortridge (1861–1952), John's close friend, personal attorney, and "mouthpiece," ca. 1921. Photo reproduced by permission of Library of Congress, Prints and Photographs Division (LC-DIG-npcc-21207).

that son was not cooperating: John was tired of the corruption that was so prevalent in the politics of his father's era. Aligning himself with Shortridge may have been the first time John did anything his father was diametrically opposed to.

John was often mentioned for the office of governor or a seat in the U.S. Senate, but he always declined in favor of family and work. Behind the scenes, he was known to be profoundly tongue-tied in front of an audience. John was bold, sagacious, and self-assured until he had to give a speech. Those who saw him as an uncompromising businessman would have had trouble thinking of him as shy, but this characteristic nonetheless may explain why he supported Shortridge, who was well known as a dignified and master orator. John was not reticent or retiring in his political views, but he was more likely to oppose his political rivals with the written word rather than the spoken one. In his unabashed support of Shortridge, though, many came to agree with Claus that John was indeed attempting to buy a senator to be his mouthpiece.[39]

With false bravado in the *Call*, John had assured readers up to the day of the nomination that Shortridge would easily defeat Perkins. This arrogance angered the dozens of the state's politicians into falling firmly behind Perkins, who had served them not only as the fourteenth governor of California but also already in the U.S. Senate. Because Shortridge did not get a single vote, many newspapers chastised John for backing a candidate who had no legislative experience and never had a chance.[40] Of course, the *Call* spun the defeat sympathetically toward Shortridge as a failed candidate, and the response by many newspapers called John and his newspaper "ridiculous enough to be pathetic."[41]

Even though John's political influence was adversely impacted by his being pushed aside at the McKinley convention, he came to be viewed with respect as a reformer against bossism and graft, and Shortridge would later serve two terms as a California senator (1921–33).[42]

John's position over time in the Republican Party was significant enough to make his opinions on policy a matter of public interest. Thus, on a trip to the nation's capital on November 16, 1899, he was interviewed by the *Saint Paul Globe* and asked for his views on the annexation of the Philippines. Following its defeat in the Spanish-American War the previous year, Spain had surrendered the Philippines to the United States. The decision by U.S. policymakers to annex the colony was very controversial, and President McKinley wrestled with that decision before ultimately assuming control of the archipelago. After John had observed what he believed to be the cruel annexation of the Hawaiian Islands, his opposition to U.S. colonial rule in the Philippines may have derived from his moral qualms concerning such rule, but he told the reporter that his views represented an economic position: "I am an anti-expansionist, and . . . I could not but think of the great good that could have been done in our own country with the money which we are now spending to maintain the army in the Philippines. If that money had been spent on irrigation in the western regions, I believe the United States would have reaped greater benefits from it than it ever will obtain by the retention of the Philippines."[43]

John was tired of the corruption that was so prevalent in the politics of the 1890s. As an outsider who couldn't be bought, he offered a stark contrast to the typical party bosses who were in the pockets of the Southern Pacific Railroad (Espee) monopoly. Some believed that John was too much of a gentleman for hard-knuckle politics, or that his desire for "pure methods and pure men" in government was idealistic. But history would prove he was simply ahead of his time. He continued to argue for reform, and with the Spreckels Republican Club, he sought to bring new blood to the party with a different moral compass, repudiating the old party bosses who wanted "the wild west" to continue. Though John's reformist attitude did not waver, he was continually examined through the lens of self-interest for his enterprises.[44] McKinley's 1901 assassination brought into power Theodore Roosevelt, whose progressive trust-busting attitude reenergized the hopes of Californians that they could root out the worst elements of the machine.

The Five-Minute Arrest: The Governor versus John

Proving he was not afraid to go after party insiders, John used his *Call* as his political mouthpiece against a Republican governor who made him a defendant in a criminal libel case. The case, labeled *The People of the State of California, plaintiff, v. John D. Spreckels and W. S. Leake, alias Sam Leake, defendants*, transpired throughout the summer of 1902, exhausting the courts and papers up and down California until the U.S. Supreme Court struck it down.

The case began in 1898, when Henry Tifft Gage of Los Angeles ran as the Republican candidate to be governor of California. Most Republican papers had climbed on the bandwagon, but not John's *Call*. The paper's managing editor, Sam Leake, despised Gage because in the past Gage had brought what Leake viewed as a frivolous lawsuit against him, over stolen sheep. He could not morally support his former accuser.

But almost as a bribe for public support, Gage promised that if he was elected, he would appoint John police commissioner of San Francisco, giving his newspaper a "great news avenue and innumerable scoops of first magnitude to the sensationalism journalism of other days."[45] The *Call* front-paged Gage for governor, and Leake remembered "grasping the point."[46]

When Gage was inaugurated as the twentieth governor of California on January 4, 1899, he publicly boasted about the acquisition of Hawaiʻi and the importance of extending the empire of the United States beyond the Pacific shore. This boasting would not have set well with John, the self-proclaimed "anti-expansionist." And that John was not appointed police commissioner was likened to somewhat of a "double-cross" by Leake. When Gage decided to run for reelection in 1902, John saw "red" and gave orders "to defeat him at any cost."[47]

Somehow the *Call* came into possession of receipts from the year 1901 from the penitentiary at San Quentin that showed evidence of a shipment to Governor Gage of furniture handmade by the prisoners.[48] Even though it had been common practice for the warden to make presents to "valuable friends," and most people turned a blind eye to it, the practice was in fact illegal. And now John could turn this time-honored practice to his advantage. In May 1902, the *Call* publicly "exposed" Gage, asserting that he was unlawfully accepting freebies for his Los Angeles home: furniture and other fine goods made by San Quentin's convicts and sent to him by the warden. Accompanying the *Call*'s headlines was a distorted picture of the governor so "as to represent him as a vicious criminal."[49]

As the *Call* continued to unleash accusations, Gage pressed charges against both John, as owner of the newspaper, and Leake, its managing editor; and criminal libel proceedings against them were instituted in Los Angeles County. This was a strategic prosecutorial move, since Los Angeles was far from Spreckels's influence. Gage's official residence at the time was Sacramento, but he called Los Angeles home; when the governor was asked to reconsider filing the charges in northern California, closer for all, he snapped, "When a man is charged with being a thief, he has as much right to be vindicated in his own home as the newspaper has."[50]

Newspapers soon reported that the Los Angeles County sheriff traveled up to San Francisco to arrest John and Leake. John was tipped off about the impending arrest warrants by Judge Victor Shaw, and he was ready and waiting with bail money.[51] After the two defendants were bailed out in five minutes, they acted as tour guides for the sheriff, who likely wondered who in their right mind, governor or not, would sue a Spreckels and think they could get away with it. As a local paper reported, "John D. Spreckels and Sam Leake of the San Francisco Call have been arrested on charges of criminal libel, by Sheriff Hammell of Los Angeles County, the complaining witness being Governor Gage, whom the Call charged with having sanctioned frauds in connection with the management of the State Prison at San Quentin. They gave bail in San Francisco in the sum of $600 each, and then took the Sheriff out to see the town."[52]

After a series of legal twists and turns, including when John turned around in August and sued Gage for criminal libel against his *Call*, it was decided that the governor had no case. As the 1902 general election approached, the Republican Party considered Gage an embarrassment and denied him renomination. His reputation never rebounded, he lost the heart for more litigation, and he "retired to private life, revenge and bitterness in his heart."[53] "A Superior Court judge on Dec. 6 expressed bewilderment as to why the case was before him since the crime alleged was a misdemeanor which should have been tried in the Police Court. The matter was remanded, but no further action was taken. This was an instance . . . of which there have been many through the decades . . . of litigation that was much publicized during an election dying a quiet death after the votes had been tallied."[54] John must have thought this was a coup because he left behind in his personal collection several yellowed newspaper clippings of this affair, even though he had been arrested for just a few minutes.

Supporting Women's Clubs

Clubs for women emerged in the mid-nineteenth century. Distinct from their male counterparts, they were not outwardly social. Women's clubs had a variety of purposes, from intellectual discussion and civic reform to how best to engage in community service. Such clubs became an important source of support for the suffrage movement and the subsequent political emancipation of women.

By the end of the century, there were more women ready to entertain new ideas, to take risks, and to challenge the old guard. In California, the first statewide vote on the question of women's suffrage took place in 1896, and Susan B. Anthony was asked to organize the campaign. Suffragists from all over the country traveled to San Francisco and joined locals, including Charles and Samuel Shortridge's legendary sister, Clara Foltz, San Francisco's first female attorney, in their campaign for the vote. The women faced formidable obstacles in the city because many men feared that if women got the right to vote, the first thing on their agenda would be to shut down the liquor industry. It was well known that San Francisco had a wealth of liquor stores and saloons. Not only was it a social custom to meet in saloons for both business and pleasure but liquor consumption was an important tax base for the city. Men freely spoke out against the suffragists; the *Chronicle*, for instance, repeatedly denigrated Anthony and Elizabeth Cady Stanton as "female agitators," making their photos look like criminal wanted posters.[55]

John was not one of those men. He supported the suffrage movement and took pride in having raised his daughters in a progressive fashion. His *San Francisco Call* praised Anthony and Stanton as "champions of suffrage." Both the *Call* and his other paper, the *San Diego Union*, advocated a progressive agenda, one that encompassed rights for women to a degree that was radical for its time. In the months prior to the 1911 election, de Young of the *Chronicle* refused to cover the suffrage campaign, leaving the public to speculate about his stance. Subscribers to the *Call*, however, knew exactly where the leadership of that paper stood. When they opened the Sunday paper on August 6, 1911, they saw the headline "Hereby the Call Pledges Its Aggressive Support to the Political Emancipation of California's Women."[56] Aside from its advocacy, the *Call* provided throughout the campaign an accurate accounting of the activities of the suffrage movement.

Voters cast their ballots on October 10, 1911, and on the next day, both the *Examiner* and the *Chronicle* declared suffrage dead even before all the votes had been counted. The *Call*, however, reminded San Franciscans to not get discouraged before all the votes had been tallied. It still predicted victory—which is what happened: California women gained the right to vote. Nobody was prouder of her father than was Grace, who had been his companion in many "male" adventures both on and off the sea.

A month later, however, one bitter judge found an opportunity to send all women a message—and to John D. Spreckels a personal message through his daughter:

> The right to the ballot carried with it a $10 fine in the case of Mrs. Grace Hamilton, daughter of John D. Spreckels, who appeared in court a few days ago to answer a charge of driving an automobile in excess of the speed limit. Mrs. Hamilton admitted her violation of the ordinance, whereupon Police Judge Weller said: "Under the old order of things this defendant would have been released with a reprimand. She has been fair in her statements to this court and the fault was not great, but now, by the laws of this state, woman have all the rights and privileges that are granted to the sterner sex and by the same token she be subjected to the same penalties. I fine the defendant $10." The fine was paid and Mrs. Hamilton departed smiling.[57]

The voters of California had granted women the right to vote nine years before the Nineteenth Amendment extended the vote to women throughout the United States. John Spreckels is remembered today as a partner in the suffrage movement of California.

8

Building San Diego's Infrastructure

Bankrupt Village

San Diego's building boom of the mid-1880s brought many infrastructural improvements to the city, including a sewerage system and horse car transportation, but they had been "shoddily" done.[1] Furthermore, the streets were unpaved and dusty.[2] Deferred maintenance was taking its toll on the city's facilities. Most of the transportation systems were obsolete, as were the public utilities.

When the city's population swiftly declined and its real estate plummeted in value during the ensuing bust (the recession of 1887–88 and the depression of 1893), John, still residing in San Francisco, proceeded to initiate a variety of capital improvement projects in San Diego. Even though some regarded his acquisitions to support the infrastructure of the city frenetic, he had plans: to rejuvenate and expand the city's aging public works for future building investments. As these development plans took shape, however, he realized he had to rebuild, not just rejuvenate, and the plans therefore grew in scale.

Like his father, John didn't partner well. He needed to be in charge, and this need required his buying out existing public conveniences or pulling them from bankruptcy. His construction efforts materialized into graded streets, mass transit networks, a reliable water source, a municipal park, and more—all of which helped to shape San Diego into an established community. His developments energized and motivated prospective residents, who could see that John D. Spreckels, a famous capitalist, was building for the future. A modern metropolis was easy to imagine.

Even before his efforts were noticeable, John justified his huge financial investment in a struggling little "bankrupt village" by the bay. He knew San Diego was the opportunity he had been looking for. As he explained,

> Men like me get a reward in the very activity of doing, or of trying to do, big things. It is my life. I was out to find a big opportunity to do big constructive work on a big scale—and in San Diego I thought I foresaw just such a chance. So I started in to buy real estate, to erect buildings, to finance enterprise, and to develop our local resources. In short, I began to lay foundations deep and wide enough to carry the big ideas I had of helping to turn a bankrupt village into a city. I realized of course, that all these investments would never amount to much. And that San Diego would never grow, and our dreams would never be anything between us—unless we secured those fundamental necessities, water and transportation. So I set to work to develop a system of impounding dams in the back country, and a street railway system which could reach out to even the outlying sections of the city.[3]

It was not until John's heavy financial investment—with his brother Adolph's full support—that San Diego was able to revitalize its municipal infrastructure after the hard times of the late 1880s and early 1890s. Most of the sixteen thousand residents populating the city during the century's final decade were eager for basic amenities and enthusiastically supported John's efforts.

The San Diego Electric Railway Company: Just Plain Horse Sense

One of the first undertakings that sparked John's interest was updating and expanding San Diego's transportation. Elisha Babcock and Hampton Story had organized the first public transit company in the city in 1886.[4] Their San Diego Street Car Company had been inefficiently operated on 8–1/2 miles of flat-bottomed iron rails using 148 slow-moving horses and 30 cars.[5] After only three years of existence, the company went bust. In 1892, John, seizing the opportunity, pulled the horse-drawn railway out of bankruptcy, and by 1897, the entire system had been converted to electricity. He renamed it the San Diego Electric Railway Company (SDERy).[6] San Diegans were overjoyed with this innovation, as were the hardworking horses that were finally put out to pasture. When accolades poured his way, however, John quashed notions the public might have had that his moves were altruistic, stating pragmatically, "I made those larger investments to protect the investments I had already made. It was just plain business sense. The city would not grow without adequate streetcar facilities. If San Diego did not grow, my big investments would not pay."[7] In the same way, John acquired the previously converted electric cable cars and lines of the Citizens Traction Company in 1898, when it went bankrupt. He was quick to modernize his new acquisition and extend the existing streetcar line of the SDERy in order to "grow" his city by encouraging local development.

And that's exactly what happened. Wherever the tracks went, development followed. Improvements in the transportation infrastructure made the northern reaches of the city accessible, and building activity began to extend into the undeveloped areas there.[8] By 1901, when the population was only fifteen thousand, the SDERy made possible the development of many suburban neighborhoods. Individuals could now own small parcels of land on which to build a house, achieving what previously had been available only to a few rich families with large houses and ample land. Leaving suburban development to others, John nonetheless benefited because homebuilders bought materials from his company and obtained loans from the various banks on whose boards he sat.

That time saw, in San Diego, the first pay-as-you-enter streetcars in the United States. San Diegans thought John was crazy to spend his money on such innovations during these "hardest of hard times."[9] But for those who found employment building the roads and streetcar system, John was quickly becoming known as the "Savior of San Diego," a moniker he scoffed at. Despite the many attempts to unionize the electric railway,

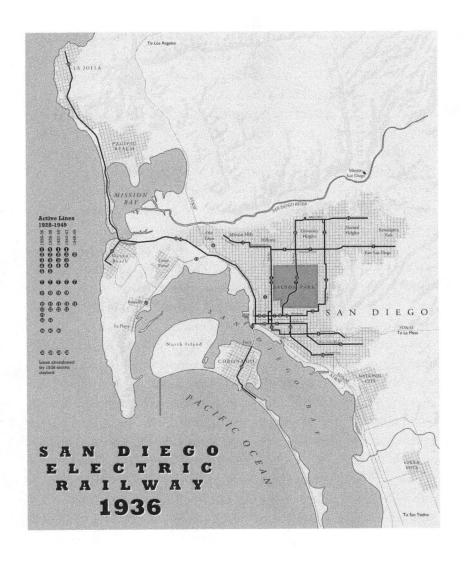

16. The San Diego Electric Railway Company (SDERy). As the SDERy extended, San Diegans were able to leave the congested city and venture into the outskirts, thereby creating the suburbs. Courtesy of Randolph Ruiz, AAA Architecture. Permission granted from AAA Architecture.

Spreckels employees were not willing to jeopardize their employment with a company that gave them higher wages and health care than a union could offer them. In fact, within five years of opening the SDERy, John announced that he would increase the salaries of eighty men by 6 to 16 percent, based on their longevity with the company.[10]

On the Rails: Mission Cliff Gardens

As the SDERy extended, San Diegans were able to leave the congested city and venture into the outskirts. Local politicians had introduced the slogan "Smokestacks versus Geraniums" around the turn of the century, depicting the local debate over development as a war of industrial dreariness against natural beauty. One mayoral campaign between banker/developer Louis J. Wilde and prominent department store magnate George White Marston became distasteful, albeit using these seemingly benign terms. Wherever he could, Wilde and his backers belittled Marston as "Geranium George," portraying him as anti-business, when in fact he simply advocated beautification along with city planning. In the end, Wilde won the voters over with his pronouncement that only the smokestacks of factories would bring prosperity to their homes. Though there was no question that John favored Wilde's "smokestacks," he was not diametrically opposed to Marston's views, because he too loved bucolic scenes; for example, while still living in San Francisco, he developed San Diego's first park, known as Mission Cliff Gardens, in University Heights.[11]

This exquisite park, on the bluffs overlooking peaceful Mission Valley, quickly became a popular place for families to picnic on Sundays. John hired a talented Scottish gardener, personally collaborating with him on the "horticultural masterpiece," as it was soon termed. He even built an aviary and brought in many different species of exotic birds, including a parrot that delighted young and old alike by shouting "Shut up!" when spoken to.

Soon John added a Japanese miniature tea garden with materials and vines imported from Japan. His desire for structure and order may be seen in his preference for the tranquil Japanese landscaping that bordered both his private home in Coronado and in Mission Cliff Gardens. He was often found strolling alone on meandering paths that crossed over bridges spanning creeks jumping with koi fish, paths that wound around an orderly landscape of bamboo, bonsai, and pine.

In the midst of the park's development, however, John refused to defend himself against relentless critics who charged that he financially benefited from Mission Cliff Gardens by owning the streetcar company that transported people there. "Maybe my faith in San Diego has fooled me into running a little ahead of the game. But if I have extended the streetcar lines ahead of population . . . I can see that this may not be a reflection on my business sense, but for the life of me I cannot see that San Diego has any cause for complaint. Whether or not any investment paid me, I paid taxes on it."[12] Nevertheless, the extensive horticulture, bandstand, and gazebo were jaw-droppingly beautiful and provided many happy memories for families—including, in fact, those of his vocal critics, who also spent their Sundays among the serene landscaping in the only groomed public park in San Diego.

On the Rails: Old Town, "Ramona's Marriage Place"

When John began to expand the SDERy route to Old Town, he immediately saw an opportunity to merge history and tourism for the benefit of all. Old Town is considered the birthplace of California because, in 1769, Father Junipero Serra established there the first of the twenty-one missions that would anchor the development of California for Spain. In 1821, Mexico won its independence from Spain, and San Diego became part of the Mexican Republic. In 1846, the Mexican-American War shifted control of the city to the United States. It has been said that the first American flag in California was raised in the plaza of Old Town. Despite that historical significance, the entire area of Old Town slid into deterioration in the 1860s, as the population migrated south to "New Town" at the direction of an enterprising businessman, Alonzo Horton.

John had an idea for the dilapidated and historic ruin Casa de Estudillo, which faced Old Town's historic plaza. It had been built in 1828 and was the former adobe home of José María Estudillo, a prominent

Mexican political figure of the time. John believed that he could romanticize tourists' perceptions of San Diego's early history by capitalizing on the popularity of Helen Hunt Jackson's 1884 bestseller, *Ramona*, a heart-tugging novel set in southern California after the Mexican-American War. There was a fictional adobe home described in Jackson's novel, so John bought Casa de Estudillo and renamed it "Ramona's Marriage Place," and it instantly became an important cultural attraction at the end of his streetcar line. He chose architect Hazel Wood Waterman to restore the integrity of the house, and due to her extensive research and expertise, the house is one of the oldest surviving examples of Spanish architecture in California today. Due to the success of John's restoration efforts, renewed interest in the city's early heritage sparked a widespread preservation effort, seen today in the historically accurate Old Town.

With the same "gratitude" they had shown for Mission Cliff Gardens, John's critics alleged that he had restored the adobe home only to get riders on his line. But even acknowledging that increased ridership might well have been one of the intended results, he could have picked anyone to do the renovation, at a much lower price; instead, he had chosen an esteemed architect, thereby showing that he wanted the work done with excellence and authenticity. He had also demonstrated that he was progressive in his time for hiring a woman. Nonetheless, he soon had another set of critics; scores of loyal Helen Hunt Jackson fans protested the historical inaccuracy of Ramona's Marriage Place.[13]

Riding the Rails to Tent City

Under John's ownership, the Hotel del Coronado achieved a level of distinction that had eluded even the dreams of her founders, Babcock and Story. John had traveled the world, stayed in the most elegant hotels, and participated in his father's expansion of the lavish Aptos hotel. He knew what luxuries a first-class hotel should have, and he knew that the rich craved nothing less than perfection.

Business correspondence between John and the hotel's humbled and some say humiliated manager, Elisha Babcock, reveals that John, still residing in San Francisco, micromanaged the hotel, even down to the quality of ingredients in the meals. The fact that they were business partners in outside ventures didn't deter John from holding Babcock accountable for the day-to-day affairs of the hotel that Babcock had built but that John now owned. If John heard even a whisper of displeasure from a guest, he demanded clarification from the frustrated Babcock, who in turn would ask to know the names and dates of stay of any dissatisfied hotel guests, but to no avail.[14]

John demanded excellence for those wealthy enough to afford the Hotel del Coronado. However, not many tourists at the turn of the century could afford the nightly rate of $3.50. But, in June 1900, during a necessary renovation of the hotel, John put guests in tents in an adjacent encampment he called Camp Coronado. Here was another opportunity; he transformed the temporary measure into a permanent second-class option. At Camp Coronado, later renamed "Tent City," a guest could rent an oceanfront tent for a more affordable option at a weekly rate of $4.50. The numerous attractions there—an open plunge with a sand bottom, carnival rides, evening band concerts, and plays—became popular among the locals and especially East County San Diego residents who sought relief from the inland heat. Tent City was an instant hit.

The canvas city combined the joys of camping with all the comforts of home; it came with beds, chairs, cooking utensils, electric lights, housekeeping, laundry service, and more. The area, about a mile in length, functioned like a real city, with a daily newspaper and its own police department. Entertainment attractions included a soda fountain, floating casino, dance hall, carousel, shooting gallery, and high dive. An early brochure described the surprising array of services for the family-friendly resort:

> The many comforts and conveniences at the resort include well-kept streets and alleys, perfect sewerage and water systems, also ice-water supplied free to all campers, electric lights, street cars, long-distance telephones, telegraph offices, drug store, photographic supplies, book

store, barber shop, ladies' hairdressing parlors, grocery store, market, delicatessen, confectionery, laundry, mails twice a day delivered at each camper's tent by special carriers, and the San Diego morning papers delivered at your tent before breakfast! Could anything be more perfect and convenient?[15]

In August 1903, after fifteen years of managing the hotel he had built, Babcock suddenly "quit the hotel business for good!"[16] He was completely frustrated with John, who he believed had stolen his dream out from under him. It's also likely that the burden of managing Tent City along with the main hotel was the last straw. A Spreckels representative announced that Babcock's ill health forced his retirement, but the fact that his son Graham was unaware of it tells a different story.[17] Rumors had been flying that the Babcock-Spreckels business partnerships in other areas were also troubled. Babcock had been acting as an agent for John and Adolph in many transactions outside of Coronado, and, in some of them, he was evidently duplicitous, and it "became difficult to determine if he was acting as J.D.'s representative or in his own behalf."[18]

Trouble had obviously been brewing between the two men for some time because John, as if he had been expecting a change in hotel management, was ready with a strong German to take charge of Tent City. He hired George Schonewald, who had nineteen years' experience at the most luxurious hotels, to completely take over the dining at the Tent City Café and elevate it to a new level. Like Claus, Schonewald had emigrated from Germany to escape army service and had arrived broke in San Francisco in 1866. There, he had worked in a German bakery until he rose to management, first at San Francisco's renowned Palace Hotel, where John maintained a suite for entertaining, and then at the celebrated Del Monte Hotel in Monterey. Schonewald had been fired from those posts, due to his overbearing personality, but the son of Claus Spreckels thought that this forceful personality could be useful in inspiring the staff to work.[19] Soon, the Tent City Café sparkled with twinkling glass, polished silver, snowy linens, and fragrant floral decorations. But Schonewald was anything but submissive to John's requests, and he was not popular with staff or clientele, so, after only a couple of years, he was let go.

Bringing in William Clayton

John knew just he who wanted to bring over to mend employee relations at the hotel—William "Bill" Clayton. In or around 1893, Clayton had arrived destitute in San Francisco from Hawai'i, having lost all his money in a diamond hoax. His daughter, Emily, later recounted that he had to sell most of his clothes and jewelry in order to pay off his valet and get to California. At one time, his hardship and poverty in San Francisco was enough for him to consider suicide. Circumstances improved only slightly after he decided on "selling axe handles office to office." It's likely, on one of those office visits, that his professional and efficient manner caught the attention of Adolph Spreckels, who, with John and some smaller investors, bought San Francisco's pioneer electric railway company, the San Mateo Electric Railway Company, in 1896. Clayton began as Adolph's secretary and quickly became indispensable. Clayton's luck further changed when he married Augusta Dohrmann, from a prosperous family.

Adolph had a demeanor with the business world that was far friendlier than that of his elder brother. John had little interest in practicing good public relations. His difficulties with business associates had begun to surface; his brutal frankness and brusqueness to the point of being rude had begun rubbing people the wrong way. In San Francisco, he had Adolph to soften business relationships, but he needed someone like that in southern California to run his budding transportation empire. He realized that Clayton's gentlemanly ways and diplomacy could help him there. In 1901, John gave Clayton a hefty raise and sent him to live in San Diego along with his wife and daughter, Emily.[20] At the Hotel del Coronado, his "magnificent physique and commanding presence," combined with his crisp British accent, won over the employees, just as John predicted.[21]

Dinner hour at Tent City was a special time, when German-born Henry Ohlmeyer conducted the Tent City band, filling the café with excellent music. For nine summers, the stout and smiling bandmaster swayed from side to side with baton in hand, in front of the thousands who had come to love his music. John too loved his music and personality and, because of this, overlooked a lot of his peccadillos. His contract ended only because he was jailed in 1914 for writing checks "for which there were no funds on more than a dozen Oakland business houses."[22]

Tent City thrived as a small town, and its daily newspaper reported on the doings within and around the canvas community. When the Spreckels children spent their school vacation in Coronado, the paper reported on the various activities they engaged in. If one of them rode the Ferris wheel or the carousel or engaged in a children's competition, the event was sure to be published.

John revealed in an interview that he never thought much about religion: "I believe a man can be just as good a Christian if he never goes to church as if he goes three times a day. So many professed Christians are hypocrites. I hate a hypocrite."[23] He nevertheless ensured that the Tent City population would honor the Sabbath, as described in the community's brochure:

> The gaiety of the week is temporarily laid aside on Sunday. In the morning there is Sunday school for the children and church services for those who are in the habit of observing the Sabbath. In the afternoon the band gives an outdoor concert. There is no unseemly hilarity in the camp, but those who wish, go fishing, riding, boating, cycling, visiting and sight-seeing, as on other days. The Sunday services at the camp are non-sectarian. No regular pastor is employed, but invitation is extended to visiting clergy, regardless of creed, to preach. To encourage a liberal supply of clerical talent, all ministers and their families are given half rates on tents during their stay in camp.[24]

Tent City flourished as a popular vacation spot for almost forty years. In the twenty-five years that John oversaw the canvas city, it operated at a yearly loss. He knew the community relied on it for its social and recreation needs, and the middle class relied on it for an affordable

17. Edward Willis Scripps (1854–1926), ca. 1912. The eccentric multimillion-aire who constantly fought John Spreckels with his *San Diego Sun* was John's lifetime archenemy. Photo reproduced by permission of Special Collections, Ohio University Libraries, Athens, Ohio.

holiday alternative. When the Spreckels children had their own children, history repeated itself; Tent City became a fond memory for each generation.

Extending the Franchises

By 1910, John had successfully obtained and consolidated several failed transportation lines into a single massive system. It had never been easy. When he encountered difficulties in financing improvements for the roads, he sought to obtain a charter amendment to extend the city franchises that were about to expire. Unfortunately, in an effort to impede John's domination of the city's infrastructure, a vigorous public campaign led by the *San Diego Sun* railed against extending the franchises. The *Sun*, a scrappy, left-leaning evening daily, had been founded by the wealthy and eccentric newspaper tycoon Edward Scripps. A muckraker at heart, Scripps used the *Sun* to attack every business interest of John (and Adolph), including their 1910 bid for a fifty-year city streetcar monopoly: "To Hell with Spreckels! We are sick and tired of being a one-man town. If Spreckels wants 50-year franchises the downtrodden common people must see that he does not get them."[25]

Since the California constitution provided for popular initiatives and referendums, San Diegans were given a say in the matter, and it turned out that they were not "sick and tired" of John Spreckels. Despite the *Sun*'s harping on capitalistic greed, the public voted three to one to extend the life of the city franchise from twenty to fifty years. John was buoyed by their confidence, and he poured even more money in to upgrade the streetcar system: "I love San Diego, I believe in San Diego. And on several occasions, when the carrying out of some of my larger projects has required their votes; the people of San Diego have shown their confidence in me by refusing to listen to the insinuations of the vilifiers."[26]

Other critics accused John of grandiosity—that he was extending the streetcar system to transport people to places he was going to create—but he knew that no city could expand without an adequate streetcar system. "Any fool can see that," he declared.[27]

Quenching the City's Thirst: The Southern California Mountain Water Company

Many early tales were told about the scarcity of water in early San Diego. John remembered that "water was peddled like milk" and a "bath was looked upon as a selfish luxury to be enjoyed only on pain of being considered an enemy of the people."[28] In fact, it was said that many locals chose to bathe in the bay and drink beer rather than the expensive cloudy water that was drilled from the bed of the San Diego River, a process that had been in place from as far back as 1875. As the city grew in area and population, however, well water became inadequate for irrigation.

In 1881, author and lawyer Theodore S. Van Dyke and engineer William E. Robinson assessed the bleak situation and saw a financial opportunity to generate a dependable water source in the mountains. They resolutely persuaded others to invest in their water venture until the San Diego Flume Company was formed in May of 1886. With a capital stock of $1,000, construction was begun in 1887 to collect rainwater in the elevated Cuyamaca Lake. The stored water was then piped down to San Diego along a wooden flume through a complex series of access roads, bridges, tunnels, and trestles to the Eucalyptus Reservoir. By all accounts, the building of the flume was a "stupendous task." The six-foot-wide and four-foot-high redwood-planked flume was completed in 1889. Flume riding at that time became a great local sport for San Diegans on Sundays. As the entrepreneurs predicted, the San Diego Flume Company became *the* source for water, quenching the thirst of parched San Diegans for many years.[29]

Unfortunately, ventilating valves had not been installed on the pipes; water passing through them air-locked, which slowed the flow to a trickle, a terrible situation for a city where very little rain fell. By the time John began investing in San Diego, the wooden flume was also in a deplorable condition.

Babcock worked on the construction on the Lower Otay Dam as part of his master plan for completing his Coronado dream and achieving a water solution. In 1896, when both money and water became scarce, he brought John in to be an equal partner. John remembered that he sort of fell into the water business when Babcock "turned to me for help when the inflated balloon collapsed, and I completed the building of Hotel Coronado and the lower Otay Dam. So you see, circumstances forced me to get deep and deeper into the big game of helping to develop San Diego."[30]

Babcock's Otay Water Company, in partnership with John, evolved into the Southern California Mountain Water Company. With these two powerful and influential men in charge, the company soon became a force to be reckoned with. In 1897, they completed the Lower Otay Dam, began the Morena Dam, and planned construction on Barrett Dam, with the goal of providing an "exhaustless water supply."[31] Their system of water distribution involved twenty miles of redwood pipes from Otay to San Diego, with branch lines to supply farmers in the outskirts. These were not easy projects, and construction on each reservoir had its unique set of obstacles. John was in San Francisco, but Babcock was local, so the weight of dealing with engineering problems on the dam fell on his shoulders. John, on the other hand, dealt with all the problems via correspondence and telegrams; he was undaunted and reported through the *San Diego Union* on January 1, 1901, "Neither men nor money will be spared in hurrying the water into San Diego at the earliest possible moment."[32]

Wrangling over Control of Water, Legal and Otherwise

Babcock must have known trouble was brewing when John arrived in San Diego on February 15, 1904, to attend the yearly meetings of companies, which heretofore Babcock had run as managing director. Even though Babcock had stepped away from his long association from the hotel he had built, he was still very active with John in other companies: the Coronado Water Company, the Coronado Railroad Company, the San Diego and Coronado Ferry Company, the San Diego and Coronado Transfer Company, the Southern California Mountain Water Company, the San Diego Electric Railway Company, the Spreckels Brothers Commercial Company, and the Marine Ways & Drydock Company.

It's unknown what went on behind the scenes to turn John against his partner—perhaps it was because Babcock had stepped down from running the hotel—but John did turn against him almost immediately after that resignation. He had a specific agenda when he arrived, and he called for elections, covertly prearranged, to be held in order to reassign duties and regain complete control of every company. Before the meeting was over, each company was under new leadership, with John as president, William Clayton as managing director, and Harry Titus as secretary. Babcock's services were no longer needed.[33]

Babcock did not quietly knuckle under, however. With his son and business partner, Graham, he filed a legal suit against John in the summer of 1905 to secure control of the Southern California Mountain Water Company. San Diego real estate developer Ed Fletcher, who thought highly of Babcock and detested John, remembered that it was an ugly public "falling out" between the two men with "the court washing their linen."[34] The Babcocks alleged that they had a controlling share in the company until John gave his son Jack 147 shares on August 21, 1905, thereby wresting control away from the Babcocks. They in turn alleged that the stock had been issued to Jack in violation of the bylaws of the company.

On September 2, 1905, "Babcock and Spreckels Fight" and variations of those words were the headlines in papers up and down California. The *Oceanside Blade-Tribune* succinctly laid out the lawsuit and described it as a battle to decide who "shall have supremacy in the management of the Southern California Mountain Water company."[35] The public was informed that it would be an interesting case to keep an eye on because "a majority of the stock of the water company is held by E. S. Babcock, but the board of directors is still controlled by the Spreckels interests."[36]

On November 6, 1905, while all this legal commotion was going on, the mayor of San Diego approved an ordinance that authorized the purchase of a significant supply of water from the Southern California Mountain Water Company for ten years at four cents per one thousand gallons, a price low enough for the city to stop buying water from the

San Diego Flume Company.[37] This undercutting almost immediately sent the San Diego Flume Company to the auction block.

The lawsuit that had begun in August dragged on until March 9, 1906, when the Superior Court of San Diego ruled in John's favor.[38] The judge pointed out that when Babcock had partnered with John in the late 1800s, they had agreed to be fifty-fifty partners. The judge found that Babcock had in fact violated that agreement when he began to "secretly" purchase stock in his son's name in order to "wrest the control of the corporation from the Spreckels Company."[39] In the end, some legal maneuvering led to a buyout of all Babcock's interests in their joint ventures, and the suit was dismissed. (Only two years after losing the court case, Graham Babcock, only thirty-three years old, died from an unspecified cause. His brother, Arnold Edgar, would die soon after at only thirty-nine, leaving Elisha and Adella without any children to take care of them in their old age.)

In 1910, developers James Murray and Ed Fletcher purchased the floundering San Diego Flume Company at the fire sale price of $150,000 (it had cost more than $1 million to construct), renaming it the Cuyamaca Water Company (CWC). Over the next five years, Murray and Fletcher greatly upgraded the entire water system, hoping to transform it into a profitable business.

In 1911, the California Railroad Commission was legally granted the power to regulate not only rail companies but private corporations delivering other public systems, including telephone, power, and water. By 1912, Fletcher received permission to increase the water rates of the CWC as long as the flumes were repaired with expensive concrete, ensuring high-quality water to the customers. He successfully used a less expensive repair and lined the inside of the flume with a rubber roofing material. He then began to develop La Mesa and its environs, including the Grossmont Reservoir for additional water storage in 1913.[40]

Despite the improvements, the CWC remained as troubled as it had been when it was the San Diego Flume Company, due to its proximity to the San Diego River, which made it susceptible to flooding episodes. Even so, the CWC began to sell water to the city of San Diego. The farmers who had previously been served in El Cajon, an East County suburb, then filed a complaint, saying their water supply was being depleted, due to its diversion to the city. Fletcher created more enemies among the farmers in 1914, when he began selling "surplus" water to the city; John, who insisted that all the water should be sent to the city, became an antagonist.

By 1912, San Diego's municipal water officials resolved to buy John's water supply. John needed capital for other big projects and agreed to sell at actual cost plus 6 percent interest on his investment, a total sum of $4.5 million. The city offered only $4 million, and John accepted. The bonds carried at popular election by sixteen to one. When it was discovered that this bond issue would exceed the city's debt limit, John agreed to sell the system, exclusive of the Morena Dam, for $2.5 million in bonds, which was within the debt limit, and to lease the dam at a rental of 4.5 percent. By February 1, 1913, the city of San Diego took over John's system, which consisted of "four reservoirs, having a total capacity of 27,675,000,000 gallons and several miles of connection conduits and pipe lines."[41]

Babcock first, then John and Fletcher, had realized that water was the essential component for the growth of San Diego and that wealth would accrue to whomever controlled it. All had built dams in different parts of the county, Babcock, and then John in the south and Fletcher with others in the east and north. All their water facilities eventually became an important part of San Diego's water supply. John had already sold reservoirs to the city for $2.5 million in 1912, and Fletcher sold the Cuyamaca system to a conglomerate of East County cities a few years later for $1.2 million. They both made out fine. Babcock, the first one to catch the vision and begin building dams in the area, made nothing, however.

After the streetcar and water companies were in place, there were those who believed that John was on a charitable mission to save San Diego, a notion that he balked at:

I want to disclaim any idea that some of my critics accuse me of cherishing. It is insinuated that because I undertook those basic developments [the supplying of water and transportation], I have set myself up as a sort of "special providence" or "savior" of San Diego. Nonsense! I made those larger investments to protect the investments I had already made. I am a business man, and not a Santa Claus—nor a fool. Any man who claims to invest millions for the fun of being looked up to as a little local tin god is either a lunatic or a liar. I, gentlemen, am neither. I simply used plain, ordinary business sense. The city would not grow without an abundant water supply.[42]

The *Union* and the *Evening Tribune*

Publishing newspapers was a profitable commercial venture, mainly due to the revenue from advertisements, but that is not what drove Claus and John Spreckels to purchase them. Their philosophy, dating back to the 1880 purchase of Hawai'i's *Pacific Commercial Advertiser*, was akin to "If you can't beat them, buy them." The *San Francisco Call*, besides being an innovative newspaper, had served and was serving its purpose to influence public opinion: endorsing the Spreckels business investments and representing the Republican Party's viewpoints. With his assets multiplying in southern California, John was quick to purchase the *San Diego Union* in 1890 for similar purposes.

When the rival *San Diego Evening Tribune* began to warn the public that a rich San Franciscan was turning their community into a "one-man town," John solved the problem in 1901 by buying the *Tribune*, after considerable litigation and settlements.

Although his motives might have been questionable, John respected the world of journalism. After he took over the *Union* and *Tribune*, he filled the newsrooms with high-spirited journalists. Even though workdays were long and wages low, it was said that "Spreckels had happy newsrooms."[43] As long as the writers and editors were "well-disposed toward Spreckels' numerous enterprises" they had creative autonomy.

John was determined to outsell his competition, particularly Edward Scripps's *San Diego Sun*, which began to oppose the *Union*'s positions immediately after John had purchased that paper. Since Scripps was a multimillionaire, there was no chance to buy his paper out, and it would be forever a thorn in John's side.

John was a creative publisher who knew how to increase readability. In the days before photographs displaced drawings, he maintained a roster of such esteemed artists as Maynard Dixon and Arthur James Cahill, who provided beautiful and striking illustrations for the *Call*. He also added magazine supplements, comics, and serial novels, which increased both subscribers and advertisers. It is not surprising, then, that he knew what to do with his San Diego newspapers. He added an innovative puzzle series, political cartoons, lively illustrations, and more. What ultimately pushed the paper ahead, though, was the increase in breakneck news reporting.

While staunchly conservative, the *Union* and *Tribune* soon earned reputations for an appreciation of diversity and sympathy for the common man. African American citizens in San Diego were longing for social justice. Before John had bought the *Tribune* from its previous owner, Frederick Kimball, the paper was known for using insulting language and illustrations in its stories, and it was "unrelenting" in its bigotry toward black citizens. They were commonly and disrespectfully referred to by first name only, or simply as "Aunt" or "Uncle," or a combination of both, and the N-word was prevalent, even in the headlines. "And it was not until 1901 when the newspaper was bought out by John that the stream of hateful language subsided."[44]

From his desk in San Francisco, John Spreckels soon dominated San Diego politics, using the *Union* and the *Tribune* to support his Republican interests from the top to the bottom of the state of California. To counter the stances of both the *Union* and the *Tribune*, millionaire Scripps used his *San Diego Sun* to relentlessly attack anything John had to say. While championing the downtrodden workingman, Scripps lived the life of luxury from his four-hundred-acre villa or on his yacht *Ohio*. John looked for every opportunity in the press to characterize him as a hypocrite.[45] In his often repeated words, "I hate a hypocrite."[46]

9

Earthquake, Death, and Legal (and Romantic) Chaos

Claus Spreckels's Stroke

When John's father was in his late fifties, contemporaries described him as a man who refused to age:

> He is of medium height, compactly built and dresses neatly. He has the face of a typical German, with the high cheek-bones, fair skin and blue eyes of the Fatherland. His eye is as clear as that of a young man, and his skin though browned by exposure, is also clean and healthy. His round head is covered with a thick growth of hair, rapidly changing from gray to white. This is the only indication of his years. He has the alert look and movement of a man of thirty, and in his steel-blue eyes is a look which goes far to reveal his character.[1]

Even in his seventies, Claus was still the proverbial "picture of health." His piercing blue eyes, big smile, firm handshake, and the ever-present cigar in hand fooled most observers, but family members knew that the stress and strain of building his sugar empire had taken its toll and that his appearance was only a superficial image of health. He probably had high blood pressure, exacerbated by his overly rich diet and his chronic cigar smoking. He was also well known for his intense outbursts of anger. Whenever he was under the weather, he would check himself into a European spa in order to restore his health. Such spa "cures," or "taking the waters," had long been the solution for the rich and famous to treat a variety of ailments. Since he had been in his forties, he had traveled, as time allowed, to several elegant spas throughout eastern Europe to calm his nerves and lose weight.[2]

In November 1903, seventy-five-year-old Claus—looking, by all reports, refreshed from one of those relaxing European spa cures—had a paralytic stroke. He then suffered a second stroke the following month that left him unable to speak clearly, thus forcing him to turn business matters over to John and Adolph. This was a staggering blow to Claus, who liked to be in control; the temporary loss of speech meant he was no longer able to ensure that his demands were being met. The finest doctors that money could buy were brought to the Van Ness Avenue mansion, creating a spectacle in Pacific Heights. The Sugar King's strokes were newsworthy enough to keep reporters on John's doorstep at midnight in the hopes of landing a headline story. John, obviously cranky, told the press that "reports of his serious illness are exaggerated. I have nothing more to say." He then slammed the door.[3]

A little more than a year later, Claus, only slightly stable enough to travel, returned to Hawai'i with Anna to rehabilitate in the mild climate and to enjoy the relative privacy. Daughter Emma accompanied them on the voyage. It had been nearly twelve years since his last visit, and Claus Spreckels was now praised in the Hawaiian press. Instead of referring to him as a ruthless interloper or an invader, as the media had done when he'd left during the overthrow of the Hawaiian monarchy, they praised him as a loyal supporter of the monarchy and the greatest entrepreneur to ever have landed on their shores. He must have basked in this warm reception.

It is probable that the mellowed royalist would have visited the aged Queen Lili'uokalani at her private home, Washington Place. At this meeting, he would have found that, even as the life of old Hawai'i was slipping away, the queen remained as loyal to her culture and as "royal" as she had ever been. She was the most high-profile personality in Honolulu, beloved by both residents and visitors. This was not only out of sympathy; indeed, she was revered and given more respect and

18. Praise in Hawai'i for Claus Spreckels for his loyal support of the monarchy. The profusion of fragrant long leis draped over the Spreckels family conveyed a great amount of affection, admiration, and respect for them. *Left to right, in leis*: Claus, Emma, and Anna, ca. 1893. Permission granted from the Terrence and Virginia Wilson Private Family Collection.

ceremonial courtesy after her dethronement than she had ever received as the sitting monarch. She became a cherished link with Hawai'i's past, and many notable figures paid homage to her throughout her life, several of whom also recognized her musical abilities.

Once back in Hawai'i, Claus and Anna thought that they might spend their last days in their opulent Honolulu home in the Punahou District, and they asked John and Lillian to retire there with them. However, John, whose business concerns made this offer impractical, was also experiencing severe health issues of his own and thus could not be persuaded. Claus and Anna, not wanting to be so far from family at their advanced age, returned to their San Francisco mansion.

John's Grave Illness

As 1904 began, John was only fifty, and he had a great deal of money, power, and fame, but his health was waning. Even so, he was in better shape than his father, who had not improved much from the strokes and was suffering complications from diabetes. In 1905, Claus stepped down and told John to assume the role of president of the Spreckels Sugar Company. If that were not enough, his brother Adolph suffered a stroke of his own and went to Berlin in July 1904 for an undisclosed operation to treat his "apoplexy."[4] His father's directive must have added untold stress to John's compromised condition. The best physicians could not pinpoint the source of his persistent illness, and they ultimately diagnosed an "obscure and obdurate digestive disorder." His family was more than alarmed when the illness reduced a "175-pound man to less than 100 pounds."[5]

News of John's illness became public nationwide in June 1904, when he was unable to attend the Republican National Convention in Chicago. He and Lillian went to Coronado with the hope he would recover enough to make it to the convention, but, as he explained, he was unable to muster up the strength to do so: "I was in ill health when elected a delegate and came to San Diego a week ago for the purpose of resting and recuperating. My journey down convinced me that I would certainly jeopardize my health by taking the trip to Chicago at this time. I therefore decided not to attend the national convention."[6]

Not only was unwanted news of his private illness being published but John's public losses were receiving attention. In 1904, John told the stockholders of the Oceanic Steamship Company that a drought in Australia had "seriously affected the business of all steamship lines." He told them things were looking bad and they had suffered a net loss of $234,672.01 along with a net loss for the preceding year of $439,303.72.[7] But he attempted to encourage his stakeholders by reporting that Australia was recovering from the "misfortune" and that the situation was improving for resumed service. Unfortunately, between late 1905 and early 1906, the press circulated stories that the Oceanic Steamship Company had suffered yet another money-losing year. John defensively provided a statement indicating that the loss was due to strong competition and the effects of Australia and New Zealand's unfavorable tariffs. A year later, the Oceanic Steamship Company lost the mail contracts to Australia, and the *Pacific Commercial Advertiser* reported that John's company was in a "hapless condition," with no comment from its owners.[8]

Likely, the stress of his beloved steamship company losing millions did not help John's state of mind, and he stopped offering statements to the hungry press. In January 1906, he was unable to digest food, and he stopped eating. He was nourished intravenously for three months, but it was said that he kept his sense of humor throughout. At a very low point, he asked to see his lawyers, despite the fact that his legal affairs had already been put in order. When Lillian questioned the request, he retorted, "Why shouldn't I have a lawyer too? There is a doctor in the next room all the time; the undertaker has been sitting impatiently at the front door for weeks and you know the cast of this show isn't complete without a lawyer."[9]

On March 24, the family was deeply alarmed by John's "precarious condition," which had left him unable to get out of his bed.[10] On the same day, the *Oakland Tribune* reported that Jack Spreckels had been working for the past five months at the *Call* office, "familiarizing himself with the business" due to his father's "dying condition."[11] At the end of March, Grace was summoned home from her trip abroad in order to see her father one last time.[12] By all accounts, John was near death—until the greatest natural disaster yet experienced by an American city occurred, an event that inexplicably healed him of his mysterious ailment.

The San Francisco Earthquake

San Francisco's moment of destiny came at 5:12 a.m. on Wednesday, April 18, 1906. John and Lillian were jolted awake in their Pacific Avenue mansion by a deep and terrible rumble, followed by a tremendous shaking. The 7.9-magnitude earthquake and the subsequent fires drove every San Franciscan to flee for their lives. From his home, John could see the whole skyline swaying below. Within seconds, streets buckled, water pipes broke, chimneys snapped off, and houses collapsed and crumbled into rubble. The most severe damage, however, followed the quake, when damaged gas lines led to widespread fires. Many heart-wrenching cries for help were heard until they fell silent. The unimaginable loss of life and property sent many into shock. John, barely able to walk, needed assistance to escape from his home.

James Stetson, a neighbor, recounted that the exterior of John and Lillian's beautiful house "had cracked and crumbled and fallen like so much spun sugar out of a wedding cake."[13] Walking down the same street, Stetson saw Rudolph Spreckels's mansion and noticed, amid the blocks of crushed cement, that Rudolph, his wife (eight months pregnant with Claudine), his little son, his mother-in-law and sisters-in-law, and maid servants "had set up their household on the sidewalk, the women wrapped in rugs and coverlets and huddled in easy chairs hastily rolled out. They were having their morning tea on the sidewalk and the silver service was spread on the stone coping."[14]

John's aged parents fled from their brownstone mansion on Van Ness Avenue. Fire then swept through their home, destroying their priceless collections of art and furniture. On one archival photo of the ruined mansion, a handwritten caption told a story: "One time when money did not count. The offer of a million dollars by Spreckels to the firemen had no effect."[15] Fortunately, Claus and Anna had never sold their comfortable old house on Howard Street in the Mission District, because it was one of the few houses to escape major damage. When an old friend asked Claus how he liked being back on Howard Street again, he said, "I wished I had never left it and I never intend to leave it again."[16] He never did.

By noon on April 18, the magnificent Call Building—only nine years old—was seen spewing large plumes of black and gray smoke. Structurally, the building had withstood the quake's effects, and damage at first was minimal, but a fire soon ravaged the interior. Only twenty-four hours after the quake, San Francisco's tallest skyscraper was one of the very few buildings that still stood, albeit a hollow shell silhouetted in

19. Earthquake rubble. John's son-in-law Alexander "Alec" Hamilton is standing amid the devastating ruins of his family's Baker & Hamilton hardware store after locating his bank vault. April 1906. Courtesy of author.

the sky. Within three days, approximately 25,000 buildings on 490 city blocks were destroyed, but the gutted Call Building survived.

John's tugboats were called into action to fight the flames. The rest of the Spreckels family, including Grace's husband, Alec, had the presence of mind to run to their respective ruins to locate their bank vaults in the rubble.

John was so weak that he practically had to be carried to the harbor by Lillian and Grace. He was helped aboard the *Breakwater*, recently purchased by his company in 1904 to ply coal and passengers between Portland, Oregon, and San Francisco for his newly purchased Beaver Hill coal mine in Oregon's Coos County. The children who assisted him on his journey to San Diego were Grace, Lillie, and eighteen-year-old Claus Jr.[17] The other men, including his son Jack and sons-in-law, Harry and Alec, stayed behind to protect their interests.

On that dark Wednesday afternoon in April, John must have felt his whole world had crashed down around him. As he watched the smoking ruins of his home and discovered the burned-out shell of the Call skyscraper, he stood at a personal crossroads. When Lillian asked him what the future held, he drolly replied, "I'm a crackerjack mechanician [mechanic] so I can get a job as a chauffeur." Lillian responded, "And you know what a good needlewoman I am, so I can always earn money by doing embroidery and other fancy-work."[18] Of course, they did not need to wonder where to find a comfortable bed. John owned an entire island and a luxurious place in which to take refuge: the Hotel del Coronado.

New Beginnings in Coronado

Once John and his family, all noticeably traumatized, arrived in San Diego, the *Breakwater* was placed at the disposal of San Diego's Red Cross. It then returned to San Francisco with a large shipment of citrus fruits, clothing, blankets, and medical supplies.[19] The news was also spread in San Francisco that John had offered Coronado's Tent City as a refuge for earthquake evacuees.

Perhaps it was due to being in Coronado, a place with happy holiday memories and a warmer climate, that John's health, to the astonishment of his family, revived. As his health began to return, no question remained: They would stay permanently in the mild climate of Coronado, away from the stresses of San Francisco. By all accounts, John's miraculous recovery gave him a sense that he was starting life anew, away from his feuding brothers and domineering father. He had been "to hell and back," and now it was time to retake his life.

Still, while the hotel was fine as a temporary haven, John and Lillian would need the privacy of their own home. They soon found for a home site a five-acre bluff overlooking the picturesque Glorietta Bay, which ensured that John could keep one eye on business (his hotel) and the other on pleasure (his yacht). This was the site that Hampton Story had begun to build his own home upon when construction had halted during the bust.[20]

To design their personal residence, John enlisted Harrison Albright, a self-trained architect from Pennsylvania who had earned a reputation for his use of reinforced concrete. This method of encasing steel in concrete so that a structure could withstand both an earthquake and fire was more than appealing to John and Lillian after what they had lived through in San Francisco. The architectural style of their home embodied the era's fondness for Italian Renaissance forms under the Beaux-Arts movement. This is seen in the formal symmetry and the ornamental columns, pediments, and balustrades, all of which were designed to make a grand and imposing architectural statement without being overly pretentious.

During the building of the Glorietta Bay mansion, a relationship of mutual respect developed between John and Albright that would endure for decades, a relationship that made the architect a very wealthy man after they collaborated on numerous concrete buildings around the region. But according to one source, money was not a motivator to the architect, because Albright was not attached to the "luxuries of life."[21] John, who worked frenetically at times, was likely calmed in the presence of a practicing theosophist who often retreated into mediation.

20. The Spreckels mansion sat on a five-acre bluff overlooking the picturesque Glorietta Bay, ensuring that John could keep one eye on business (his hotel) and the other on pleasure (his yacht), ca. 1909. Courtesy of Hotel del Coronado Records.

Albright was quoted as saying of theosophists, "We love the physical things, but are not a slave to them!"[22] At this time, Katherine Tingley, today regarded as the godmother of the New Age movement in southern California, was in control of San Diego's theosophy movement. She guided her followers, likely including Albright, from her 132-acre oceanfront commune atop Point Loma.[23] Even though John was not a theosophist and would have rejected their tenets of reincarnation, history shows he enjoyed collaborating with Albright, whose countenance resonated as one who was at "peace with the world."[24]

After a good deal of this thoughtful collaboration, John and Lillian's home was completed in 1908. When photographs of the interiors of both the San Francisco and Glorietta Bay mansions are compared, it is clear that the need for comfort in Coronado trumped the former ostentation of their Pacific Heights home. Still, the new home did have some lavish details, including a brass cage elevator and a marble staircase with leather-wrapped railings. The building included six bedrooms, three baths, a parlor, a dining room, and a library.

When it was clear that the Glorietta Bay mansion would be a permanent home, John added a third-floor solarium to take advantage of the spectacular views as well as an eight-hundred-square-foot music room, furnishing it for comfort with deep blue, thickly cushioned couches and chairs against walnut paneling embellished with gold scrollwork. Lush Persian rugs covered the floor. Inside the music room he installed an impressive Aeolian player pipe organ, housed in a rich dark walnut console.

John took music very seriously and had been taking piano lessons since he was a child. In time, playing music had become an antidote for stress. Now he would become proficient at the organ, thanks to private lessons from an old San Francisco friend from the Bohemian Club who had also relocated to San Diego. Humphrey John Stewart was a London-born musician and composer who was also a founding member of the American Guild of Organists.

When John arrived home in the evenings, he would play for an hour or so before dinner. The Aeolian's forty-one sets of pipes re-created the sound of an orchestra, which resonated throughout the mansion and all the way to the water's edge. His friend Henry Adams said that the organ "inspired the Dreamer in him and sustained and solaced the Doer."[25]

Reconciliation in the Aftermath of the Earthquake

Back in San Francisco, the city was laboring hard to rebuild itself after the earthquake with money appropriated by Congress and donated by wealthy citizens, including Claus Spreckels, who provided funds from his dwindled fortune. The completely gutted Claus Spreckels Building— the Call Building—was seen as a metaphor for the aged Sugar King. Like the eviscerated skyscraper standing forlorn on Market Street, he too was nothing but a shell of his former self, with his fortune reduced to $10 million ($282 million in today's money).[26] The reduction of his fortune was due not only to the heavy losses he had incurred from the earthquake. From 1896 to 1904, he had gifted John and Adolph a combined total of roughly $26 million.[27] In these dire circumstances, he knew he had little chance of recouping his fortune.

In the aftermath of the disaster and intense reflection, Claus became well aware of his mortality and mistakes, and he sought to rebuild his fractured relationship with his estranged younger children, Gus, Emma, and Rudolph. At the age of seventy-eight, suffering intensely from diabetes, he realized that more than a decade had passed since the 1895 litigation that had split the family, and cost him a fortune in legal fees, and he could sense his own end approaching.

The reconciliation began when Claus, hat in hand, approached Rudolph immediately in the days after the earthquake. It was a huge relief for Anna, who had always felt a special connection to her youngest, Rudolph. She had never gotten to form a relationship with her grandson, Rudolph Spreckels Jr., before his sad death at three years old in 1901. She, who had lost so many young children, would have had some motherly wisdom to share with her son. Rudolph and Eleanor had three other young children: Howard (born 1898), Eleanor (born 1902), and Claudine, born just weeks after the earthquake. The newspaper had reported that Rudolph was "dangerously sick" in the months prior to the earthquake and Anna begged Claus to let her visit him. But the local San Francisco press reported that Claus Spreckels was a "good hater" because he "sternly forbade his wife to visit her son" during his illness.[28] A *Los Angeles Times* article asserted that even so, Anna had worked tirelessly behind the scenes to reunite her "cast off sons and daughter" so they "might participate in the joint wealth of her husband and self, share and share alike" and she could enjoy her grandchildren.[29]

After the earthquake, Claus and Anna decided that John and Adolph had had their fair share of Spreckels money, and they sought to split the remaining $10 million in equal shares to their youngest children. According to Rudolph's account, Claus explained that age had caused a

21. Rudolph and Eleanor Jolliffe Spreckels, sitting on the steps with their children, ca. 1909. (From left) Claudine (1906–1996), Eleanor (1902–1984), and Howard (1898–1939). Courtesy of the estate of Eleanor Walsh de Limur.

reassessment of his feelings toward John and Adolph, and he sought to make it right.[30] And that "reassessment" meant that John and Adolph would *not* be beneficiaries of their parents' money.

Rudolph, aged thirty-four, had likely faced his own mortality in the face of the earthquake and was eager to restore relationships with his elderly parents, and he urged Gus, forty-eight, and his sister, Emma, thirty-six, to also be amenable to a reconciliation. As Gus remembered it, "Not long before my father died, he sent for me and told me that he had discovered his mistake and was sorry. He said it was the biggest mistake of his life, and to rectify it as far as possible he intended to make me the executor of his will."[31]

It's unknown whether Claus and Anna took one bold last move to unite all five of their warring children in their last years, but such a move would have been futile in the case of John. He would not consider reconciling with the brothers and sister who had caused him so much heartache and aggravation. John understood that his brothers were back in their father's favor, but his reaction suggests that he was not told that Rudolph and Gus had been named as executors, a role that he and nearly everybody expected him to fulfill as the eldest and, heretofore, favorite son.

With John preoccupied with restoring his health, his relocation to San Diego, and his investments there, Rudolph and Gus began managing much of their father's business. Emma was living in England during this period. Adolph was still involved in his father's sugar enterprises, but he was also engrossed in a secret love affair with a significantly younger woman, whom he knew would never pass the approval of either his parents or John. His interests were also focused on his racehorses; it was known that he attended the racetrack daily, likely infuriating Claus, whose own work ethic would never have allowed such an indulgence.[32]

In direct contrast with Adolph was Rudolph, whom Claus considered a hardworking and serious businessman like himself and who had become a millionaire at the age of twenty-six.[33] It's likely that he was very proud of Rudolph, who had made a name for himself as a business reformer because of his participation in the graft investigations in San Francisco in the early 1900s. Muckraking journalist Lincoln Steffens glorified Rudolph as a millionaire businessman who should be respected for his willingness to fight political corruption.[34]

The reconciliation confused the San Francisco elite, who for more than a decade had ensured that Claus's younger sons and older sons were never on the same invitation list. "Society hosts and hostesses had to be very particular about dinner invitations to the members of the Spreckels family."[35]

With both John and Adolph out of sight and preoccupied, Claus quietly had his will redrawn in New York on May 11, 1907. The location was likely strategic, so that his eldest sons, with their many San Francisco connections, would not catch wind of what was happening and stir up trouble. Not only did he name Rudolph and Gus as executors, but he stipulated that upon Anna's death, his estate was to be split among the three younger children; he was leaving the older brothers completely out: "I have made no provision in this will for my sons, John D. Spreckels and Adolph B. Spreckels, for the reason that I have already given to them a large part of my estate."[36]

Auf Wiedersehen, Claus

Early in December 1908, Claus caught a nasty cold while in Washington DC, testifying before the Ways and Means Committee of the House of Representatives regarding tariffs on sugar. That cold eventually turned into pneumonia by the time he got back to San Francisco. During the last week of the month, it was clear to all in attendance that this would be Claus Spreckels's last Christmas. Anna put everyone on alert, but John was the only child who could spend a week at his father's side before Claus died from acute pneumonia at four a.m. on December 26. Rudolph, who had been in Honolulu, barely made it to his father's bedside; he arrived just a few hours before the passing. Adolph, Gus, and Emma were all traveling abroad and missed the final farewell.

Since John had been by his father's deathbed for a week, it's hard not to wonder what that long goodbye held for both of them. Notwithstanding their conflicts and differences, their relationship had endured though mutual respect for each other's self-directed nature and independence. There was no question that, throughout the years, John had been Claus's preferred child, but that all changed when that child left to live permanently in San Diego. Perhaps Claus felt betrayed when he needed his eldest son and protégé the most. But it's not unfair to say that the strongest bond between Claus and John might have been the family fortune. Money and business might have preempted any chance of real father-and-son intimacy.

The Reverend Julius Fuendeling of St. Markus Kirche officiated at Claus's service in the home at 2027 Howard Street. He had been their pastor since 1883. St. Markus played a vital role for German immigrants such as Claus and Anna, who could hear Sunday sermons in their native tongue. Its outreach to San Francisco's German community had flourished because it preserved the tenets of Evangelical Lutheranism and the German culture. In his appreciation for the role the church played in his life, Claus had commissioned for St. Markus a Schoenstein organ and chandelier from Germany.

For two days, there was a continuous line of mourners waiting their turn to enter the Howard Street home to view Claus Spreckels's body, placed in the bay window among an enormous number of flowers. The ornate bronze coffin had a full-length French plate-glass top that equaled that of the assassinated President McKinley.

Many San Francisco office buildings, banks, stores, and factories flew the American flag at half-mast for the passing of the "Sugar King." Although John and Rudolph, bitter enemies, acted as pallbearers at their mother's request, neither looked into each other's eyes nor spoke a single word to each other.[37]

Fighting the Will

When John discovered, following his father's December 1908 funeral, the remarkable turn of affairs—that he had been disinherited—his hurt and fury were unmatched. Not only had he been replaced as the executor, but in a sense, he had been disowned by the father whom he had stood by throughout his life, particularly when the youngest children, who were now replacing him, had disrespected and sued their father.

John summoned Adolph home from New York, and the two jumped into action; through their lawyers, they declared Claus's will invalid due to coercion. They claimed that their father had been "mentally and physically incompetent" and that Gus and Rudolph had forced their father to sign over bequests to them.[38]

In April 1909, Gus and his wife, Oroville, arrived from their home in New York and moved into the Howard Street home to reside with Anna. Their primary purpose was to supervise her health; the secondary purpose was likely to safeguard her from John and Adolph's influence.[39]

On May 19, 1909, John told a journalist that he would never compromise with his brothers and would contest the validity of the will to "the bitter end": "This proceeding has been started with no idea of a compromise. It is a matter of principle and there can be no settlement. I haven't spoken to Rudolph or Claus A. [Gus] for 14 years; nor do I think Adolph has, neither are we likely to."[40]

In the midst of the contentious legal battles, Anna, unable to battle with her sons or with the lingering effects of the flu she had contracted almost immediately after Claus died, took to her bed. She had for years suffered from myocarditis, but the stress of the situation exasperated the "irregular action of [her] heart."[41] Some believed she never favored recuperation and that she felt adrift without her husband.[42]

John's sister, Emma, who had married for the third time, to John Ferris, and was living in England, made a three-week visit home to see her ailing mother for the first time in many years. She was pregnant with her first child, Jean, and this fact alone, according to Anna's niece and bedside companion, Anna Brommer, gave John's mother a fresh impetus to live.[43] She talked about going to Europe in June of 1910 to assist Emma with the new baby. She even mentioned that she might restore her Pacific Heights home to live her life out.

However, after Emma returned to England, Anna ceased all talk of going to Europe or of moving back up to her former mansion. She was now once again being forced to take a side between brothers, this time on the opposite side. In the protracted span of fifty-six years, she had delivered twelve children and had buried eight of them. She had stood by and watched her surviving children and husband fight for decades and thus had been deprived of establishing a relationship with some of her grandchildren. She had lived through the horror of the earthquake and had watched her home and city tumble around her, only to bury her husband when she needed him the most.

On January 17, 1910, after the physician C. M. Reichter visited their mother and reported that her heart was failing, John and Adolph, concerned for her emotional well-being, abandoned their proposed contest of the will. A public statement by Rudolph and Gus downplayed their elder brothers' "altruistic" move:

There were absolutely no grounds upon which a successful contest of the will could be maintained. If there were it is most improbable that any consideration for their mother could have prevented it in view of the fact that since our father's death neither John nor Adolph ever called upon or communicated with her. During his lifetime Claus Spreckels advanced to his sons, John D. Spreckels and Adolph B. Spreckels, property of great value by millions of dollars than the combined value of all the property he gave to his widow and all other children in his lifetime and by his will. Any sense of wrong that they may feel is inconsistent with the honor they claim to have extended to their father as the neglect of their mother in her old age is inconsistent with their declaration of consideration for her.[44]

Auf Wiedersehen, Anna

On February 16, 1910, in the midst of the feud between her children, Anna Christina Spreckels, aged seventy-nine, closed her weary eyes for good. Contradicting Rudolph and Gus's published statement that implied his neglectful absence, John stated that neither he nor Adolph were notified that their mother had been "in any imminent danger [of passing] until after [she] was dead."[45] If that weren't bad enough, John, miles and miles away, was not even informed she had died until after her funeral. Because he believed his mother's health had improved, this withheld information left him with "intense bitterness."[46]

Unlike her husband's very public funeral and memorial service, Anna's (according to her well-known wishes), though also officiated by Reverend Julius Fuendeling, was private, open only to family members. In that era, it was said that a lady had her name in a newspaper only when she was born, married, and buried—unless she was seeking publicity for a charitable event. Since there do not seem to be any public causes that she championed, there were few comments at Anna's memorial. Justifying the lack of press she received, one death announcement noted, "Mrs. Spreckels never cared for the gayety of society. She preferred the home."[47] Her remains were placed beside her husband's in the impressive Spreckels mausoleum at Cypress Lawn Cemetery.

22. Anna Christina Mangels Spreckels (1830–1910). She preferred to stay in the shadow of her dominant husband. She lost eight children and raised five to adulthood. Despite her best end-of-life efforts, she was unsuccessful in reuniting her adult children. Permission granted from the Terrence and Virginia Wilson Private Family Collection.

Anna's Will, Following Claus's Wishes

Following Anna's burial, John learned why he might have been intentionally left out of the funeral. He might have upset the solemn affair if he learned that his mother had fulfilled his father's last wishes and left her entire estate to Gus, Emma, and Rudolph. Her will made it very clear that her two eldest sons were intentionally omitted from sharing a single dime of her $6 million estate: "I intentionally omit making any provision in this will for my sons, John D. Spreckels and Adolph B. Spreckels . . . because I do not desire my said two sons or any of their issue to take any part of my estate. This I do for the reason that my deceased husband, Claus Spreckels, prior to his death, had already given and advanced to my said sons a large part of his estate, and for other reasons satisfactory to me."[48]

The press urged the public to prepare for "the hottest legal fight ever staged in San Francisco."[49] Readers were guaranteed that the ongoing litigation would "develop into one of the biggest will contests the West has ever witnessed" and were reminded of the irony, noting the peculiarity and the reverse of allegiance between the parents and the children.[50]

John and Adolph had reopened the contest over their father's will, and on the same day that Anna died, their legal efforts paid off (but only temporarily): The will was declared invalid on February 16, 1910.[51] But, in March 1910, the three youngest children appealed the decision, and *their* legal efforts paid off permanently on April 10, 1911, when the state supreme court reversed the lower decision, which had favored John and Adolph, and stated that the $10 million estate was to be distributed per Claus Spreckels's wishes.[52]

Feeling victorious and perhaps a little vindictive, Gus, Emma, and Rudolph, together as executors of the wills of Anna and Claus, turned the tables and sued John and Adolph in December 1911, asserting that each of them should return $12 million, which was one half of the money on record as having been previously gifted to each by their father. The suit alleged that their father had provided lifetime gifts to the two older sons of community property valued at roughly $26 million total, while the property remaining at the time of Claus's death was valued at less than $10 million.[53] In their lawsuit, the three youngest alleged that because their mother had not provided written consent to the monetary gifts made by their father, those gifts were void, had to be accounted for as part of the community estate, and had to be returned to the estate, as it rightfully belonged to them under their mother's will.

The irony that their legal objection was based on the written-consent statute made the public scratch their heads in disbelief because the younger siblings were using the same legal weapon that their father had unsuccessfully used against Gus in 1897.

John and Adolph legally objected and provided sufficient evidence that their mother had known about the money—specifically, that Anna had been well aware of the total money that Claus had given to John and Adolph—because in their father's will, admitted to probate in 1909, the gifts Claus had made to John and Adolph were specifically mentioned, indicating that Anna had known exactly her husband's desires. The court ruled in favor of John and Adolph: On May 30, 1912, Superior Court Judge James V. Coffee ordered the Spreckels estate distributed according the terms of Claus's will, thereby invalidating the younger siblings' demand that John and Adolph each return $12 million. This decision did make it possible, however, for Gus, Emma, and Rudolph to appeal the decision to the Supreme Court.[54] Finally, at the end of a long legal struggle, the Supreme Court of California upheld the will in *Spreckels v. Spreckels*, 172, Cal. 775 (1916).

The Romantic Disruptions

During the legal wrangling over the wills, John's brother Adolph and John's son Claus Jr. were disrupting John's focus on legal proceedings with disruptive and out-of-control love affairs.

ADOLPH AND ALMA

Alma de Bretteville, the daughter of nineteenth-century dirt-poor Danish immigrants, was a San Francisco legend in her time, a story of rags to riches. In her teenage years, she had delivered the laundry her mother washed for the gentry, but she had also posed nude for paintings that hung in private homes and in some of the city's better establishments. Legend holds that the six-foot-tall Alma had modeled for the figure of scantily clad Nike (the ancient Greek goddess of victory) that stands atop the eighty-five-foot monument, which was dedicated in 1902 to Admiral George Dewey, in San Francisco's Union Square.[55] Aside from this, when Alma was twenty-one, in a high-profile court case, she sued the millionaire Charles Anderson for breach of a marriage contract—or as she later told her friends, "personal defloration."[56]

Alma was resolved to marry a rich man. "I'd rather be an old man's darling than a young man's slave," she once said.[57] The *San Francisco Chronicle* often made racy jokes about the city's swanky Poodle Dog Restaurant and the indecencies that took place in private rooms upstairs. It was there that Alma met Adolph Spreckels, more than two decades her senior.[58] It was said, "their knees touched and they dined no more."[59] He became her "sugar daddy," as she called him, in 1903. He insisted that the relationship remain secret, though, knowing that neither John nor his parents would approve of Alma. Nonetheless, after five years as his mistress, Alma became Mrs. Spreckels on May 11, 1908. It had taken that long to convince the confirmed fifty-one-year-old bachelor that they should marry. Only after the fact did he inform John, who was disgusted, since it was well known that he hated Alma. He thought her crass, and he worried that she would drain the company's bank account.

The newlyweds moved into Adolph's Sausalito residence. It wasn't until Alma gave birth to their first child, Alma Emma, in 1909 that she learned about Adolph's dark secret of having contracted syphilis. After this, they moved back to San Francisco, where Adolph Bernard Jr. was born in 1911 (which sent Adolph Sr. over the moon), and Dorothy Constance was born in 1913. Surprisingly, neither Alma nor the children ever contracted syphilis, because during the years the couple was intimate, Adolph's disease was latent and thus not contagious. It's likely, however, that she held this marital deception over his head, even though she appeared devoted to him. After the birth of their first child, Adolph tore into shreds the prenuptial agreement that Alma had been forced to sign.[60]

Since the house was full of servants and nannies, Alma was free to switch her attention from childrearing to becoming a high-society hostess. The three children loved their kindhearted father, who was often debilitated by the advanced symptoms of his disease. By 1911, he had had two syphilis-induced strokes that kept him home with the children. Daughter Alma Emma once said that her mother "did a lot of wonderful things for us but she did not really take care of us."[61] In contrast, despite the pain caused by his disease, Adolph smothered his children with love and adoration.

Elated at being a father in his fifties, Adolph purchased a Victorian home in a prime area of Pacific Heights (2080 Washington Street) as a Christmas present for Alma. It was soon torn down to make room for a new French château that would take up an entire block. Adolph bought and demolished eight of the surrounding houses to give his wife the panoramic view she desired. The locals referred to it as the "Sugar Palace." John found it vulgar, however, and he was appalled at the way Alma was using their money.

Alma enjoyed all the material benefits of her new role as Mrs. Spreckels, but she was, for the most part, snubbed by both John and San Francisco society; both apparently could not forgive her dubious past.

Left behind today is a silent home movie, with subtitles, professionally made on August 23, 1922, for the thirteenth birthday of "Little Alma." The ostentatious party, filmed at the beautiful Napa Stock Farm, uses magnificent racehorses as props. Butlers and a uniformed staff are seen indulging the children's needs. Adolph is confined to a wheelchair due to his advanced stage of syphilis. John is seen playing the part of a "baby," drinking gin out of a baby bottle and being pushed around in a cart by a servant. It appears that the elegant Grace has joined the party from San Francisco, and the parental affection between father and his firstborn daughter on film is more than apparent, seen in a tender kiss.

CLAUS JR.'S PARIS LOVE AFFAIR

The rigid structure of the Belmont School for Boys had not been a good fit for Claus Jr., so he was sent to Europe to study under a private tutor.

23. Claus Jr. (1888–1935) as a young man. The youngest of John and Lillian's children, he was a carefree and headstrong lad with a preference for music over business. Permission granted from the Laurie Fletcher Guidry Private Family Collection.

Like his mother, he had a wonderful singing voice, and his European education included the study of music and voice training. Still, his parents intended him to return home to Coronado after his studies, where he would begin a practical career in one of his father's businesses.

It was in a Parisian vocal studio that Claus met and fell in love with the "tall, slim, black-haired girl with a rich contralto of unusual range."[62] Mary Adele Case was a gifted young piano player and opera singer from Portland, Oregon. Her way to Paris had been paid by a wealthy blind singer who brought her along as an aide. Mary's talent was soon noticed in Paris, and she received training, free of charge, from the renowned vocal coach Frank King Clark, whom Claus was also studying under.

The romance blossomed in Paris, but Claus hid it from his mother when she stopped in Paris on her way to Germany in the spring of 1909. During that visit, Claus took his mother to the opera where Mary was performing. Lillian had much in common with the talented Mary: Both had spent some formative years in Honolulu, both had sung in the Honolulu Opera House, and both loved Claus Jr. However, this last commonality was to be kept secret for the time being. Lillian had no idea that her son was smitten with the singer and later recalled that "Claus at that time showed only admiration for her as an artist."[63]

Without discussing his plans with his parents, the twenty-one-year-old Claus formally proposed marriage to the twenty-five-year-old Mary Adele in May 1909, shortly after his mother had continued onward to Germany. His family had acknowledged his talent as a singer, but it was only when Mary told him that he had such "a beautiful singing voice" that he believed he could make it on the stage.[64] The couple decided to return to America, marry immediately, and pursue careers as "public singers."[65]

Mary wrote home to her family, telling of her engagement to an heir to the Spreckels fortune. Her hometown papers announced the romantic tidings, and other papers across the country picked up the news that the wealthy "Sugar Boy" was to wed the "songbird." It is not known whether or not this is how John heard of the engagement, but he immediately wired Lillian in Germany with the startling news and directed her to return home. He also wired Claus, stating that the idea was preposterous and would not be tolerated. Once he learned that his son would be arriving in New York on the SS *Cincinnati*, John sent a further urgent dispatch, commanding his son to do nothing until they could talk. He then left for New York in order to prevent any attempts to elope.

Claus and Mary, looking very much in love, disembarked from the *Cincinnati* at New York Harbor on June 6, 1909. A throng of reporters and photographers were assembled on the pier to report on the upcoming nuptials of the young heir to millions and his songstress.[66]

Claus chose to obey his father and met him at the Hotel Wolcott. While John waited for Lillian to arrive, he secluded himself with his son, likely threatening to cut him off financially if he attempted to wed the singer, whom he regarded as a gold digger. Within hours of this meeting, a sullen young Claus stated to reporters staked outside the Hotel Wolcott, "I have no money to support a wife." His statement was delivered without a smile; he looked defiantly submissive. The press reported, "Claus Spreckels, Jr. decided that he would give up his study of music and enter business."[67] That evening, Claus went to Mary's hotel, and during a taxi ride, he broke the news of their "postponed" wedding. When she returned to her hotel, she left word with the night clerk that she would "see no one."[68]

Mary was brokenhearted and angry, and she publicized the fact that Claus had been forced to comply with his father's wishes. With defiant pride, she told the press that Mr. John D. Spreckels personally notified her that "no daughter-in-law of his should sing on the stage. I leave for Seattle tomorrow," she went on, "and was never so happy in my life."[69]

However, when John was interviewed on June 7 about the broken engagement, he denied that he had gone to New York to stop the marriage and claimed that his son was "at liberty to marry as he pleased," even offering the rhetorical question, "What would you give for a young man who didn't have spunk enough to get married when he had picked out a girl for himself?"[70] Despite his comments, the papers freely quoted Mary, who continued to insist that Claus had been forced by his father to break off the engagement.[71] On June 8, she said she was leaving her former fiancé and preparing to go home.[72] Some hesitation followed, and on June 10, she suggested that she still "*might* wed Claus Spreckels, Jr., *despite* the opposition of this father."[73] This suggests that a clandestine meeting between her and Claus might have taken place.

Reporters were also present when John met Lillian as she arrived from Europe. Lillian downplayed the engagement as mere "puppy love" on the part of her young son and "laughed when talking about the engagement."[74] She found it "very silly," since "Claus is too young to know his own mind. Boys of his age frequently fall in love with women who are much older. Miss Case is too old for him."[75] Reporters then surprised the parents with a statement from Claus Jr. in which he lamented that "he could not be happy because he was too rich to get married." John reportedly remarked, "He's getting to be a humorist," while Lillian stated, "This is very funny, indeed."[76]

John had told Claus that after he had spent two years working in the family business, he could marry whomever he liked. However, Mary went back to Oregon, and Claus went back to Coronado. On the rebound, she quickly married Willard Metcalf Beam in January 1910, but the marriage would not last; she left her husband in September of the same year. Beam was the nephew of a former secretary of the navy, and the prominence of his family invited further media attention; Mary had already earned some notoriety as both a solo singer and the jilted lover of a scion of the Spreckels family. The press covered the runaway newlywed, as well as her subsequent divorce in 1913, repeatedly reminding the public that her true love, Claus Spreckels, had abandoned her. It is likely that Claus followed her career in the newspapers in the subsequent years, including a performance she gave at Carnegie Hall.

CLAUS JR. AT THE ALTAR

Claus did not wait the requisite two years before marrying another. Less than a year after leaving Mary brokenhearted in New York, he married Ellis Ethel Moon on April 26, 1910. The ceremony was private, conducted without any "Splash and Dash" in the library of the Ellis family home in San Jose.[77] It is unclear why these children of two prominent families decided to have a small and private wedding. Instead of the expected gown and veil, Ellis wore a tailored suit and hat. The Spreckels family was well represented. Claus's brother, Jack, was his best man; his sister Lillie came, without her husband, Harry, because their marriage was in serious trouble, as did his sister Grace and her husband, Alec, as well as his uncle and aunt, Adolph and Alma Spreckels.

Claus had known Ellis since childhood, as she was the sister of Frank Moon, his classmate at the Belmont School. The Moons were a rich and well-known San Jose family; the father (also Frank), who had died two years earlier, was the son of Delos Moon, a wealthy lumberman from Wisconsin. Ellis, their only daughter, had been carefully groomed for an upper-class marriage, first in a Notre Dame convent and then at the Washburn Preparatory School in San Jose. She had also been sent to Miss Mason's School in Tarrytown, New York, and to Miss Head's School in Berkeley. This poised young woman appeared to John to be a daughter-in-law who would not embarrass him among his neighbors in Coronado, or his business associates in San Diego, where his reputation was very important.

10

Influencing San Diego Politics

"Progressive" to "Old Guard"

The colorful political history of San Diego at the turn of the twentieth century featured bitter struggles that mirrored what was happening up and down the state of California. John and his family relocated to San Diego at the height of the Progressive Era's municipal reform movement, an effort by local politicians to purify city governments of oppressive bossism, to eliminate special-interest groups, and to restructure those governments for greater efficiency—in essence, to take a much more rational approach to city planning and transportation. Unsurprisingly, the movement met strong resistance from the entrenched interests that had benefited from the status quo.

During the days leading up to and during the 1896 Republican National Convention, John had been branded a "progressive" for his efforts to rid San Francisco of "Old Guard" Republicans, those entrepreneurial men who had flourished in San Francisco after the Gold Rush days, with his father most prominent. But, ten years later, with Claus Spreckels's generation long gone, the tables were turned, and John, now in his mid-fifties, represented the Old Guard to San Diego's younger Republicans, who labeled themselves progressives and civic reformers. In San Diego, the progressives were led by Ed Fletcher, twenty years younger than John.

John was deathly ill and still living in San Francisco in 1905, when self-anointed reformer Captain John L. Sehon, a retired army officer, arrived on the San Diego political scene. He had been nominated for mayor by the independents but was fully supported by the Democrats and the *San Diego Sun* tycoon who had already become John's worst adversary, Edward Scripps. The *Sun* depicted San Diego's political structure as ineffective, wasteful, and corrupt, and Sehon ran on an anti-corruption platform and was elected, a victory that did not make established Republicans, such as John Spreckels, happy.

A lawsuit was filed to keep Mayor-Elect Sehon from the position, "questioning the right of a retired military officer to serve in public office."[1] But on the advice of his attorney, Edgar A. Luce, Sehon snuck out of town to prevent being served legal papers until he could take office. Many a barroom was told about how Sehon literally broke into city hall and then the mayor's office at two o'clock in the dark morning of the day he was to assume the mayoralty. When the sun rose, Mayor Sehon was seen sitting smugly in his official chair, looking through broken glass doors, defiantly claiming that possession was nine-tenths of the law.[2]

In late 1906, John, now living in beautiful Coronado and enjoying a complete restoration of his health, charged full speed ahead to build San Diego's superstructure and, in particular, the critical infrastructure of the dam and the water that it would provide. The progressives running the city resented the way that John, now their fellow citizen rather than a mere outside investor, was singlehandedly pouring millions of dollars into municipal projects without garnering any public opinion about them.

At the beginning of 1907, following a number of graft prosecutions in San Francisco, progressive activists in California organized a coordinated statewide movement for reform. The Lincoln-Roosevelt League, a coalition of Republican progressives, quickly formed reformist clubs up and down the state not only to oppose the domination of the Southern Pacific Railroad (Espee) magnates but also to advocate a direct primary system; the voter initiative, referendum, and recall; the direct election of U.S. senators; "the regulation of public utilities; the conservation of forests; the outlawing of child labor, prostitution, and gambling; hospital and prison reform; women's suffrage; a minimum wage law for working women; the systematization of public finance; charter reform; [and] public transportation."[3]

Soon, established Republicans, led by Fletcher, William Smythe, Edgar Luce, and George White Marston, saw themselves as San Diego's civic crusaders (under the label "Reformer" or "Progressive") and aligned themselves with Mayor Sehon's agenda.[4] To gain public support, that agenda was touted as a benevolent, even Christian type of governance, and for the most part, it worked to sway the "moral" public.[5] Fletcher represented San Diego at one of the first league meetings, but he was later joined by Marston, Luce, and all who had helped elect Sehon in 1905.[6]

The reformers were opposed by Old Guard Republicans John Spreckels and political "boss" Charles S. Hardy. Hardy had come to the city with his brother, George L. Hardy, in the late nineteenth century as an indebted cowboy. By the turn of the century, Hardy, as a meat processor and distributor, had become one of San Diego's most prominent businessmen; he served on the board of police commissioners, and he was a "respectable" citizen and father of five girls. His brother, George, was John's neighbor in Coronado, and Charles was given preferred space to run a profitable delicatessen at Tent City during the tourist season.

Charles Hardy controlled municipal politics through ward bosses, who selected the city council as well as the police and fire commissioners. Most bosses during this era served an important function for their cities: Large groups of immigrants from many cultures as well as former farmers had moved to the cities after the Civil War. The city governments were small and thus ill equipped to handle the explosive growth, but the newcomers needed political representation. For example, who would help the poor Poles or Italians living in tenements? Responding to this need, the ward bosses kept the peace in each neighborhood, usually with a combination of street muscle, patronage jobs from city hall, and payments to police and other "enforcers." The new residents repaid the bosses at the ballot box and by doing business with the bosses' friends. There was deep loyalty, and the ward system concentrated the vote of the poor to offset the middle class and the wealthy.[7] But wards were often seen as pernicious because a resident could easily favor his ward against the general welfare of the city.[8] The ward system entailed considerable corruption as well as some violence.

Even though boss Charles Hardy had in his hands "a real political power and [was one] to whom many went for advice and support before they decided to enter the political arena," he was reputed to be "a 'good boss,' one who was in the 'game' for the mere fun of the thing rather than for sordid gain."[9] But Marston and his progressive allies were able to get rid of the ward system in 1908; San Diego was one of the first western cities to eliminate the practice, thereby bestowing greater power to the voters for direct selection of representatives. Reformers wanted direct elections, recalls, and referendums—and, above all, no bosses. They were taking the concept of reform further than was perhaps good for John's business affairs, which came under attack by San Diego's progressives.

By 1909, Mayor Sehon fully embraced the municipal reform movement by shifting the established mayor-council model to a system of city commissions, which gave executive authority to a small board of commissioners, each responsible for the administration of different municipal entities. This system worked well in other small cities, but San Diego had a unique situation: One man, John Spreckels, owned most of the city's municipal entities, such as transportation and water. Now, instead of one mayor to answer to, John had to deal with multiple commissioners, a situation he detested.

During his mayoral campaign, Sehon had emphasized the idea that only the public should own the water supply. This idea conflicted with John's plans to provide San Diego with its water needs; his private water company created access to the desperately needed resource. After a proposal to give John's Southern California Mountain Water Company a monopoly was vetoed, John was absolutely antagonistic to Sehon; in retaliation, he "opposed reform under Mayor Sehon in every guise."[10]

John recruited candidates for office from within his organizations, and he poured thousands of dollars into city council races in order to overturn Sehon's veto. When John's supporters won seats on the city council, Sehon found himself "stranded amidst the hostility."[11]

John and Espee

A paramount goal of the Lincoln-Roosevelt League was to free the Republican Party from the domination of the Southern Pacific Railroad (Espee), which had been controlling California's politics for decades. In 1908, John, hoping to sustain a continuing opposition to Espee's power, seemingly (on paper) supported the league and their progressive agenda because he had an "unrelenting quarrel" with the railroad, focusing on its "attempts to advantage itself through the corruption of public servants or control of political parties."[12] In 1906, John became the front man for Espee owner Edward Harriman's building of the San Diego & Arizona Railway (SD&A), so this apparent opposition of John's might be interpreted that he was just bowing to the political mood at the time—in essence, that he was being hypocritical. But John, though himself a monopoly man like Harriman, was not a "ruthless profiteer" but a "God fearing, hardworking, good hearted, civic monopolist."[13] John acknowledged the much-needed service that railroads provided to the public, and he believed they were rightly rewarded as transportation agents, but he disparaged the practice of some rail magnates to corrupt governments.

Espee's corporate history is the story of four greedy men who created an organization of almost inconceivable power. Leland Stanford, Charles Crocker, Mark Hopkins, and Collis Huntington had been instrumental in the construction of the nation's first transcontinental rail line, hundreds of miles of track across some of the roughest terrain in the world, completed in 1869. The completion was a seminal moment, celebrated across the United Sates: The entire nation was linked by a single transportation system for the first time. (Many, including John's daughter in-law, Edith Huntington, a grandniece of one of the "Big Four," found themselves somewhat famous by association, and later very wealthy.) The Big Four's accomplishment deserves acclaim, but the way these men grabbed land and the methods they used were dubious. In the years before the 1887 legislation that restricted monopolies, the Big Four members had such undisputed power and influence that they were dubbed "the Octopus." In order to defend its domain, the huge monopoly deployed an arsenal of weapons, including bribery, power politics, and economic reprisals, and as a result, they were widely hated.[14]

In 1910, after a dramatic political contest, Hiram W. Johnson, a lawyer who had won renown in San Francisco graft trials, won the California governorship under the campaign slogan "Kick the Southern Pacific Out of Politics!" Progressive Republicans were determined to break the railroad's stranglehold. Even though John had early supported Johnson's opponent, Charles Forrest Curry, the secretary of state, his newspapers bowed to the inevitable and urged a straight Republican vote. John ultimately endorsed Johnson but without any obvious enthusiasm; he was uneasy with Johnson's bringing sweeping reforms to the state; for example, in 1911, Johnson and the progressives in Sacramento would give the people the power to recall elected officials and directly change or enact legislation. John was especially uneasy with the governor's constant gloating that he "threw the bums out."[15]

Dealing with Enemies

In 1914, *Harper's Weekly*, a political magazine based in New York City, called John a dangerous threat to Governor Johnson's administration. The article included a most unflattering and disheveled picture of John, clearly in need of a shave. He was labeled San Diego's "dollar king" and its "political king"; the article likened him to a "Big Frog in a small puddle." John was described as the "potential destroyer of California's progressive movement."[16] Readers were told that John had made San Diego, because of its geographical isolation, a "virtual principality," where he alone controlled every political decision.[17] It's unknown what John thought about this harsh portrayal, but in general, he did not take criticism lightly. Even though he often said he did not give a damn, there is little evidence to support his having a thick skin.

John's political aspirations in San Diego were strictly about supporting his business interests. Having worked for years alongside his
father, he knew how to manipulate the political system to achieve his
goals. In Hawai'i, for example, John and Claus Spreckels had together
established a formula that might be considered a template of the one
John would implement in San Diego:

- Go big and dominate your market.
- Make friends in the government. Claus had befriended King David
  Kalākaua.
- Make those friends owe you. Claus had lent the king money, and
  he acquired access to lease or purchase land he would not other-
  wise have had.
- Act and don't ask permission. Claus illegally bought crown lands
  from Princess Ruth Ke'elikōlani after realizing his leases did not
  extend long enough to cover his infrastructure investment.
- Control legislatures. Claus put his supporters in influential places.
- Own the transportation of your product.
- Buy the press. Claus owned the *Pacific Advertiser* in Honolulu.

But, in building San Diego, John did not have Claus's killer instinct;
his weakness was that he wanted to be liked too much! His defensive
editorials reveal considerable hypersensitivity.

The first few years of the twentieth century are today remembered as
the heyday of the progressive movement in America. Teddy Roosevelt's
administration busted many of the trusts. Laws were passed to regulate
abusive corporations (including Espee) for the public interest, to curtail
child labor, and to support conservation.

But, beginning in 1914, at the onset of World War I in Europe, public
support for "progressiveness" waned; the progressive sentiment faded
into near oblivion.[18] Until the United States entered the war in 1917,
with domestic industry cut off from European markets, many Americans
were unemployed. By 1915, all pretenses for reform in San Diego were
abandoned, and the city's government reverted to a mayor-council
model. In the following year, John informed one and all that the chaotic

days of "wishy washy political fads" were over and that the times called for a return to partisan "sensible political methods."[19]

After the war, John continued to dominate the political and financial life of the city. To profit from his businesses, he took an approach he had learned at his father's knee and from other business magnates at the time: Remove competitors at all costs. With his business monopolies on the rise, John's stature in San Diego's business community continued upward, and with that came more enemies who began to sardonically call the city "Spreckelsville-by-the-Sea."[20] "Every man who fights makes enemies," John said, "and I suppose I have mine."[21] Some of San Diego's prominent and wealthy residents did not share his enthusiasm for growth. They had fled congested cities and were not willing to give up their adopted hometown's open spaces and small-town atmosphere. They used whatever power they could to hinder John's rapid progress in developing the city.

Most critics worked behind the scenes in attempts to thwart John's progress, but Edward Scripps and his *San Diego Sun* spoke out continuously. An employee remembered that the *Sun* was "absolutely antagonistic to Spreckels—he couldn't do anything right in their eyes."[22]

Scripps averred that his newspaper catered to working-class readers, whereas John's *San Diego Union* catered only to the privileged rich. Scripps routinely opposed anything or anybody John supported, and the two had become bitter enemies. At one point, Scripps charged that John would destroy San Diego with his monopolies: "We look John D. Spreckels squarely in the eyes and say: We defy you! Upon that issue there can be no middle ground. Either you are the master and hold in your hand the welfare of every man, woman and child in this town, or the people are their own masters, and will know how to deal with your insolent challenge."[23]

As Scripps grumbled about John's power, John used the *San Diego Union* as his preferred method of communication to directly challenge Scripps about how many millions he planned to devote to San Diego's citizens, and to remind readers of the need for growth and the benefits they would receive as a result of his investments.

The *Union*'s front-page masthead provided running economic data under the words "Watch San Diego Grow." John's money and commitment to development could not be ignored by the city's average citizens—ironically, the target audience of Scripps's *San Diego Sun*. Later, John's pent-up fury erupted in a rare instance, when he unambiguously denounced Scripps: "He has gone on piling up his millions by hypocritically pretending that if it were not for the watchful eye of his San Diego Sun, the people would be like poor, dumb sheep, devoured by those hungry wolves—the Spreckels interests, the gas company, the banks, the big merchants and manufacturers, and everybody else who is trying to build up San Diego."[24]

Scripps and his supporters may have detested him, but the voting public believed that John's prosperity was their prosperity, and they consistently supported his public expansions.[25] San Diego's future was looking brighter for those who were investing in the city. John's companies were at one time estimated to be paying 10 percent of all city and county taxes.[26] Already by 1910, just four short years after John had relocated to San Diego, approximately one of every fifteen residents in San Diego worked for a Spreckels-owned company.[27]

11

Coronado's Uncle John

From a Village to an Incorporated City

After the boom burst in 1888, the city of San Diego, desperate for money and realizing that Coronado was within its boundaries, sought tax revenue from the island's residents and the Coronado Beach Company, which was then controlled by the wealthy John Spreckels. San Diego's city leaders moved quickly to assess the land and demand taxes from the Coronadoans. The Beach Company refused to pay, however, and residents, emboldened by the company's stance, followed suit. After drawn-out legal disputes, the California Supreme Court ultimately ruled that Coronado was indeed within San Diego's city limits and was therefore subject to taxation. To their collective dismay, the company and Coronado residents were assessed $50,000 ($1.4 million in today's money) in delinquent taxes.[1]

Coronadoans were outraged that they had to pay taxes for municipal benefits that did not directly benefit them, and a legal separation from San Diego became the topic of every conversation, on every corner, and over every fence in Coronado. After all, they had neither a police nor a fire department, and they needed to take care of their own community, because, unlike in San Diego, there was in Coronado no "hospital on island, illness was common, including tuberculosis, typhoid, diphtheria, smallpox, whooping cough, and measles."[2]

Throughout the summer of 1888, 2,250 full-time residents of Coronado were encouraged to sign a petition with the promise that "each signature drives a nail in the coffin of San Diego's hopes of levying unjust taxation."[3] The *Coronado Mercury* saw no way out of this predicament except by incorporation: "A community by incorporating secures full control of its own affairs. . . . [It] takes charge of its own health matters, it guards its own citizens from lawbreakers, and by ordinance, curtails the liquor traffic, and punishes those who break through the laws of decency and morality. In short, the incorporation of Coronado means full and complete control by the citizens of Coronado, of Coronado's affairs."[4]

The *Mercury* hit the public hard on the "decency and morality" issues—specifically, the controversial control of liquor. The Anti-Saloon League, formed at the end of the nineteenth century, had become the most powerful grassroots lobbying organization in the nation. The league systematically applied pressure to politicians, and it drove support for Prohibition to a feverish pitch. San Diego's downtown Fifth Avenue had a lawless reputation due to the overabundance of saloons. When Elisha Babcock and Hampton Story formed the Coronado Beach Company in 1886, they were determined to take the moral high road and support the temperance movement. It was during the company's stewardship of the island that Coronado's property holders were prohibited by a clause in their deeds from making, selling, or drinking alcohol anywhere but in the Hotel del Coronado's bar. In spite of this clause, however, there were at least seven clandestine saloons operating throughout the island. The saloon owners and their customers, many of them employees of the Coronado Beach Company, were worried that incorporating Coronado might bring teetotaling regulators too close to home and thereby threaten their illegal operations.[5]

Surprisingly, even though many of Coronado's residents were vocal in their disgust with the "evil drink," the public election of September 24, 1888, to gauge interest for secession, revealed apathy, and the issue was dropped.[6] It seems that there were reasons other than temperance to consider for the average homeowner. Joseph Hartupee, Coronado's first homebuilder, spoke publicly to his neighbors against secession. He had calculated how much money the Coronado Beach Company spent on their island upkeep, and he warned that incorporation would relieve the company of that financial burden, transferring the burden onto them. As a small but significant example, Hartupee explained that the company had planted thirty-five thousand trees throughout Coronado and had assumed an estimated cost of "50 cents per year for the care of them." He forewarned that the "cost of running the city would be in the vicinity of $40,000," a figure that gave his neighbors pause.[7]

In January 1889, Coronadoans grudgingly paid their taxes to the city of San Diego, causing ill feelings on the side of those who advocated incorporation, including John Spreckels, who desired a complete separation, even though he had overlapping business interests on both sides of the bay. His downtown properties would certainly be disadvantaged by the loss of tax revenue that San Diego would suffer as a result of Coronado's secession, thereby necessitating a tax increase on remaining San Diego properties, but the cost of his running Coronado outweighed whatever tax benefit he was currently enjoying downtown, where he was engaged in multiple building projects. The maintenance of the thirty-five thousand trees Hartupee had made an issue of was merely a drop in the bucket for the Coronado Beach Company. The Coronado Beach Company had built and was maintaining the entire infrastructure of Coronado. Incorporation promised to be a huge financial relief for the company and its president, John.

But incorporation again became a topic of conversation: After paying a hefty amount in taxes, Coronadoans were made aware that they would soon be taxed *even more* to pave streets in San Diego and pay for schools they did not desire their children to attend. These two issues ignited the fury of the community; even Joseph Hartupee reversed his stance and asked for a new election. By 1890, a majority of residents believed it was in their best interest to incorporate, and John's Coronado Beach Company propagandized on these feelings.

After a year of twists and turns, John was among those who celebrated the victory on December 6, 1890. Coronado was officially incorporated

24. View of Coronado, which was founded in the 1880s and officially incorporated in 1891. Early in the 1900s, Coronado's beautiful beaches, mild weather, and remote location placed it at the forefront of moviemaking and aviation. The sparkling Pacific Ocean was virtually the only thing within sight that was not owned by John Spreckels. Courtesy of Hotel del Coronado Records.

in 1891, and a board of trustees (city council) headed by a president now governed the island. John was not worried about a separate governing body, because his employees controlled the board right from the start.

Trouble in Paradise: The Liquor License Feud

When John relocated to Coronado in 1906, George Holmes, purchasing agent for the Spreckels companies, was president of the city of Coronado's board of trustees. Having an officer of his company as head of the city's governing board ensured stability for John's business interests. But that would all change when Holmes stepped down as board president in 1912. Banker Wilmot Griffiss stepped up within days. John was at first pleased with the succession. On the surface, he appeared to have so much in common with Griffiss, a conservative banker, married to Katharine Hamlin-Evans, the daughter of a wealthy New York horse breeder and sugar magnate, with a stepson, Townsend "Tim" Griffiss, who played polo, a sport about which John was most passionate. But, as mutual friend and colleague Julius Wangenheim recalled, unlike previous board presidents, Griffiss "was not willing to be merely a rubber stamp" for John's business interests.[8] He had sat quietly on the board since 1910, but now was his time as president to make his mark in Coronado, an effort that required raising taxes for his own projects and diminishing the power of John and his company.

John's frustration began when numerous agenda items from the Coronado Beach Company brought before the board were constantly tabled, put aside with the never-ending response from Griffiss: "Let's look into it." Wangenheim recalled John's great uneasiness with the change in city council leadership: He knew his friend John never liked to be interrogated on his business decisions and took it very personally when it occurred. He also knew his friend Griffiss was as stubborn as John. After numerous Beach Company projects had been summarily dismissed, Wangenheim remarked that nobody had ever done in Coronado what Griffiss was doing, likening it to an act of lèse-majesté, a French term meaning "to do wrong to majesty," a punishable offence against the dignity of a reigning monarch.[9]

When Griffiss began using "Anti-Beach Co." as a campaign slogan in anticipation of a new election for city council members, Holmes was infuriated and published a one-page supplement reminding citizens how much Spreckels had done for Coronado without any of their tax money. He referred to the widening and pavement of roads, electrical upgrades, fire hydrants, gifts in both land and property to uplift the community, thousands of dollars to churches and charities, and more, whereas the city had done *nothing* for John and the Beach Company. Holmes pointed out that John still supported a private fire and police department for Tent City and the hotel out of his own pocket, even though he could have asked the city to pay.[10]

Griffiss strongly favored Prohibition and wanted people on the city council who would support his stance. In 1916, he found such a man in William Templeton Johnson, a wealthy architect. Running against Johnson for the open seat was John's candidate: Wilfred Charles Harland,

Coronado's first real estate agent, founding member of Christ Church, library trustee, and John's Masonic brother.

John would do all he could to get Harland that seat, especially when Griffiss and another trustee, Newton S. Gandy, made a very vocal campaign promise to remove the liquor license of the Royal Inn in Tent City, claiming that John received undue consideration for a liquor license in Coronado that others could not receive. When Griffiss and Gandy also promised to remove the liquor license from the Hotel del Coronado, John went on the offensive.

On February 18, 1916, John took out advertising space to publish an open letter to the city council, circumventing the open-seat campaign with a shocking edict: The Royal Inn and the entire Tent City for the 1916 season would remain closed; therefore, a liquor license would no longer be a campaign issue.

> The Spreckels Interests have never asked for one favor from Coronado and its people. On the other hand, millions of dollars have been invested in Coronado and hundreds of thousands of dollars have been spent by Spreckels Interests in their policy of building up Coronado—a policy that benefited every resident or property owner. Unfortunately, we seem to have come to a parting of the ways. There will be no tent city in 1916. Consequently, there will be no saloon question before the voters. . . .
>
> Yours respectfully,
> John D. Spreckels, President[11]

John had spent tens of thousands of dollars on upgrading Tent City for the 1914–15 Panama–California Exposition crowd to the delight of the Coronadoans. This was money he knew he would never recoup, but it had been an investment of the heart. He knew how important Tent City had become, as evidenced when more than ten thousand people passed through the turnstiles in the summer of 1914.[12] With news that Tent City, the center for fun for local residents, would be closed, the *Coronado Eagle and Journal* reported that "'great gobs of gloom' hung over Coronado after the announcement, in the morning paper, that there will be no Tent City this year. Visions of a dry summer without music or pretty girls were not pleasant to contemplate, and the gay young blades are wondering what they will do for excitement and amusement when the days get warm and long."[13] To dispel any rumors, John then made it clear that Griffiss and Newton Gandy (the council member who sided with Griffiss) were to blame: "I closed Tent City entirely on account of the activities of Mr. Wilmot Griffiss and Mr. Gandy, and for no other reason. They had announced in positive terms that they would not permit another license for the Royal Inn and if necessary it was their intention to carry that issue before the people, which meant that the election of trustees would resolve itself into a saloon campaign."[14]

Dick Henderson, editor of the *Coronado Strand*, addressed the community's imminent loss of the free summer band concerts, a dance pavilion, and other Tent City amusements. He wrote scathing editorials against the Spreckels companies that rapidly divided the town over the issue of drinking alcohol at the Royal Inn. Coronadoans could not wait for April 10, 1916, to have the whole election over and done with. John was incensed over the *Strand*'s editorials, and Griffiss's "pernicious hostility" toward him. He made one "final statement" on April 8 to the people of Coronado in a paid advertisement in the *Coronado Eagle and Journal*:

> To the People of Coronado:
>
> I want to say a few more words to you before the election of April 10th. . . . I have made Coronado my home. I think I have done all that any other man would do to help build up Coronado, to make it attractive, to enhance the value of the property and make the place as prosperous as I could. I never had any difficulty or trouble with the people of Coronado during the time I had known them until after Mr. Wilmot Griffiss, assistant to the President of the Bank of Commerce,

went on the Board of Trustees. This gentleman has shown an active and I might say, pernicious hostility toward the Spreckels Interests, and has sought, whenever he could, to bring them into discredit and knife them whenever the opportunity offered.

In reference to closing down Tent City, he defended his actions:

> Now I want the people of Coronado to ask themselves what would they have done had they been in my place? If they had spent large sums of money in trying to build up a community, had done everything that they or anybody else could be expected to do, carried along unprofitable interests for years rather than let go of them for fear of the detriment such an action might be to the town, and then were constantly attacked by the Chairman of the Board of Trustees in season and out of season without one real, genuine complaint being brought against them of having done one single thing to the injury of the place—what would they have done? How much more of that sort of attack would they stand?

His hurt at being referred to as "arrogant, overbearing, unjust and dishonest" by Griffiss is seen in this humble plea to remain friends with the community:

> Personally, I would like to have a real, genuine friendship existing between the people of Coronado and the Spreckels Interests. I have always tried to be a friend of yours and I certainly would like you to be friends of mine. I think you will agree with me that no man cares to live in a community and be regarded as an arrogant, overbearing, unjust, dishonest man, and that is how I have been represented.[15]

President Theodore Roosevelt had promoted a set of progressive policies labeled the "Square Deal." He had hoped to ameliorate the negative effects of industrialization and to improve the quality of life for Americans. These Square Deal policies focused primarily on controlling corporations, the preservation of nature, and public welfare. John's overuse of the term indicates that he saw himself in a similar role in Coronado, but with a warning:

> I have never asked for anything but a square deal. I have never wanted anything MORE than a square deal, and I have always been willing to give a square deal. I have nothing to ask from Coronado. I owe Coronado nothing except my good-will, and if I do not have the good will of the people, I do not owe that much. . . .
>
> Yours respectfully,
> John D. Spreckels.[16]

Coronadoans had a lot to think about as they opened their newspapers on April 8 because in the same edition as John's letter "to the People of Coronado," others published their own opposition to Griffiss. As an example, Coronado realtor Sylvester Kipp warned voters that Griffiss was intent on driving up the taxes, and he begged to have peace and harmony return to Coronado.

> It is said that for many years prior to the arrival of Mr. Griffiss in 1909, John D. Spreckels ruled all Coronado. In all those years there was peace and harmony. Our city taxes were just about half what they are now. Our city government was fairly economical. Our city treasury had not yet sprung a leak. Coronado had a good name at home and abroad. May the good Lord deliver us and take us back to those good old days, and help us escape this everlasting raid on our pocketbooks. . . . No man can charge that I am a Spreckels henchman. Mr. Spreckels don't care a picayune for me, and I don't care a picayune for Mr. Spreckels. On that basis we are friends. But as a heavy tax payer on Coronado, I can see on which side my bread is buttered. Let us have economy, peace and happiness on our beloved Coronado.[17]

On April 10, the *Riverside Daily Press*, under the headline "Spreckels or No Spreckels?" told their readers, who lived one hundred miles from the island, that on that very day "Coronado is voting to see if the people shall rule" or if the Spreckels regime would continue.[18] "The voters of Coronado, the fashionable home of many millionaires, is today voting on whether John D. Spreckels, son of the San Francisco sugar king, shall be dethroned or continue as patriarch of the little city."[19]

The question was answered in the next day's press: By a three-to-one margin, Coronado citizens voted in John's candidate for city trustee.[20] *The Wine and Spirit Bulletin* cheerfully reported that the city guard band serenaded John on the lawn of his home, at which time he was pleased to share that Tent City would not be closed as previously threatened.[21]

In the end, though Griffiss may have left the board, his big agenda of "no alcohol" won: After more than a decade of contentious debate across the country, Americans were prohibited from manufacturing, selling, or transporting intoxicating beverages. Prohibition, ratified in 1919, became a part of the Constitution, holding equal status with "freedom of speech" and the "abolition of slavery." The Eighteenth Amendment stirred up a hot-blooded debate between "wets" and "drys" that will forever cement Prohibition's place in both America's and Coronado's history. The ink on the amendment hadn't dried before Tijuana, Mexico, became a boomtown where Americans could drink legally. John paved the Silver Strand Road in 1924 for development purposes, making it easier for Coronadoans to cross the border into Tijuana, prompting the town's ministers to call it "the road to hell."[22]

Many Coronadoans made their own small stills at home. Others, including the Spreckels family, had secret areas in their attics for stashed alcohol. Jonde Northcutt, Claus and Ellis's granddaughter, remembered being toured throughout the house by grandmother "Omie" Ellis. She vividly remembers being shown a small crawl space in the attic that was used during the Prohibition era for the secret storage of "all varieties of liquor held in beautiful wooden cabinets. . . . Each shelf was hand-labeled by a depressed script in the wood."[23]

For John, he had only to take his yacht *Venetia* out on the ocean beyond the three-mile limit in order not to violate the law. One Prohibition story involves Sam Shortridge, who in 1921 had finally become a California senator. After taking off on the *Venetia* to have a drink with John, Shortridge became violently seasick and asked to be immediately returned to shore. His seasickness was well known, but it had seemed worth the risk for an alcoholic beverage. Back on the beach, he requested a shot of whiskey to ease his pain. Within earshot of many, John laughingly refused to comply, stating that a "senator must not violate the law." It was worth the agony of seasickness to return to the ocean for the whiskey, but laughter must have abounded when Shortridge returned to land sicker than ever.[24] Prohibition continued to be a failure until it was repealed in 1933, the year Shortridge ended his senatorial career.

In retaliation for the negative press during the election, John pulled all Coronado Beach Company advertising out of the *Strand* and stopped all subscriptions to both home and business. To ensure that John read the *Strand*'s reaction, however, Henderson published a very snarky response in the *Coronado Eagle and Journal*, and hit John below the belt by referring to his most hated enemy, Edward Scripps, and his *Sun* newspaper:

> Dear Uncle John:
>
> Well, well, so you stopped both your papers did you Uncle John? Your other two papers are slowing up a little. The Union's circulation is 14,768 and the Tribune's average is 13,382. That is considerable less than I had been led to believe, 'cause the Sun's circulation is 15,658, yet the Union claims a much larger circulation than any other San Diego paper. You ought to get those birds in the circulation department to give away a few more clocks or dishes or something, and see if you can't boot it up a little.[25]

The Coronado Bank Building and the Silver Strand Theatre

With all the stress and rancor of the election over with—the defeat of William Templeton Johnson and the temperance issue behind him—John threw a victory celebration at the Hotel del Coronado. He climbed up on the bar and announced to the jubilant crowd that Harland's election victory meant prosperity to Coronado. He promised his supporters that he would build a bank and a "first-class" theater. In typical Spreckels fashion, he had building permits for both within a week.[26] The Coronado Bank Building (officially the Spreckels Security Company Building, which would house both bank and theater) was completed in 1916, its triangular structure following a unique curve for 372 feet along Orange Avenue. In addition to the bank and theater, it was built to house twelve shops, office suites, and an upper story divided into small apartments for proprietors of the stores below.

In November 1916, John incorporated the Bank of Coronado, with Frank von Tesmar as manager. The first order of business was to establish the bank on the ground floor of the new building. Apparently, John's morning constitutional in Coronado was to walk from his home to peer through the windows of the bank under construction. It's unknown what Lillian thought when the local paper published the following: "A good looking young lady asked, 'Who is that handsome, distinguished looking man that walks past the new bank building nearly every morning, and looks in all the windows?' We told her, 'Mr. J. D. Spreckels, Coronado's uncle.' Her eyes lit up some more, and she sighed. Believe us, Uncle John, you'll have to come back, 'cause this girl is there with the wonderful eyes. Name furnished on request."[27]

The Spreckels Security Company Building was also designed with a one-thousand-seat movie theater for the community. It was leased to the Broadway Amusement Company from Los Angeles to manage. By that time, Coronado had grown to more than three thousand permanent residents, and the excitement was palpable.[28] The theater was ornate and elegant, with an orchestra pit, elevated box seats, and a well-stocked concession stand.

The official 1917 opening night of the stunning Silver Strand Theatre was a gala affair for the citizens of Coronado. John's friend for twenty-five years, Sam Shortridge, with a well-known gift for oratory, came down for the occasion to give, as it turned out, the speech that John could not. Once all the dignitaries from Coronado and over the bay were seated, the footlights turned on at exactly eight thirty. The curtain rose to find the two old friends on the stage, sitting side by side in two easy chairs. One observer said, "Uncle John was smiling, and I never saw him look so happy." Another said he "looked just like a man who was entertaining his friends, in his own house, and was having a good time, and wanted everybody else to have one too."[29]

When John was introduced, the crowd stood and applauded for several minutes. When the clapping subsided, they sat, expectantly waiting to hear from the benefactor. Instead, he remained sitting and told the audience that he "wasn't much of a hand for speeches, [that he would] rather *do things* than talk about them." With that, Senator Shortridge stood and gave his friend's speech. One local reporter sensed that the audience might have preferred a short "You are welcome for this theater, dear Coronadoans" from Uncle John, because it was noted that the politician's speech was way too long and extended the program "beyond reason."[30]

Following the speech, John went behind the curtain and ushered a dear friend who had come to supply the star power for the evening: Madame Ernestine Schumann-Heink, who sang two numbers. After many successful seasons in Germany, she had moved to the United States, where she received rave notices at the Metropolitan Opera. She had come to San Diego in 1911, and later, in 1922, she bought a three-story, gray stucco mansion in Coronado from John, paying a bargain price reserved for family and friends.

The Silver Strand Theatre did its best to keep the community engaged with comedies, cartoons, and "talking dramas." It was also used for charitable fundraisers, where the proceeds would be turned over to the Red Cross. Today, the theater is a playhouse for the Lamb Players.

The beautiful and unique curved Spreckels building stretched out along Orange Avenue is still the heart and soul of downtown Coronado.

The Ferry to Home

Since 1877, when he first met Lillian, John's preference for commuting on the water to "sooth his soul" continued to be met on a ferry.[31] After a hard day of work in San Diego, he could unwind by strolling a short distance down Broadway from his office in the Union Building to the pier and ferry home on his *Ramona*. By all accounts, John loved the "modern" 118-foot ferryboat he had commissioned from Oakland's Risdon Iron Works for his San Diego and Coronado Ferry Company. John liked to be "first" in everything. The fact that the *Ramona* used the "new" oil-burning system and was the first vessel to use the steam turbine on the Pacific Coast attracted, to his delight, the attention of marine engineers.[32] John's tug *Relief* had assisted her in her 460-mile maiden voyage from San Francisco Bay to San Diego on July 3, 1903, making it just in time, as promised, to transport passengers for the huge Fourth of July celebration sponsored by the Coronado Beach Company.[33] Two years later, the *Ramona* (along with the tug *Santa Fe*) was at the right place at the right time to help rescue navy sailors who dove overboard when the USS *Bennington* exploded in San Diego Harbor.

Instead of the twenty-three-mile drive around the Strand, it took only one mile, or five minutes, to ferry across San Diego Bay to Coronado, but what John saw on the other side made it seem like a hundred miles. The small village of Coronado, surrounded by soft ocean air and glittering sea and filled with charming Victorian and California bungalows set down on wide and leafy streets, was in stark contrast to the hustle and bustle of downtown San Diego and concrete, "gray" Broadway.

The aloof "Mr. Spreckels" stepped on the ferry in San Diego, but he stepped off in Coronado as jovial "Uncle John." The moniker "Uncle John" has an unknown origin, but that is what he came to be called by the residents and in the local press, across different publications. On the Coronado ferry landing, John could finally light up his cigar (having been reproved by the *Ramona*'s captain) and could greet his neighbors, as they went to and fro on the ferry.

From Monday through Friday, Coronado village was quiet, but the weekend throngs that converged on the ferry building created a circus atmosphere. Once visitors arrived, they found that riding

25. Opa Spreckels at home in Coronado with a few of his beloved grandchildren from daughters Grace and Lillie and son Jack. *Left to right:* Adolph Bernard II (1906–1974), Grace Alexandria (1907–1977), John Diedrich III (1910–1973), Harriet (1911–1997), and Marie (1903–2001). The swing hooks still remain in the ceiling today at the Glorietta Bay Inn, which is what the Spreckels mansion became. Permission granted from the Terrence and Virginia Wilson Private Family Collection.

the Coronado Beach Railroad's streetcar was fun all by itself. Some cars, pulled by steam engines, were the same models used at New York's Coney Island. The sides could be opened to allow the salt-water breeze to waft through the car. The twenty-minute ride down spacious Orange Avenue, sitting on rattan seats and listening to the rattling floorboards and the clanging bells, was a romantic and unforgettable way to get to the epicenter of fun: Tent City and the Hotel del Coronado. The sparkling Pacific Ocean, which his holdings sat upon, was virtually the only thing within sight that was not owned by John Spreckels.

Opa Spreckels

John seems to have enjoyed the title of "Uncle John," but a title he enjoyed even more was that of "Opa" ("Grandfather" in German). Soon after his son Claus married Ellis in April 1910, they moved to Coronado, and John gifted the newlyweds a beautiful oceanfront mansion designed by Harrison Albright in 1908. The couple gave John and Lillian grandchildren who would reside only a short distance away. First came Claus Jr. "Junior" (1911), followed by Frank "Frankie" Leslie (1912), and then Barbara Ellis "Tookie" (1917). (Claire would follow a decade later, in 1928.) Claus and Ellis's children—along with their lively Irish terrier named "Jiggs," whose antics around Coronado were covered in the local newspapers—gave Opa and Oma Spreckels great joy.

John and Lillian's granddaughter Harriet Holbrook, born in 1911 by their daughter Lillie, lived at 831 Adela Avenue, on the bay side of the island, near them. After Lillie's second husband, Paul Wegeforth, died in 1923, Lillie and Harriet lived alone (besides their servants) in the fourteen-room pink Italian Renaissance Revival mansion. It was an easy walk for young Harriet to see Oma and Opa at the Glorietta Bay mansion.

Coronado became a welcome retreat after the earthquake for John's San Francisco children and grandchildren too. Jack's three children by Edith Huntington—Marie (born 1903), Adolph B. II (1906), and John D. III (1910)—were often in Coronado during their summer vacations, as were Grace and Alec Hamilton's two daughters, Grace Alexandria (1907) and Mary Leila "Happy" (1909). In all, including Jack's daughter Geraldine Anne by Syida Wirt (born 1919), John and Lillian had ten children to occupy their thoughts and hearts at home in what became their paradise, Coronado.

John was the very best version of himself around his grandchildren, and the bond between them was deep and genuine. In the Glorietta Bay mansion, John had placed the organ so that his back was against the wall. This orientation ensured that he could capture the expressions on the faces of his small audiences, which often consisted of his grandchildren. Granddaughter Harriet remembered that "Opa" played

26. Harriet Holbrook (1911–1997) with her mother (John and Lillian's daughter), Lillie. Harriet was Opa's little buddy in and around Coronado. Permission granted from the Terrence and Virginia Wilson Private Family Collection.

27. John and Lillian's grandchildren from son Claus Jr., ca. 1928. They had a privileged childhood in the "Beach House." *Left to right:* Junior (1911–1969), Claire (1928–2018), Tookie (1917–2005), and Frank (1912–1948). Permission granted from the Terrence and Virginia Wilson Private Family Collection.

"with a great deal of emotion."[34] She also remembered that he disliked the jazz that was growing in popularity at the time, favoring classical music, with a special preference for Chopin. She recounted that all the grandchildren were encouraged to experiment with the "rollers" and taught to "use all the stops."[35]

Junior Spreckels and the Coronado Public School

Prior to incorporation, Coronado had been part of the San Diego school system, requiring some young people to ferry to school. The first public school in Coronado opened in 1887 and was held in a tent on a dirt lot. The following year, a proper building was built and looked more like a Victorian home than a school. By 1917, the "Beautiful Coronado

One-Story School" made it into a trade journal due to its beauty and modern features.[36] There were classrooms to accommodate eight grades, and some of John's grandchildren were among those pupils.

For example, Harriet and Junior, eleven-year-old cousins, were likely in the same classroom with teacher Josephine Drewisch during the 1921–22 school year. While Harriet was entering and winning flower shows with her roses, Junior was causing trouble for principal Fred Boyer.[37] Report cards left behind from that school year reveal that the only subjects Junior Spreckels didn't fail were music and drawing. His lack of "application" in all core subjects resulted in a lack of promotion to the next grade, as seen in his final report card of June 16, 1922. Miss Drewisch, with a tenure of twenty-two years, was one of Coronado's most respected teachers, but it was likely a daring move on her part to hold back the grandson of the man who virtually owned Coronado.

The next bold move was made by mom Ellis Spreckels: Almost immediately, she sent Junior, now twelve years old, along with his brother, eleven-year-old Frankie (likely for companionship), to the William Warren School, an all-male military school in Menlo Park. (Opa also sent Junior's first cousin Jack, now twelve years old, likely to provide him with some structure after the death of his father, John Diedrich Spreckels Jr., the year before.) Ellis received a written assessment of Junior, completed only a month after he had left Coronado, by Major Charles T. Vandervort, which states that young "Claus is troubled a little by over-confidence. This is really a good trait in a boy, but Claus really has a little too much."[38] On the same day, rambunctious Junior fell and had to have stitches for "deep cuts in his little face." Later that day, he broke the windshield of the car.[39] On the basis of his juvenile letters, he may not have been overly academic, but he was tender and had great affection for his entire family, especially for his Oma Lillian.

And like both his grandfather and father, Junior loved guns. One month after arriving at William Warren, he wrote to Ellis, "Mother, one thing I want what pretty near every boy has is a gun for shooting deer and shooting match[es]."[40]

Junior's father, Claus, an outgoing bon vivant, blended easily into the upscale community of Coronado, while his mother, Ellis, with her gracious demeanor and generosity, became the quintessential society hostess, in charge of many charities. The 12,751-square-foot mansion at 1043 Ocean Boulevard had twenty-seven rooms, including six bedrooms, four and a half baths, a basement, and three separate wine cellars.

That mansion has a rich social history today due to a surprise visit from a British prince on April 7, 1920. Throughout the 1920s, Edward, as Prince of Wales and heir apparent to his father, King George V, represented the king abroad on many occasions. When San Diegans learned that their city would be one of the prince's scheduled stopovers while sailing the HMS *Renown* en route to Australia and New Zealand, prominent citizens jumped into action. John offered the Hotel del Coronado's Crown Room for a formal banquet, which he used as leverage to get the most out of the royal visit for his family. He "penetrated protocol" and persuaded the prince to stop off at Claus and Ellis's oceanfront mansion on the way to the hotel.[41]

Ellis was at home preparing for the ball when her maid burst in with the news of British royalty on the doorstep. Caught completely off-guard, she collected her wits and pulled off an impromptu cocktail party for the prince and his cousin Lord Louis Mountbatten. According to an anecdote she was later fond of relating, two-and-a-half-year-old Tookie escaped from her nanny to see what the commotion was all about. She was less than impressed when introduced to His Royal Highness because, as Tookie herself remembered, she told him that his lack of a white horse indicated that he was no real prince. Ellis recalled the prince's exact statement: "It was charming to be snubbed by a lady— they're always willing to meet me."[42] That the prince was known as a womanizer makes this comment particularly accurate.

John and Lillian took their sixteen-year-old granddaughter Marie (Jack and Edith's daughter) with them to the event, and Opa Spreckels made sure she took a spin around the floor with the prince. At the banquet, John manipulated the seating arrangements at the last

28. Ellis Ethel Moon Spreckels (1888–1967). John was very close to his daughter-in-law. With her gracious demeanor, Ellis became the quintessential society hostess, in charge of many charities in Coronado. Permission granted from the Laurie Fletcher Guidry Private Family Collection.

moment, moving Ellis to the right side of Prince Edward—a strategic decision because his daughter-in-law was a sophisticated conversationalist. Indeed, historical photos show the Prince of Wales and Ellis in tête-à-tête throughout the dinner. Ellis wrote, "So many later asked me what we were discussing at the time. The answer is simple—Hollywood, the movies, and all the glamorous gals of those days."[43]

One American navy wife, Wallis Warfield Spencer, lived in a small house near the Spreckels mansion in Coronado and was a close friend of Ellis's. Rumors persist that Ellis is the one who formally introduced Wallis to Prince Edward, a meeting that would later lead to the marriage that caused a British constitutional crisis compelling Edward (then King Edward VIII) to abdicate the throne.

At the end of August 1920, John invited daughter Lillie along with nine-year-old Harriet to accompany him on the *Venetia* for a three-week cruise to Honolulu. This was the era when long-distance communication was sent by signals over telegraph cables. But Italian physicist Guglielmo Marconi had suspected that invisible radio waves might offer a better solution. When John and his family arrived in Hawai'i, Marconi was on his yacht *Elettra*, conducting experiments beyond those that had earned him the Nobel Prize nine years earlier. Also, in Hawaiian waters was the Prince of Wales on the HMS *Renown*. It's unknown if the meeting had been prearranged at the April banquet in Coronado, but John gave little Harriet a historic opportunity when she went "aboard Marconi's yacht with Opa and talked on Marconi's newly invented radio-telephone to the Prince of Wales, who was aboard the *Renown*."[44] During the 1920s, the Marconi Company linked the entire British Empire by radio, and Harriet never forgot that eventful experience on her first trip to Hawai'i and relayed it throughout Coronado. Being a grandchild of John Spreckels meant having extraordinary opportunities and lasting memories to pass down.

Guarding the Grandchildren

Among the memories shared by the Spreckels grandchildren include one about a rare spanking from Opa.

Kidnapping for ransom came into notoriety in the late nineteenth century, beginning in 1874 with the abduction of four-year-old Charlie Ross, the child of a wealthy merchant from Germantown, Pennsylvania. For decades, particularly after the 1932 kidnapping of Charles Augustus Lindbergh, the twenty-month-old son of Charles and Anne Morrow Lindbergh, newspapers stoked fear into the hearts of parents across the nation, particularly wealthy parents. For example, John's great-grandson, Harriet's son, John Garrettson Belcher, recalled the widespread use of watchdogs stationed outside their bedroom doors at night in order to prevent a kidnapping.

Virginia Wilson remembered asking her mother, Harriet, if she had ever been spanked as a child. Harriet told her about an incident seared in her memory that took place one afternoon on the lawn of her grandparent's mansion. John had two imported German shepherd guard dogs. Harriet had learned a few German training commands that her grandfather used. When young Harriet became exasperated with the pranks of her cousin, Johnny Spreckels, one year older, she likely gave the dog the command "*Fass!*" which sent the dog to hold the boy down. Opa drove up the driveway in the nick of time to remove the dog, who was a breath away from hurting Johnny. Harriet always remembered her grandfather as a gentle and kind man, but on that day, he took her up to the solarium and gave her a spanking for the severity of her actions.[45]

All was forgiven for a grandfather who loved his grandchildren, and they loved him back. On his sixty-seventh birthday, he arrived home to find the Tent City Band on his front lawn, playing "Happy Birthday," as all of his smiling grandchildren carried in a huge cake decorated with his favorite theme: Hawai'i.[46]

Pranks

Opa, the larger-than-life figure, provided his grandchildren with some of their fondest and earliest memories. From singing with him as he played the organ or sailing with him on the *Venetia*, one never knew what prank he would pull, because their Opa was a fun-loving prankster. He loved his practical jokes.

One day, the grandchildren got to see a prank played on their grand-father. On his birthday in 1918, seven hundred people, including his grandchildren, were invited to a grand celebration at the Hotel del Coronado given by his company's executives. To mark the event, Arthur James Cahill, an illustrator from the early days of the *Call* who had become celebrated for his portraiture, was commissioned to use his artistic talent to play a practical joke on his former employer. He was more than happy to comply.

It was announced in advance that the noted artist would be unveiling a life-size portrait of John D. Spreckels at the end of the birthday merriments. John, who had sat for the portrait, was also looking forward to the "sur-prise." When the time came, Spreckels company chairman George Brobeck stood beside the heavily veiled easel and ceremoniously spoke: "And now, Mr. Spreckels, on behalf of my associates and myself, I have the honor and pleasure to present to you, and beg you to accept, this lifelike portrait of him whom we admire and esteem above all other men: yourself."[47]

A hush of expectancy went around the Crown Room as the veil was drawn away. Instead of applause, however, "a ghastly silence fell" on the crowd as they viewed a painted distortion of the man whom they had come to celebrate. The caricature, as it was later revealed, exposed a heavyset and disheveled John Spreckels seemingly out of character in a tuxedo that was being strained at the buttons due to a paunch. The ever-present gold watch fob and the ever-present cigar and lapel pin were also distorted. It was said that John's face "was a study" as he pondered "why in the name of thunder had Cahill" done that to him.[48] After what seemed an eternity, the real portrait was revealed: The tall, slim, and handsome John Spreckels in his sixties, blue-eyed, silver-haired, sporting a handlebar moustache, wearing a crisp white, high-collared shirt, tweed vest, and casual Norfolk jacket with his gold watch fob. The nervous laughter didn't subside for what also felt like eternity. It was noted that John was among the last to laugh.[49] But when he did laugh, he laughed hard and insisted on keeping both paintings.

The capers of Opa Spreckels's dogs were also reported in the news-papers. Coronadoans, including the Spreckels family, loved their dogs, as evidenced by the sheer amount of references to the town's special dogs in the papers. Ellis chaired the first annual dog show at Tent City, starting a series that attracted newspaper coverage all over the country because of the distinguished judges and breeds. (The shows were short-lived, however, because the ferry trip over the bay traumatized too many of the champion dogs.[50])

"Uncle John" was known to stroll around Coronado with Bear, his faithful unleashed companion. When Bear "chased a turkey around the block, returning with a mouthful of tail feathers," it made news.[51] John might have been greeted at the ferry landing with "Good afternoon, Mr. Spreckels. I hear Bear's favorite food is turkey!" Since the board of trustees had enacted a ban on chickens and other fowl running at large, John likely guffawed that his dog was just helping enforce the town's ordinances.[52]

An anonymous delivery of a puppy of the "purest pedigree" was dropped off one day at the Glorietta Bay mansion. But as it grew into a dog, it became clear that there had been no blue-ribbon blood in the puppy—that it was, in fact, an adorable mutt. After two years of "running through the list of friends" who might have played this joke, John learned the identity of the man who had done it, and he patiently waited to "get even." When the dog eventually died, he placed its body in a crate, which he had delivered to the man's residence. After the gruesome discovery, the unnamed friend realized who had sent the crate, and the following dialogue ensued:

"See here, J. D., what the devil do you mean by sending me that dog?"

"What dog?"

"Oh, you know well enough. That dead one."

"Well, you see, he's the one you kindly lent me; and I always return a loan."

"You win."[53]

Perfecting His Paradise: The Del

By the turn of the twentieth century, as taste for domestic travel flourished, every city with a natural resource, especially one with a seashore, seemed to sprout a grand hotel that offered luxuries once seen only in Europe. John's earliest mission for the Hotel del Coronado was to redesign it to mimic a European luxury hotel.

Babcock and Story had intended the hotel to be a large fishing and hunting resort. Although feminine in its Queen Anne Revival style, it had a masculine interior. The two-story lobby was richly paneled with a coffered ceiling in dark wood, giving it a refined lodge appearance. The stunning Crown Room, with its thirty-foot-high Oregon sugar pine ceiling, was considered an architectural achievement. With no nails except wooden pegs to hold the arched ceiling together and no pillars to obstruct the view, John made sure this room would be worthy of royalty, which it became. There were dedicated rooms, fairly masculine, for billiard tables, cards and chess, smoking, and bowling.

Soon after he acquired ownership, John redesigned the interior to be less masculine and more elegant. Midwesterner L. Frank Baum, author of *The Wizard of Oz*, spent many winters in the warm and welcoming sunshine of Coronado beginning in 1904. He wrote at least three of his Oz books while staying at the Del. When Baum wanted to upgrade the look of the Crown dining room, John was only too happy to allow him to design the impressive crown chandeliers. John purchased fine china and linens from Paris, carpets and furnishings from the Far East.[54] Antiques from all over the United States were placed in the public rooms. The "rich, thick ripe-red carpets, great deep inviting divans, and big, wide alluring armchairs" adorning the hotel soon justified its description as a "European Victorian Palace."[55]

The mystique and international allure generated by "the Del," as the hotel became known, hinged on the very real possibility that one could come face to face with a president, a famous movie star, royalty, or such prominent businessmen as Henry Ford, Harvey Firestone, or Thomas Edison, all of whom were guests at the same time. Many millionaires from the cold climates, attracted to the sunshine and modern amenities, wintered for months on end at the hotel, arriving with their children and their retinue of servants. A school that employed a classical curriculum was opened on hotel grounds for the children. It was said that some children spoke flawless French after their winters at the Del. John often used his own private Pullman railroad car (numbered 050), a "lavish suite-on-wheels," and for the wealthy that traveled across country in their own private railroad coach cars, he built a railroad spur.[56] This secondary track allowed privacy for the Del's most affluent and privacy-seeking guests.

Christmas was always a big deal in the Spreckels family, and John was well known for his generosity during the season. The Del was full with Spreckels family members enjoying one another's company from Christmas through New Year's. Mrs. Babcock had begun a tradition, still alive today, of hosting a children's Christmas party at the Del. For years, as the children were sitting on wicker chairs in the decorated ballroom enjoying Christmas goodies, Santa Claus arrived. Above the white beard were familiar bright blue eyes, and under the red and white costume was the "invisible host," John D. Spreckels.[57]

In 1888, in the Hawaiian Kingdom, the Spreckels family had made history with the electrification of their sugar mill. The royal monarchs had been impressed enough to confer with Thomas Edison and light up the 'Iolani Palace, beating America's White House. At seven p.m. on Christmas Eve 1904, the Del made history as well when it unveiled the world's first electrically lighted outdoor living tree.[58] The 250 colored lights, strung between the Del and the Norfolk Island pine, were a wonder to behold in an era where the few who had trees inside their homes lit them with candles. A *San Diego Union* reporter captured the wonderment of two children during this history-making event: "All evening long, the radiant tree was the object of admiration. All evening long, two barefooted children, a boy and a girl, stood . . . and gazed upon the beaming tree. The little girl held her brother's hand close within her own. They spoke scarcely a word. The imprint of their little feet is even yet visible in the rain-softened earth."[59]

John had a long tunnel built from his home to the Del, so he could walk out from his music room and under the road unnoticed. He could easily visit Coronado's city health officer and his lifelong personal physician, Dr. Raffaele Lorini, recruited from the French Hospital in San

Francisco to be "house surgeon" for the Hotel del Coronado. Lorini, born in Italy, trained in France, was a brilliant acquisition; he co-wrote the *National Medical Dictionary*, which he personally translated into five languages, and he was instrumental in developing methods and standards for the medical profession.[60]

John could also get his shoes shined or get a shave and haircut at Burge's Barber Shop in the Del. James Burge related how one could earn John's favor:

> I was shaving him in the hotel barber shop when he first came down from San Francisco, after the earthquake. He had been sick. Some man called him to the telephone and kept him standing 10 minutes, then another man called him and did the same. When he was called out of the chair the third time, I said, "Yes, Mr. Spreckels is here but he can't come to the phone, some damn fools have kept him standing too long." That pleased Uncle John, as everyone called him, so he set me up in business in the block with the bank that he built. I was there until a few years ago. Had another shop in Tent City, too.[61]

John's grandchildren continued to be well known by the Del's staff for years after the boss's passing. Claus and Ellis's youngest daughter, Claire, remembered herself and her brothers running wildly through the hotel, amusing the staff, who turned a blind eye to them. Their youngest son, Frank, and his buddy Arthur Messner were well known by the hotel baker, Steve, who allowed the boys to help themselves to hot rye bread out of the oven and his famous delicious black currant sorbet.[62] Many of those longtime employees remembered the shenanigans of these very children's parents—their boss's children: Grace, Lillie, Jack, and Claus Jr.—when they were young. During the years before the move to Coronado, the family stayed in the hotel during the summer months. One story passed down is about "Grace and the garden hat." Evidently, Grace often wore a hat with an extraordinarily wide brim to keep the sun away. Lillie recounted that the tall Grace, when nobody was looking, went behind the bar and ran alongside the top shelves to see how many glasses she could knock off with her brim.

In the Court of Hotel Del Coronado.

29. John and Lillian's children in the Del's courtyard. *Left to right:* Jack, Lillie, Grace, and Claus Jr. The Del's staff knew when the rambunctious Spreckels children arrived for the holidays. Permission granted from the Terrence and Virginia Wilson Private Family Collection.

Lillie, much shorter, used a stick to sweep the glasses off the lower shelves. Other times, they went to the top floors in search of room service trays outside doors. They cleared off the used food and dishes to the floor, and then they converted the wooden trays into sleds to go down the stairs of the hotel.[63]

Polo and Then Golf

Coronado and the Del, established simultaneously, grew together, side by side—each equally benefiting the other. When John set down roots in Coronado in 1906, one of his first acts was to build a stunning clubhouse near the Del for the game of polo and transfer it to the city. The Coronado Country Club, the first polo facility of its kind in southern

California, quickly became known throughout the country for the quality of its barns, fields—and climate—as well as the proficiency of its skilled players and its beautiful horses. The club grounds were groomed by a herd of hungry guinea pigs, and John raised a flock of young ducks on his lawn to eat "trespassing bugs."[64]

John became the sport's most passionate advocate. He brought to Coronado players from around the world. The world-class facility attracted the rich and famous, and starry-eyed locals flocked to the polo field to catch a glimpse. The first John D. Spreckels Cup in polo was a solid silver punch bowl offered at the club that year. Due to the significance of it being the first tournament, each player received a silver goblet as a personal memento. In 1908, the "All America Polo Trophy" competition was held in Coronado. Any team was eligible, but John personally presented a silver punch bowl only to those teams from California.

In 1909, the Coronado Country Club became the first polo club on the Pacific Coast to affiliate with the United States Polo Association. When the Hawai'i Polo Club affiliated with the association in 1912, John brought them to Coronado to play.[65] The history of polo in Hawai'i is intertwined with the culture of the *paniolo*, the Hawaiian cowboy. Polo was often played on fields amid the sugarcane. The polo players from Hawai'i revealed through their names—Dillingham, Baldwin, Castle, Milliken, Rice, and Spalding—that they were descended from missionaries, and sugar planters themselves, who had detested the Spreckels name in Hawai'i during the days of its monarchy. It's likely that both John's love for Hawai'i and his competitive nature brought the men in to compete.

For more than a decade, Coronado hosted championships, with John defraying most of the costs. In 1921, when an edict went forth from the Spreckels companies that golf would replace polo in Coronado, the community pleaded for a reversal of that decision. Even though they understood that polo was too costly to sustain, they claimed that from a "sentimental standpoint it is [was] a tragedy."[66] They were going to miss seeing from the grandstands the likes of Charlie Chaplin, Douglas Fairbanks, Rudolph Valentino, and Gloria Swanson.[67]

But now the community had the use of the beautiful golf course, one that Supreme Court chief justice and former president William Howard Taft loved to play on. "Two or three times" John offered the course as a gift to the city of Coronado, but they refused the offer, preferring the tax revenue they received from John's bank account. It was well known that he felt slighted by that decision.[68]

The Coronado Library

John knew that the sporting events, the weather, the natural beauty of Coronado, the beachfront hotel, and Tent City attracted visitors, but he worried that, without cultural amenities, it would be impossible to convince the "right type of people" to relocate to the island. And those who were his island neighbors, including his family members, needed more than Tent City to entertain them. His love for books was well known, as evidenced by his gifting in 1903 of a rare collection to form the Karl Weinhold Library at the University of California, Berkeley. Soon after the turn of the century, when its need was clear, John gave Coronado a lovely public library. Some speculated that the gift was not entirely altruistic, that he did it as a "trade," or "in gratitude" after the city complied with his request to eliminate the small street Clarita Row so he could enlarge his mansion grounds.[69] Whatever the reason, the community was excited!

The library, dedicated in 1909, was built on the main thoroughfare of Orange Avenue at a cost of $10,000. The 1,600-square-foot building, while not large, could hold five thousand volumes. The classically themed building, designed by John's favorite architect, Harrison Albright, makes quite a statement, with its decorative frieze inscribed with the names of ancient authors Homer, Cicero, Horace, and Virgil. The library was completely furnished, with "reading tables, book shelves, chairs and other necessary furniture."[70] Coronadoans adopted the library as a special project. To fill the shelves, John donated space in the Del to be used for fundraisers. The library mattered deeply to the village, and "New Books at the Coronado Library" was a regular column in the *Coronado Eagle and Journal.*

When construction was completed, Story Hour for the children was held daily at one p.m. On Saturday mornings, only the children of Coronado had access to the library "in order that they may obtain a broader knowledge of books and also have help in the selecting of them." Literary Clubs were organized, and prizes were given for attendance.[71] The West Plaza, a large, lush park directly across the street from the library, was renamed Spreckels Park as a tribute in 1927.[72]

Hollywood Comes to Coronado

Motion pictures, and the people who made them, were something of an intriguing mystery to most people at the end of the nineteenth century. Thomas Edison had invented the motion picture camera (Kinetograph) in the 1890s, and the Edison Company held the patent on it. With Edison's dogged determination, motion pictures quickly became a successful entertainment industry.

Edison filmed a few events that affected John personally. When the battleship *Maine* blew up and sank in Havana Harbor in February 1898, Edison filmed John's conscripted SS *Australia* steaming away from San Francisco's harbor, packed from helm to stern with soldiers on their way to war. Large-scale disasters were also a favorite subject for the Edison camera; thus, when the San Francisco earthquake and fire in 1906 occurred, the destruction of John's iconic Call Building was well documented. The cameras were there in the good times for John as well. Hollywood director Allan Dwan used Coronado as a backdrop for *A Girl of Yesterday*, starring "America's Sweetheart," Mary Pickford, with scenes filmed onboard John's yacht, the *Venetia*.

Early filmmakers such as Edison recognized the advertising potential of motion pictures, and so did John, who believed there was no better way to promote his island paradise for both recreation and relocation than by encouraging filmmakers to film on Coronado's beach, Tent City, and the Del. In 1901, Edison captured a ferryboat entering the Coronado slip, people frolicking on the beach in their woolen Victorian beach apparel, children playing in Tent City, and others waving from their sailboats.

When film producer Siegmund "Pop" Lubin turned his eyes on San Diego in 1915—with his immense prestige and stature—everyone took notice. Lubin was considered a giant in the silent film industry, and that fall, John gave Lubin a five-year lease to open a film studio on a choice parcel of his land near Coronado's ferry landing, at First and Orange. He had an unusual stipulation, though: He would charge only one dollar per year as long as everyone working for the studio dwelled in Coronado, thereby ensuring that the local economy would benefit.

Throughout the following year, actors, directors, writers, and cameramen strolled throughout Coronado, providing loads of entertainment for the residents. Not surprisingly, most of the films that Lubin's company produced in Coronado included a battleship or several navy vessels and featured such titles as *Sons of the Sea*.[73] Particularly fascinated were the young ladies, who enjoyed watching the handsome actors dressed as sailors "at war" on their beach.[74]

Despite Lubin's best efforts, he went bankrupt in 1916, due to the instability of the economy.[75] But Lubin's departure did not stop other filmmakers, and by the end of the silent movie era, there were "eighty-five films made in Coronado from 1898 to 1929, not counting newsreels or military films."[76]

Once a celebrity went home to Hollywood, the word was passed that the Del was a destination not to be missed, favored for its seaside setting and seclusion, and it became a playground for Hollywood's first film stars. Also, with its close proximity to Mexico, where drinking alcohol was legal, Coronado became a good cover during Prohibition. When William Desmond Taylor, a popular figure in the gilded age of Hollywood, was interviewed about his recent visit to Coronado, the reporter ended the story this way: "He denies, however, that he visited Tijuana."[77]

Patriotic German around Town

World War I stirred an anti-German sentiment that reached into all parts of the United States, even though German immigrants had brought to their newly adopted homeland an expertise in farming, education, science, the arts, and more. Now German-language newspapers were forced out of business, and colleges dropped the German language from the curriculum. Churches that had been founded as German-speaking were "encouraged" to discontinue their German services. Words and phrases that sounded German were changed; as an example, the hamburger became a "liberty steak," and dachshunds became "liberty hounds." Even music by such German composers as Bach, Beethoven, and Brahms was removed from orchestral programs. As a result of this wholesale persecution, many German Americans concealed their ethnic identity and "over-proved" their loyalty to America. On the other hand, John was one who over-identified with his German roots, as seen in many of his hiring preferences for both home and businesses. John even built a German Garden in Tent City as a place to relax and remind himself of his roots. It was said that the garden was "as thoroughly foreign as though it existed beside the Rhine, instead of on the shores of the Pacific."[78] It's impossible to know John's feelings during America's anti-German delirium, but it likely saddened him while he displayed his great patriotism for America.

Theodore Roosevelt helped popularize the Preparedness Movement to convince Americans of what could happen to an unprepared country. The idea behind the "preparedness parades," which took place nationwide, was to support the bolstering of the American military in case the so-far-neutral nation entered the war. The village of Coronado, which was surrounded by the military on Spreckels land on North Island, joined such big cities as New York and Washington DC to hold its own little preparedness parade, which marched down Orange Avenue on July 8, 1916. John demonstrated his endurance and patriotism when he marched the entire distance at the front of the line of Coronado's first troop of Boy Scouts (which he had cofounded), waving the Boy Scout flag to the cheering onlookers. The press was amazed: "How many other men of his years and station would have deigned to get out and march?"[79]

Wake Up!

In 1920, *El Patio*, a self-effacing, amusing, society-oriented twenty-page weekly newspaper arrived on the Coronado scene. Welford Beaton, the witty editor, publisher, and old-time journalist, was dumbfounded over the apathetic spirit of Coronado, which left him bored for any kind of entertainment outside of the Del and Tent City. In one of his first publications on September 18, 1920, Beaton ruffled some feathers of Coronadoans when he told them to "Wake Up!"

> Nature has made Coronado one of the finest places of residence in the world. During its many years of existence the hotel has brought thousands of people here from all parts of the world and every winter the available houses on the Island are filled with families from all over the country. Yet the last federal census gave us a resident population of 3,200. We have room for 25,000 people, and this limit seems a long way off at the present rate of progress. Why? The reason for the slow growth is the lack of a community spirit. If we are going to be a playground, what are we giving the residents to play with? Nothing. What Nature did not do, we have left to Mr. Spreckels to do. There is nothing else that Nature can do and nothing else that you should ask Mr. Spreckels to do. It is time the rest of us were doing something.[80]

By January 15, 1921, Beaton narrowed his criticism to the "idle rich":

> Coronado is too much in the habit of sitting back and allowing the Spreckels people to do everything for the advancement of the Island. To ask them to [be] a sort of amusement manager—would be riding a good horse to death. We refer to those rich people whose only interest in Coronado is confined by the walls of their homes and the boundaries of the Country Club. Their business interests are elsewhere and they are satisfied with the Coronado of today. They have a perfect right to their feelings. We have no quarrel with them. Their lack of a reason for a community spirit merely places the burden of creating one on the shoulders of the rest of us.[81]

Beaton had come from outside California and was amazed to discover the width and breadth of the contributions made by one man to both the infrastructure and the superstructure of San Diego and Coronado—and yet John Spreckels received nothing but criticism from both sides of the bay. Beaton wryly and sarcastically addressed that never-ending criticism in the October 16 issue of *El Patio*. He commented that "the luckiest thing that ever happened to Coronado and San Diego is that the 'D' in his name stands for 'demented'—Mr. John Demented Spreckels."

> Until I discovered this, some years ago, nobody could understand why Mr. Spreckels kept on dumping one million after another on our devoted (and thankless) hole-in-a-corner—when he might have invested all his wealth in government bonds, lived in any one of the world's most delightful spots, cruised over the seven seas in his palatial yacht, and let us scrub along the best way we could under the uplifting guidance of the San Diego Sun. Thank Heaven that Mr. Spreckels isn't entirely sane. I live in terror lest he may have a lucid interval one of these days, suddenly realize what he has been doing all these years, and then clear out, bag and baggage! Let us pray that his dementia has now become incurable. Amen![82]

That article clearly resonated with John because, four years later, he could still recite it, albeit paraphrased in Spreckels style:

> Some years ago, when some of our peanut politicians were warning San Diego not to fall for the crafty schemes of the foxy "Spreckels interest," a certain well-known wit and sage said that my name must be J. D. Demented Spreckels because if I were not crazy, I would not subject myself to this constant yelping of village curs but would sell out my whole business, put all my money in Government bonds, sail away on my yacht, and let San Diego go to hell—or look to the bunch of anti-Spreckels knockers to save the city, under the high-minded leadership of the *San Diego Sun*. Gentleman, he did not know me, or he would never have suggested a surrender on my part. Whatever else I may or may not be, I am not a quitter.[83]

Bored living among the "idle rich," Beaton folded the clever little *El Patio* after only a year and left Coronado to publish the *Hollywood Spectator*. When he wrote, "Mr. Spreckels—poor, patient Mr. Spreckels who desires only to live in peace and to continue to do good to the community to make it more pleasant for his neighbors," he was right.[84] He only wanted to live comfortably among the community, to be their "Uncle John," and to be Opa Spreckels to his grandchildren.

12

The So-Called Impossible Railroad

At Long Last: The San Diego & Arizona Railway

San Diegans at the turn of the twentieth century were discouraged over their inadequate land transportation. Though the city's short-haul railroads carried a variety of products, they lacked any semblance of integration. The only way a passenger could travel out of town eastward was to first go to Los Angeles on a branch route of the Santa Fe Railroad. The isolation alone caused many early San Diego settlers to abandon the city. Finally, in 1901, the San Diego Chamber of Commerce established the Eastern Railroad Committee to secure a direct transcontinental railroad out of San Diego. George White Marston, Ulysses S. Grant Jr., and other influential San Diegans raised an impressive $42,000 after an attempt to get federal aid to build had been denied.[1] Unfortunately, despite their repeated attempts, the committee was unsuccessful, and the donated funds stayed in the bank.

Therefore, subscribers to the *San Diego Union* must have jolted their coffee cups on the morning of December 14, 1906, when they read the headline "Railroad from San Diego to Yuma Is Now Assured!" The pronouncement came as a complete surprise to most in the community. Now there would indeed be a railroad that would bypass Los Angeles and provide San Diegans with a direct transcontinental rail link to the East, and people would finally be able to travel directly to places like Chicago and New York City.[2] The public learned that the construction of the proposed San Diego & Arizona Railway (SD&A) was in the very capable hands of the city's builder, John D. Spreckels, a fact that made the proposal a credible possibility and that right away opened up all sorts of opportunities for both businesses and citizens. Supporting this venture, at least on paper, would be John's usual posse: his brother Adolph Spreckels, his son Jack Spreckels, his right-hand man William Clayton, and Harry Lewis Titus, his corporate attorney. Everything John touched in their city seemed to profit both him and the city. Although city leaders had made promises for decades, now the direct railroad to the eastern United States seemed assured, even to skeptics.

The concept behind the SD&A had originated with Edward Henry Harriman. After investing his own money in railway stocks and even marrying into a railroad family, Harriman had become by the turn of the century one of the leading figures in American railroads. During the nationwide financial panic of 1890, he had been able to seize control of the bankrupt Union Pacific Railroad. He soon acquired the Southern Pacific Company (Espee) and some eastern lines as well. After finishing a job in the Imperial Valley region for President Theodore Roosevelt in 1905, he was regarded as a hero when his railroad crews arrested the flooding of the runaway Colorado River, averting disaster in that fertile farming region. During this experience, he realized the potential of developing the agriculture of the Imperial Valley. To do this, he would need to extend the Espee line directly into San Diego.

Unfortunately, Harriman's hero status had diminished by 1906, particularly with President Roosevelt, due to his unpopular monopolistic control over several railroads. Some began referring to Harriman negatively as the "Napoleon of Railroading."[3] He had a remarkable ability to persuade others over the years to join in his ventures, John D. Rockefeller and Cornelius Vanderbilt among them. Now he needed to influence one more millionaire to be a front man in a secret train venture: John D. Spreckels. He and John were already well acquainted; earlier that year, Harriman had purchased all of John and Adolph's Oregon coal mine properties, including a twenty-mile railroad, for

$13,000. Harriman (and many others) thought he'd secured a really good deal, but John said, "I was glad to get rid of it."[4]

By that time, John had lots of experience with railroads. He and his father were well known, first for the railroad in Maui and then for railroads in California: the Santa Cruz Railroad in 1875, the Pajaro Valley Railroad in 1889, and the San Francisco and San Joaquin Valley Railway in 1895. John agreed to supply the name, the fame, and the local connections for Harriman's vision. John was convinced that this rail line would contribute to the population growth of San Diego, increase the quality of life for San Diegans, and increase his own wealth to boot. Now the Eastern Railroad Committee, unsuccessful in their efforts to build a direct transcontinental line, relinquished to John all their "properties, franchises, rights of way, and incorporations."[5] Along with their pledge to provide their "most hearty and unwavering support," they also turned over to John the $42,000 they had raised, which he immediately returned, crowing later that it was due to his "code of chivalrous consideration."[6] Marston remembered that this single act converted some Spreckels naysayers and made "John D. a veritable Santa Claus."[7]

Difficulties and Disappointments

In record time, the San Diego & Arizona Railway Company was incorporated, and a well-attended groundbreaking ceremony took place. On September 7, 1907, the city's aged founding father, Alonzo Horton, smiled as Mayor John Forward turned the first shovelful of dirt from the foot of Twenty-Sixth Street just south of downtown San Diego. Although the ceremony garnered plenty of community excitement, the difficulties and disappointments for the SD&A began almost immediately.

Just as grading was to begin, a nationwide economic depression dried up funding for the railroad, delaying the onset of work until 1908. And then engineering surveys determined that El Centro should replace Yuma, Arizona, as the connection for Espee and that a route through parts of Mexico would be smoother and cheaper. "Cheaper" was the motivator for negotiations, and in March 1908, a dispatch from Mexico City announced that "John D. Spreckels, the millionaire California steamship and railroad man, left for home tonight after having secured from the Mexican government a concession granting him the right to build his Yuma–San Diego railroad through Mexican territory for a distance of fifty miles."[8]

As it would turn out, convincing a foreign government to grant John a permit to build a rail line through its country was the easy part. Just as construction had finally begun in earnest, John received the shocking news that Edward Harriman had unexpectedly died on September 9, 1909. "Things went along very nicely until the year of his death," John later remembered. "He was furnishing the money and I was spending it."[9] Now Espee backed out of the financial contract, leaving John adrift, without the assurance of continuing funds. It wasn't long before the secret was out that John D. Spreckels had only acted as a front man for Harriman's planned railway.

Upon hearing that no more money was coming his way, John called Espee's backing out "a staggering blow," which he likened to his favorite sport, boxing: "It was tantamount to a knock-out, but gentlemen, let me tell you, before the count of 10 arrived I said, 'then let me do it.'"[10] He resolved to continue construction, using his own funds. It's likely that he deeply regretted his magnanimous gesture of returning, in 1907, the $42,000 back to the public fund managed by Marston's committee. Though he was outwardly confident of raising money, inwardly he knew the challenges of securing subscriptions.

Meanwhile, the line was dubbed the "Impossible Railroad," due to the immense logistical challenges of getting over and through mountains, across rivers, and through deserts. John loved a challenge. He was at his best when confronted with such seemingly impossible situations as continuing the railway. It may have been, in a sense, a matter of sport, as he pitted his mental powers and personality against the physical challenges the railroad brought. John consulted with innovative engineers, however, and whatever he was told, he was likely motivated by a well-known quote from an engineer who had helped build the transcontinental railroad across America: "Where a mule can go, I can make a locomotive go."[11]

John would not allow the moniker "Impossible Railroad" to define his project, even through the engineering obstacles, mounting natural disasters, and the disruptive Mexican Revolution.[12] "It was just one damned thing after another," he said.[13] The only time his countenance weakened was in February 1912, when he received notice that Espee was suing him for the $3 million it had invested under Harriman. But, with typical fire, he fought the suit until it was legally dismissed four years later: Espee conceded and reentered the venture as a partner.

Throughout the calamities, John's family members, concerned for his health, asked him to consider letting go of the project. Business partners, concerned over the millions of dollars fleeing from his bank account, asked him to cut his losses. Some stakeholders of the railroad slyly said that SD&A stood for "Slow, Dirty & Aggravating."[14] Even San Diegans had lost the vision and were tired of the construction mishaps. Particularly unenthusiastic about the venture were those who owned property that was being condemned to obtain a right of way for the planned route. The "colossal condemnation proceedings" angered many, and they vocally came out against John.[15] But, his well-known quote came into play: "Whatever else I may or may not be, I am not a quitter."[16]

When the United States entered World War I, it looked like the decision to quit was being made for John because the federal government, in an effort to conserve resources, seized control over all American railroads and halted construction of those being built. But John was able to navigate bureaucratic red tape triggered by the war and convince President Woodrow Wilson of the need to resume construction of the railroad line. John recalled how he attacked this "last obstacle at the White House" by arguing the strategic benefit of his train: "I personally went to Washington and there, by pointing out the value of our completed road as a military asset in case of an attack either on the Pacific Coast or on the Mexican border, I was successful in getting permission to go ahead."[17] Insiders, who knew the immense stress John was under, breathed a deep sigh of relief that he had been persuasive enough with President Wilson to get a special exemption. The SD&A was released from federal control, and John got his workers literally back on track.

Completion: A Party Atmosphere

When the railroad was finished on November 15, 1919, John was told that he was expected to make a speech before a thousand spectators during the golden spike ceremony. Those who knew of his "stage fright" told him to just prepare bulleted items of the "interesting events."[18] Prior to the event, John declared, "That speech has more terrors for me than building another railroad." John, chatting with one of his journalists and likely assured that what he said was off the record, described his terror: "Once I was scheduled to make a speech and I spent a week in rehearsing it before the glass and learning it word for word. When I got up to deliver the Oration I could not remember even the first sentence. I am scheduled to speak next Saturday, but I may upset the program to the extent of making somebody else do the speaking. I would much rather build a railroad with all of its trial and tribulations [than give a speech]."[19]

When he made the formal address, he followed his plan of succinctly covering the high and low points of the endeavor but then veered off topic to tell the assembly of dignitaries, "I am not the talker that some of those connected with me in the railroad are. I am better at action. I never did get very far by *talking*."[20] Then, showing his agility at age sixty-six, he jumped down from a flatcar, stripped off his coat, and with great ceremony attempted to drive the final spike into the track. However, he missed the "sweet spot" on the spike, which caused it to awkwardly bend. This illustration of humanity only made the crowd love him all the more on that day. But even this last act gone wrong was symbolic of the fiascos of a railroad that had at last became "possible" after everyone said it was "impossible."

The party atmosphere continued as everyone jumped on board and the train launched its maiden voyage. All along the way, the train was greeted by celebrations at a variety of stops. A touching moment occurred when the train stopped in Tecate, Mexico. Juan Prieto Quemper, a distinguished Mexican magistrate, acting the part of a preacher more than that of a judge, looked straight into John's eyes and said,

> This date . . . will be hailed by the people of this community as a day never to be forgotten; young and old ones will ever think of it as a token of God, because we come nearer to you in a spirit of justice and fairness, and it equally brings you closer to us in a spirit of friendship and hope. . . . You are great, powerful and prosperous; we are passing through a painful evolution of our life as a nation; but we are supremely confident of our future, we have deep faith in our destiny and we firmly believe in better days. If God Almighty made us forever neighbors, let Him make us forever friends.[21]

The day could not have gone better for John, and when the sun went down, he said this day was "the happiest moment of my life."[22] The next brightest day in his life that momentarily overshadowed twelve years of frustration occurred a couple of weeks later, on December 1. More than two thousand San Diegans packed Union Station, spilling out into the streets, to get a glimpse of the first round-trip train returning from its inaugural run to the Imperial Valley. The cheering crowd was surprised to see a "white moustached, blue eyed man at the engine throttle" and discovered it was none other than John D. Spreckels at the helm.[23] As soon as the train glided to a stop, it was garlanded with a multitude of flowers, Hawaiian style, and several warships of the Pacific fleet anchored in San Diego's Bay "thundered a greeting."[24]

Later, when the euphoria had subsided, and John realized that he had spent more than $18 million of his own money (that would be $265 million today), John summed it up nicely for posterity: "It was up to me to bring into San Diego a direct train from the east or go back on my promise. Well, in spite of hell, and it was hell believe me, a direct train from the east slid into our Union Station on December 1, 1919, and San Diego got what I had promised."[25]

30. John declared, "In spite of hell, and it was hell believe me, a direct train from the east slid into our Union Station on December 1, 1919," and it was "the happiest day of my life." Permission granted by Pacific Southwest Railway Museum, Campo, California.

Promoting the Carrizo Gorge and Mexico

John was particularly proud of the engineering feat it had taken to get the trains through the brutal hazard of the Carrizo Gorge.[26] Many engineers had told him it was impossible, but he persevered. His stubborn pride cost $4 million alone for laying track through this granite gorge. He rightfully boasted "we had to bore through 17 of the 21 tunnels through solid granite, which geologists said was the hardest and toughest in the whole North American continent."[27] Nobody could argue with the man when he crisply stated that it was "one of the most formidable places that a railroad was ever built in."[28] One tourist magazine's flowery language about the vistas seen while crossing through the Carrizo Gorge captured the imagination of many: "Across its precipices, its gulfs and crags, and its mountain pinnacles, are spread gorgeous blanket-patterns of color, measured in miles and woven from fluid rocks when the world was made."[29]

Regular passenger service on the train provided captivating views for day-trippers on a run to Yuma. Long-distance passengers could then hop on Espee's "Golden State" to Chicago, where Pullman sleeper cars were available.[30] Espee locomotives, running the brand-new 148-mile winding route between San Diego and El Centro, were heavily promoted in magazines and newspapers across the country.

One month after the SD&A began its passenger service, Prohibition began in earnest. One journalist wondered why anyone would want to ride a train through treacherous Mexico. That is, until he rode the train and gleefully reported that alcohol was legal in Mexico, and one needed only to step into the "buffet car" to enjoy the libations every time the train made its dip below the border. All praise, the reporter stated, should be given to "John D. Spreckels' foresight [in] running the railroad into Mexico."[31]

Continuing Obstacles

It was in the transporting of building materials that the railroad played its most significant role in the development of San Diego during the first two decades of the twentieth century, but it had come at a tremendous financial cost for John and later for his heirs. All in all, though the SD&A proved to be a great engineering achievement as well as a monument to the perseverance of one man who accepted that life and business are unpredictable, the obstacles and difficulties continued long after the twelve years of laying train tracks through seemingly impenetrable terrain—obstacles and difficulties that cost John more and more of his fortune. A short time after completion, landslides collapsed tunnels, and floods swept away bridges and miles of tracks, each calamity requiring an astonishing amount of repair money. Ultimately, the impact of the railroad was modest at best, since the era of highway development was just beginning. Certainly, John had seen this, but his tenacious and stubborn spirit would not allow him to accept defeat.

13

Building Up Broadway

"Sweetening San Diego"

Once John had established his home in Southern California, he detached himself emotionally from the day-to-day operations of the various sugar businesses. Even as their president, he viewed the various sugar ventures as an indifferent investor and left the superintendence of the ventures to others. Even though he and Adolph controlled two-thirds of the Hawaiian sugar plantation interests, they left the lion's share of the work to William G. Irwin, their financial equal partner. Irwin, however, along with others in the sugar companies, grew weary of shouldering all the responsibilities while the Spreckels brothers grew richer from their labors. The following correspondence that Irwin sent to his friend Walter M. Giffard in 1908 reveals John's complete lack of interest in plantation problems in Hawai'i: "John D. [Spreckels] has simply lost all interest in business matters, so far as the Islands are concerned and he seems to have taken up his residence in San Diego, where I trust he may make a better success of it than he has the Island business. I have held business for the firm single-handed for many years past, but there is a limit to what I can do, especially when the firm with which we have been so intimate, fails to do their share of the work."[1] In California, William H. Hannam, managing director of the Spreckels Sugar Company in San Francisco, also grew impatient because "J. D.

Spreckels was spending most of his time, and the company's money, on his interests in San Diego."[2]

Both men were right: John had "lost all interest in business matters" outside of San Diego—but especially in the sugar business, a career path he had been forced into. The Oceanic Steamship Company and the other Spreckels businesses that were still headquartered in San Francisco were managed capably by Adolph and were run by others, but John now focused all his energy in San Diego. He jumped in with whole heart and wallet in order to make his own mark. He had been in his father's shadow for most of his life, and San Diego, in his own words, presented a "big opportunity to do big constructive work on a big scale. . . . So I started in to buy real estate, to erect buildings, to finance enterprise, and to develop our local resources."[3] John had a single-minded goal: to pick up where Alonzo Horton had left off and pour millions of dollars from his outside investments in order to turn San Diego into a metropolis.

The "Father of San Diego," Alonzo E. Horton

"Modern" San Diego's history began in 1867, when fifty-four-year-old Alonzo Erastus Horton arrived from San Francisco and saw potential in the "little old remnants of a Spanish town."[4] He determined to develop a "downtown" near the appealing waterfront and away from the historic Spanish settlement. With $265 ($4,808 in today's money), his life's savings, he purchased 960 acres of cactus and sagebrush four miles south of "Old Town" and named it "Horton's Addition."[5] Horton, a retired furniture shop owner, had apparently found his calling late in life, because he embraced the role of real estate developer with gusto. Before long, he was selling acres for double the amount he had paid. To encourage commercial development, he sold lots cheap, or he gave them away to individuals he deemed would increase business to his "New Town." Horton's enterprise exceeded even his own expectations. One of San Diego's first newspapers, the *Union*, reported on November 21, 1868, that "Mr. Horton is selling from $600 to $1000 worth of lots every day. Restaurants, bakeries, livery stables, furniture stores, blacksmith shops, hotels, doctors' offices, wholesale and retail storerooms, saloons and residences are going up."[6]

By late 1869, hundreds of people had bought Horton's vision and land on the assurance of a railroad "organized under a congressional charter" that would connect San Diego directly to the East.[7] In 1871, the Texas Pacific Railway began to grade the transcontinental line from the Mississippi Valley toward San Diego. Horton delightedly watched his land holdings increase in value—until the financial "Panic of 1873" shut down all talk of a train. Development in San Diego then remained at a standstill for almost a decade, and only 1,500 disappointed but optimistic citizens stayed during the long sleep.[8] The standstill was the point of no return for the aged "Father of San Diego"; he never recouped his fortune (though it became well known that he held no bitterness). It would be up to the "Foster Father of San Diego," as John Spreckels was later called, to expand Horton's vision for a metropolis by the bay.[9] Horton was in the background, watching John taking a path similar to the one he had taken but on an even more spectacular scale, turning dollars into hundreds, then hundreds into thousands, and then thousands into millions.[10]

The "Foster Father of San Diego," John D. Spreckels

At the turn of the twentieth century, San Diego's economy rebounded, mainly due to John's visible infrastructure efforts, notably with transportation and water. The economic clout of the Spreckels name was legendary. As it became known that the scion of the San Francisco Spreckels family was rebuilding San Diego from the ground up, outside investors, particularly venture capitalists in Los Angeles, took notice. Their investments helped boost the economic recovery, generating optimism for future prosperity.

Even though investors saw great potential, most non-westerners had not heard of San Diego. A glance at the 1901 *XX Century Cyclopædia and Atlas* revealed little to say: "San Diego, San Diego co., Cal., pleasantly situated on bay of same name, 15 [miles north] of the Mexican border, is a popular resort for invalids, its climate being perhaps mildest and most equable known."[11]

But John was making sure that the name San Diego would soon be known for something more than as a "resort for invalids." Already he was undisputedly the city's largest landholder and its wealthiest citizen. San Diegans expectantly wondered what he would do with all the real estate he had been continually purchasing. By now, they regarded him as unstoppable in his quest to build up the City of Spreckels.

To create his new downtown, John needed a blank canvas. He wanted to leave the "Wild West" atmosphere of the Stingaree District (today's Gaslamp Quarter), with its vermin-infested brothels, gambling halls, opium dens, and clapboard saloons crammed together. It is well known that Wyatt Earp had come to San Diego around 1886 and helped the city earn the moniker "Sin City West."[12] During every city election campaign in San Diego candidates promised to clean up the Stingaree, but nothing ever happened. John turned his sights elsewhere to create a stately commercial boulevard that would reflect his character and upgrade the city's image. The unexploited D Street would provide the blank canvas he needed. His plan would require reorienting the city's commercial hub from Fifth Avenue, which ran north to south, to D Street, which, like the sun, ran east to west. Preparing to build offices and hotels, he had been acquiring prime commercial properties; in addition to some nearby lots, he and Adolph now owned the entire south side of D Street from Fifth Avenue to the waterfront.

And the waterfront was where the Spreckels coal wharf enterprises had been prospering since 1888. John's new plan made perfect sense to a man who liked order: He could wake up on his island of Coronado, hop on his ferry for a short ride across the bay, and immediately step onto property he owned on the other side. It seemed like a good business plan to keep all his properties in a nice, neat, orderly row of modernity.

With the SD&A in progress and the completion of the Panama Canal in clear sight, there was no doubt in John's mind that these two events would make his money multiply, and, in 1906, he began his transformation of D Street into a grand commercial boulevard, constructing commercial buildings that mirrored Chicago and New York. He also

31. View of the south side of Broadway, ca. 1915, all owned by John. The Spreckels Theatre, prominently lit by the morning sun, was but one of his notable buildings along downtown's thoroughfare. The Spreckels streetcar is seen moving up Broadway (named by John) from the waterfront (passing the Spreckels coal wharf), making it easy for one to take the Spreckels ferry back and forth across the bay to Coronado Island, virtually owned by John Spreckels. Photo reproduced by permission of Library of Congress, Prints and Photographs Division (LC-DIG-det-4a24661).

wanted to change the name of that boulevard where he was shifting all the commercial, office, and hotel space. D Street was not a fitting name for the model thoroughfare he envisioned, and, in 1914, he successfully enticed the city leaders into renaming the street Broadway.

Since John's allegiance had shifted solely to San Diego and he needed capital to build his metropolis, he sold the *San Francisco Call* in 1913 to the man whom his brother had shot twenty-nine years earlier. It was an ironic twist of fate when Michael de Young bought the *Call* and then sold it to William Randolph Hearst, who merged it with the *Evening Post*.[13]

By 1926, John had six major buildings along the thoroughfare: the Union Building, the Spreckels Theatre, the Hotel San Diego, the Golden West Hotel (just off Broadway on Fourth Avenue), the First National Bank Building, and the city's first skyscraper, the John D. Spreckels Building.

The Union Building

John's first office building on the thoroughfare was built on land formerly owned by Alonzo Horton. The collapse of the boom had been disastrous to Horton, and John acquired the land from him in 1901 as an investment for $10,000. In 1906, after deciding that San Diego would be his permanent home, John laid out the plans.[14] San Diego's first reinforced-concrete structure, designed by Harrison Albright, was the Union Building, on D Street (not yet Broadway), which occupied the entire block between Second and Third Avenues. Since it was San Diego's first concrete building, Albright explained to the public that his inspiration had come from a mosque in Lucknow, India, which had been built by filling the bricks with concrete: "Although the building has been standing for 122 years, it is said to show no sign of decay or deterioration."[15] He fully expected the Union Building to become "better with age."[16]

The Union Building was erected to house both the *San Diego Union* and the *San Diego Evening Tribune* newspaper interests in the same way that the Call Building in San Francisco housed the *San Francisco Call.* In direct contrast to that ostentatious San Francisco skyscraper, however, the Union Building was only six stories high. In response to the earthquake and fire he had lived through with the Call Building, John's offices and companies in the Union Building were housed in the first two floors instead of up in a tower. The plans that John had drawn up in 1906 set aside space for a dozen businesses under the Spreckels companies. In addition to the two newspapers that employed 152 people, he needed to provide office space for the managers of other entities of his, including the street railway system, the water supply system, the Coronado Beach Company, the Coronado Railroad Company, the

Coronado Ferry Company, the Coronado Water Company, the Coronado Hotel Company, and the National City and Otay Railroad Company.[17]

John came up with a clever marketing plan. In order to attract attorneys, he strategically built the "Union Law Library" on the fourth floor for $10,000 and provided more than five thousand legal references.[18] As he had predicted, attorneys were pleased to relocate to the Union Building, understanding the clear benefit, both in accessing the resources and in conducting their legal practices alongside other attorneys. In short order, this portion of the street became referred to as "lawyers block" due to the sheer number of legal contracts that were signed in the building.[19]

In 1909, John successfully enticed the Cuyamaca Club, a prestigious social club for San Diego businessmen that had been established in 1887, to relocate to the Union Building, and he devoted the entire swanky sixth floor to them. There the club had offices for private business deals as well as separate rooms for card playing, billiards, reading, lounging, and sleeping. There was even a kitchen and two dining rooms for entertaining. The luxurious furnishings and rich mahogany paneling mimicked San Francisco's Pacific-Union Club. There was also a rooftop garden, a feature John favored in many of his building projects and likely encouraged by architect Albright, who favored meditation retreats.

The building had electric elevators manned by uniformed operators to take occupants to their spacious offices, which were surrounded by luxurious and comfortable amenities. There were also modern toilets on each floor, with separate facilities for women—a rare feature in its time. Also rare for San Diego were three practical conveniences: The building was heated by steam, lit by electricity, and cleaned by a vacuum suction system.[20] Immediately upon its opening in 1908, the Union Building, beautiful inside and out, was *the* building to work in and play out of.

The Spreckels Theatre

There is no building then or now more closely associated with John's spirit than the Spreckels Theatre. He purchased the land where the

32. Interior of the opulent Spreckels Theatre, cutting edge in its era, resistant to earthquake and fire damage, with the ultimate in mechanical equipment for heating and ventilating. Two outstanding features set it apart in its day: It was all open space, with no pillars blocking views, and there were outstanding acoustics. Photo reproduced by permission of Library of Congress, Prints and Photographs Division (HABS CAL, 37-SANDI, 24–5).

Diamond Carriage Company housed their horses and buggies in 1906 from the Security Savings Bank and Trust Company for $10 and "other considerations."[21] Diamond Carriages were the forerunner of outdoor advertising in San Diego. Madam Ida Bailey used the topless carriages to trot her best-looking prostitutes up and down the streets on Sundays. "Decent housewives" were happy to watch John Spreckels spend more than $1 million on that $10 investment.[22]

John told outsiders that he built the theater to boost the economy and employment. To illustrate this, John had Neptune in a chariot, bringing prosperity to San Diego, pictured on the stage's proscenium arch. But insiders knew that this was a labor of love. John regarded San Diego as much more than an economic marketplace. He loved music, and he knew that a public theater would be a valued cultural element in his metropolis. Like all of his buildings, the theater was built out of reinforced concrete, but he took the extra step to protect against fire by placing all the wiring in conduits, which was cutting-edge technology in those days.

John had hired Harrison Albright to construct the venue, but he was very much involved in the details. His sentimentality can be seen in the symbolic touches. For example, it was essential that the theater open in 1912, to correspond with the projected opening of the Panama Canal (which actually did not open until 1914). The theater's original seating capacity was projected to be 1,915, in honor of the approaching 1915 Panama–California Exposition. When construction commenced in 1910, the city's population was only 40,000 residents, so making the case for 1,915 seats was ambitious, but, for John, these emblematic details were important.

The theater had two salient and unique features for its time: It was entirely open-spaced, with no pillars blocking views, and the acoustics were stellar. The stage at the center of the Baroque-designed interior was one of the largest ever constructed. And to fill that stage, John negotiated a unique lease with managers John "Jack" Mason Dodge and Harry Hayward: If there was no net profit during the year, then nothing would be due on the rent. He wanted top-shelf productions. Dodge remembered that John told him to "book every high class road show."[23]

The evening opening of the Spreckels Theatre on August 23, 1912, was the most notable occasion in the city's history up to that time. "Street curbs were lined for blocks with autos and carriages," and astonished people entered a foyer described as "luxuriously fitted with rare Persian rugs and hangings, palms, ferns and the stately Egyptian lotus."[24]

When the sophisticated audiences were in their luxurious seats, described as "a gleaming harmony in old ivory and gold,"[25] the clapping for John D. Spreckels to deliver a speech was deafening. And those just getting to know the tongue-tied millionaire were surprised when the man of the hour came to the stage only after being cajoled, said only a few words acknowledging his gift to the city, and quickly retreated back to his box.[26] For the opening, John, as usual, used his paper to speak for him. For those who felt the theater was too grandiose for small-town San Diego, he told them: "The town is ready for it now, and its growth has been hampered without it. Let's get that fixed in our minds; the Spreckels Theatre is none too big and none too good for San Diego right now!"[27]

A dazzling list of stars from the concert, drama, and variety stages played the Spreckels Theatre during those early years before motion pictures took over. A few of the prominent ones included Will Rogers, Anna Pavlova, Al Jolson, Ina Claire, Enrico Caruso, Lionel Barrymore, Bela Lugosi, Joe E. Brown, Ronald Colman, William Powell, Mary Pickford, and John Barrymore.[28]

And when touring symphonies were in town, John made sure that local schoolchildren were given the cultural opportunity to attend:

> What a happy thought that was of Mr. Spreckels to buy hundreds of tickets to the great symphony concert for the school kids. That's the stuff, Mr. Spreckels! You can't spend money to better purpose than in giving our youngsters just such opportunities to enjoy something finer than the awful "movies" and "jazz" records ground out on machines. Culture becomes the pose of "highbrows" only because the things that make for culture are usually within the reach of the rich alone. Give the people—especially young people—a chance to see and hear the best, and, believe me, sir, they'll eat it up.[29]

At one point, John offered, at no cost to the city, the elegant offices above the Spreckels Theatre for city officials to use as a city hall. Chairman Julius Wangenheim of the planning commission later recalled the offer was rejected because "Spreckels already was too powerful without owning the City Hall."[30] The mayor, furious at the rejection of the princely offer, responded by firing the offending staff member. Regardless, John, offended, would not reinstate his offer. Here is how John later regarded the rejection: "If anybody suspects that my ulterior motive was to make San Diego a one-man town and to make myself the dictator of city hall politics—well, gentlemen, all I can say is: 'Let the imbeciles enjoy their Sun-inspired imbecility.'"[31]

Today, as it did then, the Spreckels Theatre lights up the darkness of Broadway and transforms the night into a glittering space of amusement, thanks to the stalwart guardianship by owner Jacquelyn Mae Littlefield, who cherished it till her death at age ninety-six in 2019. Walking into the opulent theater conveys a true feeling of John's time and place.

The Hotel San Diego: Competing against Buck Grant

If John had to share the limelight with anyone in San Diego, it was with the popular Ulysses Simpson "Buck" Grant Jr., son of former president Ulysses S. Grant. Buck moved to San Diego at the age of forty-one and reinvented himself, dropping politics and law for real estate development.

The two men weren't always on friendly terms. In 1898, when Grant was a candidate for the U.S. Senate, he purportedly asked John and the *San Francisco Call* to publicly support him. He vowed that after he was elected, however, he would serve only a token year and then withdraw, thus allowing John to take his Senate seat. In his published accusation of Grant's duplicity, seeking election but then conspiring not to serve his full term, John described in his own words what happened:

> Grant visited me at my office at 327 Market St., and broached the subject of the election of the United States senator. He said he had a mission to become a senator solely for the owner of the position it would give him. He solicited my support for his candidacy and said he would, if elected, hold the position a year or two, and then resign in my favor. I listened to his kind offer, and replied that I was not seeking the position, did not want it, and would not accept it.[32]

Unlike his father, Buck never completely yielded to the lure of politics, so the fact that he did not ultimately win the seat in 1899 might have been a relief, but it is unknown whether he retained any bitterness against John Spreckels, the new force in San Diego, who in all likelihood cost him the seat with the bad press about his character. But all would be forgiven when the two of them, now representing the conservative Republican Party, needed each other as the city's new "reformers" and "progressives" rose in office.[33]

John's million-dollar Hotel San Diego was only the second luxury hotel on Broadway. The first hotel, Buck Grant's opulent U.S. Grant Hotel, had been completed in 1910 with the needed help of investors as a monument to his father, the former president. It's hard to believe that architect Harrison Albright found time to work on the U.S. Grant, considering how busy John was keeping him on his other projects, including the Hotel San Diego, the third building he had commissioned Albright to erect for him on the south side of Broadway, after the Union Building and the Spreckels Theatre. As with the other two, this structure stopped at six floors and reflected John's taste for stately simplicity, often referred to as the "Chicago Style." Completed in 1914, the hotel became part of a uniform skyline south of Broadway, all of it carefully laid out by John.

Both men had designed their hotels with upscale amenities they knew would appeal to the people of wealth and importance who would be attending the upcoming Panama–California Exposition. John realized that the son of a former U.S. president, with a hotel named after his father, had an advantage in attracting dignitaries for the expo, but he competed hard with his luxurious amenities.

Both of these hotels were a triumph of concrete construction, beautiful inside and out. Virtually across the street from each other, they made quite an impression on the visiting dignitaries throughout the exposition years. Though the Hotel San Diego opened just in time for the exposition, it never achieved as high an occupancy rate as the U.S. Grant during the exposition years. The lavish and historical U.S. Grant Hotel stands today as a somewhat mirror image of the Hotel San Diego.

The Golden West Hotel

San Diego's economic development caused an influx of a substantial number of single working-class men and, as a result, posed a huge housing problem. John, in particular, needed an affordable hotel to house all the workers who were laboring on his many projects. He brainstormed with architect Frank Lloyd Wright over the plans for an inexpensive hotel. After executing a rough architectural rendition, Wright turned the project over to his second-oldest son, nineteen-year-old John Lloyd Wright, who was being mentored by Harrison Albright. Soon after construction started in 1913, young Wright left for Chicago to join his father, but he supervised the project long distance.

The sprawling, three-story-high Golden West Hotel on Fourth Avenue, just south of Broadway, became universally known as the "workingmen's hotel." It stressed function and utility over ornamentation; for example, unlike John's other buildings, it had no stained-glass windows, no columns or cornices on the outside, and not much more than a bed and sink in each eight-by-twelve-foot room.[34] Today's structure retains all the architectural designs and the configurations of its various spaces, and even some of the furniture is authentic to the hotel's beginning.

The First National Bank Building

In 1915, John acquired a majority interest in the stock holdings of two banks: the First National Bank and the American National Bank. The latter was in a serious financial crisis, which was threatening the local economy. Seeing that the situation was "exceedingly precarious," John quietly (at first) paid off more than $400,000 in debt (more than $10 million in today's money) out of his pocket.[35] Then he merged the American National with the First National, which he housed in a ten-story building on Broadway. He was chairman of the board of directors, and his close friend, Frank J. Belcher Jr., was president. In 1922, the bank became a branch of the First National Trust & Savings Bank of San Diego, with John continuing as chairman of the board and Belcher continuing as president. Continuing with the merger, John's granddaughter Harriet married Belcher's son, Frank Garrettson Belcher, in 1930.

A Personal Monument, the John D. Spreckels Building

When he turned seventy in 1923, John decided to build his personal monument. The Florentine Renaissance–inspired two-hundred-foot skyscraper at 625 Broadway would be a departure from his other six-story, quietly understated buildings. Using prominent Los Angeles architects John and Donald Parkinson, John went high and big with the flourishes. To promote excitement for his commercial office building, the John D. Spreckels Building, the brochure boasted the planned features admirably:

> San Diego's newest office building represents exhaustive and most exacting efforts on the part of owner, architect and builder. The building, a modern, steel frame structure with its exterior facing of terra cotta, gives the appearance of a solid granite edifice. The cost of the thirteen-story building, land and equipment will be approximately $3 million, the largest investment ever made in any San Diego office building up to the present time. The balcony will surround the 13th floor, completely overlooking all sections of the city, suburbs, mountains of California and Mexico, San Diego Bay, Coronado, North Island, Point Loma, and beaches on the Pacific Ocean.[36]

The thirteen-story building would be San Diego's first high-rise office building. The bottom floor was designed to accommodate John's new banking acquisitions and the top floor, naturally, to house a businessmen's club. For the floors in between, John desired tenants in the medical and dental professions. Using the same techniques he had used to attract lawyers for the Union Building, he told prospective tenants: "There are 143 offices equipped with x-ray and other electrical outlets and special sanitary and laboratory conveniences for group occupation."[37]

When it was completed in 1927, the John D. Spreckels Building was the tallest in San Diego—until three years later, when the El Cortez Hotel surpassed it. Today, the historically designated building is dwarfed among the twenty-first-century glass buildings.

Boss Spreckels

At the height of building his metropolis, in the second decade of the twentieth century, John was pulled in many different directions. He held the title of president of many companies: the Western Sugar Refinery Company of San Francisco, the Spreckels Beet Sugar Company at Salinas, the Oceanic Steamship Company, the J. D. Spreckels & Brothers Company of San Francisco, the Spreckels Brothers Commercial Companies of San Diego, the Pajaro Valley Consolidated Railroad Company, the San Diego Electric Railway Company, the San Diego & Southeastern Railway Company, the San Diego & Arizona Railroad Company, the San Diego Light & Fuel Company, various of John's companies listed earlier that were housed in the Union Building, and many more. In short, there were thousands of people who called him "boss."

Running multiple companies came with financial rewards but also a lot of risks. To ameliorate the risks, he surrounded himself with loyal managers and responsible employees. He was impatient with stupidity in all forms and chose his employees for their intellect. His philosophy for hiring was simple: He believed in matching talent to task, stating, "I believe that every man should work according to his ability and opportunity."[38]

Once employees had the job, they knew they had a hands-on boss who led by example, and that example was typified by hard work, day in and day out. Long hours were the norm for him and his employees alike—so much so that it was noteworthy when he was not the first at his desk: "I have worked all my life, worked hard, and hope to until my time comes. I worked from four o'clock in the morning until seven at night for several years. I know what manual labor means."[39] His tenacity was legend, his working style systematic and structured. He despised waste and worshipped efficiency. In an article for *Hearst's Magazine*, journalist Erastus Brainerd asked John to share his philosophy of life: "The little crinkles came in the corners of [Mr. Spreckels's] humorous eyes and then went away. The steel jaw set. The fighting head thrust forward. His words jumped like bullets from a Maxim. 'I believe God put man on earth to work. I do not believe He meant man to be a drone. I believe He has no use for drones.'"[40]

When John was at the office, work was his center of attention; he was goal-oriented. If employees digressed from the business at hand, he could become impatient. He may well have felt that he lost time if he engaged in small talk, as noted by one worker: "He was a good-hearted fellow in his own way. But he was a gruff fellow to approach because he was very short in speech, he wouldn't give you too many words. When you went in there, it was 'Yes' and 'No' and 'Goodbye' and that was it."[41]

John had an insatiable thirst for information on his projects and asked blunt questions that were impossible to evade. Each of his managers understood that he expected up-to-date information immediately upon request, so all of them made sure to have it at all times. His employees were impressed at how quickly he could reduce their multitude of facts to the nub.

Those who knew John as an uncompromising employer would have had trouble thinking of him as "shy," but that characteristic may actually explain much about him: his refusal to engage in small talk, his sparse words when speaking with or listening to employees, and his tight focus on his work. He seems to have been very much an introvert. His dogged nature in business was arguably an exception, but it does fit with his belief in hard work and his emphasis on the same. He did not back down often, but then, he was more likely to face his rivals with the written word than with the spoken one. He certainly wasn't shy on paper—he always felt he was a better writer than speaker—but when it came to blunt verbal confrontations outside his companies, he preferred to let his lawyers speak for him.

Still, Spreckels company insiders knew that their boss was painfully shy. Anderson Borthwick, a banking employee, recalled a reception at the Hotel San Diego that John gave for all Spreckels employees. At the appropriate time, John climbed up to the podium and stood silently. After "what seemed like an eternity" to spectators, Claus Jr. rescued his father by going up on the stage, taking his father's written speech, and reading it to the assembled employees. Borthwick asked his superior the next day, "Was Mr. Spreckels sick?" He remembered his superior's exact words: "No, your brain starts growing from the day you are born, but it stops the minute you get up before an audience." Borthwick recalled, "He couldn't open his mouth in the presence of an audience, he was just tongue-tied."[42]

If John couldn't even speak to his paid employees, giving a speech to an audience of strangers was even more terrifying. The San Diego Advertising Club was founded to help promote the upcoming Panama–California Exposition and the city as a whole. President Ed Davidson conducted a one-on-one interview with San Diego's empire builder. Pleased with the interview and finding John "very fluent" and a great conversationalist, Davidson asked John to present at a club meeting and publicly share "reminisces." Davidson was stunned at John's immediate refusal and recalled that he "had that millionaire panic stricken, and there's no two ways about it. If I ever go to him again to try to sell him anything I'll ask him to make a speech somewhere and close the sale before he comes to."[43]

Among the things John prized most were family and friendship, and loyalty to both. This may explain why so many of his employees were relatives, either on his side or Lillian's. Many of his in-laws, nephews, and nieces worked in his California enterprises. Having family around helped buffer the hate he received from many different sources.

The Price of Loyalty

There was nobody more loyal to the boss than William Clayton, John's right-hand man in every San Diego business venture. Because John was pulled in every direction up and down the West Coast, it was Clayton that often stepped in for the boss. Clayton's efficiency, along with his polite and personable British deportment, was well received inside and outside the Spreckels companies. He was highly respected by Spreckels employees because he was "hands on." Clayton's daughter, Emily, remembered that her father spent "the last hour of every day visiting the men" throughout the Spreckels companies in the Union Building, making sure they knew they were valued.[44] He was the very face of the Spreckels Companies in San Diego, and employees and managers knew he spoke for the boss at all times.

With that level of responsibility, he was guilty by association one afternoon in March of 1917, and it almost cost him his life. As Clayton left work from the Union Building, he was shot in the abdomen by

Lorenzo Bellomo, a disgruntled former employee who had been crippled in a streetcar accident. Despite the fact that the man was found at fault for jumping from the car without signaling the conductor, the Spreckels Company had paid all the medical bills. Later, Bellomo was given a position in the street railway company, but it did not last long due to his poor job performance. Bellomo was bitter at his misfortune, and after shouting, "He is rich and I am poor!" he shot Clayton twice, once in the abdomen and once in the back.[45] Despite the seriousness of the injuries, Clayton miraculously pulled through the surgeries due to his "strong constitution and splendid physique."[46] John's loyalty to Clayton increased exponentially after this shooting.

Not a Philanthropist

During John's lifetime, many people resented him. In building his metropolis, he was determined to get his way, and critics such as Edward Scripps constantly accused him of building up San Diego just so he could prosper. That may have been at least partly true, but as John was well aware as a yachtsman, a rising tide lifts all boats. Some of his critics felt he did too much (apparently threatening the city's independence), while others felt he should have done *more*, since he was so wealthy. Andrew Carnegie was very popular during this era for advocating that multimillionaires such as John Spreckels should be as aggressive as possible in their pursuit of wealth and then give it back through private philanthropy. Carnegie was known for his mantra, "A man who dies rich dies disgraced."

Even though Andrew Carnegie is known today for being a pioneer of philanthropy, he was disliked in his community. Working conditions in the steel magnate's mills were appalling. Employees worked in a harsh environment even by tough nineteenth-century standards that compromised their health. So, when Carnegie chose to give his profits away, rather than raising his impoverished workers' pay, labor leaders and clergymen of the day condemned him. Carnegie argued that by keeping profits high, he could serve society with such charitable acts as funding libraries across the nation. During the infamous Homestead

Steel Strike of 1892, nearly four thousand workers snarled at that logic, asking, "What good is a book to a man who works 12 hours a day, six days a week?"[47] Carnegie is on record for replying, "If I had raised your wages, you would have spent that money by buying a better cut of meat or more drink for your dinner. But what you needed, though you didn't know it, was my libraries and concert halls. And that's what I'm giving to you."[48]

Like the striking steel workers, San Diego's philanthropist Ellen Browning Scripps wryly noted that Carnegie was a hypocrite: "He has amassed $20,000,000. The question of benefitting mankind should have been considered and solved at a time and in a way that should have prevented his becoming a millionaire."[49]

John was blunt about Carnegie's so-called philosophy of "Carnegie-ism," and even though he valued music and books, the area of Carnegie's charities, he set the record straight: "I am not a philanthropist, and do not believe in Carnegieism."[50] He also set himself apart by making it known that his kind of philanthropy, which he curiously likened to a hobby, would benefit his hometown alone. "Carnegie spends money on libraries and Rockefeller in other directions. My particular hobby is to do what I can for San Diego and Coronado."[51]

In the profile for *Hearst's Magazine*, journalist Brainerd captured "Boss" Spreckels's views and philosophies on labor, which were contrary to those of Andrew Carnegie: "I do not believe in indiscriminate charity. We have too much of it, and it tends to pauperize men and make drones out of them. I believe the best charity you can give a man is work, and [to] pay him so well that he is satisfied. I believe that the man who works is entitled to be comfortable, and I try to make everybody who works for me feel so. I may be mistaken in my methods, but I do the best I know how."[52]

Unlike Carnegie, John preferred to give without fanfare and where it was personal. As good friend and former state senator Martin Luther Ward stated, "No one knows" how much exactly, "for Mr. Spreckels would never tell the extent of his charities" but "he paid out money with a lavish hand."[53] Ted Williams, professional baseball player and manager who was inducted into the Hall of Fame, often recalled his early years of poverty in North Park, a suburb of San Diego. The little house at 4121 Utah Street, where he grew up, had a mortgage of only $4,000, but it was far too much for his mother, May Williams, who was raising both him, six years old at the time, and a brother. May had earned an angelic reputation throughout San Diego and Tijuana by helping the impoverished. She was an officer in the Salvation Army, raising charitable contributions on the streets near John's offices on Broadway, with little Ted following behind. Though his mother's activities, which had her dressed in full uniform and accompanied by drumbeats, embarrassed young Ted, they earned admiration from John. In May 1924, when John was made aware of the mother's poverty, he quietly paid off the note on her house.[54] Like many of his philanthropic gestures, this one was never broadcast.

14

John and the Wobblies

Battle-Ready Union Workers

The Industrial Workers of the World—aka the IWW, or the Wobblies—was founded in Chicago at the turn of the twentieth century. The Wobblies aimed at merging industry workers into "One Big Union." The concept behind the IWW was revolutionary, and its members during John's time were, in many respects, revolutionaries themselves—militant, determined, and unyielding. The Wobblies motto, "Abolition of the Wages System" (borrowed from Karl Marx[1]), was reflected in one pamphlet that read, "The worker on the job shall tell the boss when and where he shall work, how long and for what wages and under what conditions."[2] Their opposition to capitalism, their ready use of strikes, and their provocative street-corner organizing and oratory made the Wobblies both hated and feared by such employers as John Spreckels, who was vehemently antiunion.

In 1909, the IWW received nationwide notoriety for leading a strike of six thousand workers against an affiliate of the U.S. Steel Company. They defied the Pennsylvania state troopers and pledged to take a trooper's life for every striking worker killed. In one gun battle, four strikers and three troopers died. In the end, the strikers won the fight.[3] In addition to strikes, the IWW employed boycotts, slowdowns, and other forms of direct action to achieve their ends, including sabotage. Tactics included shipping materials to the wrong destination, damaging machines, and alienating businesses' customers. Years earlier, the Spreckels family had experienced similar tactics at their Pennsylvania sugar refinery when saboteurs—in this case, agents of the rival Sugar Trust rather than militant workers—sought to destroy their profits by damaging their machines.

John was no stranger to strikers. In 1877, a financial depression had hit the country hard, causing San Franciscans to view the influx of cheap Chinese laborers as unwelcome competition for a scarcity of jobs. Socialists, numbering in the thousands, voiced their anti-Chinese sentiments on the infamous "sand lots" in front of city hall and started a two-day riot in the city's Chinatown.[4] John recalled that Dennis Kearny, a "fiery demagogue," organized a mob to "run down and butcher luckless Chinese, shoot up the town, burn, rob, murder and raise hell generally."[5] But San Francisco's vigilantes had been battle-ready against such lawlessness since they had formed in 1856 during the wild Gold Rush era. John, twenty-four in 1877, joined the "pick-handle brigade" of vigilantes to protect the Chinese and quell the rioting. Later in his life, John made a big deal of his vigilante involvement, boasting that he had organized his own subgroup of vigilantes, rejecting "pick-handles" for "bullets." He told his friend and authorized biographer Austin Adams that he "mobilized a hundred of his own husky employees, issued rifles to them and personally drilled them every night in the seclusion in the [sugar] refinery yard."[6] It is unknown if any murders took place, but there is no doubt that John welcomed vigilante justice.

Another example involved John's steamship business. Working below decks in John's Oceanic Steamship Company vessels were skilled "stokers," or "firemen," who shoveled coal from the bunkers and maintained the fires in the boiler rooms. John experienced his first strike in June 1886, when the Marine Firemen's Union instructed his employees to riot over a dispute on the number of stokers required on an ocean crossing. Likely anticipating the event, John and his brother Adolph were on board the steamer in Sydney, Australia, when the firemen engaged in mutiny, hoping to strand the ship. Seeing an opportunity, "Chinese stokers" were standing by, and John hired them on the spot to replace his seamen. When the mutinous firemen threatened violence against the ship and her passengers if they left the harbor with the Chinese scabs aboard, John took matters into his own hands. He "stationed armed members of the crew at the portholes; loaded the ship's gun with boiler-punchings and trained it upon the entrance to the pier."[7] John had refused to negotiate with the firemen or arbitrate their requests for lighter workloads; in the end, his fortitude won, and the strikers who were not fired went back to work. He won admiration among other shipping owners for his strong stance. Ensuring further success against strikers, he was instrumental in creating the Ship Owners' Protective Association, which required all seamen to be vetted by a central shipping office to ensure that no active unionists would be hired.[8]

One more example involved John's newspapers. "There was a stereotyper's strike at the *Call* once," John recalled, "and though I had never cast a plate in my life, I took off my shirt and cast all the stereotype plates to print the paper on for a whole week."[9] The name John D. Spreckels became known throughout labor union circles as a strong anti-union contender.

By 1901, however, John became more willing to negotiate after an offshore union strike had cost his company a net loss of $200,000. In 1902, four hundred workers went on strike at the Western Sugar Refinery after John allegedly fired dozens of employees who had become secret union members. After publicly denying any policy of anti-union discrimination, he settled the dispute by reinstating fired workers, increasing their wages, and promising to be amicable at the union bargaining table.[10]

But John had had his fill of union tactics, and he despised the Wobblies, composed mainly of unskilled migrant workers. Press reports of IWW activity infuriated John. For example, in Montana, a lumber and mining region, hundreds arrived by boxcar after some strikers had been prevented from speaking due to an anti-speech ordinance. Strikers were arrested one after another until they clogged the jails and the courts, ultimately forcing a repeal of the ordinance.[11] Their energy, dogged persistence, and ability to mobilize thousands in one place at one time made the Wobblies a formidable nationwide opponent.

John and Scripps Battling It Out in Their Newspapers

The emboldened IWW began moving farther west toward Spreckels territory. The political atmosphere in California became increasingly reactionary after James and John McNamara, members of the International Association of Bridge and Structural Iron Workers, dynamited the Los Angeles Times Building on October 1, 1910. The blast killed twenty-one newspaper employees and injured many more. When the McNamara brothers went on trial for the bombing, which was described as "the crime of the century," they pled not guilty and gained the support of the American Federation of Labor (AFL) and John's antagonist, the influential and wealthy Edward Scripps, publisher of the *San Diego Sun.*[12]

Using the *Sun* as a platform, Scripps asked his working-class readers to question whether the bombing was merely "revolutionary warfare between the classes." He wrote, "Must James McNamara, who set the explosive, be condemned as a murderer? Or could he be considered a martyr or patriot?" He asked whether "the real disturbers of the peace" were the "very selfish and very few who oppressively and unfairly take to themselves the greater share and far too great a share of the joint product of labor and capital and management."[13]

Meanwhile, both of John's papers, the *San Diego Union* and the *San Diego Evening Tribune*, condemned the McNamaras as union thugs and criminals and put those who supported them, such as Scripps, in the same category. John's feelings about the *Sun* and its publisher were clear: "[The *Sun*] is a scurrilous, unscrupulous, and hypocritical newspaper, whose life depends upon stirring up discontent, arousing suspicion, and pandering to the envy and jealousy of the man in the street. . . . [It] is one of a numerous string of similar sheets owned by a multi-millionaire who has publically [*sic*] admitted that he made his millions by hounding other millionaires and by posing as the champion of the poor, down-trodden working man!"[14]

San Diego, with a population around fifty thousand, was going through a period of growth as the economy began to stabilize and mature. From 1910 to 1915, the city experienced widespread development and planning in anticipation of the Panama–California Exposition, with which John was actively involved. The exposition would celebrate the opening of the Panama Canal as well as tout San Diego as the first port of call in the United States for ships traveling northward after passing westward through the canal. New roads and infrastructure were being built all over the city. With so much construction going on, builders feared that the rise of the labor force threatened those paying its salaries.

In May 1911, the state legislature gave San Diego the right to control its own harbor. And in November, a bond issue passed for dredging the channel and building an eight-hundred-foot-long pier. The city's frenzied pace of growth drew workers from all over the country. In particular, it drew the attention of the Wobblies.

By the turn of the century, John owned the city's utilities, its ferry system, two of its three newspapers, its short-haul lines (local railroad tracks used for hauling), most of downtown and the waterfront, and a controlling interest in the Southern California Mountain Water Company. In a word, John D. Spreckels reigned, and he knew he was a big target for the Wobblies.

John hoped he could use his enormous influence to keep the threats of organized labor out of his city by turning the citizens against the workers before they arrived. He used his newspapers as his weapon, and his editorials began to curb public support for the Wobblies.

The Wobblies and Mexican Revolutionaries

John also had business interests in Mexico to worry about. His San Diego & Arizona Railway (SD&A), being built to extend to Yuma, Arizona, went through a part of Baja California. The *San Diego Union* ran long articles on the need to protect American investments in Mexico. This was triggered by the activities of Mexican revolutionaries adjacent to San Diego's borders who sought to overturn Mexico's existing social order, seize control of the banks, and redistribute land and factories to the workers. In 1911, hundreds of Wobblies joined the revolutionaries and supported their call to "take the land." On May 8 of that year, they began cutting telegraph wires along John's railroad track that led into Tijuana. On May 19, the IWW raided a construction camp and took over a train, although the conductor was able to regain control and return to San Diego. Back in San Diego, John vowed he would rather lose everything than have one of his employees harmed.[15] The revolutionaries and the Wobblies held Tijuana for over a month before falling to Mexican federal forces and surrendering to the U.S. Army.

In the summer of 1911, a group of revolutionaries who had been captured at the Mexican border were released into San Diego. They quickly joined labor unionists, socialists, street speakers, and working-class minorities. Their speeches could be heard daily in San Diego's commercial center, where they congregated near John's Union Building. The IWW began to organize workers, such as those John employed on both sides of the border who were not already protected by the AFL, and they soon began to unite those who worked for the city's streetcar franchise, which John owned. There were only fifty members in the IWW's Local 13, but John viewed the Wobblies' effort to go after his employees as a profound threat to the symbolic order of his budding empire.

Fighting over Freedom of Speech

In November 1911, Harrison Gray Otis, the owner of the *Los Angeles Times*, urged San Diego businessmen to fight unionism by restraining free speech, as Los Angeles had done through restrictive city ordinances. John, present at that meeting, was aligned.

On January 8, 1912, the San Diego City Council passed Ordinance 4623, banning street speaking in a forty-nine-block area encompassing the commercial district. The ordinance was purportedly to expedite street traffic, but the IWW knew the real issue underlying it: to stop them from recruiting workers. Several hundred Wobblies flooded San Diego, openly challenging the ordinance by speaking from soapboxes and car hoods. Police arrested scores of IWW members testing the new law, and news of these arrests drew hundreds more Wobblies to San Diego to take turns speaking at the banned corner of Fifth and E before they were hauled away.

Scripps's *Sun* opposed the direct action and predicted that "this ordinance will start a fight that will last for a long time and will be bitter all the time."[16] Though many San Diegans shared neither the

Sun's overall views nor the IWW's aims, they supported the fight for free speech because they felt that if the Wobblies' rights could be taken away, *everyone's* rights were at risk. It seemed as if every San Diegan was forced to take an ethical and moral stance on the issue of free speech in the early months of 1912.

The freedom-of-speech conversation among San Diegans changed drastically, however, when Vincent St. John, general secretary of the IWW, sent San Diego's mayor James E. Wadham a letter from Chicago with the following threat: "This fight will be continued until free speech is established in San Diego, if it takes 20,000 members and 20 years."[17] When the word got out, reactionary vigilante groups quickly formed, taking the threat as a challenge: They sought out protesters, attacked them with knives and clubs, forced them to kiss the flag and sing "The Star-Spangled Banner," and then drove them to the edge of the city.[18]

The vigilantes were backed by so many of San Diego's prominent citizens, in addition to John, that the police looked the other way. In effect, the vigilantes had become an unofficial arm of the city's power structure. When John later told a group of fellow businessmen, "I defy any man to point to any instance of my ever having tried to influence any member of the city government against the best interest of the city, or to my ever having tried to circumvent or evade the law in any way,"[19] some may have looked at their feet, remembering his coerciveness with the city council in 1912 in getting Ordinance 4623 passed as well as his support of vigilante violence generally. They might also have recalled the warning to the Wobblies in John's *San Diego Union*: "And this is what these agitators (all of them) may expect from now on."[20]

The free-speech protests continued. On March 4, 1912, John's *Evening Tribune* published an editorial about the IWW, declaring that "hanging is none too good for them and they would be much better dead; for they are absolutely useless in the human economy; they are the waste material of creation and should be drained off into the sewer of oblivion there to rot in cold oblivion like any other excrement."[21]

One month later, 141 Wobblies hopped a freight train from Los Angeles to San Diego on their way to join a series of free-speech protests.

At one o'clock in the morning, the train slowed to a stop. Some four hundred angry vigilantes armed with rifles, pistols, and clubs met the Wobblies. Albert Tucker, one of the Wobblies, described what happened next:

> We were ordered to unload and we refused. Then they closed in around the flat car which we were on and began clubbing and knocking and pulling men off by their heels, so inside of a half hour they had us all off the train and then bruised and bleeding we were lined up and marched into [a] cattle corral. . . . They searched us several times, now and then picking out a man they thought was a leader and giving him an extra beating. Several men were carried out unconscious.[22]

Sympathy began to sway John's way when six men, known IWW members, were arrested on August 22, 1912, before they could carry out their plan to dynamite the Spreckels Theatre during an opening-night performance the following night.[23] The resulting arrests, beatings, and other violence subsided in the fall of 1912, and the movement gradually died a natural death. Afterward, John commented, "I know the I.W.W. people do not like me. I would not give much for a man who did not have some enemies. But I do not mean to be unjust to anybody. If I am I want to remedy it if I can. My greatest pleasure is in affording the opportunity to work to as many people as I am able to supply with it. I have only tried to help San Diego help itself."[24]

John hated the union's tactics, and he believed he had to defeat them—quickly, unambiguously, and completely—no matter what the cost. He used his newspapers to sway public opinion on many issues, but this time, many, including feminist Ellen Browning Scripps, a bystander, believed that he had gone overboard. She publicly stated: "I think women would have managed the Industrial Workers of the World better, and less to the discredit of the city."[25] The actions of John Spreckels, the role of the *San Diego Union*, and the events of 1912 are rehashed today as topics surrounding the constitutional rights of freedom of speech, the press, and public assembly.

15

Gifting the Panama–California Exposition and the Zoo

Showcasing San Diego

For hundreds of years, world travelers had dreamed of building a canal that would cut through Panama to shorten the long, arduous, and harrowing journey around South America's Cape Horn to travel from the Atlantic Ocean to the Pacific. As a child, John traversed the treacherous Isthmus of Panama through rivers, jungles, and formidable mountains to avoid that voyage. He knew firsthand the engineering challenges that had been faced during the thirty years it took to create a water path so that ships could shave months off their journeys. As a mariner, John could not wait to remake the journey on his yacht *Venetia* through the yet-to-be-completed Panama Canal.

As the historic canal neared completion, John was among the San Diego city leaders who recognized how crucial it was to showcase San Diego as the first American port of call for ships traveling north from the canal. A world's fair, a staple of American entertainment since the middle of the preceding century, could display the city's enthusiasm and confidence for being a major player in global trade. If the city were successful in convincing the world of its importance, there would be new revenue streams for local businesses, and investments within the city would be encouraged. As John bluntly and unapologetically later said, "If San Diego did not grow, my big investments would never pay."[1]

Vice-President Spreckels of the Board of Directors

The president of the San Diego Chamber of Commerce, banker Gilbert "G." Aubrey Davidson appointed a committee in the summer of 1909 to explore the viability of an exposition to open in 1915 to celebrate the opening of the Panama Canal. When the chamber voted in favor of forming the Panama–California Exposition Company, it was undoubtedly assured of success because two of San Diego's most influential men agreed to serve on the board of directors: John Spreckels and Ulysses "Buck" Simpson Grant Jr., whom John had contended with both in California politics and during a hotel rivalry.

John was appointed vice-president of the board, and the chairmanship went to Grant. The influential David "Charlie" Collier was given the title of director general. Collier, an immaculate dresser, always with a Windsor tie and five-gallon black hat, looked the part. Many of the other directors on the board were men on the Spreckels payroll or close friends of John's. Both John and Grant each pledged to sell $1 million in exposition stock. In fact, to the committee's relief, John personally pledged an impressive up-front purchase of $100,000 of stock.[2] That huge amount fired the chamber into action, and the promotion began in earnest.

With the advent of the automobile came a pressing need for road improvements. San Diego's roads had plenty of hazards, and the papers were replete with stories of the tragic results of cars and horses using the same roads. The city, now flush with bond money, desired influential road commissioners to get the project moving in time for the exposition. Who would be better as commissioners than the wealthiest—and, therefore, the most powerful—men in town: John Spreckels, Edward Scripps, and Albert Spalding. Ellen Browning Scripps, half-sister of Edward Scripps, humorously called the three rich men the "Triune S's—Scripps, Spreckels, and Spalding."[3] That two of the triune, John and Scripps, were placed on the same committee ensured that it would not be successful. Despite the fact that John had stated in a recent published interview that he sought amends with those who had crossed him, his actions told a different tale when he stormed off the committee: "I will not again sit on the highway commission or any commission with Mr. Scripps who is inimical to my interests and to the best interests of the city."[4] From then on, Scripps was never appointed to any committee that had anything to do with planning the exposition.

Silver Gate versus Golden Gate

In January 1910, James McNab, president of the San Francisco Chamber of Commerce and one of the planners of the Panama–Pacific International Exposition to be held in San Francisco in February 1915, urged San Diego, known informally as the Silver Gate, to abandon its competing exposition plans.[5] Evidently, McNab was unaware of the fortitude of San Diego's exposition committee. *Sunset* magazine was puzzled by the announcement of two competing world's fairs in California: "Why can't the big San Francisco Exposition be made to include all that San Diego may wish to mark?"[6]

Indeed, others wondered the same thing; in the early planning stages for San Diego's Panama–California Exposition, there was that fierce competition to consider. San Francisco's own world's fair had a similar purpose: to celebrate the completion of the Panama Canal. President William H. Taft implored the U.S. Congress to financially back the San Francisco expo, primarily to support a city that had been through so much devastation following the earthquake and fires of 1906. San Franciscans wanted to prove to the world that their city still existed, that it was indeed open for business and thriving.

But San Diego had something to prove too. John Spreckels himself would ensure that San Diego, with one-tenth of San Francisco's population and with less money and no federal blessing, would create an exposition to rival—if not exceed—that of San Francisco. Not having the federal government's support only empowered John and the committee to push ahead and take control of all aspects of the expo without any of the federal parameters that came with government money. Instead of a world's fair in the strictest sense, they would compete against San Francisco's more formal and traditional fair with a more "cultural and regional" celebration of similar proportions.[7] Those in San Francisco who knew the Spreckels name must have known that nobody carrying that name would back down from anything he or she ever started.

City Park to Balboa Park

The logical location for the Panama–California Exposition was San Diego's City Park, but its dreary, uninspiring name would have to be changed.

San Diegans had long lamented their lack of a proper public recreational park. John's Mission Cliff Gardens had been serving the public admirably, but it was only five acres. The larger City Park had never really served the public as a viable recreational option; its hilly, undeveloped grounds at one time or another had held a dump and a dog pound as well as a home for Kumeyaay Indians, as Ellen Browning Scripps observed when she toured the "Indian encampment" in 1890.[8]

Now City Park would serve as the site for the expo, but a better name was needed. The names Cabrillo Park and Canyado (little canyon) Park had been suggested in 1908, but nothing came of it.[9] In 1910, the park commissioners chose the name Balboa Park. It seemed appropriate, as Vasco Núñez de Balboa had been the first European in the New World to see the Pacific Ocean in 1513, after crossing the Isthmus of Panama, and now the new canal would enable ships to cross it as well.

John versus Olmsted Brothers

By the end of 1910, people were impressed when they learned that the nationally acclaimed landscape architect John Charles Olmsted, representing the Olmsted Brothers firm of Boston, had been contracted as lead landscaper for both San Diego's exposition and the 1,400-acre Balboa Park, which would outlive the expo.[10] The Olmsteds had been a strong advocate throughout the late nineteenth century for more localized green areas in developing cities. Their focus right from the beginning was to keep the project area in San Diego as natural as possible.[11] In January 1911, the renowned New York architect Bertram Grosvenor Goodhue joined Olmsted Brothers as the consulting architect.

His assistant was San Diegan architect Irving J. Gill. The last to join the team was Frank P. Allen, a veteran exposition construction engineer from Seattle.

With these four experts on the job, nobody could have predicted the discord that almost immediately happened. Allen instantly rejected the Olmsted Brothers' preliminary sketch for the exposition. He was dissatisfied with the projected hilly terrain they were expected to build upon, and Goodhue soon concurred.[12] They proposed instead a central location for easy access to the construction site. John also concurred—but for a different reason. He had always stipulated that the fair buildings needed to be centrally located for the streetcar line he was going to build. The directors saw the wisdom in Goodhue's change of plans, but Olmsted Brothers would not reconsider any alteration to their vision, insisting that buildings were unnatural intrusions into nature and should blend harmoniously with the landscapes, not lord over them. Goodhue didn't seem to mind that John, a major funder of the exposition, was visibly and vocally upset over the Olmsted Brothers' refusal to reorient the buildings.

John as well as Director General Collier also opposed the Olmsted Brothers' romantic Greek theme, which they felt had been overdone in other expositions. They had already decided on an "Indian, mission, and pueblo" theme, which Olmsted Brothers refused to consider. In June 1911, John and his supporters resigned from the board, suspending their participation until the Olmsted Brothers firm would be willing to see things their way. The firm asked the chamber, who had hired it, to support its artistic judgment, but any appeal would fail because Scripps and others knew that "the Chamber of Commerce is recognized as being a body packed and controlled by Spreckels."[13]

On September 2, 1911, the Olmsted Brothers firm formally submitted its resignation to Julius Wangenheim, who was president of the board of park commissioners: "We regret that our professional responsibility as park designers will not permit us to assist in ruining Balboa Park. We tender herewith therefore our resignation."[14] Nobody was happier when the Olmsted Brothers firm was off the project than John, who had already begun building two hotels and investing in an electric streetcar line to support the exposition.

Goodhue in Charge

John wanted to retain Goodhue, who agreed with him that Greek architectural styles did not correlate with the beauty and past of the San Diego region. With this change of plans, Gill stepped down as assistant architect and was replaced by an upcoming young architect, Carleton Winslow, from Goodhue's firm in New York.

As both historian and architect, Goodhue wanted California's early history perpetuated long after the fair with an opulent Spanish Baroque style, another factor making Balboa Park an appropriate name. John realized in a very personal and profitable way why the Panama–California Exposition should utilize a romantic Spanish atmosphere. The love story of Alessandro and Ramona in Helen Hunt Jackson's novel *Ramona* saturated regional boosterism at the turn of the century, which was exactly why John had promulgated the "Ramona's Marriage Place" myth and used that name for the abandoned Casa de Estudillo in Old Town at the end of his streetcar line. The *San Diego Union* offered many articles on Jackson's fictional Ramona, behaving as if she were real. Ramona's Marriage Place proved to be a big success before, during, and after the exposition.

John used the *Union* to take one last dig at Olmsted Brothers by reporting that the exposition "might have erected buildings of Greek or Roman types" (exactly the predictable choice that Olmsted had proposed), "which have appeared at all world's fairs of the past," but this fair instead chose to combine the sentimentality of Spanish-themed literature with a vibrant Spanish Colonial Revival architectural theme.[15]

Goodhue's new plans allowed access to the expo grounds from what was to become Park Boulevard on the east, thus making it possible to build the electric railway desired by John's companies along the right of way. This railway was to consist of a unique fleet of electric streetcars, built in St. Louis, to transport the multitudes of the soon-to-be-infatuated tourists to the romantic Spanish expo city in Balboa Park.

When Europe went to war in 1914, the world's fair plans in both California cities were interrupted. Thirty-seven countries pulled their San Diego exhibitions out "overnight." John and the other board members had to decide whether to "cancel or go ahead."[16] One of John's former employees, Anderson Borthwick, recalled that more money was required to continue. Based on the circumstances, no bank in San Diego would lend sufficient working capital. So, John arranged and endorsed a loan of $250,000 to the exposition from the Continental Illinois Bank. Frank J. Belcher Jr., president of First National Bank, came back from Chicago with the money in hand, and it was full steam ahead.[17]

It's a Family Thing: The World's Largest Outdoor Pipe Organ!

John had considered placing an outdoor pipe organ at Mission Cliff Gardens, his private property, and it's not clear when he decided to relocate it to public land, in Balboa Park. Even though the world's fair exposition was to be temporary, he intended to leave the organ as a permanent gift to the city of San Diego.

In this John was recapitulating how his father had gifted the Spreckels Temple of Music, or the "band shell," to San Francisco's Golden Gate Park. No doubt John and his family were among the thousands in attendance when that gorgeous temple was dedicated during the summer of 1900, and heard orator W. H. L. Barnes praise the structure.

Claus Spreckels had offered the beautiful outdoor concert hall to San Francisco in gratitude for the support he had received, as an immigrant, when building his sugar empire. It was therefore natural for John to leave his legacy in San Diego in the form of a musical structure designed by architect Harrison Albright; the prototype had already been established by his father. John loved the organ and believed, as Mozart had when he wrote in 1777, "The organ is in my eyes and ears the king of all instruments."[18] John planned on surpassing his father's massive structure by embedding within Balboa Park's pavilion the world's largest pipe organ.

This colossal instrument instantly appealed to San Diegans. In the early years of the twentieth century, music was not readily accessible.

Radio was in its infancy, and Victrolas had to be hand-cranked and could produce only a tinny sound. To hear a full orchestra play symphonic music was a rare privilege for the common man. Such cultural elites as Andrew Carnegie felt it was their duty to provide "monster organs" to be placed inside municipal auditoriums so that everyone could afford an orchestral concert in which a single musician passably imitated an entire orchestra.

Carnegie, like many other music-loving magnates, engaged private organists to play on their pipe organs for them in their mansions, but nobody had to be hired to play on John's home organ. He had become quite accomplished throughout the years, keeping pace with his old friend, the renowned organist Humphrey John Stewart, whom he had hired to play during the run of the exposition.

During the late nineteenth and early twentieth centuries, pipe organs were central to American musical life. These were boom years for organ companies. When John pitched the idea to several of them of installing an organ in the great outdoors, most thought him mad and ignored his proposal. Organs require stable temperatures and humidity to stay in tune. John's proposal sounded like a plan for failure. Only the Austin Organ Company of Hartford, Connecticut, responded with a plan that would allow the possibility of success in a mild climate such as San Diego's. English-born brothers John and Basil Austin had installed other municipal organs and were trailblazers with their organ technologies, and $35,500 sounded like a fair deal to John, considering the pavilion to house the organ cost another $65,500.

When John was shown what he felt was a substandard location for his organ pavilion, he flat out refused it. He wanted a particular site in the middle of the exposition grounds but was told it was promised to ten Sacramento counties for their exhibitions. His justification was that the pavilion would exist long after the years of the exposition, and he was uncompromising on his preferred location. He "threatened to place the bandstand outside the exposition grounds" if "the site was not given up" for his needs. The term "noblesse oblige" was thrown around in a snarky manner in the *Sacramento Union* when it was learned that their confirmed exhibit area was being moved to accommodate the privileged John D. Spreckels. However, the Sacramento contingency was appeased when they learned their new upgraded site would have $5,000 more in amenities. It seemed everyone was content.[19]

When the organ pavilion was completed, assistant architect Winslow was very critical of the orientation of the pavilion site because spectators would not be protected from the sun's direct rays. But he was an architect and not an organist and did not take under consideration that this orientation was preferred because it offered the organ protection in case of rain.[20] Winslow later then criticized the Spreckels Organ Pavilion as being "too ornate." The pavilion and colonnade could have benefitted from less ornament, he averred, and from more refinement in the ornament used.[21] He continued in his criticism of Albright's work in reference to a disproportion of scale between the organ and its pavilion. But only by looking carefully at photos of both San Diego's Spreckels Organ Pavilion, designed by Albright, and San Francisco's Temple of Music band shell, designed by James and Merritt Reid, can one discern any distinguishing features that separate them. They are uncannily similar in design, featuring the characteristics of classical architecture, with highly decorative friezes, massive tympana (recessed spaces), and grand columns. The band shell in Golden Gate Park is seventy-five feet tall, as is John's Organ Pavilion in Balboa Park. Likely out of respect, John ensured that his own pavilion did not exceed his father's in height.

The 1915 Expo's Grand Opening!

By seven p.m. on New Years' Eve 1914, the entrance into the "Spanish City on the Hill" was thronged with thousands upon thousands of "merry visitors" peering through the gates to get an early glimpse of the exposition that would not be available to them for another two hours. The first attendees were there for the opening program that was to begin at nine p.m. The pomp and circumstance would last for three hours, until the official grand opening at midnight. A crowd of enthusiastic volunteer citizens was ready to showcase San Diego when

33. The ornate Spreckels Organ Pavilion, built and donated to the city of San Diego in 1914, houses the world's largest outdoor pipe organ. A civic organist performs free weekly Sunday concerts at two p.m. Courtesy of Robert E. Lang, Spreckels Organ Society, 2016.

the exposition gates were thrown open once the clock struck nine. The smiling volunteers were identified by buttons bearing the inscription, "I live here. Ask me."[22]

The masses were directed to the Spreckels Organ Pavilion site for the opening program that would begin with the dedication of the magnificent organ. At the appointed time, John climbed the steps to the vast stage of the Organ Pavilion. With moist eyes, he turned to the president of the park commission, John Forward, and said only a few words: "I beg you to accept this gift on behalf of the people of San Diego." Forward looked to John and loudly proclaimed: "In the name of the people of San Diego and of those untold multitudes who in all the coming years shall stand before this glorious organ and be moved by its infinite voices, I thank you."[23]

Many of the attendees, especially the dignitaries, likely expected John to give a short speech, but instead, the words, once again, came from his friend Samuel Shortridge, who extolled the power of music as a benefit for the soul. Giving the speeches John should have given afforded Shortridge the opportunity to influence powerful politicians in his continuing quest for a seat in the U.S. Senate, which is exactly what he would achieve in 1920.

During the five years of planning and construction obstacles in the expo project, many had wondered whether this day would ever come. Also, John had been distracted with other difficulties and discouragements surrounding his massive railroad project. But here at last was a triumphant night to celebrate. More hoopla followed John's gift to the city, until the stroke of midnight, when President Woodrow Wilson touched a Western Union telegraph key in Washington DC, sparking the exposition's electric power. A special balloon, outfitted with a hanging light, lofted 1,500 feet above the Plaza de Panama and lit up a three-mile radius around Balboa Park. The sound of celebratory gunshots exploded in the air from both Fort Rosecrans and strategically placed navy cruisers in the harbor below.

So, at the very beginning of 1915, San Diego's Panama–California Exposition opened, four months after the official opening of the Panama Canal and almost two months before the opening of San Francisco's Panama–Pacific International Exposition.

Surrounding the enormous Spreckels organ, an elaborate fireworks display commemorated the momentous event. Cheers erupted from the nearly forty-three thousand attendees. Then an orchestra of 50 presented the overture to Offenbach's *Orpheus in the Underworld*, and a people's chorus of 250 sang Haydn's oratorio *The Creation*. At John's cue, organist Humphrey John Stewart picked up the expo's Spanish conquistador theme, playing the processional march from *Montezuma*, which Stewart had composed. John made headlines around the world with his gift of both organ and pavilion. A year later, the *San Diego Union* declared that the world's first outdoor pipe organ "delights world musicians and exposition pleasure seekers," among whom were Thomas Edison, Henry Ford, Theodore Roosevelt, William Howard Taft, William Randolph Hearst, the Maharaja of Kapurthala, and "more than a hundred" politicians, from mayors and governors to members of Congress.[24]

Upon entering the park, visitors were instantly transported back hundreds of years to a time and place of Spanish colonization. Statues of famous Spanish explorers adorned the ornate buildings, and statues of priests adorned the walls of the California Tower, built to mimic a Catholic church. Strolling musicians and Spanish dancers promenaded among the buildings.

The centerpiece was the California Building, with its tiled dome and soaring California Tower, personally designed by Goodhue; it became the iconic photograph used in newspapers and magazines. And it would be permanent, as would a new bridge, the Spreckels Organ Pavilion, and an imposing arched wooden botanical building neighboring a sparkling water feature. Outside the Spanish "city" were the typical amusements found at other world's fairs, featuring ethnic minorities exploited in an Indian village,[25] a Hawaiian village, a Chinese town, and more. Housed in other buildings were exhibits from different countries and states, displaying their heritage. Then there was the Isthmus, a half-mile-long amusement zone where visitors found the Temple of Mirth and the Sultan's Harem. Fittingly, there was a 250-foot-long model of the Panama Canal.

Reporters from around the globe captured the exact reaction that the architects and San Diego's boosters had hoped for. *Sunset* magazine told readers they would be able to envision a time in San Diego's past when lanterns swung from the turret of the old Spanish lighthouse overlooking the sea that Juan Rodríguez Cabrillo had sailed in 1542 and to imagine the walls battered by the bullets of pirates dating back two centuries.[26]

The expo was designed to be practical as well as culturally romantic, illustrating new technologies in farming, medicine, transportation, science, and education. Demonstrations throughout the grounds presented products in every stage of development. For example, the Lipton Tea Company erected a working tea plantation in order to show how a cup of tea went from farm to table. Instead of providing oranges from a crate, one popular exhibition allowed visitors to pick their own bright and juicy oranges from a working citrus orchard. The exposition was strategically designed to illustrate opportunity by showing tourists, through applied demonstrations of machinery in operation and through fields under cultivation, how easy it could be to make a good living in the beautiful Southwest.[27]

The Expo's First Year

Attendance was good during the early months after the opening of the expo, but by late spring it had waned, and fears that the exposition might have to close for lack of funds circulated behind the scenes. A special finance committee led by Wangenheim devised a plan for loan guarantees from individuals in order to pay the incurred debt. A promise by one party to assume the debt obligation of a borrower if that borrower were to default was sorely needed. Wangenheim was able to persuade John to become that "one party," the lead signatory for loan guarantees up to $250,000. John must have been relieved when attendance increased during late summer and the loans were no longer needed to pay off debt.[28] He was aware that many of San Diego's civic leaders, including some on the exposition committee, referred to him behind his back as "damn Spreckels—except when the hat [was] being passed around."[29]

During that first year, former president Theodore Roosevelt encouraged the city to extend the exhibition into a second year, which is what happened. He also suggested that Balboa Park's "buildings, of rare, phenomenal taste and beauty" be retained permanently.[30] Even before the expo's second year began, though, there were deep concerns that it would not be solvent. The war in Europe was rising in intensity, and the increasing possibility that the United States would become involved had a deleterious effect on travel. The Panama Canal was also experiencing logistical problems, which reduced the much-hoped-for commercial traffic. Many who had pledged financial support had defaulted, which meant legal action. And worst of all, the biggest weather disaster in San Diego's history occurred in January 1916, when record-breaking rains followed by a horrific flood washed out transportation. When five feet of water flowed down Broadway in downtown San Diego, John did not have to worry about the survival of his steel-reinforced concrete build-ings, however. Also, once the books were ultimately balanced, debts that had been incurred were paid. Later, John supplied another $100,000, making the grand total of his contribution in excess of $325,000.[31]

Public addresses given at the Spreckels Organ Pavilion by the many politicians who attended the fair were well attended by the public. During one such address, Roosevelt criticized the sitting president, Woodrow Wilson, on his foreign policy.[32] Even though Roosevelt praised San Diegans for the "astounding feat" in achieving a beautiful exposition, John later wrote to the park commission, objecting to the use of the pavilion for political speeches. He requested that organ concerts in the pavilion be free to the public, but he felt that politics and music should not mix.

The Expo's Long-Term Influence

Even though attendance was not all that had been hoped for, the expo-sition returned dividends of another kind that would forever change the character of San Diego. U.S. Marine colonel Joseph H. Pendleton had lunch one afternoon at the fair with Congressman William "Bill" Kettner, and they discussed how San Diego was the perfect place for the U.S. Navy.[33] Pendleton then gained the support of Franklin Roosevelt, assistant secretary of the navy, who also came to believe that the Naval Training Center should move to San Diego. Kettner did much for the city in terms of civic improvement—and many of his accomplishments involved bringing federal money and facilities there. John, a rock-ribbed Republican, had this to say about Kettner: "I'm sorry he is not a good old-fashioned Republican, as I am. However, for a Democrat he comes nearer being a Republican than anyone I know."[34]

With that said, he donated $5,000 to the campaign to reelect the local Democratic congressman because Kettner was just as determined as John to help San Diego grow.[35] Because Kettner accepted that con-tribution from John, he lost the support of wealthy Democrat Edward Scripps and the *San Diego Sun*.[36] It turned out that Kettner didn't need the support of the Scripps papers, since he had the Spreckels papers behind him; he was reelected that year by a margin of twenty-four thousand votes over his opponent. Even though Scripps had refused to support the victor, after publicly conceding that John's support had been the winning factor, he was impressed that Kettner was not a "sniveling hypocrite or false pretender":

> Mr. Kettner acknowledged that he held his position as congressman by reason of the will of Mr. Spreckels and the support of Mr. Spreckels' papers and he thanked Mr. Spreckels then and there. Mr. Kettner's candor was so great as to excite my admiration. As a newspaperman my usual experience has been that after I have caused the election of some man to some important office, the new-made official has taken the first and every possible opportunity to impress upon me and the public that God and the people had chosen him and that I had nothing to do with his honors.[37]

By the time the Panama–California Exposition closed its two-year run on January 1, 1917, attendance had reached about 3.8 million, about a fifth of the total for San Francisco's competing Panama–Pacific International Exposition. But, unlike the expo buildings in San Francisco, Goodhue's key buildings had been built to last, as was John's Organ Pavilion—and they were on public land.[38] San Diego is fortunate that most of the architecture and buildings of the original expo still remain a central component of the identity of Balboa Park, something rarely achieved with world's fair structures. They are a permanent reminder of the exposition.

San Diego expanded rapidly after the exposition, nearly doubling its population—just exactly as John had hoped for and literally banked on. The expo's architectural impact and its influence on individual architects were widely seen throughout the city in the Spanish colonial homes designed in the 1910s and 1920s. Real estate developers continued to develop such "streetcar suburbs" as Golden Hill, Kensington, Mission Beach, and University Heights, while paved roads took automobiles eastbound. In 1923, a transcontinental highway connected San Diego with Washington DC, along a southern route.

The San Diego Zoo

It has been said that the world-famous San Diego Zoo "began with a roar." As the story goes, in the summer of 1916, two brothers who shared a medical practice were driving to their clinic when they heard the roars of despondent lions housed in small cages at the then-vacant exposition site. Paul and Harry Wegeforth, distinguished surgeons, had been the contracted doctors for the expo and knew exactly where those sorrowful roars emanated from. The brothers had both been ardent animal lovers since childhood, and Harry recalled the exact moment that propelled him into action: "On September 16, 1916, as I was returning to my office after performing an operation at the St. Joseph Hospital, I drove down Sixth Avenue and heard the roaring of the lions in the cages at the Exposition then being held in Balboa Park. I turned to my brother, Paul, who was riding with me, and half jokingly, half wishfully, said, 'Wouldn't it be splendid if San Diego had a zoo! You know . . . I think I'll start one.'"[39]

But first, they needed to find donors and create a nonprofit corporation. The Wegeforth brothers' talent for tugging the heartstrings and purse strings of San Diegans was legendary. They attracted three other influential men, and, within a month of hearing the soulful wails of caged lions, they were advertising their newly created Zoological Society and were looking for financial support. Paul easily persuaded John to donate. Ellen Browning Scripps, half-sister of John's archenemy, was another of the earliest benefactors.

Harry Wegeforth's inspiration in designing the San Diego Zoo came from Germany's Carl Hagenbeck, whose Tierpark eschewed the traditional cages and exhibited a menagerie of animals similar in species in large, "natural" surroundings of mountains, plains, caves, and water features. Also, Wegeforth successfully promoted the concept of a vibrant and verdant zoological garden where animals could be integrated with "familiar" plants in pleasing settings. No animal lover could resist this exciting concept.

The lions were not the only abandoned animals that were rescued. But more exotic animals were needed in order to draw the crowds. Wegeforth wanted to add elephants but learned that they were cost-prohibitive. He needed a sponsor and approached John, who had already contributed significant financial assistance during the zoo's initial fundraising. But despite John's well-known soft spot for animals, Wegeforth's animated coaxing was unsuccessful: "Fact is, Harry, I'm not much interested in elephants."[40] Known for his dry humor, John stated that he would buy the animals "providing you can get whiter elephants than some I already have."[41] He was referring to a widely spread account of the time: Showman P. T. Barnum had heard of a sacred white elephant for sale in Asia. He paid a fortune for it and began promoting it with typical circus ballyhoo. When the mythical "white" elephant arrived at his circus and was actually a light gray, Barnum had been repeatedly humiliated in the press across the country. Wegeforth recalled his next move to effectively cajole John into buying the elephants:

> The next day I bought a large can of white powder and four of the largest powder puffs I could find. I went back to the zoo and set the keepers to experimenting on the elephants. The result was eminently satisfactory. The next problem was to get Mr. Spreckels to the zoo. I mapped out a little campaign. Mr. Spreckels came over to the elephant compound where the man had been busy wielding valiant powder puffs. There stood the two snow-white, bulging beasts, looking like nothing any mortal had ever seen, their black eyes and pink mouths the only spots of color in the large white expanse. The keepers carried out the white color scheme, for they too were covered with powder from head to foot. Mr. Spreckels laughed heartily at the fantastic picture and promised to pay not only for the loan but for the elephant compound as well, and sure enough, in the first mail we received his check for $7500 [more than $175,800 in today's money].[42]

The Spreckels–Wegeforth Wedding

John's daughter Lillie ended her unhappy marriage to Harry Holbrook, left San Francisco, and moved into the Spreckels Coronado mansion in 1919 with her eight-year-old daughter, Harriet. Paul Wegeforth had a private medical practice in Coronado, and when he met Lillie Holbrook at a local social event, there was an instant connection.

John gave his blessing for marriage, even though Lillie was seven years older than her suitor. Paul was a brilliant brain surgeon and highly respected in his private Coronado practice, and John had great respect for him. John undoubtedly admired that Paul, like he, was the son of a German immigrant.

On January 19, 1920, in a quiet but well-publicized event at the home of her parents on Glorietta Bay, Lillie and Paul were married. It was a family reunion of sorts. Harriet was the flower girl, carrying a basket of Maryland roses, and John's two young grandsons by Claus and Ellis—Claus "Junior" and Frank, eight and seven, respectively— followed in white satin suits. John's dear friend Humphrey John Stewart played Mendelssohn's "Wedding March" on John's home organ. With these grandchildren now living in Coronado, John and Lillian were content.

Evidently, Lillie had finally found stability for Harriet and herself, and the building up of the San Diego Zoo became a family project. Lillie and Paul settled into their large pink mansion near John and Lillian's Glorietta Bay mansion, with the hopes of a long and happy marriage. Alas, it was not to be. Harriet later recounted that, after just three years of marriage to her mother, her stepfather, the brilliant young doctor, died at the age of thirty-five on March 29, 1923, after contracting tuberculosis from conducting surgery on an infected patient.[43]

The Australian Expedition: The Harrowing Journey Down Under

After Paul's death, Lillie likely encouraged her father to support her brother-in-law Harry Wegeforth's request to help the San Diego Zoo gain worldwide fame by obtaining "strange creatures from the bush."[44] In fact, Lillie and Wegeforth were relentless in their efforts to induce John to provide free round-trip passage in 1925 for the zoo's new director, Tom Faulconer, to sail to Australia on one of the Spreckels steamships, the *Sierra*, to obtain such creatures in exchange for animals from this hemisphere. The Australia-bound animals, including coyotes, wolves, and other species from North and Central America, were crated and shipped by rail to San Francisco.

Unfortunately, the exchange mission got off to a bad start. In San Francisco, where the animals were supposed to board the *Sierra*, the crew paled at the sight of crated and caged wild beasts that would be with them for three long weeks. The "irate company officials" had assumed that the request to make room for zoo animals was another "Spreckels joke" and were totally unprepared for them.[45] After twelve frantic hours of dealing with these officials and "reluctant" ship's officers, "cages were stashed and stowed wherever room could be found, and sadly, several birds and small animals died from exposure."[46] According to Faulconer, "between feedings, there was the cleaning of cages, doctoring the sick, and sympathizing with the monkeys, wolves, and coyotes, every single one of whom suffered from seasickness more severe even than the attacks that came upon me."[47]

And if that was not bad enough, a curious twelve-foot alligator escaped and wandered the decks among shrieking passengers until a crew member lassoed it.[48] The mayhem continued when a hungry spider monkey named Billy reached into a wildcat's cage to grab a piece of meat and had its arm bitten off. The trip, full of such animal escapades, took a harrowing twenty-one days. John, who loved to tell stories in small groups over a glass of gin and a cigar, would have enjoyed hearing about every detail—the more startling and gorier, the better.

The Koala Coup

Faulconer returned with more than thirty native Australian species, including kangaroos, wallabies, echidnas, Tasmanian devils, dingoes, kookaburras, emus, cassowaries, water dragons, and, most amazingly of all, the zoo's first koalas. The cuddly koalas were originally not supposed to be among the zoo-bound species, since their exportation was banned. Australians were worried about the fast-dwindling population of the species. Very few people outside of Australia had ever seen the teddy-bear look-alikes, and a disappointed Faulconer had remarked while boarding the *Sonoma*, the homebound vessel, "I would have traded a dozen kangaroos and wombats for a single koala." But moments before departure, two crates were delivered to the dock, with an enormous sign marked "Koala Bears for the Children of San Diego, U.S.A., from the Children of Sydney."[49]

Faulconer kept the two rare koalas near his side the entire voyage home, a fact that gave him celebrity status on board the ship: "Being a chaperone to the two little koalas, I soon was competing with a British Lord and an east Indian Maharaja for most popular man on the ship."[50] Snuggle Pot and Cuddle Pie, named after characters in an Australian children's book at the time, continued their superstar status in San Diego. They would become the first koalas ever displayed in the United States, making them the zoo's earliest attention-drawing, attendance-driving celebrities.

16

Standing Up to the U.S. Government

The *Venetia*, a Steam Yacht

There was an unexpected twist to the Panama–California Exposition: It brought naval dignitaries to San Diego, and John was more than happy to talk "sailor to sailor" with them and invite them for a cruise around the harbor on his yacht. It was his pleasure to illustrate the great possibilities in dredging the harbor to create one of the most beautiful and functional ports for the U.S. Navy.[1]

The hobby of yachting, operating a privately owned yacht, had begun to be fashionable in the mid-nineteenth century for those who could afford it, and John had taken to it with gusto. Since voyages aboard these yachts could take weeks, comfortable accommodations were vital to someone like John, who was used to luxury. When he was in his prime, he regularly hosted parties for small groups of friends on his eighty-four-foot *Lurline*. The famous parties were long and loud enough for the local paper to report that inebriated guests sat up all night on the deck to watch "the stars and pour libations in their honor."[2] The *Lurline* became so celebrated for her victorious races that she made the front cover of June 1883's *Breeder and Sportsman.* John had traveled the globe, hosted dignitaries and royalty, and won many a race with the *Lurline*, but his best memories were with his wife and children on the open seas.

As he neared sixty years of age, John desired a new steam yacht for this phase of his life. He looked around for many months until he found

34. The opulent 227-foot steam yacht *Venetia* was John's pride and joy. Permission granted from the Terrence and Virginia Wilson Private Family Collection.

the *Venetia* for sale at $125,000 (more than $3 million in today's money). He went east and purchased the imposing and luxurious 227-foot steam commuter yacht from a Philadelphia millionaire who had hit on hard times. On October 3, 1910, John began sailing it home himself from New York Harbor. Friends and family filled the ten staterooms for the leisurely five-month sightseeing journey, with stops in New Orleans and the West Indies before reaching Glorietta Bay via the Straits of Magellan on March 5, 1911.

The lavish *Venetia* was John's passion, a floating mansion and his transportation of choice for conducting business in San Francisco and even in Hawai'i. The opulence continued below the deck with floor-to-ceiling rich hardwoods and a stunning painted-glass skylight. Each stateroom had an adjoining bathroom (with salt- and freshwater taps) kept warm by central steam heat. The main deck house contained a smoking room, a well-stocked library, and an elegant dining room. There was a social lounge, where John had installed a Weber pianola so that he could personally entertain his guests. It was well known that the relaxation at sea helped John keep his stress under control and that when he came ashore, he was refreshed and restored.

To steam up and down the coast, between the Silver Gate and the Golden Gate, on last-minute business trips required a highly trained and knowledgeable crew. For most millionaires, crew members were retained seasonally, but John retained his chief engineer, William Darroch, and captain, David Nicolini, year-round. With admiration for their boss as well as good salaries, they grew old with him on a ship they all loved.

With the birth of motion pictures, Coronado, in its close proximity to Hollywood, became a hub of an emerging culture of celebrity. Mary Pickford, "America's Sweetheart," shot scenes for a movie onboard the *Venetia*. The yacht also acted as a taxi for friends and family from San Francisco wishing to stay at the Hotel del Coronado. The yacht's arrivals in and out of both San Diego Harbor and San Francisco Harbor were noted in the press.

Most yacht builders at the beginning of the twentieth century were straddling the ages of coal and oil. In 1912, John was one of the first to step over the line and convert the *Venetia*'s coal-burning engines to the more economical fuel, oil, which increased her cruising range.[3]

Military Squatters on North Island

Across San Diego Bay from the city and attached to the Coronado residential community was a half-mile stretch of water known as Spanish Bight, which awkwardly separated John's Coronado properties, North Island and South Island. North Island was a true island, albeit small, and presented a challenge for a real estate developer like John. Since he had acquired it from Elisha Babcock, he had done nothing to develop it; it was nothing more than grazing ground for cattle and a hunting ground for rabbit-tracking hotel guests, an activity John and family fully enjoyed participating in.

In 1910, John had lured aviation pioneer Glenn Curtiss to Coronado to open a flying school on North Island and charged him no rent for three years. Though John didn't want to develop North Island himself at this point, he was happy to sell it to others who would. As a

35. View of Coronado's shallow channel, the Spanish Bight, which awkwardly separated North Island from South Island. In late 1943, the navy began to fill in the Bight. The Tent City location is on the sand spit that separates Glorietta Bay from the Pacific Ocean (the lower right side of the photo). Photo reproduced by permission of Library of Congress, Prints and Photographs Division (8-AA-015–071).

promotional strategy, without spending a dime, he was using a noted aviator to provide publicity and promotion.[4]

Curtiss had his own promotional goals; on the morning of January 25, 1911, he used Spanish Bight as a seaborne "runway" for his experimental "hydroaeroplane," a prototype seaplane he named *Triad Amphibian*. It was the very first seaplane flight, and Curtiss was hoping the War Department would purchase the plane after seeing the advantages and possibilities that aviation presented. He formally demonstrated *Triad Amphibian* on February 17, showing how ships and planes could work effectively together, and the U.S. Navy almost immediately purchased the aircraft.

John's desolate, flat, sandy, sagebrush-covered island now began to attract attention—free publicity—just as he had hoped. Because John respected Curtiss's entrepreneurship, he allowed the aviator to offer free seaplane training on North Island for select army and navy officers. Navy Lieutenant Theodore Ellyson was sent first to Coronado to receive free instruction in January 1912. Ellyson established a temporary navy camp for other arrivals and began training on the three seaplanes purchased from Curtiss. In due time, the army purchased a number of aircraft from him and established their own flying school on North Island.[5] Unfortunately, within four months, all the seaplanes had crashed, and the navy transferred their aviation personnel to Annapolis, Maryland.[6] (But they would return within five years to cause untold grief for John.)

The army stayed, however. On November 8, 1912, the *Coronado Strand* announced that a large contingency of army officials invited by Curtiss had arrived for flight training, taking John by surprise. By 1913, there was a large military encampment on North Island, enjoying flight training rent-free, thanks to John, who had no idea he had extended the invitation.[7]

On January 22, 1914, John's second-in-command, William Clayton, sent a letter to Captain Arthur S. Cowan, the commanding officer of the First Aero Squadron, camped out on North Island, informing the officer that just because John had allowed "temporary" structures there, "the giving of this permission shall in no way be interpreted or construed as conferring any permanent right to maintain such structures, or as granting any interest or right in or to the land of said North Island, or any part thereof."[8] On December 1, 1915, John formally requested that Captain Cowan stop grading the land and stop putting up buildings on the land the army neither owned, rented, nor paid taxes for. He informed the captain that he had "paid out over $50,000 [around $3 million today] in taxes alone" since they had been using his land at his benevolence.[9]

The captain was further informed that the Coronado Beach Company's development plans, which had been put on hold for many years, would require their departure by March 31, 1916. John stated that the time had now arrived to get North Island ready to put on the market as a "high-class residential property." He needed to build an infrastructure, including "grading, paving, sewering, water, electric lights and street cars."[10] None of that could be done while the military was squatting on his island.

Wooing the Navy

Meanwhile, John was thrilled to show off his beloved yacht Venetia—particularly to naval dignitaries who would understand and appreciate the cutting-edge ship conversions he had made to it. He had at one time entertained the secretary of the navy and several navy admirals over the years, never dreaming that the type of impression the swift Venetia made would cost him dearly when war broke out.

After the annexation of Hawai'i, the navy had built a base on San Francisco Bay, the only one on the Pacific Coast for years. However, war scares with Japan prompted the navy to expand down California's southern coast. San Diego, with its perilously shallow bay, had never been on the navy's preferred list for a second West Coast base; instead, the service favored San Pedro, near Los Angeles.[11]

But San Diegans, hungry for a navy presence, began looking for opportunities to promote the attractiveness of its strategic location for a naval base. When President Theodore Roosevelt sent the navy's Great White Fleet around the world in a show of global maritime power, San Diegans had seized the chance to be seen, even though their city was not on a scheduled stop. After the battle fleet was seen rounding Point Loma on a beautiful spring day in April 1908, a committee went into action. Thousands of citizens waving handkerchiefs lined the waterfront to watch their city's leaders intercept the fleet as they anchored off Coronado. Armed with flowers and a gift of ten thousand oranges, they convinced the officers to stop over, enjoy the city's hospitality, and pay official naval respects to the USS Bennington's dead sailors buried in San Diego's Fort Rosecrans. The three-day celebration in San Diego "left an indelible mark on the memories of the thousands of the navy's officers and men" that affected decisions made in the following decade.[12]

According to one story, one evening following the Great White Fleet's visit, John planned a promotion prank with the commanding officer of the USS *California* in a dark corner of the Hotel del Coronado. The armored cruiser was in San Diego to escort the secretary of the navy, Josephus Daniels, to Los Angeles to celebrate the opening of the nearly finished harbor at San Pedro. When Daniels arrived in San Diego, John cordially invited him aboard the *Venetia* to steam behind the *California* in style. John planned to point out the beautiful features of his city and "bend the secretary's ear with tales of what a joke San Pedro was compared with San Diego's natural harbor."[13] As they entered the new harbor, a prearranged "bar-room strategy" went into action: A confusing number of the commanding officer's signals from the bridge to the engine room required the navy cruiser to react in a way that churned the lovely blue water into an ugly brown because the large screws of the ship brought up "swirling eddies of mud." As they steamed into the brown harbor, John apparently said to Daniels, "Not like that in San Diego Bay—eh, Mr. Secretary?"[14]

President Theodore Roosevelt's fifth cousin, Franklin Delano Roosevelt, then assistant secretary of the navy, attended the Panama–California Exposition in its first year. After being escorted around by Congressman William Kettner, FDR adopted Kettner's vision for a naval base in the mild climate of San Diego. Kettner recalled that FDR shared his distress over the sickness among the navy men working in the harsh climate of Goat Island in Rhode Island. Kettner, bolstered by FDR's enthusiasm, started the "machinery in motion" in Washington. Meanwhile, to maintain momentum when the expo closed, the navy was given the abandoned Balboa Park and the fair buildings as a temporary naval training center until a permanent site could be located.

After being toured around the shores of San Diego, Captain Arthur MacArthur found two hundred acres in Point Loma quite suitable for the navy's needs. To purchase this private land for the navy, Kettner went after the "City Dads."[15] When the hat was passed around, John, the richest "dad," gave the highest donation: $15,000 (almost $400,000 today). Once purchased, the Point Loma site became the Naval Training

Station. Fortunately, John's North Island was not then viewed as a potential base for training sailors (though the military continued squatting there). John had come to regard his island as an important acquisition; he would not easily part with that expensive acreage.

Wartime Appropriation of John's Property

The Panama–California Exposition and the famous visitors it brought as well as the 1916 opening of the San Diego Zoo were welcome distractions for San Diegans who were weary from the constant news of Europe's engagement in a war. Nevertheless, Americans could not escape the fear-provoking news that was front-paged across the nation for nearly three long and worrisome years. The United States hung back from participation until events forced its involvement. The most notorious event was the sinking of the RMS *Lusitania* in May 1915 by a German U-boat torpedo, which resulted in a massive loss of life, including 128 Americans. The next contributor to the war fervor was the infamous Zimmermann Telegram, which had been intercepted in January 1917 by the British. In the telegram's coded message, the high-ranking German official Arthur Zimmermann purportedly encouraged Mexico to make war on the United States in exchange for help in reconquering Texas, New Mexico, and Arizona (which Mexico had lost in 1848). Five weeks after President Woodrow Wilson released that provocative telegram to the media at the end of February, the United States declared war on Germany on April 6, 1917, and immediately seized German ships berthed in American ports. John's life was about to be interrupted with another telegram, informing him that his own ship, the center of his social world, was being taken from him. He also would receive news that North Island would be seized as well.

APPROPRIATING THE *VENETIA*

Soon after the declaration, Congress set aside $50 million for national defense, and the Department of the Navy began looking for auxiliary vessels. Secretary of the Navy Josephus Daniels knew just whose ship he would like to acquire; after all, he had been on the *Venetia*, as had other military brass. The navy had previously conscripted three of the Spreckelses' tugs in April 1898 to be used in the Spanish-American War, and the military was then occupying North Island. This next move by the navy would severely test John's patriotism.

On July 13, 1917, John received a stunning telegram from Secretary Daniels, informing him that "the exigencies of the Navy in war demand the acquirement of your ship *Venetia*. Under the law I am sending you notice to that effect. If you prefer to lease or tender it without this procedure wire to-day and state your desires."[16] Captain A. S. Halstead, senior member of the Naval Board of Appraisal, followed up on the telegram the next day, informing John that "the President of the United States has directed the acquisition of the *Venetia*" and that the board should report "a just compensation for this vessel." Halstead requested John to inform the board of "all the evidence you desire taken into consideration in determining the amount of such compensation."[17] John replied on July 24, stating that he preferred the navy to lease rather than purchase his yacht: "I received your communication of July 14 upon my arrival in the city to-day; hence the delay in reply to the same. . . . I would greatly prefer to lease the vessel during the term of the war, with the understanding that she would be restored to me in as good condition as when taken over by the Navy."[18]

On August 4, John delivered the *Venetia*, as ordered, to the commandant at the Mare Island Navy Yard on San Pablo Bay, northeast of San Francisco. Specialists there inspected the yacht and found her to be in "excellent" condition. Whether the navy was buying or leasing her was not yet settled, but they began modifying and equipping her for war, including the installation of gun mounts.

Responding on August 30 to Captain Halstead's request for documentation to substantiate the value of the *Venetia*, John indicated that he and his staff had been pulling paid invoices "from a large file." What he pulled, he said, did not "cover the entire cost," but he approximated a subtotal of $189,134.16, plus $26,007.29 (the cost of bringing the yacht from New York to San Francisco), yielding a grand total of $216,131.45.[19]

On September 15, Secretary Daniels wrote to John that President Wilson was interested in acquiring rather than leasing and had determined a "just compensation" of $165,000 (about $4 million today), which was far less than what John expected. With carefully selected words in his reply a week later, John was clearly insulted at the meager amount the navy was offering: "It is inconceivable upon what basis this sum was arrived at. Surely very few of the facts were taken into consideration in fixing the amount. As a matter of fact, within the last six months I have been offered three hundred thousand dollars ($300,000) [$7.5 million today] for the yacht, and I refused the offer."[20] He reiterated that his preference had always been to lease and *not sell* his ship to the navy:

> I obtained the yacht only after a long search for a vessel that suited me, and I have no desire to part with it. In answer to a personal telegram from you requesting me to determine whether I would sell or lease the yacht to the Government, I elected to lease the vessel for the duration of the war, and I assumed upon my acceptance of your offer to lease the yacht, the Government would charter the ship. Will you please inform me what monthly remuneration I may expect for the charter of this ship?[21]

Finally, on October 20, the navy notified John that they agreed to lease the *Venetia* for $2,000 per month (compensating him $165,000 "in case of loss").[22] With this mutual agreement in place, the newly commissioned *Venetia* sailed off a week later under navy command. She went through the Panama Canal to League Island Navy Yard in Philadelphia, and then to Brooklyn Navy Yard, for further retrofitting.

APPROPRIATING NORTH ISLAND

North Island's fate was also sealed after the United States entered the war. A joint army-navy board recommended that the island be acquired for permanent military use. The navy had tried on several occasions to purchase it from John, using Kettner as an intermediary, but he always declined what he believed were stingy offers.

If John and his Coronado Beach Company would not sell North Island to the United States, the United States would take it by eminent domain, and the takeover would be done quickly. On July 24, 1917, President Wilson signed an executive order to take possession of "the whole of North Island for national defense," three days later Congress approved the order, and on August 1 the president signed a "Condemnation Act" to take the 1,232-acre island as a permanent air base.[23] Thus, the ownership of North Island passed out of John's hands and into the possession of the United States. On September 8, the navy began sharing the island with the army, who had long been camped out there rent-free.

John fought the Condemnation Act, which would take his land for no compensation. Congressman Kettner, who owed his congressional seat to John's support, legally insisted that confiscation would endanger private property rights and that John should be fairly paid for the value of his property. Ultimately, after a series of court hearings regarding the appropriateness of taking possession of the island, the government concurred that it should compensate John.[24]

On April 15, 1919, a trial established the fair value of North Island at $5 million. Congress dragged their feet while they contested (and pontificated about) the dollar amount. The whole fiasco was settled in 1921, but, while they deliberated, the land increased in value, so John was paid more than a million extra.

What Happened to the *Venetia*

The USS *Venetia* was pressed into military service as patrol craft SC-431. On December 21, 1917, she left for Gibraltar as part of a twenty-eight-ship convoy; she was towing a French submarine chaser. From Bermuda to the Azores, she encountered several northwest storms. The resulting heavy strain caused the deck seams to open up, and she leaked. She also had a collision in the Mediterranean Sea. At least twice she was placed in dry dock at Gibraltar for repairs. On May 11, 1918, a torpedo from an enemy U-boat streaked past the bow of the USS *Venetia* and sunk a French ship in her convoy. The yacht's commander let loose a barrage of depth charges that drove the U-boat away, preventing even more lives from being lost, an act that earned him a commendation.[25]

Thankfully, John was unaware that his beloved yacht was being greatly wounded during the nineteen months she served the navy.

After three other uneventful round-trip convoys, the battle-scarred *Venetia* returned to the United States to be decommissioned, a gold star attached to her smokestack for war victories. In early March 1919, John was informed that his yacht was ready for pickup. On April 7, he traveled to Mare Island with every intention to sail her home to Coronado's Glorietta Bay. But when he saw the battle-worn *Venetia*, he became outraged and refused to accept her back until the navy restored her to her prewar condition, as per their agreement. It's likely that his good friend William Darroch, a fellow Mason and the *Venetia's* longstanding chief engineer, was by John's side for inspection purposes. But Darroch knew his presence wouldn't have been necessary, because, as he said, "I have never been able to slip anything over on the Boss." John's "abilities and intimate knowledge of engines" equaled his, he said, and that was high praise from an engineer.[26]

John went home and initiated a lawsuit against the U.S. government for $100,000 to cover repairs.[27] Rear Admiral Victor Blue, acting secretary of the navy, offered to settle for $76,331.83, but further stipulated: "In case the owner refuses to accept the amount as stated . . . he should be notified of his legal rights in the matter, i.e., to accept 75 per cent of the above amount and sue in the Court of Claims for [the balance]."[28] Heated negotiations ensued until September 20, when John addressed the commandant of the twelfth naval district as follows: "As you know, it has always been, and is now, my claim, which I am able to establish through competent proof, that the allowance made by the Government is inadequate to compensate me for the loss sustained, to place the yacht in condition she was in when taken over by the Government, and my acceptance of the amount to be paid must not be considered as a waiver of my claim to additional allowance and compensation therefor."[29]

On September 25, John picked up the *Venetia* and sailed her home. He accepted the sum of $57,248.87, which was 75 percent of the total award of $76,331.83 made by the board of appraisal, but he wrote on the paperwork "subject to inventory."[30] Back in San Diego, he had a marine surveyor and consulting engineer go over the yacht with a fine-tooth comb; he then proceeded to have repairs done to restore her to prewar condition. It was said, however, that she never handled with the same agility as she had before going to war.[31]

It is unknown what information was given by the navy personnel that had taken his ship to war, but John immediately published articles of mythical proportions in the *San Diego Union* regarding the *Venetia*'s supposed war exploits. The biggest myth was that the *Venetia* had sunk the German U-boat that had sunk the *Lusitania*. These stories were picked up and made into headlines by major newspapers throughout the country. With no one willing to discredit him, John sponsored the printing of the heroic tale *Venetia: Avenger of the Lusitania* in 1919.[32] After his death, this myth was finally debunked.[33]

Lillian's Wartime Aloha

While John was making wartime news by fighting the U.S. government, his wife was making news in a smaller way. A young, homesick native Hawaiian cadet who was stationed at Camp Kearny Army Base in San Diego was given a once-in-a-lifetime opportunity. He was among one of the 28,000 soldiers who had been trained to fight in the trenches of Belgium and France. He and a few men from his battalion attended church one Sunday in "Coronado City." When Lillian Spreckels, who was there that morning, noticed that a Hawaiian soldier was sitting in the pew, she approached him with an extraordinary invitation. After church, she walked him and his fellow squad members over to the Hotel del Coronado for a "seven-course dinner." The cadet noted that they felt like "clumsy country jakes" in their bulky uniforms and boots as they paraded by "monocled society folks." His experience was written up in his hometown Kaua'i newspaper. "Mrs. Spreckels treated us as though we were princes" and even introduced them to the granddaughter of John D. Rockefeller. After the meal, in Hawaiian style, they were each given gifts. The cadet emotionally reported that he would never forget Lillian Spreckels's aloha and generosity at a time that he was "homesick to desperation."[34]

On December 30, 1921, Lillian waited in Coronado when John went to Los Angeles Federal Court to receive a check for $6,098,333.33 ($5 million for North Island and $1,098,333.33 in interest, which reflected the increase of the land's value).[35] With the cashing of that check, which would be valued today at around $88 million, John's little island became the sole property of the United States. There was little joy in receiving those millions, however, because John and Lillian were then dealing with the most heart-crushing pain that parents could ever experience.

17

The Cruel 1920s

Jack Spreckels's Tragic Death

Jack Spreckels and Edith Huntington's romance, once regarded as a great love story by those who knew them, crumbled in 1913 after one or both had strayed from the marriage. The high-profile drama covering their divorce, finalized on August 22, 1915, had become acrimonious after Edith made public allegations that Jack was having an affair with a certain "Miss X" and then charged Jack with cruelty.[1] John put his friend and attorney on the case: Samuel Shortridge, who assured the court that his client had never "inflicted either mentally or bodily injuries upon Mrs. Spreckels."[2]

Sometime during this ordeal, Edith had found a new romance. Three days after the divorce decree was final, Edith married Franklin W. Wakefield in Honolulu. Unlike the Catholic wedding she had insisted upon with the Lutheran-oriented Jack Spreckels, her wedding to Frank Wakefield was conducted in the Mormon Church. After Edith left for Honolulu with Wakefield, her and Jack's children—Marie, Adolph Bernard, and John Dietrich III—went to Coronado to stay with their grandparents.

Exactly one month after her marriage to Wakefield, Edith's father, Willard B. Huntington, the nephew of the famed Collis P. Huntington, was killed in an automobile accident, leaving John Spreckels as the three children's only living grandfather. This fact would play out prominently less than a decade later.

By marrying in Honolulu, Edith did not escape the San Francisco gossipmongers, who were quick to report that "San Francisco society matrons have not looked with much calm upon the new adventures of the new bride."[3] Due to the notoriety of the Spreckels family, Edith's divorce and quick remarriage made headlines in most major papers until it was eventually subjugated to the back pages, to the relief of the public, especially of John and Lillian Spreckels.[4]

Edith wasn't the only one who quickly jumped back into wedlock. On September 15, 1915, Jack married a vivacious blonde, thirteen years his junior, a beauty by the name of Syida Wirt, who worked as a dancer and singer. Interestingly, not a single Spreckels attended the home wedding at 2009 Pacific Avenue. Amusingly, Syida changed the spelling of her name often; she was variously known as Syadia, Sidia, Syida, Sadie, and Sydi. Official documents use "Syida." They had a daughter together, Geraldine Ann, who was born on October 15, 1916.

One of Jack's closest friends was Charles Herbert Veil, who lived in Paris. Veil liked fast planes and fast women. He was a highly decorated American fighter pilot who had flown with a French air force unit in World War I. He had earned celebrity status when he flew his airplane through Paris's Arc de Triomphe by rolling the plane on its side just before passing through the arch.

Following the war, Veil had become well known for living life on the edge in Europe. In 1920, when Jack and Syida visited Paris, "the most beautiful city in the world," Veil was their escort. Things turned topsy-turvy, however. In his autobiography, *Adventure's a Wench*, Veil recounted the numerous sexual exploits he and Jack had together with various women on that holiday, which likely caused Syida to file for divorce.[5] It's not known where Syida was for most of the time, but out of her sight, the "handsome, wealthy, captivating" Jack Spreckels was the life of every Parisian party. With the Spreckels sugar millions in the background, Jack was generally successful "around a lovely face and shapely legs." When he and Veil gave a dinner party for twelve "dancing girls" at the famed Hôtel Claridge, Syida unexpectedly walked in. After a "supercilious glance at Jack," she retreated to a dark and lonely corner. Veil wondered how Syida had overlooked Jack's "two weaknesses: liquor and women." In the end, she could not, and in December 1920, she went to Reno to file for divorce.[6] Veil recounted how heartbroken Jack was and told him his "one vulnerable point was that he remained in love with his own wife."[7]

By the second decade of the twentieth century, it was well known that Jack liked to drive fast. He had numerous car accidents, one a near-death experience when he hit another car head on. And, of course, he received several speeding tickets.[8] One memorable ticket for having headlights brighter than California law permitted sent him to jail in Redwood City. He dismissed the idea of a lawyer and conducted his own defense, likely confident of a positive outcome. His defense was that he attempted to dim the headlights by "rubbing tobacco juice on the headlight lenses." Unimpressed, the plucky Judge George Seeley threw Jack in jail for two days to teach him a lesson, stating that a "fine would serve no purpose with a man of Spreckels' wealth."[9]

As it turns out, Jack didn't have such a horrible time in jail. It was reported that he played many rounds of a competitive card game called "Pedro" with three other prisoners over the two days. Not finding his bed as comfortable as he liked, he sent someone out to buy him a "pair of blankets." And because he "declined to eat the prison fare," he also had "his meals specially prepared on the outside."[10]

Papers across the country reported on the "millionaire's son" in jail. One Chicago reporter humorously wrote that Judge Seely was guilty of "treason, insubordination, and heresy" for taking down the son of John D. Spreckels. He predicted a horrible outcome for the poor judge when John's lawyers went after him. The newspaper headlined the story "Seely for Governor," extolling the judge's audaciousness and nerve and suggesting that he was wasted as a mere justice of the peace.[11]

With another divorce proceeding in progress, John insisted that his son stop playing around and get to work. With four children to support and two alimonies to pay, it was time that Jack find a place in the Spreckels companies and earn a living. And he did and more. In and around Los Angeles, the development of the oil industry was helping to put the nation on wheels and enticing investors such as John Spreckels, who approved of Jack's enthusiasm to find his footing in that stirring industry.

John had stealthily moved into the oil industry at the beginning of the century, long before such mega-companies as Standard Oil and General Petroleum did. According to the *Pacific Oil Reporter*, the Spreckels family was gobbling up land in the Devil's Den District of Kern County, but information was limited because "outsiders are not allowed on the grounds."[12] One insider, Jack, had at last found a purpose, much to John's relief, and was soon known as an "oil man." San Francisco's *Town Talk* looked at the "underground" investment humorously, implying that the family patriarch, Claus Spreckels, might be rolling over in his grave because Jack had "broken the rules, shattered the tradition" by gambling on "mines and oil wells." Claus had always been clear with the family to stay away from speculating "on what the earth might produce" and to stick with sure ventures that "were made in the upper spaces of the earth."[13]

Jack, aged thirty-nine in 1921, became president of the Spreckels Oil Company, but his personal life was still in shambles. His first wife, Edith, sued him for back alimony in the amount of $10,000, which drew a great deal of media notice. And even though his divorce with Syida had not been made final, she made it clear that there was no turning back. She was making bigger news with her claims that she gave a man in London an $80,000 pearl necklace to take it to be cleaned. She had bought it on credit on June 3, 1920, from Tiffany's in London under the name "John D. Spreckels," but she had left off the "Jr." When Tiffany's wanted either to be paid or to get the necklace returned, Syida claimed that the man had stolen it and that she was not going to pay for something she no longer had. The store initiated a lawsuit against her soon-to-be ex-father-in-law, John Spreckels, claiming that he had authorized the purchase. John was furious and told Jack to clear up the situation with his legal team.[14]

Suffice it to say, Jack had a lot on his mind on August 8, 1921. He was in the middle of negotiating with Syida and had offered to pay the Tiffany's bill in exchange for sole custody of Geraldine, claiming that Syida was as unfit a mother of Geraldine as Edith was of his three children by her. He visited one of his company's oilfields near Bakersfield, California, at eleven a.m. and left in a hurry for his next destination, the town of Taft. He was driving too fast to successfully navigate a curve, ran into a telephone pole, and overturned his car. A trucker unsuccessfully attempted to save his life after finding him pinned under the car. Sadly, John and Claus Jr. arrived at Bakersfield's Mercy Hospital in a hastily chartered special train too late to say goodbye. Jack, just thirty-nine years old, twice divorced, the father of four, died from a hemorrhage of the brain at four o'clock that afternoon.

Charles Veil eulogized his friend in his book, saying, "Poor Jack is dead. . . . If there is a place in the hereafter for a prince of good fellows with more recklessness than moral sense, I trust he is there."[15]

It took a long time for John to recover from Jack's death. He dove into new business ventures to bury the intense grief. Some say that Lillian never recovered and went into a steep decline, but her Coronado grandchildren helped: Lillie's daughter, Harriet, and Claus Jr.'s three children—Junior (called "Junie" by family members),[16] Frank, and Tookie—were all living within walking distance of the Glorietta Bay mansion. The official results are unknown, but John fought hard for custody of all of his deceased son's children. Jack left behind Marie, not quite eighteen; Adolph B., going on fifteen; and John D. III, eleven (his children by Edith)—and Geraldine Ann, his daughter by Syida, who was not yet five years old.

Immediately upon his son's death, John set about preparing for the financial welfare of these four grandchildren beyond his own life. Especially when Edith's marriage to Wakefield ended the same year she married him, John transformed his grief into concern for those grandchildren. As Syida was about to depart for Europe with Geraldine, she boasted to the press that she was "plentifully supplied with funds, which came from John D. Spreckels, Sr." in order for them to get out of town.[17] John's financial payoff to Syida would allow him to administer his son's estate to Geraldine. He did not trust that Syida would allow his son's fortune to benefit his granddaughter in the future.

Reporters ran to the San Francisco dock on August 22, 1922, after a sighting of the well-known *Venetia* steaming through the Golden Gate. John's stated reason for a visit was that he was arriving "to look after the interests of his grandchildren."[18] Months after his son's death and furious over Edith's "ultra-modernism in love and marriage," John filed for guardianship of Jack and Edith's three children.[19] The custody hearing came as a response to a lawsuit filed against Edith by a Mrs. Rodney Kendrick, who alleged that Edith was romancing her husband. Edith admitted that she offered Mrs. Kendrick $100 a month for life to quietly divorce Mr. Kendrick so that she could make him her third husband.[20] The details of any custody suit are unknown, but by August 1922, and in the years that followed the tragedy, Jack's three oldest children were often in Coronado with Opa and Oma Spreckels.

The Problem of the Heir Apparent: Claus

After Jack's death, all eyes were upon John's youngest son, Claus, to see if he could adjust to the new and demanding role of heir apparent. Society gossip held that Claus spent his money on extramarital affairs, gambling, and buying influence. Evidently, he enjoyed the status of being the son of San Diego's most prominent man as well as the social deference that went with that position. He got by just fine with his playful personality and good sense of humor. As the only remaining son, Claus was certain to inherit, so he might have succumbed to idleness and overindulgence. Perhaps he also felt so intimidated by his father's and grandfather's accomplishments that he never attempted anything of his own; having to measure up to the Spreckels name might have proved too daunting. His father might have been too busy maintaining and multiplying his wealth to teach Claus how to keep it. Speculation aside, the fact was that when Claus was out on the town, the money flowed, and women and false friends followed.

36. Claus A. Spreckels Jr. (1888–1935). After the death of his older brother, all eyes were upon him to see if he could adjust to the new and demanding role of heir apparent. Permission granted from the Laurie Fletcher Guidry Private Family Collection.

Some worried that if Claus was ever pushed too hard to succeed, he would cave under the pressure. By most accounts, he was both emotionally immature and intellectually unexceptional. In order to succeed in a Spreckels company and meet his father's perfectionist creed, he would have to undergo a dramatic personal change.

It was clear that Claus did not have his father's superhuman drive for business, nor was he interested in acquiring it. What he enjoyed doing most was playing with his children and singing, and he had a voice that inspired admiration. Newspaper stories tell of events where "Claus stopped the show cold" with his vocal talent, often getting two encores. After a performance at the Hotel del Coronado on August 18, 1917, the press noted that his talent was superb and that it was "a pity he is so seldom heard in public."[21]

Perhaps he would have been happier married to Mary Adele Case, his short-term fiancée from the Paris love affair back in 1909, who shared his musical passions. Perhaps he never forgave his father for breaking up that engagement, but in any case, it appeared that his marriage to Ellis was less than a happy one. His dalliances with other women were getting hard to suppress from the public, and the money he spent exceeded both his salary and the monthly allowance he was given. John had quietly—likely at Lillian's urging—paid his son's debts. Ironically, Claus's title at the Spreckels companies was "Treasurer."

Finally, to rein in his spendthrift son, John directed money to be sent directly to his wife, Ellis. On September 27, 1918, an interoffice memo instructed George Brunton, the company's auditor, to keep money out of Claus's hands: "Mr. J. D. Spreckels today verbally instructed that hereafter we send a check for $500.00 monthly to Mrs. Claus Spreckels, Coronado, and charge to his account, instead of making monthly credit of similar amount to Mr. Claus Spreckels' account, as heretofore."[22]

After Jack's death, Claus had either made promises for better behavior, or it was an act of good faith by John, because money was allowed to flow back to his youngest, as seen in the September 15, 1921, interoffice memo written by Claus to Brunton, informing the auditor to reverse his father's decision and reinstate the $500 monthly allowance (more than $7,000 in today's marketplace): "Kindly make voucher payable to me, for five hundred dollars every month, and charge same to Mr. J. D. Spreckels' account. Mr. John D. Spreckels has given me authority for this transaction."[23]

Claus's "Play Toy"

In a surprise move on February 20, 1922, John gave Claus "a new suit and a new car and a new job" and named him general manager of the San Diego Electric Railway Company (SDERy).[24] The ever-faithful William Clayton promised that he would remain quietly in the background and would serve as John's eyes and ears. Knowing how much his father hated Ed Scripps and his paper, one wonders why Claus spoke to a reporter from the *San Diego Sun*. The *Sun* quoted Claus as saying "that he and the Public have a 'lot of troubles to settle,' and he'll do his part as fast as he can; but don't rush me, Public."[25]

In March 1922, the *Electric Traction* magazine told railroad enthusiasts that the thirty-three-year-old son of John Spreckels had been elected general manager of the San Diego Electric Railway, the Point Loma Railroad, and the San Diego and Coronado Ferry Companies. The announcement noted that Claus "assumes the strenuous duties and responsibilities, not only in the full vigor of youth and enthusiasm necessary for coping with transportation problems; but possessing a deserved popularity among employees."[26]

One interoffice memo written on June 13, 1924, by Claus, who had now been promoted to vice-president as well as general manager of the Spreckels companies, reveals that he may not have been as popular with employees as the *Electric Traction* article had stated. The communication was in response to a letter from George Holmes, a longtime purchasing agent for the Spreckels companies, informing Claus that he would be using vacation time to attend an industry convention. Claus's response is negative:

Dear Sir:

Replying to your letter on under date of June 11, relative to the matter of your vacation and the California Railway Association Purchasing Agents Association Convention, I would say that it is not essential to leave town in order to take a vacation and would suggest that you stick around town.[27]

There are several other memos left behind from other employees who were seeking clarification for new policies that Claus had put into place, policies that an employee could easily view as threatening. Claus's responses essentially reminded the employees that the policies should have been put in place a long time before.

In October 1924, the American Electric Railway Association published a less-than-flattering portrait of Claus under the heading "Claus Spreckels' Play-Toy."[28] The *AERA* article portrayed Claus as a spoiled kid and stated that John had put his son at the head of the street railway to "keep him out of mischief."[29] In a defensive response, Claus stated, "Oh boy, but this was a broken up play toy he handed me."[30]

As vice-president and general manager of SDERy, he obviously wanted to make his mark; he announced a $2.5 million construction program to upgrade the entire system.[31] He commissioned fifty new streetcars, choosing a variety of the best new models at the time. His stated purpose was to make the company the best in the country, and the grand sum of this upgrade was $8 million (around $120 million today), a sum that likely made John and his financial managers shudder.

Mission Beach's Residential Playground

As a real estate developer, John understood the axiom "location, location, location" and had bought in 1913 a barren sandbar between the Pacific Ocean and Mission Bay. The fifty-foot-high sand dunes had discouraged development prior to his purchase, but to John, the potential gains appeared to outweigh the troubles: In June 1914, he formed the Mission Beach Company with some other investors. He entered as a 50 percent partner, and the company began grading and constructing a bridge to lay down rails for his trolley. The company filed a subdivision plan for "Mission Beach," which included the entire length of the peninsula.[32] Advertisements promoted the natural advantages of Mission Beach to potential property buyers, who would have access to a multitude of water sports after a hard day's work.[33]

In the midst of those promotions, unforeseen economic troubles began to crop up in 1915, and development came to a grinding halt. For one thing, the war in Europe had created worldwide financial instability, and then a flood of historic proportions hit San Diego in January 1916, causing considerable damage. Meanwhile, John was financially overextended in many other project developments—most notably, the San Diego & Arizona Railway, whose financial troubles never seemed to end. It seemed prudent not only to postpone development but to sell a portion of Mission Beach's northern peninsula to another developer, Josephus Marion Asher, who had also relocated after living through the horrors of the San Francisco earthquake. In 1916, Asher put up a "Tent City" at Mission Beach, hoping that those who had loved the Hotel del Coronado's Tent City would enjoy an even more affordable option. And while vacationers were there, they might be enticed to purchase a residential lot. Although Asher did sell a few lots, his timing was unfortunate; for the next several years, Mission Beach remained largely a seasonal vacation destination for visitors to San Diego.

However, by the early 1920s, business conditions had turned around: The navy had proved to be a financial boon for San Diego. In August 1922, John began revitalizing the Mission Beach development project with vigor. His $6 million sale of North Island the preceding December enabled him to buy out the smaller investors, and he now owned 75 percent of the company.

To create interest, in April 1923, John began advertising Mission Beach as a "residential playground" by showcasing its crowning glory, a seventeen-acre seaside playground to be called the Mission Beach Amusement Center.[34] He knew that to get people to move to his suburb, they must be shown "that they can get there quickly, comfortably and, above all, cheaply."[35] He replaced the dormant streetcar line with a modern, double-track express line that stretched from downtown San Diego to Ocean Beach—and then north to Mission Beach and La Jolla.[36] Residents would be transported effortlessly through the center of Mission Beach, with a station conveniently located at the brand-new amusement center.

Predictably, shortsighted critics accused John of being an overzealous developer looking to bilk a few more dollars from the public. On the contrary, opening an amusement park revitalized a floundering development effort by suburbanizing the city's growing middle class. Simply extending a streetcar line into a certain subdivision would not automatically guarantee growth, but installing an amusement park there might. John's strategy for urban planning and development was unique to the West Coast in the early twentieth century; he likely drew inspiration from successes on the other side of the country—most notably Brooklyn's Coney Island, which had been in place since the 1880s—that were designed to give the middle class an escape from urban life and all its drudgery. Catering to California locals, John presented a more uplifting objective: a place to live, play, and work all at the same time. After all, as was proposed to prospective residents, "Why not live happy and healthy?"[37]

The early decades of the twentieth century were a period of profound innovation in roller-coaster technology. With the thrill of danger at the heart of the experience of amusement parks, coasters rose to new heights and rocketed their riders through the air faster than ever. John had prominent coaster builders Frank Prior and Frederick A. Church build the Giant Dipper wooden roller coaster. He followed this with a roller-skating rink, pools, a "fun zone," and more. Meanwhile, so-called dance madness was sweeping up young Americans, and people were rushing to dance halls to learn the latest steps. To capitalize on this craze, John built a two-story dance hall with a large stage for the Mission Beach Orchestra; he also installed a café on a balcony above for the public to watch the dancers.

John emulated Bertram Goodhue's architectural style used in the Panama–California Exposition in Balboa Park: All the amusement park buildings were constructed in the same Spanish Renaissance style. As with the expo, the design reflected an idealized vision of California's Spanish history. Moreover, unlike other amusement parks, the Mission Beach Amusement Center was not fenced in, restricting visitor access through turnstiles. Instead, the park was designed to be a fantasyland, a smaller version of the expo. The buildings were placed along a beach-front boardwalk open to all, adjacent to a 1,600-foot-long sea wall, where visitors could sit and enjoy panoramic views of the ocean.

The Speech: "Gentlemen, I Love San Diego"

With Claus seemingly dedicated to the Spreckels companies, it was time for John to garner support from the business community for his many ventures, which would be left in the hands of his son. It was also time to explain his motives and his vision for San Diego to an audience of business leaders, many of whom had often criticized or thwarted his plans throughout his thirty-year career.

Those who knew John intimately worried that because of his reputation for shyness, he would not be able to deliver his long-awaited speech and redeem himself in front of the most influential politicians and businessmen in San Diego. But he rose to the occasion.

On the evening of May 19, 1923, nearly one hundred of the city's leaders arrived at the Hotel del Coronado for an elegant dinner in the stunning Crown Room, where it was rumored that John would be the keynote speaker. There were very few outside his companies who had ever *heard* him speak of his views, having only read them in his newspaper. Few would have refused this dinner invitation.

When John walked up to the podium, the only noise he likely heard was the rapid beating of his heart. He unfolded his six-page, single-spaced, typed speech, looked over the assembly and then down to the papers, and—after a long breath—began:

Gentlemen: I have asked you to do me the honor of dining with me tonight for three reasons: First, I want to know you better. Second, I want you to know me better. And, lastly, I want you to understand precisely what I have tried to do in the past.

"Actions speak louder than words" had become a familiar refrain of John's in the few years preceding his speech. This is how he justified not giving public talks.

> If I have not spoken my mind before, it was because I am a man of action rather than words: but I have foreseen the time when I must speak— right out in meeting as man to men. Well, gentlemen, that time is now![38]

He followed with a strong statement of his belief in the city:

> In fair weather or foul . . . I have gone steadily forward in my effort to help build the San Diego I saw in a vision on that far-off day thirty- six years ago when I first sailed the old Lurline into our splendid harbor. I had faith in San Diego. I still have. That is why I am still here. Faith!

Then he identified what it took to build a city such as San Diego:

> [Faith] may be able to move mountains, but, gentlemen, no amount of mere faith ever built a city. Only one thing can build a city, cooperation. It is team-play alone that can put a city on the map and keep it there.

John chronicled his arrival in San Diego as a young adventurer, and he relayed some of his undertakings that became more charitable than fruitful, such as the railroad and water companies, his bailing out a major bank, and more. He expressed his many private disappointments due to "persistent opposition and almost constant malicious misrepre- sentation," which had made him feel like quitting:

> There have been times—lots of them—when the game did not seem worth the candle. But, gentlemen, I am here yet!

John claimed that if the businessmen of the city would only work together, nothing would be too big to expect for San Diego. Lack of cooperation, he averred, was the reason San Diego had yet to become a metropolis, that it always seemed to "miss the train," as he put it—a lack of cooperation that he identified with the small-town mentality of his critics:

The moment anybody appears with any proposition of a big constructive nature, the small town undertakers get busy digging its grave. And if anyone dares to invest too heavily, he is warned that San Diego objects to being a one-man town. Well, gentlemen, if being a one-man town is bad for the town, it's hell for the "one man" in a one-man town!

He strongly denounced the popular saying that he always "played politics" and asked those in attendance to

try to put yourself in my place for a moment. . . . As long as candidates proclaim themselves anti-Spreckels, can you blame me for defending myself and supporting the other man? I am no coward. Quit making me an issue, and I will quit "politics." Surely, there must be men available for our city government with something more constructive in their minds than the popular slogan "to hell with Spreckels!" If that is the only necessary qualification for office, then God help San Diego!

How long do you progressive men mean to stand for this sort of small-town stuff? It paralyzes progress, it punctures prosperity; in short, it hurts San Diego, not me. Think it over, gentlemen, and see if you do not think it is about time to make up. I do.

He poignantly encouraged San Diego businessmen to offer support for Claus,

on whose shoulders must soon rest the heavy burden of my responsibilities and the carrying out of my future plans. All I ask for him who is to follow me is your support and sympathy in his efforts to realize, after I am gone, the dream and hope I cherished for San Diego.

When the long speech was over, his critics also learned that John D. Spreckels was not made of iron. The papers in his hands shook on the lectern, and, as he finished speaking, there were tears in his eyes. Developer Ed Fletcher recalled that John never looked up from the papers the whole time until the end, and then, looking out for the first time from the manuscript that trembled in his hands, this city-builder seemed to forget for a moment all the strangeness, embarrassment and uncertainty of his unwonted place as the speaker of the evening. He looked out over the silent assemblage. Tears filled his eyes and his voice came unsteadily as he spoke a short sentence not written in his manuscript: "Gentlemen, I love San Diego."[39]

Among family papers is an unsolicited letter from an average citizen who had read the published speech the following day in the *Union*. For one who had received letters from admirals, presidents, and royalty, the fact that this letter was saved in the family archives meant it was important to John.

> *May 20, 1923*
>
> Mr. J. D. Spreckels
>
> San Diego, Calif.
>
> It is my belief that it is the duty of a citizen to inform his public official of his opinion of their actions in order that it may aid them in the performance of their duties. How are they to know otherwise, for in few cases do they have the opportunity of finding out what their constituents really think? I have just finished reading the address which you gave at the Coronado Hotel last evening with a great deal of pleasure. It has been a wonder to me during the past 10 years that you have so much vilification without protest. I am glad that you have taken your admirers more into your confidence by giving this speech.
>
> It is with diffidence that I signed this as an individual for I believe that it is the opinion of a great many.
> Yours sincerely, [illegible name][40]

Although John's impassioned speech fostered an admiration for his principled stand among those in attendance as well as citizens who read it in the *Union*, Ed Scripps predictably savaged the speech and described it as a dramatic "swan song":

> You've done too much in your full life to go out in a towering, thundering rage, singing your own praises at a banquet paid for by yourself, and damning all those who oppose you. An old man singing his swan song is not a pretty picture. Passing along his crown to his son and seeking to pass along his prejudices and intolerances with his Sceptre.[41]

Only two weeks after that impassioned speech, the tables were turned. On June 13, 1923, six hundred businessmen attended an impromptu appreciation dinner for John at the U.S. Grant Hotel. The surprising toastmaster for the event was Ed Fletcher, John's longtime opponent on a number of issues. Fletcher recollected that he was astounded when Frank Belcher asked him to be the emcee because of the consistent fights he and John had had over water rights: "There never had been any love lost between Mr. Spreckels and myself."[42] John looked at the assembly and told them emotionally that they should "expect from my son all that you have from me."[43] When he sat down, there were loud cheers to the "Daddy of San Diego."[44] At the end of the evening, Fletcher ushered Claus to the podium, and John's son offered assurances to both father and the business community: "My father has promised you tonight that I will go through with the rest of the game and further build up what he has started and he is not going to break that promise."[45] Did anyone present think it peculiar that Claus made a promise that held his father accountable rather than himself?

Auf Wiedersehen, Lillian

It has been said that well-behaved women rarely make history, and in Lillian Spreckels's case, there are no truer words. There is little on record about how Lillian lived. She was the wife of a newspaper publisher, and she prided herself on discretion: She knew what the media could do with any loose slip. The only notable exception was the publicity she received for the trips she took for the cure at Karlsbad, Bohemia.[46] Bathing in or drinking Karlsbad's mineral waters was thought to cure a wide variety of ailments, but the place was predominantly viewed as a weight-loss spa. Having struggled with her weight over the years, Lillian joined the well-heeled of Europe who were put on a strict regimen that included drinking regularly from the "curative springs."[47] One "victim" portrayed a graphic picture of the costly road back to health: "In Carlsbad [*sic*] you drink often and drink deep. Drinking is your main occupation. Your drinking glass is strapped over your shoulders as you wander, sipping from spring to spring. Your misery begins at 6 o'clock. If you had not been a miserable sinner, you would not be here, but you have done those things you ought not to have done, and your penalty is Carlsbad [*sic*]."[48]

Lillian was extremely private; she really was in many ways like her mother-in-law, Anna. She preferred home to society. Though she had her European excursions, mansions, yachts, and millions of dollars at her fingertips, her primary focus through it all was her children and her grandchildren.

Adorable notes to her grandchildren found in baby books reveal a very engaged grandmother. Not wanting to leave the children behind in Coronado, she took them on trips with her. On one holiday trip to Honolulu, where she took Claus and Ellis's two sons, she wrote home to John, "Dearest . . . our little Frankie grows like a weed and is strong as a lion. He can pat-a-cake very nicely and say ta-ta. He loves to come in my room each morning for a visit, I play with him and he laughs so heartily."[49]

Lillian seems to have had a special relationship with Junie, a year older than Frankie. In regard to a train set she had bought him in Hawai'i, she proudly reported to a grandfather who knew trains well that their grandson

knows the names of all [the cars] and you should hear him say caboose. It really is the cutest thing I ever heard. He told me tonight to get in the caboose and he would take me for a ride. I let on as though I were climbing in and then I put my finger through the caboose window and said bye-bye June, and he said bye-bye Oma, and started off on fast speed and he said,—Oma fell out and broke her neck—cry, Oma, cry, and of course I cried to please him, and he laughed so heartily.[50]

37. Grace Alexandria (John and Lillian's eldest child) with her two daughters, Grace (b. 1907) and Mary Leila "Happy" (b. 1909). Courtesy of David Lewis.

And when Lillian was away, she wrote letters to be read to her grand-children by their nannies or parents. On a trip to San Jose, when Junie was only three, she sent him letters with details that would interest a toddler, events surrounding autos and butterflies, and included sketches. She ended the letter as only a grandmother would: "Write another letter to your Oma, for she loves her little Junior and . . . kiss dear little brother Frankie for me and I send you a kiss too in this letter. Kisses from Oma."[51]

But, after the death of Jack, there was a sadness that never left. Also, around the same time as her son's untimely death, both her mother and her sister Etta Elise passed.

Lillian never established herself as a Coronado society hostess; she let her daughter-in-law Ellis do that. Her idea of good entertainment was playing bridge both in her home and on the decks of ships. Lillian was dignified, always reserved, a little aloof. She had no real need for outside friends, since she had always been close to her younger sisters, and they were frequently together. She was also close to her daughters and often traveled to San Francisco to pass time with her eldest daugh-ter, Grace, and her two granddaughters there.

Lillian's charities centered on children's education and on children in need, and her contributions consisted of both cash and song. When she herself was not singing, she had Ernestine Schumann-Heink to provide the famous face for fundraisers. Madame Schumann-Heink was considered the greatest contralto of her era—perhaps of all time—and she became Lillian's vocal teacher and close friend.

John's world was turned upside down when Lillian died in the first month of 1924. She had been sick for a year, bedridden for a month, so her death was not unexpected. Feeling that her husband should have the last public word, she was likely the one who had encouraged him to give his keynote address at the Hotel del Coronado.

Lillian's private memorial service was officiated by Reverend Charles Barnes of St. Paul's Episcopal. Considering that she had loved music so passionately, it's surprising that her brief service was devoid of music. She was cremated and transported to the San Francisco Bay Area to rest beside her son Jack in Cypress Lawn Memorial Park. In Coronado, flags

38. Lillian Caroline Siebein Spreckels. John's world was turned upside down when she died in the first month of 1924. Permission granted from the Terrence and Virginia Wilson Private Family Collection.

were lowered to half-mast.[52] John donated $300,000 ($4.4 million in today's money) to Mercy Hospital for a "Spreckels Memorial Wing" in his wife's name.

Pushing Claus Out

It was during the last year of construction at Mission Beach that Lillian died, and John's enthusiasm for his project there waned. However, he hoped that the playground would be a fitting project for Claus, a kid at heart, to take over—even though none of the other businesses were thriving under Claus's authority. Spreckels employees were concerned about his lack of business sense. Family members were also taken aback by rumors of his extramarital affairs. Certainly, John hoped that the Mission Beach project would finally help his son establish himself.

The amusement center officially began operation on May 30, 1925, but the grand opening was a less-than-joyous occasion for John, due to his grief and problems created by Claus. Unfortunately, it had become clear that Claus could not be trusted with his family's legacy. Behind-the-scenes particulars remain unknown, but, in the summer of 1925, Claus was stripped of his titles and told to step down from all responsibilities within the Mission Beach Company as well as involvement within all the other Spreckels companies. He no longer had his mother to stand up for him. Samuel E. Mason took over Claus's titles at both the SDERy and the San Diego and Coronado Ferry Company. John softened this blow by appointing his son figurehead over an advisory committee, essentially "kicking him upstairs," where he would have no real authority in any Spreckels companies. To effect this demotion, John sent a formal letter to his son:

June 22, 1925

Dear Claus:

Referring to numerous conversations with you, you are all aware that the activities of the Spreckels organization have been enlarged very considerably within the last few years. Under these circumstances, it is necessary and advisable to have these activities very closely coordinated, in order to function properly, and I have been thinking of this matter for a number of months past, with the thought in mind of bringing these activities to one focus, as far as possible.

Within the next few days an advisory committee will be appointed to advise on all activities connected with all San Diego companies, and I should like you to consent to assume the chairmanship of this committee.

At the present time, you are directly connected with only some of these activities, and in order to take up the chairmanship of this broad advisory committee, I think it would be advisable for you to sever your direct connection with the few companies you are directly connected with, in order to assume the chairmanship of this broad Advisory Committee, for in that way you will be in a position to look at the coordinating of all efforts so that they will function to one head.

This has been a matter which has been discussed with you on many previous occasions, and I want to thank you for being willing to take up these new duties. It seems quite appropriate to make this change at this time, when the work you have been devoting so much time to relative to the opening of Mission Beach has been brought to such a successful conclusion.

I am writing this letter to you with two thoughts in mind: to formally put in writing the thoughts discussed between us, and to thank you for your willingness to take on these new duties, as outlined above.

I am, very sincerely yours,
John D. Spreckels
President[53]

Claus was humiliated by this public stripping of power. He knew this new role was offered just to appease him. He did not suffer the insult long, however, as he had no interest in playing the ineffectual, impotent figurehead. In April 1926, he made an ostentatious display of quitting, declaring, "I felt that I did not have to work under such conditions. My services will be more valuable elsewhere."[54] While Claus was deciding where that "elsewhere" might be, attorneys were called down from San Francisco to confer with the board members on the subject, a move likely purposed to keep John out of the fray, as his health was poor. Friends later revealed that Claus never recovered from this embarrassment and "seemed crushed by the turn of events" that ended in his parting from the company.[55]

After Lillian

The loss of Lillian's companionship was difficult for John. The comforts she had brought, the memories they had shared, the disappointments and tragedies they had endured together, the ever-important stability they had enjoyed—all were gone. There was no longer any reason to rush home from the office. John didn't even have his faithful chow dog Bear to go home to: Four weeks before Lillian had died, his beloved companion, his blue-ribbon champion, had been poisoned by a "maniac" on a "dog-harming spree" in Coronado.[56]

It was time to take a trip. John had a good reason because he was a California delegate for the Republican National Convention, to be held in Cleveland June 10–13, 1924. Not only did he hope to see Calvin Coolidge retained as president, but he would witness female delegates, who for the first time had been given equal representation in a political convention (following the ratification in 1920 of the Nineteenth Amendment, granting women's suffrage nationwide). John was well known to influential suffragists because he had supported women's rights for decades, so this convention would be momentous for him. Also, this would be the first convention to be broadcast over the radio.

John chose the *Venetia* as the method of transportation, which would require him to steam down the west coast of Mexico, through the Panama Canal, and then northward to New York. The trip in its entirety was shaping up to be the distraction he needed and a meaningful experience, both on and off the water. His twenty-year-old granddaughter by Jack and Edith, Marie, looking very much like a favored grandchild (based on the sheer number of references to her being seen with him at events), made plans to accompany her grandfather.

As John was packing for the long trip, his sister Emma Claudine Hutton died on May 2, 1924. She had been on her third marriage, she lived in England, and she left behind a thirteen-year-old daughter by her second husband, Jean Ferris, whose stepfather, Arthur Hutton, was her guardian. John hadn't seen his sister in years, due to the hurt and angry feelings after much litigation, but he was likely contemplative about their joint childhood.

It was on this trip that John decided to ensure his legacy. He asked preacher-turned-playwright Henry Austin Adams to write the story of his life. Since the trip would take several weeks, he invited Adams to make the trip with him so they could have hours of uninterrupted discussions. Adams was being handsomely compensated for his efforts, but he chose a curious way to negotiate payment, as seen in this letter John composed en route:

PANAMA CANAL

My dear Mr. Adams:

Referring to our conversation of recent date concerning the question of compensation for writing the story of my life, and for sundry other services that you have rendered me in the past, I acquiesce to your preference for a small monthly payment in the future, rather than for an immediate payment in full. I consider this a wise choice on your part, in view of your inexperience with the investing of money. You will, accordingly, henceforth be paid the sum of two hundred and fifty dollars ($250) [$3,722 in today's money] the first of every month.[57] While I appreciate your announced intention to "volunteer" as a "free lance" on my behalf in the future as well as you have in the past, I want it to be clearly understood that the proposed monthly payments to you are in no sense a salary, still less a pension, but simply deferred payments for past services.

Don't live too long, or you yourself may feel that you have been overpaid.[58]

With best wishes for your health and happiness.

Yours very truly,
John D. Spreckels[59]

Auf Wiedersehen, Adolph

On July 1, 1924, after the convention, as John was on his way home at a stop in Florida, he received the devastating news that Adolph, sixty-seven, his brother, business partner, and best friend, had died on June 28. For twenty years, syphilis had ravaged his body to the point that "memory loss and seizures evolved into brain hemorrhages and strokes. Heavy drinking became his escape." His niece Harriet further speculated that "as his last years slipped into a downhill slide," he likely welcomed his own death.[60]

Unable to make the funeral, John disembarked in Miami and made the mournful journey to San Francisco, in order to provide a stabilizing influence where needed. Austin Adams, who had planned using this long stretch of sailing time to finish John's life story, sailed back to San Diego and filled in the blanks as best he could.

Six months later, John made his last trip to San Francisco to create a lasting legacy for his brother in the city Adolph loved. As a tribute to him, John commissioned Ernest M. Skinner to build a magnificent indoor/outdoor pipe organ as a gift to the city of San Francisco—in the same way he had gifted San Diego with a municipal organ.

On the summit of one of San Francisco's hills overlooking the sparkling Pacific Ocean still stands a breathtaking structure, the California Palace of the Legion of Honor, which was planned and funded by Adolph and Alma Spreckels to be a replica of the original Légion d'Honneur in Paris. It is a memorial to the California soldiers who fell in World War I.

January 11, 1925, was a bitterly cold day, and John, in a long black coat and scarf, somberly made his way up the steps of the Palace of the

Legion of Honor to dedicate the organ. The fact that his brother had died before the palace opened its doors the preceding November must have added a deep sorrow to the ascension of those steps. Looking out over the assemblage, he said only a few simple words: "You have it in your hands; it is yours. I have bought it for the people of California."[61]

39. One of the last photos of Skipper Spreckels. "Sunset and evening star, /
And one clear call for me! / And may there be no moaning of the bar, / When
I put out to sea . . ." Permission granted from the Terrence and Virginia Wilson
Private Family Collection.

18

The Departed Skipper

When John returned from San Francisco after dedicating the organ in tribute to his brother, the record shows that he went downhill. He spent less time at the office, letting the "office" come to him. His persistent back pain was becoming less tolerable. Back pain was a medical enigma in the twentieth century, and it is unknown what treatment was given to John, but it was ineffective. Newspaper articles throughout his life referred to a broken collarbone, a broken leg, a broken nose—and there were likely more due to his boxing activities. All these may have contributed to the pain along his spine that had become debilitating.

With so much downtime, what did he dwell on? He must have felt his mortality keenly after the deaths of Lillian and then Adolph. He might have worried that his name and role in the history of San Diego would be forgotten. Did he find sadness when he gazed at the *Venetia*, which had been too long at anchor? Or did he find satisfaction savoring the memories of his many racing victories? On the ocean, as in life, he was relentless—never satisfied. He certainly would not have been satisfied with the enforced sedentary lifestyle.

So, in the fall of 1925, in a burst of hopeful energy, John planned a sailing excursion on the *Venetia* down the coast of Baja California to the isolated Magdalena Bay. This 850-mile trip would provide some solace from the loss of Lillian and Adolph as well as from his disappointment with Claus. Granddaughter Harriet remembered that "twenty old friends" agreed to accompany him.[1] The warm turquoise waters and pristine sand beaches of Baja seemed a good remedy, but then John's back gave out during the journey preparations, and he was told to lie flat in bed. His longtime personal physician, Raffaele Lorini, soon diagnosed him with "spinal disease." By December of that year, John was spending most of his time in bed.

By the following spring, rumors were circulating that John was near death. Inundated with queries regarding his condition, the *Coronado Eagle and Journal* downplayed John's ailments on June 1, asserting that his condition was "much better," and quoting a bulletin from Dr. Lorini: "Mr. Spreckels' condition is, in the main, comfortable, notwithstanding an evident ebb and flow of symptoms. He suffers no pain or apparent discomfort, the use of narcotics has never been required and the patient is receiving the sympathetic and devoted care of a staff of most competent nurses."[2]

Watching from the Sunroom

Fifteen-year-old Harriet, who lived just a stroll away from Opa, remembered that during his bedridden days, he "spoke at length of his plans for the future of San Diego and regretted his inability to see them to fruition."[3] He might have suspected that one of those plans he would not see to "fruition" would be the completion of his personal monument, the John D. Spreckels Building on Broadway, a massive structure designed to dominate downtown the way he had dominated daily life in San Diego for nearly forty years. In 1913, John had a rooftop sunroom built for his mansion, and this sunlit space, surrounded by beautiful foliage, offered him deep solace in the first part of 1926. The panoramic view afforded him a look across the bay at the progress of his downtown skyscraper. After four decades of development, his namesake building had become the most important project to him. When he became housebound, the building's shell had already risen above all the other buildings to its planned height of thirteen stories, but the sides were only halfway built out. It's easy to imagine that he must have felt each day as if he were racing against the clock to see his monument finished.

From his vantage point, John could see the Hotel del Coronado, the business venture that had brought him to San Diego many years earlier, when he was a "young skipper." He must have felt a deep sense of satisfaction as he gazed upon the gleaming white hotel, with its sprawling layout, multiple red turrets, and dormered windows. Undoubtedly, he sensed the important part in American history his hotel had played; its designation as a national historic landmark was assured.

Harriet remembered "he had the *Venetia* moved to a spot in the bay where he could easily see her entire form from the solarium."[4] He kept a close eye on his beloved yacht, listing in the sparkling bay by day and under the white shimmering moonlight at night. But curiously, during his days of confinement, he would not talk directly with the *Venetia*'s overseer of many years. In early 1926, the yacht's longtime engineer, William Darroch, conveyed his anxiety in private letters, referring specifically to his boss's "mental condition" and the fact that he was prevented access to visit.[5] It's easy to imagine in those last days, after the customarily exuberant, larger-than-life John D. Spreckels had become helplessly frail, that a visitor like Darroch might have outwardly shown pity.

Another visitor denied access was Rudolph Spreckels. The news of John's serious diagnosis prompted Rudolph to seek amends with his long-estranged older brother. In January 1922, he and Adolph had mended their estrangement publicly in San Francisco society; evidently, "their mutual admiration for horses" had inspired them to "discard their differences."[6] Now he apparently hoped for a similar outcome with John, but it was not to be. When he arrived in Coronado from San Francisco, he was refused entrance to the Glorietta Bay mansion. John could not bury the resentments he had long harbored against his brother.

John isolated himself in the solarium, which overlooked his first love, the deep, and dark, ever-restless sea. It's hard to know what his mental capabilities were, but one wonders what he thought about during this period of forced quiet. Was he surprised that he had made it to the winter of his life when so many of his siblings had not made it past childhood? Did he regret his role in the numerous lawsuits that had divided his family irreparably, precluding any possibility that brothers Gus and Rudolph could recollect with him the days of their shared youth? Did he think about his beloved son and namesake, who had died too soon? Or about his other son, who had just left the family company in a burst of anger?

He must have suspected that, after his death, his empire would fall to ruin. For without motivated and ambitious successors among his family, how could it survive? That thought must have been profoundly bitter, to be pushed away as soon as it entered his mind. He had worked so hard to build his empire that he could hardly imagine it dismantled. Moreover, that such a sad outcome was partly his own fault could not have escaped him. Even so, his pride prevented him from acting to secure his legacy while time still permitted. Other family members— particularly, his younger brothers Gus or Rudolph—might have stepped up to ensure the survival of his legacy, but it was much too late to renew those long-lapsed relationships. John did not easily forgive and forget.[7]

Crossing the Bar

It's not hard to imagine that John would ask his long-time faithful German butler, Hans Tiedemann, to help him traverse down the marble stairway so he could sit in his favorite blue-cushioned chair in the music room during one of his final nights, where, as most knew, he had spent many of his happiest hours with Lillian and the grandchildren. He would have turned a thoughtful gaze upon his beloved pipe organ. He may even have taken a seat at the precious instrument and pressed a wistful note or two on one of the keyboards. The venture downstairs would have been painful, however, due to his chronic back pain and his compromised breathing, and his feisty Lillian was no longer alive to tell him precisely when it was time for bed. Hans was never the one to give his boss an order, but he would stay with John, ensuring that all his needs were met before retreating to his own cottage behind the mansion.

Six months after Dr. Lorini's diagnosis, John died at the age of seventy-two. He took his last breath at 2:40 in the afternoon on Monday, June 7, 1926. The official cause was respiratory paralysis, common with sufferers of spinal cord injuries.[8]

John's casket was placed in the music room. The funeral at the mansion on Glorietta Bay was simple, per his wishes. Reverend Roy Campbell of the First Congregational Church of San Diego concluded the short ceremony with Tennyson's poem "Crossing the Bar"—fitting verses for one whose great love had been the sea:[9]

> Sunset and evening star,
> And one clear call for me!
> And may there be no moaning of the bar,
> When I put out to sea,
>
> But such a tide as moving seems asleep,
> Too full for sound and foam,
> When that which drew from out the boundless deep
> Turns again home.
>
> Twilight and evening bell,
> And after that the dark!
> And may there be no sadness of farewell,
> When I embark;
>
> For tho' from out our bourne of Time and Place
> The flood may bear me far,
> I hope to see my Pilot face to face
> When I have crost the bar.

"Crossing the Bar" seems to voice a compliant attitude regarding an imminent death. It is very probable that John himself selected this poem to provide comfort for his family. He might have envisioned himself on the *Venetia* at twilight, waiting for the tide to free him from the sandbar—his pain—lifting him "out to sea," ready and content to move on to meet God, his Pilot.

After Reverend Campbell read the poem, John's old friend Humphrey John Stewart slipped over to the organ seat and struck up the chords of Chopin's "Funeral March" as the casket was lifted for transport. The honorary pallbearers consisted strictly of men who had been John's loyal employees for more than thirty years. Children from the local school in Coronado walked to the ferryboat *Ramona* ahead of the casket, silently scattering flowers in the path.[10]

The funeral cortege traveled quietly past the *Venetia*, whose stars of gold signifying war victories, both mythical and real, twinkled in the sunlight, whose flag hung at half-mast, and whose engine ran in a final farewell to her skipper.[11] The *Ramona* rocked gently in the bay, "banked high with flowers and ferns," waiting to take the skipper for one last trip across the bay he had loved.[12]

His coffin was driven through the streets of downtown San Diego, where white flags had been hung at half-mast throughout the city as the solemn cortege passed by. Hundreds upon hundreds of his employees had stood for "a period of two minutes of silent tribute" at a prescribed time. Every ferry, streetcar, and even the train was stopped at the same exact time in a tribute to Mr. Spreckels.[13]

John was cremated at Greenwood Cemetery, and then his ashes were transported to San Francisco to rest beside those of Lillian and Jack in Colma's Cypress Lawn Memorial Park. The following week, Mayor John Bacon of San Diego ordered a citywide memorial service and issued a proclamation that public buildings would shut down during the hours of the service, saying, "This is little enough tribute to pay at the passing of a great San Diegan."[14]

Memorial to the Empire Builder

Nobody was surprised on August 25, 1926, when more than two thousand citizens bade their final farewells on that bright Sunday afternoon service at the Spreckels Organ Pavilion in Balboa Park. Because most of the family had traveled up north with John's ashes, there was only a small representation of family members in the front row; Lillie and her fifteen-year-old daughter, Harriet, and Claus and Ellis's nine-year-old daughter, Tookie. For many of the mourners, it was the first time they had seen any of the publicity-shy Spreckels clan in public. Intensely private, family members were rarely photographed or interviewed, almost never seen. John had made sure of that when he was alive.

Mayor Bacon told the assemblage that John's "name will live" because "everywhere you turn, transportation systems, great buildings, banks, parks, beach construction, water development, everything that touches our city life has been advanced by his work, and it seems particularly fitting that we should hold his memorial service here today in the shadow of this great Organ which he gave to the city of San Diego."[15]

Martin Luther Ward, state senator and Masonic brother, took to the podium and with "cheeks wet with tears" gave a lengthy memorial address, with the theme "An Empire Builder Passes."[16] This address was preceded and followed by those of several influential men with whom John had dealt with in the four decades during which he had amassed one of the largest fortunes in California.

Humphrey Stewart then sorrowfully climbed the stairs of the pavilion and sat at John's other organ for one last tribute. Stewart knew that John had two favorite compositions: one a tribute to his heritage, "Träumerei" (Dreaming) by German composer Robert Schumann, and the other a tribute to one of Hawai'i's greatest composers, "Aloha 'Oe" (Farewell to thee), whose melody was by John's old friend Queen Lili'uokalani.[17]

After the speeches were given, the songs sung, and the tears dried, what remained in the memory of San Diegans was the one short, unscripted sentence John D. Spreckels had spoken to city leaders at the conclusion of his one and only formal speech: With trembling hands and tear-filled eyes, he had looked out over the masses and said, "Gentlemen, I love San Diego."

Epilogue

Breaking Up the Empire

At the time of John D. Spreckels's death, almost every household in San Diego had been touched by his life. He had employed thousands of people, and, at one time, he was paying 10 percent of all the property taxes in the county. At various times, he owned all of North Island, the San Diego and Coronado Ferry Company, the Union-Tribune Publishing Company, the San Diego Electric Railway Company, the San Diego & Arizona Railway, and the Mission Beach Amusement Center, which became Belmont Amusement Park. He had built several downtown buildings that established the modern and stately skyline, including the Union Building, the Spreckels Theatre and office building, the Hotel San Diego, the Golden West Hotel, and much more. Besides the companies already mentioned, he had been president of the Oceanic Steamship Company, the Coronado Water Company, and the San Diego and Coronado Transfer Company. (Outside of San Diego, he had been president of the Western Sugar Refinery Company of San Francisco, the Pajaro Valley Consolidated Railroad Company, and other interests in Los Angeles and Hawai'i.) He had organized the Southern California Mountain Water Company, which built the Morena Dams, the Upper and Lower Otay Dams, the Dulzura Conduit, and the necessary pipeline to the city. He had contributed to the city's cultural life by donating land to those who would elevate the arts, music, and literature; he himself had built theaters and a library. He had given generously to transform City Park into Balboa Park for the 1915 Panama–California Exposition, and he had donated the Spreckels Organ Pavilion (along with its outdoor pipe organ) there. In other words, his footprints were everywhere.

So, it was shocking that the empire of John Diedrich Spreckels was broken up quicker than anyone in his era could have imagined. In 1979, fifty-three years after John died, San Diego's elder statesman, bank president Anderson Borthwick, was still expressing his utter disbelief at how quickly the "Spreckels Empire" had been dismantled. Borthwick, who had worked for John as a young man, concluded that the empire had broken up because some heirs wanted quick "cash."[1] And there was plenty of cash to be had; John had died rich, making his middle name, "Died-rich," very apt.

Many of his smaller holdings around San Diego were sold quickly and quietly. The first round of liquidation of John's biggest assets was believed by many to be retaliatory because they were sold "at ridiculously low prices."[2]

Selling Off the *San Diego Union* and the *San Diego Evening Tribune*

It was well known that Adolph Spreckels's widow, San Franciscan Alma de Bretteville Spreckels, intensely disliked John and had "an abnormal disdain for San Diego." After John's death, she seemed "to delight" in undervaluing and "selling short" the prized holdings of the brother-in-law who had never fully accepted her into the family.[3] Before Adolph married Alma in 1908, it was likely John who had insisted they have a prenuptial agreement to protect the J. D. and A. B. Spreckels Securities Company's assets. But as Alma began having children, Adolph, elated that he had not been made sterile from syphilis, took the prenuptial agreement and "tore it into shreds."[4] The erratic "Big Alma," as she came to be known, spent freely following Adolph's death in 1924. The book *Big Alma: San Francisco's Alma Spreckels*, currently in its seventh printing, chronicles her colorful life of unrestrained excess until her death in 1968 at age eighty-seven.[5] Her excesses reduced her inherited

$8 million fortune (half of $16 million; three kids split the other half) to a paltry $1 million.[6] Following John's death, Alma looked at her inherited interests in the J. D. and A. B. Spreckels Securities Company for liquidation possibilities, and the first to go was San Diego's leading newspapers and the Union Building, which housed them.

In 1928, Ira Clifton Copley, an Illinois newspaper magnate on a press-buying spree, knew a bargain when he saw one as the *San Diego Union* and the *San Diego Evening Tribune* went up for sale. He purchased the papers at such a ridiculously low price that he bragged that "he was offered several hundred thousand dollars more than he paid for the property a few hours after he bought it."[7]

Soon after the purchase, Copley hosted a celebration dinner at the Del and told the assemblage that his operating style would be far different from that of John Spreckels: "These papers are not to be personal organs of myself or anyone else. I have no political ambitions."[8] But such words did not ring true for those who knew Copley. Like John before him, Copley was a conservative Republican, and he supported those who sustained his political leanings. Edward Scripps had died just a few months before John, but his *San Diego Sun*, with its socialist leanings, continued on until Copley solved that problem, as John would have, by buying it out in 1939. When Copley merged the *Sun* with the *Evening Tribune*, the colorful era of the dueling papers of Spreckels versus Scripps ended.

The Fate of the Broadway Buildings

Many of the supposedly lasting memorials that John had envisioned would survive him, those steel-reinforced concrete buildings on Broadway emblazoned with his crest, instead vanished quickly after his death. San Diego's Save Our Heritage Organization (SOHO) stood up many times in the twenty-first century for Spreckels buildings but could not save all of them.

Copley's newspaper acquisition had come with the stately Union Building on Broadway, the city's first steel and concrete building. The popular building had not only established Broadway as the commercial hub of the city, it had also set the tone for the uniform "Chicago Style" skyline of modern San Diego. It was where John had his personal office and where most of the Spreckels business interests were housed. Despite its historical designation, though, it was demolished in 1974.

The beautiful and stately six-story Hotel San Diego, which had been built just in time for the 1915 exposition, was listed as an official San Diego Historical Site in 1983 for its significance in both architecture and cultural importance. Despite the valiant efforts of SOHO, though, it was demolished and replaced by a federal courthouse annex in 2006. Its rival, the exquisite U.S. Grant Hotel, still stands on Broadway as a reminder.

The thirteen-story John D. Spreckels Building at 625 Broadway was John's personal monument, though it was only half completed at his death and was one of the first properties to be sold, in 1927 to the Bank of Italy, and some say at a "ridiculously low price" of $2,250.[9] John's masterpiece was given a historic designation in 1983 and became home to several other banks, including Bank of America and Home Federal Savings. Today, it is dwarfed not only by the El Cortez Hotel, which surpassed its height in 1930, but by a number of more modern buildings, and it is in the middle of being converted to high-end residences.

The Spreckels Theatre is today the building most associated with the name John D. Spreckels. It has sat proudly on Broadway for over a hundred years, thanks largely to Louis B. Metzger, who managed the theater for ten years until his death in 1944. When it came up for sale in 1962, Metzger's daughter, Jacquelyn Littlefield, and her husband purchased it, returning it from a movie theater back to a historically restored live-performance venue. She cherished it until her death in 2019, and, as of the date of this publication, the building is for sale once again, and its future is unknown.

Selling Off the Oceanic Steamship Company

Oceanic was the venture that had given John the impetus to chart his own course in life, and he considered the business personally and emotionally important. The company had thrived with a fleet of passenger/

cargo steamships that operated from California to New Zealand and Australia via Hawai'i, but it was economically dependent on government transpacific mail contracts, which, in John's era, were awarded by acts of Congress. Thus, it prospered when it had the contracts but fell into deep economic problems when it did not, such as in the year that John died. Fred S. Samuels, the longtime vice-president of the Oceanic line, had worked hard behind the political scenes to retain the contracts, but in the months before his boss's death, it was a futile endeavor. On May 17, 1926, John's beloved steamships *Sierra, Sonoma,* and *Ventura* became subsidiaries of the Matson Navigation Company. After forty-five years, this must have been a hard blow to an ailing man.

Dispensing with the Spreckels Wharf

In 1886, in John's very first San Diego venture, he built a brick warehouse and an imposing black-timbered coal bunker on a huge wharf near today's corner of Pacific Highway and G Street. For many years, this wharf had been essential in San Diego's growth, receiving and processing such bulk commodities as coal, oil, cement, wood, fertilizers, and railroad iron. In 1922, seeing that the lease on the land would expire in three years, John had purchased the wharf for a cheap price. In the ensuing years, however, as the metropolitan environment in downtown San Diego changed—in particular, as coal was replaced by oil as the primary fuel for heat—the numerous piers and waterfront warehouses associated with the wharf slid into obsolescence. Downtown redevelopment put a spotlight on the city's former workaday warehouses, especially a "modern" one John had built in 1924. That warehouse was one of the few surviving Spreckels buildings, serving as a Cost Plus World Market store for decades. It was on the "most endangered list" of SOHO. Ultimately, though, the city council overturned its historic designation, and, in 2019, it was razed and replaced by a six-story apartment complex.

Selling Off the SD&A

Though the San Diego & Arizona Railway (SD&A) had been a great engineering achievement, the continuing calamities described at the end of chapter 12 required the input of an astonishing amount of repair money. A conservative estimate of the cost was $16 million (more than $237 million in today's money) from John's personal fortune, about the same cash he left his heirs, who likely imagined their bequests would have been doubled if only John had abandoned the project, an abandonment that many had asked him to consider.

As early as 1929, Southern Pacific Transportation Company (Espee), equal partners in the railway, approached the Spreckels heirs with an offer to buy their share at 50 cents on the dollar, or $5,500 (more than $82,500 in today's money). Espee likely thought this was a good offer because, as documented two years earlier, the railway had been operating at a deficit of $737,263. But the heirs did not accept the offer; when they saw there had been an ever-so-slight rise in both gross and net earnings in 1928, they hoped that the railway's fortunes would turn around.[10] But their faith never materialized into earnings. Landslides and weather calamities continued to play havoc with the railroad, and, in the years following the offer, the SD&A's financial condition was not enviable.[11]

In 1932, when the operating costs were more than twice its operating income and there was a deficit of $1,110,350, the Spreckels heirs knew it was time to cash in.[12] They sold the SD&A to Espee for $2,795,400. The line was rebranded as the San Diego & Arizona Eastern (SD&AE) and commenced operation on February 1, 1933, with new and improved freight service. SD&AE also acquired the Tijuana & Tecate Railway, which owned that part of the line between those Mexican cities. Familiar cronies were named as SD&AE directors: William Clayton and John's attorney and brother-in-law, Read G. Dilworth.

The Carrizo Gorge section of the line was subsequently battered by years of violent storms. In 1979, faced with a daunting bill estimated at $1.27 million to repair a line that was already hemorrhaging money each year, Espee pulled the plug on its "Impossible Railroad" and sold it to San Diego's Metropolitan Transit Development Board for $18.1 million, after agreeing to first restore the line to operational status.

Ultimately, the impact of the railroad was modest at best, since the era of highway development had begun. In 1951, with the advent and ease of air travel, passengers abandoned the line. In 1976, after a fierce storm caused irreparable damage, its use as a freight line was discontinued. The six-hundred-foot-long, two-hundred-foot-high, freestanding wooden trestle, built after a tunnel had caved in, today sits abandoned in the canyon but is a popular destination for serious hikers.

Selling Off the Spreckels Sugar Company

The death of John D. Spreckels marked the last time that any Spreckels sat on the board of directors of the family's sugar business.[13] The industry that had first brought the Spreckels family enormous wealth and worldwide recognition through its contributions to agriculture brought nothing but discord among the heirs after his death.

John was succeeded in the company management not by sons but by in-laws. Lillie's daughter, Harriet, recorded that she and the other John D. heirs attempted to stabilize proposed liquidation proceedings, but there was a "hectic family situation" on the "other side," meaning Adolph Bernard's side of the family, when Adolph Jr. sued his mother, "Alma de Bretteville Spreckels, for funds of the company that she had claimed were earned dividends, while Adolph Jr. contended they were capital disbursements."[14] This lawsuit resulted in Alma retaliating by selling her stock to "an outside financial company, which in turn sold it to the American Sugar Refining Company," a large, publicly traded company based in New York, which already owned 50 percent of the Spreckels Sugar Company by this time, and therefore gave "American Sugar the upper hand in Spreckels Sugar."[15] In 1963, American Sugar Refining absorbed the Spreckels Sugar Company (including the Western Sugar Refinery Company of San Francisco) as a fully owned subsidiary.

On the East Coast, the company was identified by its yellow Domino label. On the West Coast, the Spreckels label was seen on grocery shelves but always in second place to the pink-packaged "pure cane sugar from Hawai'i" created by C&H Sugar. While refined sugars from beet and cane are used interchangeably for most purposes, the strongest markets for Spreckels beet sugar became commercial food manufacturers. Within a few years, the company was renamed Amstar Corporation. The name "Spreckels" remained a division of Amstar until 1987, when it went private and separated itself. In 1996, it merged with Holly Sugar Corporation. In 2005, Southern Minnesota Beet Sugar Cooperative purchased Holly Sugar from Imperial Sugar Company (which had owned it since 1988), and the name Spreckels Sugar Company, Incorporated, was chosen.[16] After the buyout, according to Harriet, "although control of the Spreckels Sugar has passed out of the family's hands, our allegiance to it remains strong. This is evidenced by the fact that when we dine at a restaurants or hotel, Lyn (Harriet's daughter) carefully checks the brand of sugar served, and if the management has had the good judgment to choose Spreckels sugar, it puts us all in very good humor."[17]

Selling Off the Del

John's granddaughter Harriet recalled that after the Depression and throughout the turbulence of World War II, "opinions of family members continually clashed, meetings became heated and vindictive. Shortly after World War II, in order to relieve the tensions, the J. D. and A. B. Spreckels Company was liquidated. All properties were disposed of and the liquid assets were distributed to the individual family members."[18]

One of the last remaining assets was the world-famous Hotel del Coronado, purportedly the last surviving Victorian wooden hotel in the United States. It remained in the Spreckels family trust through World War II and did not come up for sale until January 1948. The sale of the iconic hotel was one of the major real estate transactions in an otherwise slumping post–World War II real estate market in San Diego.

Peter DeLancy Lewis married (for his second time) the second daughter of Grace Alexandria Spreckels Hamilton and Alexander "Alec" Hamilton: Mary Leila "Happy." (It was Happy's second marriage as well; she was recently divorced from Phillip Neill and had two sons by him.) Lewis convinced the other heirs to sell the Del and all Spreckels holdings in San Diego and Coronado.

The heirs sold the hotel and 470 acres of Coronado acreage to Bostonian financier Robert A. Norbloom and a small group of investors for $2 million. The ink was barely dry on the purchase contract before

Norbloom curiously sold the property to Jewish Russian immigrant and hotelier Barney Goodman of Kansas City in April 1948 for $17 million. Goodman then spent $2 million in major renovations to modernize the hotel. Only half of the 360 rooms had baths. He added 60 rooms, each with a bathroom, and operated the hotel until his death in 1951.[19]

Spreckels's longtime employee, Ernest R. Tiedemann, provided the much-needed stability for both the community and the employees as the Del's general manager. His considerable knowledge of the hotel's history and culture was invaluable during the years following Spreckels's death. Tiedemann had met Spreckels in San Francisco in 1912, soon after he arrived from Hamburg, Germany, with his bride and needing a job. John was looking for loyal staff at the Del, and his instincts were good: The "tall, stately, gracious and soft spoken" Ernest (brother of John's butler, Hans Tiedemann) served in many capacities at the hotel, stayed on after the 1948 sale, and retired as general manager in 1960, after forty-seven years of service, when the next new owner stepped into place. Ernest died in 1964 at the age of 71.[20]

In 1960, San Diego's colorful John Salvatore Alessio, who gained fame through his ownership of Tijuana's famed Agua Caliente racetrack, purchased the Del. He was one of seven enterprising sons of an Italian Immigrant who arrived in San Diego in 1920 in a "beat up panel truck" from West Virginia.[21] From shoeshine boy to banker, businessman, restaurateur and race-track operator, he made millions and then spent two of them upgrading the public interior areas with the help of a Hollywood scene designer, hoping to attract conventions and the money they could bring.[22] In 1962, Alessio lobbied the City Council of Coronado to finally build a bridge across the bay, which would make the Del more accessible to travelers. Spreckels himself tried to get a bridge built in 1926. But the idea, as before, was rejected by a popular vote. Many Coronadoans did not relish giving up their small-town atmosphere and worried about the amount of people who would trample their island via the bridge. Alessio, disgruntled, sold the hotel after only three years. Alessio might have hung on to ownership of the hotel had he known that a bridge would be approved in 1964. After two years of construction, the gracefully curved San Diego-Coronado Bay Bridge, high enough for the tallest navy ships to pass, opened on August 2, 1969. In the course of a colorful and controversial life, Alessio gave generously and is known today as the developer of safety helmets for jockeys. He was a force in California politics until 1970, when he was convicted and served two years of a three-year sentence for federal income-tax evasion. Before his death in 1997 at the age of eighty-seven, he told friends that, before prison, his "life was little short of fantastic."[23]

In 1963, Maurice "Larry" Lawrence, a millionaire developer, bought the deteriorating hotel from Alessio. The sale included lands just south of the hotel. Lawrence invested $150 million on top-to-bottom renovation and expansions that included new foundations, electric wiring, plumbing, heating, and, most importantly, a multimillion-dollar fire alarm system to ensure the second largest wooden structure in the United States would survive throughout the ages.

With the bridge in place, Lawrence accomplished what Alessio did not and opened the Grande Hall Convention Center in 1972 that could hold 1,500 people.[24] The Del is one of the most photographed hotels in the entire world, but it is hard to find an exterior photo of Lawrence's convention center, which was built on the northeast corner of the property fronting Coronado's main artery. This is because it is a large, unembellished building juxtaposed against the decorative hotel. The architectural design tried to mimic the architecture of the Del in color, but it failed not only in its appearance but in location, as it completely blocks the views to the iconic hotel from the street that matters the most, historical Orange Avenue.

In 1973, Lawrence then built the architecturally insignificant seven-story Ocean Towers on the southwestern corner of the property. The Towers, with 214 rooms, did not even attempt to complement the historical hotel in any shape or manner. Throughout the remainder of the 1970s, Lawrence expanded the Del in many other areas, some good choices were made and some not.[25]

Lawrence, personal friend to President Bill Clinton and the Democratic Party's top donor, was rewarded with an ambassadorship to

Switzerland. When Lawrence died in 1996, Clinton provided him a waiver as a wartime Merchant Marine to be buried in Arlington National Cemetery. One year later, he received posthumous humiliation when it was revealed that his purported wartime service was a fraud, and his body was dug up and returned to San Diego in 1997.

After Lawrence's death, the hotel was then sold in several transactions between financial institutions. Travelers Insurance Company bought the hotel for an undisclosed amount in September 1996 and then sold it to Lowe Enterprises in August 1997 for $330 million. After a $55-million renovation project, the Del was then sold in 2003 to a business partnership. CNL Hospitality Properties Inc. and KSL Recreation Corporation carried out a further $10-million renovation project and in 2005 announced a first-time development of "North Beach," with an exclusive enclave of villas adjacent to the hotel.[26] The hotel was next owned by the Blackstone Group LP (60%), Strategic Hotels & Resorts Inc. (34.5%), and KSL Resorts (5.5%). In 2007, the Del unveiled the limited-term occupancy cottages and villas on "North Beach." Most of the community did not object, because Beach Village, as this development was called, was tastefully designed with the trademark white-and-red Victorian architecture that the hotel is known for throughout the world. In 2014, Strategic Hotels & Resorts became full owners of the hotel, but, by December 2015, Blackstone purchased them and became full owners.

In March 2016, Blackstone Group announced they were selling the Hotel Del to Beijing's Anbang Insurance Group. There was a great uproar in the military community due to the fact that a sale to a Chinese company could potentially pose a national security threat. In very close proximity to the hotel are a naval air station, an amphibious base, landing fields, a warfare-training center, and a training ground for Navy SEALs. It is also in close proximity to other major naval bases. The sale was blocked in October 2016 by the federal interagency Committee on Foreign Investment in the United States, citing "security concerns," and the hotel remained in Blackstone's ownership. In August 2017, Hilton Hotels and Resorts took over the management of the Hotel del

Coronado as part of their upscale Curio Collection, while Blackstone Group still retains ownership.

The Hotel del Coronado temporarily closed to the public at the end of March 2020 for the first time since its 1888 opening, in response to the pandemic. During its closure, the entire twenty-eight-acre resort was to undergo a massive $200 million redevelopment and expansion project. At the time of this writing, the Del has turned into a major construction zone, with the roar of jackhammers and bulldozers piercing the enforced quiet of the small island community, who are "sheltering in place" under the restrictions of the COVID-19 outbreak. Some of the resort's features and structures dating back to the time of John D. Spreckels's ownership are being historically restored, which excites those who celebrate the hotel's storied history. The master plan for this beautiful National Historic Landmark is scheduled to be completed by year-end 2021.

With the frequent changes in ownership, one local columnist, way back in 1969, wrote a personal note to the "Lady by the Sea," the Hotel del Coronado:

> Dear lady, you have been sold and resold. Each time, those who know and love you, hope you won't let new money go to your head. . . . Just like a woman, you have allowed yourself to be swept into the times to meet all the modern demands of the day, but never have you lost your dignity, your charm, your grace, your femininity.[27]

Selling Off the San Diego Electric Railway and Other Municipal Holdings

Coronado's Orange Avenue Line on the San Diego Electric Railway (SDERy) saw its last day of service on May 31, 1947. In the following year, the Spreckels heirs sold the SDERy privately to Jesse L. Haugh, thereby reducing the holdings of the J. D. and A. B Spreckels Company to about one hundred acres of land.[28] Haugh renamed the railway the San Diego Transit System. It was hard to compete with the new motorized buses, and the Spreckels streetcars were retired in 1949. The system was later sold to the city of San Diego.

Various other enterprises and vast holdings were also sold or disposed of. The Coronado Ferry Company, the Coronado Water Company, and the Coronado Railroad Company were all transferred to the city of San Diego at cost. Belmont Park, the multimillion-dollar amusement park that John had named the Mission Beach Amusement Center, was donated in 1934 to the state of California, which then transferred it to the city of San Diego. When eighty acres of unimproved land northwest of Miramar were sold on March 1, 1948, the selloff of Spreckels municipal properties was complete.

The Fate of Balboa Park's Organ Concerts

Following John's funeral, a reporter asked his son and heir, Claus, if he would continue to contribute the $120 a month to "maintain the organ recitals on Sundays in Balboa Park."[29] Claus's "terse reply" of "Absolutely Not!" was, in the reporter's view, "hurled." "Young Spreckels said a great deal when he said those two words. He could not have recited 10,000 words and met with more public disappointment in him. His attitude is one of the supreme authority. His wealth is his to deal with as he chooses! He does not choose to perpetuate the memory and the esteem of his father through music, which was a deep love with the little giant enterprises."[30]

John's longtime friend Humphrey John Stewart enjoyed at that time the role of paid civic organist and played daily concerts for an annual salary of $4,000.[31] John also, through the park board, had paid $120 monthly for an organ tuner. Stewart lived in Coronado, and there are some hints in the city council minutes that suggest a bit of unfriendliness between Stewart, who was chairman of the board of trustees in Coronado at the time of John's death, and Claus, who was also sitting on the city council then. Regardless of the reason, "Absolutely Not!" became the headline that made John's heir very unpopular with the community.

The Spreckels Organ Society (SOS) was formed in 1988 to ensure the continued preservation, promotion, and programming of the free-to-the-public organ concerts. Ross Porter, executive director of SOS, explained that "in the wake of Claus's [1926] decision, the San Diego City Council allocated funds to pay the Civic Organist for regular concerts and incorporated the upkeep of the organ and pavilion into its budget."[32] Today, the Spreckels Organ Pavilion is the setting for a wide variety of public and civic events.

Selling Off the Glorietta Bay Mansion and Dispensing with Its Pipe Organ

John bequeathed his Glorietta Bay mansion to his eldest child, Grace Hamilton, who he had likely hoped would live in Coronado part time.[33] But Grace was well established in northern California and probably could not bear the thought of living in the home of her adored parents. Ira Clifton Copley sought Grace and Alec out and, on May 29, 1929, purchased the mansion for $225,000. Today, the mansion is the Glorietta Bay Inn.

Hans Tiedemann, John's German butler for many years, was forced to leave his garden apartment in back of the mansion. With the $5,000 left him in John's will, he moved to a small home several blocks away, at 900 E Avenue. He became a recluse in the years after his boss died, preferring the company of his parrot and his flowers. In 1952, he hanged himself from a shower rod in his bathroom.[34]

At an unknown point in time, John's daughter Lillie Wegeforth and her friends dismantled and packed up his beloved pipe organ. The twenty thousand pieces that once composed the Aeolian Company Opus 1345 Organ were taken to a San Diego warehouse belonging to the Golden Construction Company. When Lillie died in 1965, her daughter, Harriet, was tasked with trying to ensure that the pieces were not thrown into a trash pile. Her efforts to donate the organ were unsuccessful, due to the sheer amount of money and time it would take to reassemble it.

Somehow, the organ pieces were acquired in 1982 by Wendell Schoberg, owner of the San Diego Pipe Organ Company, who then sold it in the same year to Richard F. Zipf, a wealthy eye surgeon in Carmichael, California. Even though Zipf never played the instrument, he meticulously restored John's organ to its former glory as a hobby. Zipf put it up for sale for $347,729 but, in the end, magnanimously donated it in 2012 to the George Eastman Museum in Rochester, New York, along with funds for its shipment, refurbishment, and installation. The three-manual console with a roll-player mechanism (235 rolls) and forty ranks of wooden and metal pipes is a showpiece. The museum's legacy curator, Kathy Connor, assures us that John's legacy lives on in New York, that the museum hosts pipe organ groups and conventions from around the world. "We have organ concerts the first Sunday of every month and regularly play the instrument during evening special events. Our museum docents play organ rolls for visitors on a daily basis, so all visitors get to hear this spectacular instrument."[35]

Selling Off the *Venetia*

The yacht *Venetia*, John's most prized and personal possession, remained moored near the ferry wharf for nearly two years following her skipper's death. In 1928, she was sold for $60,000 to James Playfair, a wealthy Canadian lumber baron and yachting enthusiast, who lived in Pasadena. On March 31, 1928, the yacht steamed out of San Diego Harbor under a new skipper. San Diegans and Coronadoans lined the waterfront to watch the city's mascot sail away; there was an air of a "funeral" around the departure.[36] In 1939, the *Venetia* was sold to Robert Scott Misener, founder of the Scott Misener Steamships, the largest fleet on the Great Lakes. She was scrapped in 1963, when Misener died.[37] It was highly unusual that the name of the yacht was never changed over the course of her long life. The book *Millionaires, Mansions, and Motor Yachts: An Era of Opulence* by Ross MacTaggart extensively covers the history of the *Venetia* with stunning photos.

More than likely, having been encouraged by an ailing John, all his heirs filed a lawsuit in 1927, seeking the remaining 25 percent that was still outstanding for damages incurred to the *Venetia* during her military conscription. John had received only $57,248.87 (75 percent of the damages) in 1919 and had never been successful in encouraging the government to release the balance. However, the heirs filed suit with guns ablaze and prevailed, receiving lease payments in addition. The U.S. Supreme Court awarded them $41,082.98 (nearly $605,788 in today's money) as "reasonable compensation" for the damages incurred.[38]

Disbursements from John's Will

The will of John D. Spreckels held no surprises. John's final estate was appraised at $16,740,264 (more than $242.6 million in today's money) for the inheritance tax levy.[39] After all legacies, beneficiaries, and creditors were paid—the amount of $7,000 ($107,545 in today's money)—the estate was divided evenly among his children and grandchildren, without the favoritism that his parents had shown. Grace, Lillie, and Claus each received a quarter of the amount, with the fourth quarter going to the children of his deceased son, Jack: Marie, Adolph, John, and Geraldine.

On page 11 of John's will, it's easy to see that he was worried about Jack's four children:

> It is my earnest wish that the children of my said deceased son, John D Spreckels, Jr., shall be cared for and reared in one or more of the families of my daughters, or of my son Claus Spreckels. I direct my trustees to pay to either of my daughters or to my son, who shall have custody in care of any of such children, the sum of $250.00 per month out of the income of the trust estate, for each child . . . for the proper support maintenance and education of such a child, so that it may have the best care and the best education which is capable of acquiring.[40]

The amount of $250 a month for each child was more than generous, considering that today the amount would be more than $3,600, but the record does not reveal that any of Jack's children were overseen by his siblings. Leaving a nest egg for Jack's children was being fair, from John's perspective; he wanted them to survive. But such a nest egg can go fast, particularly when you're young and have no overseer—which is what happened with every one of John's grandchildren by Jack.

To ensure accountability to one another, John had also showed no partiality and had made his three surviving children, son-in-law Alec Hamilton, and his brother-in-law, Walter D. K. Gibson, equal executors, along with the levelheaded William H. Hannam, who for twenty-five years had managed the Spreckels sugar interests and could easily be the "referee" in any family disagreement.

John also left significant amounts to Lillian's sisters, several employees, and close friends, but the largest bequest of $300,000 ($4.6 million in today's money) was given to San Diego's Catholic Hospital, Mercy, as a memoriam to his wife, Lillian.

To John's credit, his plan to divide his estate evenly succeeded because it did not result in an inheritance battle in court, resembling the one that he had with his siblings after the death of his own parents.

John's Surviving Children

CLAUS SPRECKELS

With his powerful father no longer in control of the newspapers, the romantic peccadillos of Claus were freely printed. One widely publicized love affair in 1928 with Follies dancer Hertha "Babe" Kaths almost caused him to be arrested under the Mann Act. This 1910 law made it a crime to transport women across state lines "for the purpose of prostitution or debauchery, or for any other immoral purpose."[41] Hertha's mother pressed for a conviction for Claus, who had taken her daughter to New York, but in the end, she lost the case and suffered a nervous breakdown due to stress.

Claus's independent enterprises never went well, and his financial problems were exposed. Bad market speculations and poor investments brought court cases against him and swallowed up the fortune he had been left with. In the summer of 1931, several newspapers reported that Claus Spreckels had blown through his $6 million inheritance and had filed for bankruptcy. In the summer of 1932, Ellis Spreckels had no choice but to use $250,000 from her personal $2 million trust fund and borrowed another $150,000 to fight "post-bankruptcy litigation."[42] It must have been stressful for the fiercely private family to endure the negative publicity that they had been previously been shielded from when John was alive.

In the fall of 1934, Claus, age forty-six, came down with pneumonia and was hospitalized in San Diego's Mercy Hospital—likely in the south wing, which his father had funded in memory of his mother. Having pneumonia exacerbated Claus's fight with his diagnosed lung cancer. On December 10, when he believed that his condition had stabilized, he left San Diego for San Francisco to stay with his sister Grace. Ellis had taken six-year-old Claire on a European excursion, so she wasn't consulted on her husband's decision to go to San Francisco. It was immediately evident to Grace, however, that Claus was in critical condition. He was soon admitted to San Francisco's exclusive Dante Sanitarium, where it was determined that his lung cancer had metastasized throughout his body.

Claus died in the city of his birth on January 12, 1935, from "Cancer of Lung," according to his death certificate. He was cremated and placed beside his parents and elder brother in Cypress Lawn Cemetery. He just missed meeting his first grandchild, Carol Ellis Spreckels, born January 23, 1935, to his firstborn son, Claus Jr. ("Junior"). His sister Lillie, who arrived in San Francisco to say a final goodbye to her younger brother, later gave Claus's physician, Harold Brunn, a generous grant to study lung cancer.

When Claus's estate was settled, people sighed with relief that John Spreckels, who had understood that his son might easily blow through his inheritance, had created a trust sum that would take care of Ellis and their children, Junior, Frank, Tookie, and, later, Claire.[43] After his estate was settled in 1937, the only asset left in Claus's name was a "Four-cylinder truck—not in condition to operate—$20."[44]

Ellis was able to find true love in her second marriage in 1936, to the distinguished Dr. Edward Clarence Moore. Unfortunately, the love didn't last long for poor Ellis; Edward died in 1944 at the age of sixty-two from kidney cancer.

GRACE SPRECKELS HAMILTON

John's eldest child, Grace Alexandria Spreckels Hamilton, lived a good life, dividing her time between her beautiful apartment in San Francisco and her summer country estate in San Mateo County's Menlo Park/ Atherton; she also resided part of each year in Europe. In Menlo Park, she was the happiest, spending quality time with her two daughters and nurturing the family passion for horses. Grace was one of the founders of the popular Menlo Circus Club, designed exclusively for children and offering a "circus" for the enjoyment of their community. The children performed alongside a menagerie of chickens, a cat, three dogs, a goat, and a few ponies. Over time, the event grew more elaborate until it became the social event of the summer season, with the proceeds given to the Stanford Convalescent Home for Children.

Grandson David Lewis said that even before dog purse carriers were in fashion, a sweet Pomeranian could be found peering out of his grandmother Grace's purse.[45] Grace died at the age of fifty-eight on January 23, 1937, two years after her brother Claus, from a heart attack, likely due to her heavy smoking. Her husband, Alec Hamilton, had already died on October 14, 1932, and Grace sadly died "with only a maid in attendance."[46] Her two daughters, Grace Hamilton Kelham and Happy Hamilton Lewis, donated in her memory her extensive art collection to several San Francisco art institutions, including the Palace of the Legion of Honor.

LILLIE SPRECKELS WEGEFORTH

John's second child, Lillian "Lillie" Caroline Spreckels Wegeforth, never remarried after the death of her second husband, Paul Wegeforth, in 1923. She stayed mostly in the shadows of Coronado's society, preferring to spend time with the children of her daughter, Harriet, by Harriet's first husband, Frank G. Belcher.

In 1937, Lillie had an operation on her eyes, which left her needing to wear very thick glasses. Her grandson Garry remembered that "tiny Omie" was virtually blind, and this necessitated that she retire from the popular Coronado National Horse Show, which she had founded and funded at great expense.[47]

Of all John's children, it was Lillie who most had a philanthropist's heart. Using her inherited money, she gave wherever it was needed; medical science and research, in particular, ignited her passion for giving. In 1939, she gifted Coronado, the community she loved so much, with land and funds to build a hospital.[48]

Harriet and Frank moved to San Francisco in 1946 and then to the wealthy enclave of Atherton with their children, John "Garry" (1932), Frank "Mike" Garrettson Jr. (1934), and David Holbrook (1941). Daughter Virginia Caroline was born soon after, in 1948. Wanting to be near her family, Lillie made the heart-wrenching decision to leave her beautiful home on Adella Avenue in Coronado and follow them. Being the only surviving child of John D. had given her a very special status in San Diego, a status she would never regain after her relocation.

In Atherton, Lillie built a house next door to Harriet, and grand-daughter Virginia remembers scampering between the two houses on an obscure brick footpath. After moving away from Coronado, Lillie's relationship with Harriet became terribly strained over money. Lillie begged Harriet to no avail to stop spending frivolously from her inherited funds. Like her father, when Lillie gave, it was for a purpose. To see money frittered away by her daughter broke her heart. Both of her grandsons remembered finding their grandmother in tears over the state of affairs.[49]

Despite Lillie's turbulent relationship with her daughter, the love between her and her grandchildren—Garry, Mike, Virginia, and David (who died at twenty-one in 1963 in an airplane accident)—was deep and real. Garry recalled that, as a child, he had a hard time forming "Oma," so he called her "Omie," the name that would stick for life. The grandchildren all loved "tiny Omie" fiercely and remembered her as the stability in their lives. Like Lillie's dad, she was shy, greeted everyone in the same way, loved a stiff drink, told dirty jokes, and was as tough as nails, until the pain of life became unbearable.

Lillie Caroline lived the longest of John's children; she died at the age of eighty-five in 1965. Grandson Mike recalls the sad day she died: "She simply decided she wanted to pass on, and so she quit eating, sipping only water for a couple of weeks."[50]

The Empire Builder's Legacy

Today, only a few things retain the Spreckels name. In many ways, that fact is a sad commentary on a once-great legacy and vital chapter in San Diego's history. Where John Diedrich Spreckels is remembered, it is the bull terrier part of his personality (the breed that he was regularly compared to) that has most often survived. Less known is his softer side, the gentleness of character that time seems to erode most in historical figures: his love for his family, for the sea, for art, for music. . . . Perhaps that was the true John D. Spreckels: the quiet man his father thrust into the spotlight; the man reluctant to make waves but willing to work hard to finish his goals.

John's fierce love for his adopted city was clear. That said, John was a consummate businessman. There are probably few men who were as pragmatic about making money as John Spreckels. He did not buy companies out of ego, or because they were in trending industries, or because they were well-known names. He bought them only if he believed he could elevate or advance them with the latest technology of the time and, most important, make him a profit.

Millions of John D. Spreckels's dollars changed hands over the years—years that regrettably included a number of shattered relationships. Looking back, though, it is clear that John built and expanded his empire and held it together by the sheer force of his dogged personality. What is the evidence? After his death, there was nobody in his family with the will to maintain his physical legacy.

After writing the story of John D. Spreckels's life and looking around the city he built and I live in, I looked within for some last thoughts regarding his lasting legacy and could not easily articulate them. Feeling pressured by deadlines, I struggled with the right words to express my innermost feelings. And then, to my amazement, I discovered a century-old tattered undated newspaper clipping, entitled "An Empire Builder Passes," that not only reaffirmed the book's title decision, but put into words what was in my heart:

> The city of his vision—that is not his enduing tribute, but a finer thing. His legacy is the spirit that builds a city and that spirit is his lasting memorial, enduring beyond gold or stone or steel.[51]

NOTES ON SOURCES AND RESEARCH

I have not identified any single repository for the public and private papers on "John Diedrich Spreckels" in any main institution. His industries were far and wide, and it seems those papers found their way into the archives of the various industries. Those interested in the San Diego & Arizona Railway will find bounty at the Southern Pacific Railway Museum in Campo, California. The financial records of Adolph and John Spreckels, held at the Bancroft Library, University of California, Berkeley, document the financial transactions of several joint ventures over the years from 1880 to 1925. Reports of the Spreckels Sugar Company station (1897–1931) can be found at the Peter J. Shields Library, University of California, Davis. The Spreckels Sugar Company Collection can be found at Holt-Atherton Special Collections and Archives, University of the Pacific Libraries in Stockton, California. Numerous other collections of documents comprise papers concerning John D. Spreckels.

The Hotel del Coronado Records were found at San Diego State University Library in its Special Collections until they were transferred in 2019 to the Hotel del Coronado. The San Diego History Center safeguards a large collection of general ephemera that also contains "land booklets" for property held and managed by the Spreckels companies, including the J. D. and A. B. Spreckels Company, the San Diego

Electric Railway Company, the Mission Beach Company, the Spreckels Brothers Commercial Company, and more; in addition, it is a repository for many personal documents and photos donated by descendants of John Spreckels sometime in the twenty-first century. The Huntington Library in San Marino, California, has wonderful pictorial records of the Oceanic Steamship Company.

The Coronado Historical Association houses the lion's share of the general papers regarding John D. Spreckels's San Diego and Coronado activities, but the masters of these are still found in living family members' home archives. The Hawai'i State Archives house papers regarding Claus Spreckels and his interaction with the Hawaiian government, but a deep dive is necessary to find information regarding his son John; there is little to no personal correspondence left behind. However, these archives hold correspondence by Queen Lili'uokalani to her business manager J. O. Carter that reveal her positive relationship with John Spreckels.

A very important and valuable source that helped me "see" the city of San Diego before and after John Spreckels arrived was the stack of heavy, large red hardbound books I bought at a garage sale some thirty years ago. The late Richard F. Pourade, editor emeritus of the *San Diego Union*, had been commissioned by Union Publishing to chronicle the city's history over seven volumes: *The Explorers, Time of the Bells, The Silver Dons, The Glory Years, Gold in the Sun, The Rising Tide,* and *City of the Dream*, all published between 1960 and 1977. Using these books, I was able to weave in the voices of some of John Spreckels's contemporaries.

The Library of Congress's *Chronicling America* website (https://chroniclingamerica.loc.gov/) as well as the *California Digital Newspaper Collection* of the University of California, Riverside (https://cdnc.ucr.edu/) proved to be an invaluable research source for newspaper articles highlighting the goings-on of the Spreckels family. Ancestry.com was the "go to" for conducting genealogy research on family members.

Privately printed books on the family, personal documents, including correspondence from family scrapbooks, marriage and death certificates, and treasured photographs with histories to match, were a significant contribution to the book. I wish there were space to include them all!

When I quoted primary source material, I made every effort to accurately and faithfully represent any original letter or report cited in transcription. To this end, I left errors in grammar or spelling uncorrected, with the exception of names of well-known people (for example, "Spreckels" for "Spreckles") and a few historical place names. In the interest of clarity, I shortened some sentences and inserted some paragraph breaks without disrupting the sequence of the original. In a few instances, I inserted a bracketed word for clarity and/or readability. I sometimes replaced nonessential words in a single sentence with ellipses.

It would be impossible to cover every aspect of John Spreckels's life, and I realized early on that to identify all the business ventures that he bought into or to explore every personal relationship that he was involved in would each require a book of its own. So, I ask for grace.

NOTES

ABBREVIATIONS

CAK   Charles A. Kofoid Papers. University of California, San Diego, Libraries.

CHA   Papers of the Coronado Historical Association. Coronado Museum of History & Art, Coronado, California.

HDC   Hotel del Coronado Records, 1888–1995. Series 1, bound correspondence, 1888–1907, ed. Aislinn Catherine Sotelo. Formerly at the San Diego State University Special Collections and Archives but now housed at the Hotel del Coronado, Coronado, California.

HSAL   Lili'uokalani Trust Folder M-397-8-11, correspondence: Lili'uokalani to J. O. Carter, from Washington DC, March 24–December 19, 1899. Hawai'i State Archives, Honolulu.

VW   Papers of Virginia Wilson (great-granddaughter of John D. Spreckels).

PROLOGUE

1. "A Good Story," 59; Peterson, *The Coronado Story*, 37.
2. Adams, *The Man, John D. Spreckels*, 289.
3. Bradlee, The Kid.
4. Adams, *The Man, John D. Spreckels*, 294.
5. Brainerd, "A Man of Millions," 716–17.
6. "John Demented Spreckels," *El Patio*, October 16, 1920.

1. CHASING THE SWEET AMERICAN DREAM

1. Frizell, *Independent Immigrants*, 21–22.
2. Strickland, "Ethnicity and Race in the Urban South," 21, 28.
3. O'Brien, "Claus Spreckels, the Sugar King," 516.

4. Phelps, *Contemporary Biography of California's Representative Men*, 409.

5. "Hardy Pioneer and Benefactor of State Dead," *San Francisco Call*, December 27, 1908, 18.

6. "Living on Twenty Dollars a Week: Our Millionaires Tell the People How They Could Do It," *San Francisco Morning Call*, November 12, 1892, 3.

7. Phelps, *Contemporary Biography*, 410.

8. "Living on Twenty Dollars a Week."

9. Carrie Berger (daughter of John G. Belcher and descendant of John D. Spreckels), personal communication with author, April 23, 2018.

10. "The Weather," *Sumter Banner* (Sumterville SC), August 16, 1853, 2.

11. Strickland, "Ethnicity and Race in the Urban South," 63.

12. Adolph Rosekrans (grandson of Adolph B. Spreckels), personal communication with author, March 1, 2018.

13. Ambrose, *Nothing Like It in the World*, 54.

14. Yenne, *San Francisco Beer*, 27.

15. "Living on Twenty Dollars a Week."

16. Strickland, "Ethnicity and Race in the Urban South," 8.

17. Strickland, "Ethnicity and Race in the Urban South," 10.

18. Adams, *The Man, John D. Spreckels*, 48.

19. Spiekermann, "Claus Spreckels: A Biographical Case Study," 4.

20. Hoitt, "Education in California," 1.

21. History of the College of California, vol. 1, issues 1–2 (1887), 104, in Papers of the California Historical Society, San Francisco, California.

22. "University of California: History," *Wikipedia*, https://en.wikipedia.org/wiki/University_of_California#History, accessed November 6, 2010).

23. Magnuson, "History of the Beet Sugar Industry in California," 68–79.

24. Maulhardt, *Oxnard Sugar Beets*, 14.

25. Magnuson, "History of the Beet Sugar Industry in California."

26. Hill, *Hill's Album of Biography and Art*, 412.

27. Adams, *The Man, John D. Spreckels*, 49.

28. David Lewis (great-grandson of John D. Spreckels), personal communication with author, 2018.

29. Uwe Spiekermann, personal communication with author, February 8, 2019.

30. Phelps, *Contemporary Biography*, 409.

31. Don Hefner, "Sugar Beet Roots," unpublished, undated brochure, CHA.

32. "Newport of the Pacific," *Santa Cruz Sentinel*, June 12, 1875.

2. TAKING HAWAI'I BY STORM

1. Adams, *The Man, John D. Spreckels*, 72.

2. "Spreckels in Queer Tangle," *Hawaiian Star*, June 16, 1909.

3. Emmet, *The California and Hawaiian Sugar Refining Corporation of San Francisco*, 1.

4. *American Sugar Refining Company, and Others*, 937.

5. "Living on Twenty Dollars a Week: Our Millionaires Tell the People How They Could Do It," *San Francisco Morning Call*, November 12, 1892.

6. "Living on Twenty Dollars a Week."

7. Simonds, *Kama'aina*, 42.

8. Simonds, *Kama'aina*.

9. Bonura, "Queen Lili'uokalani's Beloved Kawaiaha'o Seminary," 31–68.

10. Bonura, *Light in the Queen's Garden*, 141.

11. Kiyosaki, *Talk Pidgin*, 11.

12. Kiyosaki, *Talk Pidgin*, 10.

13. "Claus Spreckels," *Hawaiian Star*, December 26, 1908.

14. Elson, *The Musical Herald*, 205.

15. Adler and Kamins, "The Political Debut of Walter Murray Gibson," 96–115.

16. Adler and Kamins, "The Political Debut of Walter Murray Gibson."

17. Lili'uokalani, *Hawai'i's Story by Hawai'i's Queen*, 360.

18. Lili'uokalani, *Hawai'i's Story by Hawai'i's Queen*.

19. Pennsylvania State Board of Agriculture, *Agriculture of Pennsylvania*, 6:16.

20. Spiekermann, "Claus Spreckels: A Biographical Case Study," 5.

21. Hackler, "Princeville Plantation Papers," 79.

22. Carrie P. Winter to Charles A. Kofoid, January 15, 1891, quoted in Bonura and Day, *An American Girl in the Hawaiian Islands*, 73.

23. Kanahele, *Emma: Hawai'i's Remarkable Queen*, 345–46.

24. Kanahele, *Emma*.

25. Kanahele, *Emma*, 346.

26. Bob Calhoun, "Yesterday's Crimes: A Cursed Church and the *Chronicle*'s Bloody Beginnings," SF *Weekly*, September 3, 2015.

27. Adams, *The Man, John D. Spreckels*, 81–83.

28. Quoted in Kent, *Charles Reed Bishop, Man of Hawai'i*, 117.

29. "Claus Spreckels, the Sugar King, Is Dead," *Hawaiian Gazette*, December 29, 1908, 3.

30. "JD Spreckels on Hawaiian Affairs," *Hawaiian Gazette*, December 20, 1887, 1.

31. "A Royal Dinner Party," *Hawaiian Gazette*, September 2, 1890, 5.

32. *All about Hawaii*, 34.

33. "Oceanic Shipping Company," 353.

34. "Spreckels' New Tug," *Daily Alta California* 42, no. 14214, August 5, 1888.

35. "The Most Important Maritime Event of This Kingdom," *Pacific Commercial Advertiser*, August 4, 1883.

36. Scott, *The Saga of the Sandwich Islands*, 168.

37. Tate, *Transpacific Steam*, 52.

38. Spreckels, "Hawaii for Tourists," 661–62.

39. Spreckels, "Hawaii for Tourists."

40. Winter to Kofoid, January 15, 1891, quoted in Bonura and Day, *An American Girl in the Hawaiian Islands*, 6.

41. "Spreckels' System: He Refuses to Wait an Hour for the American Mails," *Los Angeles Daily Herald*, July 30, 1887, 1.

42. Quoted in Bonura and Day, *An American Girl in the Hawaiian Islands*, 9.

43. O'Connell, *The Inner Man*, 19.

44. Adams, *The Man, John D. Spreckels*, 146.

45. Brainerd, "A Man of Millions," 715.

46. Johnston et al., *Time and Navigation*, 754.

47. Spreckels, "Hawaii for Tourists."

48. Spreckels, "Hawaii for Tourists."

49. Carrie P. Winter to Charles A. Kofoid, August 27, 1890, CAK.

50. Winter to Kofoid, August 27, 1890, CAK.

51. Krauss, *Johnny Wilson*, 31.

3. CRAZED LAND BOOM AND BUST

1. Basney, "The Role of the Spreckels Business Interests in the Development of San Diego," 9.

2. Adams, *The Man, John D. Spreckels*, 290.

3. "San Diego and the Spreckels Australia Steamers," *Los Angeles Herald*, June 10, 1887.

4. Barr, "The Historians Corner," 5.

5. "Celebrate Golden Wedding," *Coronado Eagle and Journal*, July 24, 1920.

6. MacPhail, *The Story of New San Diego and of Its Founder*, 101.

7. "Spreckels' Wharf," *Coronado Mercury*, October 1, 1887.

8. "Captain Hinde Dies," *Coronado Eagle and Journal*, March 13, 1915.

9. Basney, "The Role of the Spreckels Business Interests," 31.

10. Basney, "The Role of the Spreckels Business Interests."

11. Basney, "The Role of the Spreckels Business Interests," 32.

12. "A Yacht Set Sail and a City Changed Course," *San Diego Union*, February 7, 1965.

13. "A Yacht Set Sail and a City Changed Course."

14. This successful venture into facilitating the delivery of coal motivated John later to purchase his own coal mine in Coos County, Oregon, thereby earning him even more millions.

15. Spiekermann, "Expanding the Frontier(s)," 179.
16. "Coronado: History of the Charming Seaside Resort," *Coronado Mercury* 7, no. 27, November 23, 1893.
17. "Divorces," *Chicago Daily Tribune*, November 15, 1875.
18. Hampton Flannigan, conversation with author, April 13, 2020.
19. "Argonaut Dead in San Diego," *Los Angeles Herald*, April 9, 1905.
20. "Coronado: History of the Charming Seaside Resort."
21. Coronado is referred to sometimes as an "island" (especially at high tide) and sometimes as a "peninsula." Its status is ambiguous, though "island" is generally the preferred term in quoted primary sources. Both terms are used here.
22. Peterson, *The Coronado Story*, 21.
23. Langmead, *Icons of American Architecture*, 238.
24. *Coronado Beach, San Diego County, California*, 5.
25. James W. Reid, "The Building of the Hotel del Coronado" (unpublished six-page booklet, n.d.), 3, quoted in Langmead, *Icons of American Architecture*, 240.
26. When the first Coronado lots had been sold, there was a temperance clause written into the contract stipulating that residents could imbibe only at the Hotel del Coronado.
27. *Hotel del Coronado*, 3.
28. Jacob Gruendike, busy as a bank president, as well as investors Josephus Collett and Heber Ingle, were not as deeply involved in the project as were Babcock and Story, and their reactions to its financial troubles are unknown.
29. Basney, "The Role of the Spreckels Business Interests," 12.
30. Adams, *The Man, John D. Spreckels*, 291–92.
31. Elisha S. Babcock to I. H. Mayer, Esq., June 30, 1888, HDC.
32. Carlin and Brandes, *Coronado: The Enchanted Island*, 65.
33. "Runaway Cars," *Sacramento Daily Record-Union*, December 17, 1887, 1.
34. Elisha S. Babcock to "friend," May 19, 1888, HDC.
35. Elisha S. Babcock to E. Kemp, Esq., August 13, 1888, HDC.
36. Babcock to Kemp, August 13, 1888.
37. Elisha S. Babcock to A. S. Dunham, Esq., November 19, 1888, HDC.
38. Carlin and Brandes, *Coronado: The Enchanted Island*, 67.
39. Adams, *The Man, John D. Spreckels*, 292.
40. Adams, *The Man, John D. Spreckels*, 292.
41. Elisha S. Babcock to Captain B. Scott, G. M. Interior Co. of Mexico, July 29, 1889, HDC.
42. Elisha S. Babcock to C. W. Kohlseat, Esq, of New York, August 2, 1889, HDC.
43. Elisha S. Babcock to John D. Spreckels, August 6, 1889, HDC.
44. Babcock to Spreckels, August 6, 1889.

45. Adams, *The Man, John D. Spreckels*, 292–93.

46. Adams, *The Man, John D. Spreckels*, 177.

47. Adams, *The Man, John D. Spreckels*, 293.

4. SUGAR AND STRIFE

1. *The Builders of a Great City: San Francisco's Representative Men, the City, Its History and Commerce* (San Francisco: San Francisco Journal of Commerce Publishing Co., 1891), 317, quoted in Goldberg, "A Cauldron of Anger," 247.

2. "The Sugar Trust's Foe," *New York Times*, May 18, 1888.

3. Taylor, *Under Hawaiian Skies*, 313. Some say that Adolph, Gus's elder, was bitter at not having been selected instead. Adolph had never been given the same autonomy as his brothers in the business, because he spent too much time on women and horses and not enough on business.

4. "The Spreckels Slander Suit," *Hawaiian Gazette*, April 26, 1895.

5. Bean, *Boss Ruef's San Francisco*, 73.

6. "Mr. Spreckels Wants War," *New York Times*, February 12, 1890.

7. Goldberg, "A Cauldron of Anger," 252.

8. "The Spreckels' Jar," *Salt Lake Herald*, April 5, 1895; "The Spreckels Slander Suit."

9. "Our Clever Men," *San Francisco News Letter*, February 1, 1896, 17.

10. Steffens, "Rudolph Spreckels," 393.

11. Goldberg, "A Cauldron of Anger," 255.

12. Goldberg, "A Cauldron of Anger," 256.

13. "Claus Spreckels' Hot Wrath," *San Francisco Examiner*, March 24, 1895, quoted in Goldberg, "A Cauldron of Anger," 257. The $2 million refers to the Hawaiian Commercial deal.

14. "Claus Spreckels' Hot Wrath."

15. Steffens, "Rudolph Spreckels," 392–93.

16. Goldberg, "A Cauldron of Anger," 258.

17. Goldberg, "A Cauldron of Anger," 254.

18. Goldberg, *Community Property*, 189.

19. "Some New Law for California Married Women. Wives Declared to Have No Rights in Community Property . . . A Startling Definition of the Duties and Obligations of a Husband by the Supreme Court," *San Francisco Call*, March 24, 1897, quoted in Goldberg, "A Cauldron of Anger," 268. Because John owned the *San Francisco Call*, it is hardly surprising that the paper's reaction to the decision was negative. Nonetheless, the article principally concerns the rights of married women.

20. Goldberg, "A Cauldron of Anger." The *Chronicle* suggested that the decision "might not have the support of Susan B. Anthony and Rev. Anna Shaw."

21. Spiekermann, "An Ordinary Man among Titans," 267.

22. Steffens, "Rudolph Spreckels," 391.

23. Retan, *The Iretta Hight Retan Collection*, 47.

24. "Miss Spreckels Elopes," *New York Journal*, January 3, 1897, 1.

25. "The Spreckels Family Jars," *San Francisco Daily Times*, January 1, 1903.

5. ALOHA HAWAI'I

1. "The King Abroad," *Daily Bulletin* (Honolulu), December 26, 1890, 5.

2. "The King Slept Here," *Honolulu Star-Bulletin*, January 11, 2009.

3. Quoted in "The King Slept Here."

4. Bright's disease was a nineteenth-century term that referred to a group of kidney diseases; today, the condition is described as acute or chronic nephritis.

5. Coffman, *Nation Within*, 107.

6. Adler, "Claus Spreckels' Rise and Fall in Hawai'i, 19.

7. Cordray, "Claus Spreckels of California," 66.

8. Scott, *The Saga of the Sandwich Islands*, 564.

9. It was after their ouster that Claus decided to relinquish his Hawaiian holdings, as described in chapter 4.

10. Sanford Dole, president of the provisional government, paroled her. Lili'uokalani, *Hawai'i's Story by Hawai'i's Queen*, 33.

11. Lili'uokalani, *Hawai'i's Story by Hawai'i's Queen*, 308.

12. "Lili'uokalani Is on Trial," *San Francisco Call*, February 16, 1895, 1. In spite of the family wrangling described in chapter 4, the issue of the queen's dethronement seemed to unite the family members.

13. Scott, *The Saga of the Sandwich Islands*, 707.

14. "The Man Who Bought Arms," *Los Angeles Herald*, February 8, 1895.

15. "To Honorable J. O. Carter from Lili'uokalani, Ebbitt House," June 22, 1898, HSAL.

16. "To Honorable J. O. Carter from Lili'uokalani, Ebbitt House," July 1, 1898, HSAL.

17. "To Honorable J. O. Carter from Lili'uokalani, Ebbitt House," July 8, 1898, HSAL.

18. "Friends Are to Pay Final Tribute Today to John D. Spreckels," unnamed, undated newspaper clipping, VW.

19. "Ex-Queen Secures Loan," *San Francisco Call*, November 23, 1908.

6. RAISING THE SPRECKELS CLAN

1. Uwe Spiekermann, in discussion with author, February 11, 2019.

2. Spiekermann, in discussion with author.

3. "The New Mansion Home of Claus Spreckels," *San Francisco Call,* December 19, 1897.

4. "Social Jottings," *The Wasp,* July 14, 1906, 10.

5. *The Wasp,* September 23, 1905, 39.

6. Purdy, *San Francisco,* 196.

7. Hamilton and Hamilton, *Villa Calafia,* 1:30.

8. Simpson, "John D., Miracle-Maker," 203.

9. Bonura, *Light in the Queen's Garden,* 19–20.

10. "Reconciliation of the Spreckels," *San Francisco News Letter,* February 11, 1905.

11. Carrie P. Winter to Charles A. Kofoid, January 15, 1891, quoted in Bonura and Day, *An American Girl in the Hawaiian Islands,* 73.

12. Dearborn, *Saratoga, and How to See It,* 5.

13. *San Francisco News Letter,* Christmas Number, 1902, 79.

14. Clarsen, *Eat My Dust,* 14–15.

15. "Autoneer," *San Francisco Call,* May 11, 1902.

16. *Town Talk,* January 7, 1905.

17. "John Spreckels an Enthusiast," 375.

18. *The Wasp,* September 23, 1905, 39.

19. *The Wasp,* September 23, 1905, 39.

20. Levere, *The History of the Sigma Alpha Epsilon Fraternity,* 2:223.

21. *The Wasp,* July 5, 1902, 28.

22. In 1885, the Central Pacific Railroad was acquired by the Southern Pacific Railroad (Espee) as a leased line, though it remained a corporate entity until 1959, when it was formally merged into Espee. The Central Pacific's Big Four continued to be principals of Espee.

23. *Pacific Commercial Advertiser* (Honolulu), July 7, 1902, 6.

24. *Pacific Commercial Advertiser* (Honolulu), July 7, 1902, 6.

25. "J. D. Spreckels, Jr., a Clerk in Wealthy Father's Office," *St. Louis Republic,* December 20, 1903.

26. "J. D. Spreckels, Jr., a Clerk in Wealthy Father's Office."

27. *The Wasp,* 1910, 21.

28. "A Rumor Restored," *Town Talk,* March 8, 1902, 17.

29. "The Week's Sensation," *Town Talk,* January 7, 1905, 22.

30. "The Week's Sensation."

31. *The Wasp,* November 4, 1905, 656.

32. *The Wasp,* September 23, 1905, 39.

33. *The Wasp,* September 23, 1905, 39.

34. "Society," *San Francisco News Letter,* October 28, 1905, 22.

35. *The Wasp,* September 23, 1905, 39.

36. "Society."

37. "Robert M. Hamilton," 1129.

38. "To Be a Quiet Affair," *San Francisco News Letter*, October 14, 1905, 16.

39. Lane, "Life and Jack London," 34.

40. *The Wasp*, January 2, 1909, 12.

7. ROOTS IN SAN FRANCISCO

1. *Watsonville (CA) Pajaronian*, November 10, 1887, quoted in Conway, "Spreckels Sugar Company: The First Fifty Years," 12n13.

2. Steffens, *Upbuilders*, 250.

3. By 1901, Claus's sons John and Adolph owned 50 percent of the beet sugar business, which had expanded to eight plants in California.

4. Bernhard, *Porcupine, Picayune, and Post*, 78.

5. Bernhard, *Porcupine, Picayune, and Post*, 78.

6. "Comment on Day's News," *San Pedro Daily News*, June 11, 1926.

7. Ellen Klages, "The Call Building: San Francisco's Forgotten Skyscraper," Shaping San Francisco's Digital Archive @ FoundSF, http://www.foundsf.org/index.php?title=THE_CALL_BUILDING:_SAN_FRANCISCO%27S_FOR-GOTTEN_SKYSCRAPER, accessed November 5, 2019.

8. Klages, "The Call Building."

9. Hall, *America's Successful Men of*, 2:750.

10. Adams, *The Man, John D. Spreckels*, 68.

11. Details from hand-typed essay, likely by Harriet Hamilton (John's grand-daughter), VW.

12. Adams, *The Man, John D. Spreckels*, 145.

13. Adams, *The Man, John D. Spreckels*, 92.

14. "Society," *San Francisco Call*, October 22, 1894.

15. *Sea Letter of the National Maritime Museum*, lxxx.

16. "John D. Spreckels Pined for the Helm: A Reluctant Millionaire," *San Diego Union*, May 15, 1963.

17. "John D. Spreckels Pined for the Helm."

18. "For His Welcome," *San Francisco Call*, July 18, 1893.

19. Smythe, *History of San Diego, 1542–1908*, 736. A naval court of inquiry determined that the explosion had been due to the negligence of the commanding officer and the chief engineer.

20. "John D. Spreckels Pined for the Helm."

21. Adams, *The Man, John D. Spreckels*, 94.

22. Kipling, *American Notes*, chap. 1, "At the Golden Gate."

23. Adams, *The Man, John D. Spreckels*, 92.

24. Dice, *The Bohemian Grove*.
25. It was at the Bohemian Club that John's brother-in-law created the Gibson martini.
26. "The Millionaires Had Better Not Fool with the Masses," *Oakland Tribune*, October 9, 1890, 6.
27. "Olympic Club Presents Silver Column to John D. Spreckels," *San Francisco Call*, December 26, 1901.
28. "Olympic Club Presents Silver Column to John D. Spreckels."
29. "Bimetallism, Not Bi-standard-ism," *San Francisco Call*, May 7, 1896.
30. "John D. Spreckels Is Doubly Honored," *San Francisco Call*, October 19, 1896.
31. Hanna had also promised the benefits of patronage to the southern delegates for their support.
32. "They Met at St. Louis," *Los Angeles Herald*, June 26, 1896.
33. "Unhappy End of John D. Spreckels as Meat for the Cat," *San Francisco Examiner*, September 23, 1896.
34. "The Spreckels Club," *San Francisco Call*, July 31, 1896.
35. "The Spreckels Club."
36. Perkins was already in that seat, having been appointed senator on the death of Senator Leland Stanford in 1893. That he was the established incumbent goes far to explain Claus's support of him.
37. Dicks, "J. D. Spreckels and the Reform Movement in California."
38. "Shortridge vs. Perkins and Claus," *Evening Sentinel* (Santa Cruz, CA), October 6, 1896.
39. Dicks, "J. D. Spreckels and the Reform Movement in California."
40. "Perkins on the First Ballot," *San Francisco Examiner*, January 13, 1897.
41. "Voice of the Press," *Sacramento Record Union*, January 18, 1897.
42. Dicks, "J. D. Spreckels and His Influence on San Diego City Politics."
43. "Anti-Expansionist," *Saint Paul Globe*, November 18, 1899.
44. Dicks, "J. D. Spreckels and the Reform Movement in California."
45. Leake, *The Healing of "Sam" Leake*, 15–16.
46. Leake, *The Healing of "Sam" Leake*.
47. Leake, *The Healing of "Sam" Leake*.
48. "Further Facts Prove Gage a Beneficiary," *San Francisco Call*, August 1, 1902.
49. "Warrants Issued for Spreckels and Leake," *Los Angeles Herald*, June 15, 1902.
50. "Warrants Issued for Spreckels and Leake."
51. Adams, *The Man, John D. Spreckels*, 84.
52. "Publishers Arrested," *Chico (CA) Record*, June 21, 1902.
53. Leake, *The Healing of "Sam" Leake*, 16.

54. Roger M. Grace, "Perspectives, 1902: Republican DA Rives Defies Wishes of GOP Governor," *Metropolitan News-Enterprise* (Los Angeles), January 9, 2007, 7.

55. "The Female Agitators," *San Francisco Chronicle*, July 11, 1871.

56. *San Francisco Call*, August 6, 1911.

57. "Fined for Speeding Because She Has the Vote," *Washington (DC) Herald*, November 29, 1911.

8. BUILDING SAN DIEGO'S INFRASTRUCTURE

1. Dodge, *Rails of the Silver Gate*, 17.

2. Dodge, *Rails of the Silver Gate*.

3. Adams, *The Man, John D. Spreckels*, 293.

4. Mengers, *San Diego Trolleys*, 12. The transfer of the Coronado Beach Company to John and Adolph included two steam trains, one of which Babcock and Story had used to pick up passengers from the ferry landing and take them to the Hotel del Coronado.

5. Dodge, *Rails of the Silver Gate*, 23.

6. MacPhail, *The Story of New San Diego and of Its Founder*, 120.

7. Dodge, *Rails of the Silver Gate*, 27.

8. MacPhail, *The Story of New San Diego and of Its Founder*, 120.

9. Brainerd, "A Man of Millions," 715.

10. "Spreckels Increases Pay," *Los Angeles Herald*, September 29, 1906.

11. The gardens were maintained until after John's death, but they closed in 1929, and the land was subdivided into residential lots. MacPhail. "A Little Gem of a Park."

12. Adams, *The Man, John D. Spreckels*, 296.

13. Brigandi, "'What I Sought Is That Which I Have Found,'" 7.

14. E. S. Babcock to John D. Spreckels, Esq., April 7, 1893, HDC.

15. "Conveniences," *Coronado Tent City* (1903 brochure), https://library.ucsd.edu/dc/object/bb7784398w/_1.pdf accessed November 7, 2019.

16. "Del Tidings," *Coronado Eagle and Journal*, November 11, 1971.

17. "Babcock Out at Coronado," *Los Angeles Herald*, August 30, 1903.

18. Dodge, *Rails of the Silver Gate*, 23.

19. "Loses His Job a Second Time," *San Francisco Call*, October 21, 1902.

20. William Clayton Papers (Collection 256), Library Special Collections, Charles E. Young Research Library, UCLA.

21. "William Clayton, Civic Leader, Is Called by Death," *San Diego Union*, November 15, 1934.

22. "Ohlmeyer, Band Leader, Is Held; Arrested in Oakland on Check Charge; His Friends Surprised," *Coronado Eagle and Journal* 3 (no. 17), September 12, 1914.

23. Brainerd, "A Man of Millions," 716.

24. "Sunday Customs," *Coronado Tent City* (1903 brochure), https://library.ucsd
.edu/dc/object/bb7784398w/_1.pdf, accessed November 7, 2019.

25. Quoted in Dodge, *Rails of the Silver Gate*, 54.

26. Adams, *The Man, John D. Spreckels*, 227.

27. Adams, *The Man, John D. Spreckels*, 227. The name San Diego Electric Railway
Company continued unchanged until 1948, which is quite remarkable in
street railway annals.

28. Adams, *The Man, John D. Spreckels*, 184–85.

29. Pourade, *The Glory Years*, 219–20.

30. Adams, *The Man, John D. Spreckels*, 227.

31. Richard W. Crawford, "Wooden Pipes Delivered Water to a Thirsty City," *San
Diego Union-Tribune*, May 28, 2009.

32. Crawford, "Wooden Pipes Delivered Water to a Thirsty City."

33. "Spreckels Holds Controlling Hand," *Los Angeles Herald*, February 16, 1904.

34. Pourade, *The Rising Tide*, 47.

35. "Babcock and Spreckels Fight," *Blade-Tribune* (Oceanside CA), September
2, 1905.

36. "Babcock and Spreckels Fight."

37. Ordinance no. 2212, *Ordinances of the City of San Diego, California*, approved
November 6, 1905.

38. "Spreckels Wins Suit in San Diego," *Sacramento Union*, March 10, 1906.

39. "Decision Rendered in Big Water Suit," *San Francisco Call*, March 10, 1906.

40. Strathman, "Land, Water, and Real Estate," 128.

41. "San Diego Water Works," 52.

42. Adams, *The Man, John D. Spreckels*, 294; Harris Jr., "John D. Spreckels and
the San Diego and Arizona Railway," 161.

43. Unnamed, undated newspaper clipping from Virginia Wilson (great-
granddaughter of John D. Spreckels), VW.

44. "Getting Respect from the San Diego Press," 1, 2.

45. Teel, *The Public Press, 1900–1945*, 31.

46. Brainerd, "A Man of Millions," 716.

9. EARTHQUAKE, DEATH, AND LEGAL CHAOS

1. "King of the Sugar Trade: Claus Spreckels and the Power He Wields, How
from Selling Cheese and Crackers in New York Spreckels Became the Master
of Millions," *Knowersville (NY) Enterprise*, February 14, 1885.

2. Spiekermann, "Claus Spreckels: A Biographical Case Study," 19.

3. "Claus Spreckels Has a Second Paralytic Stroke," *Pacific Commercial Advertiser*, December 2, 1903, 1.

4. "Adolph Spreckels Ill," *Los Angeles Herald*, July 14, 1904.

5. Adams, *The Man, John D. Spreckels*, 219.

6. "John D. Spreckels Reason for Absence," *San Francisco Call*, June 14, 1904.

7. "Australia Is Rapidly Recovering from Drought," *San Francisco Call*, January 22, 1904.

8. "Oceanic Is in Hapless State," *Pacific Commercial Advertiser*, March 20, 1907, 1.

9. Adams, *The Man, John D. Spreckels*, 215–16.

10. "Men and Women," *The Wasp*, March 24, 1906.

11. "Young Spreckels Managing the Call," *Oakland Tribune*, March 24, 1906.

12. "Men and Women."

13. Banks and Read, *The History of the San Francisco Disaster and Mount Vesuvius Horror*, 118.

14. Banks and Read, *The History of the San Francisco Disaster and Mount Vesuvius Horror*, 118.

15. Author's collection.

16. "Social Jottings," *The Wasp*, July 14, 1906, 10.

17. "The Latest News," *Colusa (CA) Daily Sun*, May 3, 1906.

18. Adams, *The Man, John D. Spreckels*, 219–20.

19. "San Diego Sends More Supplies," *Los Angeles Herald*, April 28, 1906.

20. Unpublished, undated Hampton Lovegrove Story family paper, Papers of Hampton Flannigan, 3.

21. Wright, *My Father, Frank Lloyd Wright*, 65.

22. Wright, *My Father*.

23. Today the commune is the campus of Point Loma Nazarene University.

24. Wright, *My Father*.

25. Adams, *The Man, John D. Spreckels*, 227.

26. Goldberg, "A Cauldron of Anger," 275.

27. Goldberg, "A Cauldron of Anger."

28. "Family Differences," *The Wasp*, January 2, 1909, 9.

29. "Late Sugar King's Vast Estate Again in Court," *Los Angeles Times*, December 22, 1911.

30. Goldberg, "A Cauldron of Anger," 278.

31. "Family Differences."

32. Goldberg, "A Cauldron of Anger," 275–76.

33. Goldberg, "A Cauldron of Anger."

34. Steffens, *Upbuilders*, 244–84.

35. "Family Differences."

36. "Spreckels Will Sole Evidence of Two Heirs: Produce No Writing to Prove That Gifts to Brothers Were Advancements, Fictitious Values Given in Answer Nearly Cut in Two by Sworn Testimony," *San Francisco Call,* June 4, 1910, 18.

37. "Warm Fight Over Sugar King's Wealth," *Tacoma (WA) Times,* May 19, 1909.

38. Birmingham, *California Rich,* 64.

39. "Of Social Interest," *The Wasp,* April 10, 1909.

40. "Warm Fight over Sugar King's Wealth."

41. Spreckels et al. v. State, *California Appellate Divisions,* vol. 22, 775.

42. "Death of Mrs. Claus Spreckels," *The Wasp,* February 19, 1910, 4.

43. Spreckels et al. v. State, *California Appellate Divisions,* 553.

44. "Answer to Announcement Made by Brothers," *Wenatchee (WA) Daily World,* January 17, 1910.

45. "Shocked by Spreckels' Quarrel," *The Wasp,* February 26, 1910, 4.

46. "Shocked by Spreckels' Quarrel."

47. "Follows Beloved Husband to Grave," *San Francisco Call,* February 16, 1910.

48. Goldberg, "A Cauldron of Anger," 274.

49. "Death of Mrs. Claus Spreckels."

50. "Death of Mrs. Claus Spreckels."

51. "Death of Mrs. Claus Spreckels."

52. "Executors Win against John D. and Adolph," *Sacramento Union,* April 11, 1912.

53. Goldberg, "A Cauldron of Anger," 275.

54. "Test of Claus Spreckels's Will in Supreme Court," *Santa Fe New Mexican,* June 1, 1912.

55. But see "Graceful Figure Modeled in Clay," *San Francisco Chronicle,* January 24, 1902, 12, which asserts that Aitken's model was Clara Petzold, who later became a noted photographer.

56. Christopher Craig, "Spreckels (née de Bretteville), Alma Emma— Philanthropist, Socialite, and Patron of the Arts," Shaping San Francisco's Digital Archive @ FoundSF, http://www.foundsf.org/index.php?title=Alma _Spreckels, accessed November 9, 2019.

57. Alexander, *America Goes Hawaiian,* 231.

58. Starr, *The Dream Endures,* 154.

59. Starr, *The Dream Endures.*

60. Starr, *The Dream Endures.*

61. Adolph Rosekrans (grandson of Adolph B. Spreckels), personal communication with author, March 1, 2018.

62. "Mary A. Case Wins Honors," *Daily Alaskan* (Skagway), October 26, 1908.

63. "'Puppy Love' Says Mother," *Pacific Commercial Advertiser,* June 23, 1909.

64. "Says She May Wed Spreckels," *San Diego Sun,* June 14, 1909.
65. "Young Spreckels Engaged to Marry; He Leaves Paris on Fast Ship Summoned by Parents," *Sacramento Union,* May 29, 1909.
66. "Spreckels Goes to Work," *Times Dispatch* (Richmond VA), June 8, 1909.
67. "Spreckels Goes to Work."
68. "Spreckels Goes to Work."
69. "Spreckels in Queer Tangle," *Hawaiian Star,* June 16, 1909.
70. "Spreckels in Queer Tangle."
71. "Papa Prevents Wedding of Musical Maid from Alaska," *Daily Alaskan* (Skagway), June 7, 1909.
72. *Vinita (OK) Daily Chieftain,* June 8, 1909.
73. "Wireless Flash Hinders Work of Cupid at Sea," *Detroit Times,* June 10, 1909.
74. "'Puppy Love' Says Mother."
75. "'Puppy Love' Says Mother."
76. "'Puppy Love' Says Mother."
77. "An Unostentatious Celebration," *The Wasp,* April 30, 1910.

10. INFLUENCING SAN DIEGO POLITICS

1. Pourade, *Gold in the Sun,* chap. 3, 43.
2. Smythe, *History of San Diego, 1542–1908,* 478.
3. Starr, *Inventing the Dream,* 236.
4. Miller, "The Origins of the San Diego Lincoln-Roosevelt League, 1905–1909," 421–43.
5. "Dr. Burnham to Talk on Municipal Reform," *San Diego Union and Daily Bee,* March 7, 1909.
6. Pourade, *Gold in the Sun,* 90.
7. Dicks, "J. D. Spreckels and His Influence on San Diego Politics: 1890–1909."
8. Bridges, *Morning Glories: Municipal Reform in the Southwest,* 61.
9. McGrew, *The City of San Diego and San Diego County,* 227.
10. Bridges, *Morning Glories,* 79.
11. Bridges, *Morning Glories,* 78.
12. "The Lincoln-Roosevelt League's Avowed," *Santa Cruz Weekly Sentinel,* August 19, 1907.
13. Dicks, "J. D. Spreckels and His Influence on San Diego City Politics: 1890–1909."
14. Dicks, "J. D. Spreckels and His Influence on San Diego City Politics: 1890–1909."
15. Dicks, "J. D. Spreckels and His Influence on San Diego City Politics: 1890–1909."

16. *Harper's Weekly*, July 11, 1914, 29.

17. "Our State in Nation's Eye," *Riverside (CA) Daily Press*, July 16, 1914.

18. Dicks, "J. D. Spreckels and His Influence on San Diego City Politics: 1890–1909."

19. "Return to Sensible Party Lines Forecast," *San Diego Union and Daily Bee*, May 29, 1916.

20. Simpson, "John D., Miracle-Maker," 203.

21. Brainerd, "A Man of Millions," 717.

22. Anderson Borthwick, interview by Robert Wright, San Diego Historical Society Oral History Program, February 28, 1979, https://library.ucsd.edu/dc/object/bb2902188s/_1.html (site discontinued).

23. Pourade, *Gold in the Sun*, 116.

24. Adams, *The Man, John D. Spreckels*, 305.

25. Simpson, "John D., Miracle-Maker," 203.

26. Basney, "The Role of the Spreckels Business Interests in the Development of San Diego," 15.

27. Kropp, *California Vieja*, 106.

11. CORONADO'S UNCLE JOHN

1. Vickie Stone, curator of collections, "Coronado's Incorporation," unpublished paper, 2019, CHA.

2. Stone, "Coronado's Incorporation."

3. "Coronado Will Incorporate," *Coronado Mercury*, June 11, 1888.

4. "Coronado Will Incorporate."

5. Stone, "Coronado's Incorporation."

6. Stone, "Coronado's Incorporation."

7. *Coronado Mercury*, July 28, 1888.

8. "Julius Wangenheim: An Autobiography," 362.

9. "Julius Wangenheim: An Autobiography," 362.

10. George Holmes, "Supplement to the Strand," *Coronado Eagle and Journal*, April 25, 1914.

11. "No Tent City," *Coronado Eagle and Journal*, February 26, 1916.

12. Carlin and Brandes, *Coronado: The Enchanted Island*, 125.

13. "No Tent City."

14. "Mr. John D. Spreckels Makes a Final Statement," *Coronado Eagle and Journal*, April 8, 1916.

15. "Mr. John D. Spreckels Makes a Final Statement."

16. "Mr. John D. Spreckels Makes a Final Statement."

17. "Another Letter from Mr. Kipp," *Coronado Eagle and Journal*, April 8, 1916.

18. "Spreckels or No Spreckels Issue," *Riverside (CA) Daily Press*, April 10, 1916.

19. "Spreckels or No Spreckels Issue."

20. "Spreckels Wins at Coronado," *Riverside (CA) Daily Press*, April 11, 1916.

21. *Wine and Spirit Bulletin* 30, 1916, 28.

22. Carlin and Brandes, *Coronado: The Enchanted Island*, 166.

23. Jonde Northcutt (great-granddaughter of John D. Spreckels), personal communication with author, June 9, 2019.

24. Peterson, *The Coronado Story*, 138.

25. Dick Henderson, "Uncle John Stops His Papers: Circulation All Shot Up," *Coronado Eagle and Journal*, October 25, 1919.

26. Peterson, *The Coronado Story*, 106.

27. "Trade Last for Uncle John," *Coronado Eagle and Journal*, April 5, 1917.

28. "The Coronado Story," *Coronado Eagle and Journal*, May 20, 1954.

29. "Silver Strand Theatre Opening," *Coronado Eagle and Journal*, July 28, 1917.

30. "Silver Strand Theatre Opening."

31. Adams, *The Man, John D. Spreckels*, 72.

32. "The Oil-Burning Ferryboat Ramona," 625.

33. "The Oil-Burning Ferryboat Ramona."

34. Edward Barr, historian of the Spreckels Organ Society, unnamed, undated, unnumbered communiqué, CHA.

35. Barr communiqué.

36. Leather, *The One-Story Schoolhouse Idea with Plans of Model Schools*, 28.

37. "Winners in Flower Show Announced Beautiful," *Coronado Eagle and Journal*, April 8, 1925.

38. Guidry, "Mother Stork's Baby Book."

39. Guidry, "Mother Stork's Baby Book."

40. Guidry, "Mother Stork's Baby Book."

41. "The Duchess of Windsor and the Coronado Legend, Part 1."

42. "The Duchess of Windsor and the Coronado Legend, Part 1."

43. "The Duchess of Windsor and the Coronado Legend, Part 1."

44. Hamilton and Hamilton, *Villa Calafia*, 1:98.

45. Virginia Wilson (great-granddaughter of John D. Spreckels), personal communication with author, June 1, 2019.

46. "Uncle John Surprised on His Birthday," *Coronado Eagle and Journal*, August 21, 1920.

47. Birmingham, *California Rich*, 68–70.

48. Adams, *The Man, John D. Spreckels*, 117.

49. Birmingham, *California Rich*, 68–70.

50. Carlin and Brandes, *Coronado: The Enchanted Island*, 163.

51. "Uncle John," *Coronado Eagle and Journal*, August 14, 1958.

52. Carlin and Brandes, *Coronado: The Enchanted Island*, 84.

53. Adams, *The Man, John D. Spreckels*, 109–11.

54. Bauer and Bauer, *Recipes from Historic California*, 217.

55. Carlin and Brandes, *Coronado: The Enchanted Island*, 71.

56. Deutsch, *San Diego and Arizona Railway*, 52.

57. Carlin and Brandes, *Coronado: The Enchanted Island*, 151.

58. "America's First Outdoor Yule Tree Lighted at Hotel del Coronado," *Coronado Eagle and Journal*, December 19, 1963.

59. "250 Lights Christmas Tree at the Del!," *Feuilleton, the Famous Hotels Newsletter*, Library of Hospitality, https://famoushotels.org/news/250-lights-christmas-tree-at-the-del, accessed November 9, 2019.

60. Black, *San Diego County, California*, 443–44.

61. "Browsing with Brownie," *Coronado Compass*, June 11, 1948.

62. "There's Nothing Better Than a Fond Memory of the Del," *Coronado Eagle and Journal*, February 25, 1998.

63. Wilson, personal communication with author.

64. Carlin and Brandes, *Coronado: The Enchanted Island*, 133.

65. Laffaye, *Polo in the United States*, 88.

66. "No More Polo," *El Patio*, March 19, 1921.

67. Later, John's daughter Lillie Spreckels Wegeforth helped promote the annual horse shows in place of polo.

68. Anderson Borthwick, interview by Robert Wright, San Diego Historical Society Oral History Program, February 28, 1979, https://library.ucsd.edu/dc/object/bb2902188s/_1.html (site discontinued).

69. "How They Are Assessed," *Coronado Eagle and Journal*, April 10, 1920.

70. "Coronado Is to Have a Free Public Library," *San Francisco Call*, July 29, 1907.

71. *Coronado Eagle and Journal*, September 21, 1926.

72. "Trustees Ignore Civic Club's Demand for City Attorney Resignation," *Coronado Eagle and Journal*, June 21, 1927.

73. Joshua Dana (Coronado independent film historian), personal communication with author, May 31, 2019.

74. "The Hotel Del Grew Up with the Film Industry," 6–7.

75. Brégent-Heald, *Borderland Films*, 37.

76. Dana, communication with author, May 31, 2019.

77. "Pickups by the Staff," *Camera! The Digest of the Motion Picture Industry*, July 10, 1920.

78. Carlin and Brandes, *Coronado: The Enchanted Island*, 100.

79. "Preparedness Parade," *Coronado Eagle and Journal*, July 8, 1916.

80. "As the Publisher Sees It: Wake Up Coronado!," *El Patio*, September 18, 1920.
81. "Coronado Business People Want the City to Get a Move On," *El Patio*, January 15, 1921.
82. "John Demented Spreckels," *El Patio*, October 16, 1920.
83. Pourade, *The Rising Tide*, 23.
84. *El Patio*, July 29, 1921.

12. THE SO-CALLED IMPOSSIBLE RAILROAD

1. Basney, "The Role of the Spreckels Business Interests in the Development of San Diego," 113.
2. "Railroad from San Diego to Yuma Is Now Assured!," *San Diego Union*, December 14, 1906; "Santa Fe and Southern Pacific Arrangements," 8–9.
3. Hofsommer, *The Southern Pacific, 1901–1985*, 20.
4. Edward H. Harriman v. Interstate Commerce Commission, 662 U.S. (October term, 1907); Otto H. Kahn v. Interstate Commerce Commission 664 U.S. (October term, 1907); Interstate Commerce Commission v. Edward H. Harriman, 618 (2nd Cir. NY, 1908), 651.
5. Basney, "The Role of the Spreckels Business Interests in the Development of San Diego," 115.
6. Basney, "The Role of the Spreckels Business Interests in the Development of San Diego," 115.
7. Marston, *George White Marston*, 6.
8. "Construction and Improvements," 15.
9. "San Diego and Imperial Now One," *San Diego Union*, November 16, 1919.
10. "Epic of Indomitability of Purpose, Writers' Name for Mr. Spreckels' Railway Work," *San Diego Union*, November 12, 1919.
11. Ambrose, *Nothing Like It in the World*, 25.
12. How the Mexican Revolution affected the "Impossible Railroad" is discussed in chapter 14.
13. "Epic of Indomitability of Purpose."
14. Hanft, *San Diego and Arizona*, 81.
15. Dodge, *Rails of the Silver Gate*, 39.
16. Pourade, *The Rising Tide*, 23.
17. "Epic of Indomitability of Purpose."
18. "Epic of Indomitability of Purpose."
19. "Epic of Indomitability of Purpose."
20. "San Diego and Imperial Now One."
21. "San Diego and Imperial Now One."
22. Hanft, *San Diego and Arizona*, 76.

23. "Crowd Cheers Train," *Omaha Sunday Bee*, December 7, 1919.
24. "New Railroad Opens Wealthy Farming Zone," *Omaha Daily Bee*, December 7, 1919.
25. Adams, *The Man, John D. Spreckels*, 300.
26. In the early twentieth century, the spelling was variously Carisso Gorge or Carrisso Gorge.
27. "Epic of Indomitability of Purpose."
28. Basney, "The Role of the Spreckels Business Interests in the Development of San Diego," 117.
29. Pontius, "San Diego & Arizona Railway," 4–5.
30. Hanft, *San Diego and Arizona*, 79.
31. "Can Get a Drink on S.D.&A. Line below the Border," *Riverside (CA) Daily Press*, December 17, 1919.

13. BUILDING UP BROADWAY

1. William G. Irwin to Walter M. Giffard, November 4, 1908, quoted in MacLennan, "Kilauea Sugar Plantation in 1912: A Snapshot," 6.
2. Conway, "Spreckels Sugar Company: The First Fifty Years," 112–13.
3. Adams, *The Man, John D. Spreckels*, 292–93.
4. Laut, "San Diego: First Port of Call," 112.
5. Vandegrift and Mecham, "San Diego City," 42.
6. Smythe, *History of San Diego, 1542–1908*, 368.
7. Vandegrift and Mecham, "San Diego City," 42.
8. Vandegrift and Mecham, "San Diego City."
9. Panama–California Exposition, the Chamber of Commerce and the Citizens of San Diego, *Makers of San Diego 1915 Panama–California Exposition*.
10. Laut, "San Diego: First Port of Call," 112.
11. Spofford and Annandale, *XX Century Cyclopædia and Atlas*, 326.
12. Innis, *San Diego Legends*, 42.
13. Its name after that merger was the *San Francisco Call & Post*. In 1929, the paper was further merged with the *San Francisco Bulletin* to become the *San Francisco Call-Bulletin*. Another merger in 1959, with Scripps-Howard's *San Francisco News*, inaugurated the *News-Call Bulletin*, which ultimately ceased publication in 1965, when it was purchased by the *San Francisco Examiner*, which then entered into a joint operating agreement with the *San Francisco Chronicle*, which had been founded by the de Young brothers.
14. Basney, "The Role of the Spreckels Business Interests in the Development of San Diego," 128.
15. Albright, "Reinforced Concrete Construction in Southern California," 43.

16. Albright, "Reinforced Concrete Construction in Southern California," 37.

17. "San Diego Newspapers Will Soon Have New Home in a Magnificent Six-Story Structure," *San Francisco Call*, September 17, 1906.

18. Albright, "Reinforced Concrete Construction in Southern California," 39.

19. Basney, "The Role of the Spreckels Business Interests in the Development of San Diego," 131.

20. Albright, "Reinforced Concrete Construction in Southern California," 39.

21. Basney, "The Role of the Spreckels Business Interests in the Development of San Diego," 132.

22. "Ida Bailey: The Most Infamous Madame of the Stingaree," Horton Grand Hotel blog page, https://hortongrand.wordpress.com/2015/05/06/ida-bailey -the-most-infamous-madame-of-the-stingaree/, accessed November 11, 2019.

23. Dodge, *"Jack" Dodge (John Mason Dodge*, 78.

24. Pourade, *Gold in the Sun*, 167.

25. Pourade, *Gold in the Sun*, 166–67.

26. Pourade, *Gold in the Sun*, 167.

27. Quoted in Gonzalez, *Architects Who Built Southern California.*

28. "Spreckels Theater Building, San Diego California," *Historic Structures*, http:// www.historic-structures.com/ca/san_diego/spreckels_theater.php, accessed November 10, 2019.

29. *Coronado Eagle and Journal*, January 20, 1923.

30. Pourade, *The Rising Tide*, 12.

31. Adams, *The Man, John D. Spreckels*, 295.

32. "The Lie Is Passed: Spreckels Directly Accuses Grant of Double Dealing," *Los Angeles Herald*, December 20, 1898.

33. Miller, "The Origins of the San Diego Lincoln-Roosevelt League," 421–43.

34. "The Proposed Working Men's Hotel at San Diego," 8.

35. Basney, "The Role of the Spreckels Business Interests in the Development of San Diego," 142.

36. Brochure from Virginia Wilson (great-granddaughter of John D. Spreckels), vw.

37. Brochure from Wilson, vw.

38. Brainerd, "A Man of Millions," 716.

39. Brainerd, "A Man of Millions," 716–17.

40. Brainerd, "A Man of Millions," 716–17.

41. Anderson Borthwick, interview by Robert Wright, San Diego Historical Society Oral History Program, February 28, 1979, https://library.ucsd.edu/dc/ object/bb2902188s/_1.html (site discontinued).

42. Borthwick, interview by Wright.

43. Ed Davidson, "The Human Side of John D. Spreckels," unnamed, undated, newspaper clipping, CHA.

44. Emily Clayton's handwritten memoir of her father, May 17, 1959, William Clayton Papers (Collection 256), Library Special Collections, Charles E. Young Research Library, UCLA.

45. Pourade, *Gold in the Sun*, 223.

46. "William Clayton, Civic Leader, Is Called by Death," *San Diego Union*, November 15, 1934.

47. Susan Stamberg, "How Andrew Carnegie Turned His Fortune into a Library Legacy," *Morning Edition* (National Public Radio), August 1, 2013, https://www.npr.org/2013/08/01/207272849/how-andrew-carnegie-turned-his-fortune-into-a-library-legacy, accessed November 10, 2019.

48. LeRoux and Feeney, *Nonprofit Organizations and Civil Society in the United States*, 176.

49. McClain, *Ellen Browning Scripps*, 157.

50. Brainerd, "A Man of Millions," 716.

51. "Clayton Said It, Too, and Explains Why," *Coronado Eagle and Journal*, April 1, 1916.

52. Brainerd, "A Man of Millions," 716.

53. Quoted in untitled, undated *San Diego Union* newspaper clipping, VW.

54. Bradlee, *The Kid: The Immortal Life of Ted Williams*.

14. JOHN AND THE WOBBLIES

1. Marx, *Value, Price and Profit*, 63–78.

2. Zinn, *A People's History of the United States*, 331.

3. Zinn, *A People's History of the United States*.

4. Rayback, *History of American Labor*, 141.

5. Adams, *The Man, John D. Spreckels*, 77.

6. Adams, *The Man, John D. Spreckels*, 78.

7. Adams, *The Man, John D. Spreckels*, 131–32.

8. Knight, *Industrial Relations in the San Francisco Bay Area*, 22–23.

9. Brainerd, "A Man of Millions," 716.

10. Knight, *Industrial Relations in the San Francisco Bay Area*, 118.

11. Zinn, *A People's History of the United States*, 332.

12. Foner, *The AFL in the Progressive Era*, 23.

13. Quoted in McClain, *Ellen Browning Scripps*, 103.

14. Adams, *The Man, John D. Spreckels*, 305.

15. Meade County Area Chamber of Commerce (Brandenburg KY), Meade County Tourism, *Meade County Colony in California, Part 2, The Devil in the*

Garden of Eden (2019), http://visitmeadecounty.org/meade-county-colony
-in-california-part-ii-the-devil-in-the-garden-of-eden/, accessed November 10,
2019.

16. Quoted in Street, *Beasts of the Field*, 618.
17. Jeff Smith, "The Big Noise: The Free Speech Fight of 1912, Part Four: Free-
    Speech Protesters Got the Fire Hose," *San Diego Reader*, June 13, 2012.
18. McClain, *Ellen Browning Scripps*, 105.
19. Adams, *The Man, John D. Spreckels*, 302.
20. Quoted in McClain, *Ellen Browning Scripps*, 105.
21. Quoted in Brissenden, *The I. W. W.: A Study of American Syndicalism*, 264.
22. Quoted in Dubofsky, *We Shall Be All: A History of the Industrial Workers of the
    World*, 110.
23. "Plot to Blow Up Theater Is Charged: Suspect Attempt to Destroy $1,000,000
    Playhouse during Performance," *Los Angeles Herald*, August 23, 1912.
24. Brainerd, "A Man of Millions," 717.
25. McClain, *Ellen Browning Scripps*, 271.

15. GIFTING THE EXPOSITION AND THE ZOO

 1. Adams, *The Man, John D. Spreckels*, 294.
 2. Gregory, "1915–1916 San Diego Panama California Exposition," 177.
 3. Ellen B. Scripps to Edward W. Scripps, November 9, 1924, drawer 3, folder
    9, Ellen Browning Scripps Collection, Denison Library, Scripps College,
    Claremont CA. Reference courtesy of Molly McClain.
 4. Lockwood, *San Diego's Hilarious History*, 125.
 5. Pourade, *Gold in the Sun*, 254.
 6. Laut, "San Diego: First Port of Call," 111.
 7. Pourade, *Gold in the Sun*, 186.
 8. McClain, *Ellen Browning Scripps*, 153.
 9. Nolan, *San Diego*, 77–78.
10. "Noted Landscape Artist Plans San Diego Fair," *Los Angeles Herald*, November
    23, 1910.
11. O'Day, "The Role of the Olmsted Firm in the Development and Design of
    Boston's Small Parks, Playgrounds, and Public Squares, 1897–1915," 22.
12. Marston, *George White Marston*, 36–37.
13. Edward Scripps to C. A. McGrew, March 13, 1914, MSS 117, series 1.2, box 20,
    folder 1, E. W. Scripps Papers, Mahn Center for Archives & Special Collections,
    Ohio University Libraries. I thank Molly McClain for sharing this source.
14. Marston, *George White Marston*, 39.
15. "Architectural Gems of Old Spain Revived," *San Diego Union*, January 1, 1915, 1.

16. Anderson Borthwick, interview by Robert Wright, San Diego Historical Society Oral History Program, February 28, 1979, https://library.ucsd.edu/dc/object/bb2902188s/_1.html (site discontinued).

17. Borthwick, interview by Wright.

18. Whitney, *All the Stops*, xiv.

19. "Valley Counties Change Location," *Sacramento Union*, April 19, 1914.

20. Edward Barr to Richard Amero, August 13, 2002, in Amero, *Balboa Park and the 1915 Exposition*, chap. 11, "The Spreckels Organ Pavilion in Balboa Park," 5.

21. Barr to Amero, 6.

22. "Ready to Open," *Riverside Daily Press*, December 31, 1914.

23. Richard Amero, *A History of the Exposition*, chap. 1, "The Making of the Exposition, 1909–1915," in Richard Amero Balboa Park Collections, San Diego History Center, San Diego, California, accessed via https://sandiegohistory.org/archives/amero/1915expo/ch1/, November 10, 2019.

24. "Celebrities Captured by Camera at Exposition," *San Diego Union*, January 1, 1916, 8.

25. Ironically, the Kumeyaay Indians had already been living in their own village in the park before they were displaced by the exposition.

26. Laut, "San Diego: First Port of Call," 113, 119.

27. Showley, *San Diego: Perfecting Paradise*, 94.

28. "1915 San Diego Panama–California Exposition Centennial 2015," 2.

29. Adams, *The Man, John D. Spreckels*, 301.

30. Pourade, *Gold in the Sun*, 198.

31. MacPhail, *The Story of New San Diego and of Its Founder*, 147.

32. MacPhail, *The Story of New San Diego and of Its Founder*, 197.

33. MacPhail, *The Story of New San Diego and of Its Founder*, 198.

34. Kettner, *Why It Was Done and How*, 19.

35. Borthwick, interview by Wright.

36. McClain, *Ellen Browning Scripps*, 272.

37. Edward Scripps to Hon. William Kent, March 23, 1914, MSS 117, series 1.2, box 20, folder 1, E. W. Scripps Papers, Mahn Center for Archives & Special Collections, Ohio University Libraries. I thank Molly McClain for sharing this source.

38. San Francisco's exposition site was built on private land and was eradicated after its single-year run. Most of the cheaply made buildings were sold off to the highest bidder. Since they were constructed only of wood, chicken wire, and faux travertine made of plaster, few remain today.

39. "San Diego Zoo Global," *Wikiwand*, http://www.wikiwand.com/en/San_Diego_Zoo_Global, accessed November 10, 2019.

40. Stephenson, *The San Diego Zoo*, 54–55.

41. Stephenson, *The San Diego Zoo*, 56.

42. Stephenson, *The San Diego Zoo*, 56.

43. Hamilton and Hamilton, *Villa Calafia*, 1:99.

44. Faulconer, "The Zoo's Pioneer Expedition," 4.

45. Faulconer, "The Zoo's Pioneer Expedition."

46. Faulconer, "The Zoo's Pioneer Expedition," 4.

47. Stephenson, *The San Diego Zoo*, 82.

48. Faulconer, "The Zoo's Pioneer Expedition."

49. Faulconer, "The Zoo's Pioneer Expedition."

50. Faulconer, "The Zoo's Pioneer Expedition," 6.

16. STANDING UP TO THE U.S. GOVERNMENT

1. Kettner, *Why It Was Done and How*, 60.

2. "A Millionaire's Yacht for Sale," *Town Talk*, September 17, 1910.

3. "The Venetia," San Diego Yesterday, http://www.sandiegoyesterday.com/wp
-content/uploads/2017/03/Venetia-1.pdf, accessed November 2019.

4. Trimble, *Hero of the Air: Glenn Curtiss and the Birth of Naval Aviation*, 105–6.

5. Pescador and Aldrich, *San Diego's North Island*, 19.

6. Pescador and Aldrich, *San Diego's North Island*, 17.

7. Carlin and Brandes, *Coronado: The Enchanted Island*, 117.

8. Kettner, *Why It Was Done and How*, 86–87.

9. Kettner, *Why It Was Done and How*, 86–87.

10. Kettner, *Why It Was Done and How*.

11. Linder, *The Navy in San Diego*, 7.

12. Linder, *The Navy in San Diego*, 17.

13. Jerry MacMullen, "Steam Yacht Era Yielded Rich Character Studies," 1972,
CHA.

14. MacMullen, "Steam Yacht Era Yielded Rich Character Studies."

15. Kettner, *Why It Was Done and How*, 60.

16. "Spreckels et al., Executors, v. U.S.," 65.

17. "Spreckels et al., Executors, v. U.S.," 66.

18. "Spreckels et al., Executors, v. U.S.," 66–67.

19. "Spreckels et al., Executors, v. U.S.," 69.

20. "Spreckels et al., Executors, v. U.S.," 70.

21. "Spreckels et al., Executors, v. U.S.," 70–71.

22. "Spreckels et al., Executors, v. U.S.," 71.

23. Kettner, *Why It Was Done and How*, 91.

24. Kettner, *Why It Was Done and How*, 91.

25. MacTaggart, *Millionaires, Mansions, and Motor Yachts*, 94.

26. MacTaggart, *Millionaires, Mansions, and Motor Yachts*, 95.

27. *Our Navy*, 22.

28. "Spreckels et al., Executors, v. U.S.," 74.

29. "Spreckels et al., Executors, v. U.S.," 75.

30. After John's death, his heirs sued the government and won, recovering the balance he never received in addition to the lease payments.

31. MacTaggart, *Millionaires, Mansions, and Motor Yachts*, 4.

32. Greene, *Venetia, Avenger of the Lusitania*.

33. MacTaggart, *Millionaires, Mansions, and Motor Yachts*, 4.

34. "Letters from a Cadet," *Garden Island* (Lihue HI), August 24, 1920.

35. Walshok and Shragge, *Invention and Reinvention*, 44.

17. THE CRUEL 1920S

1. "Mrs. Jack Spreckels' Divorce," *The Wasp*, November 15, 1913.

2. "Spreckels Denies Wife's Charges of Cruelty," *Daily Capital Journal* (Salem OR), December 24, 1913, 4.

3. "What They Say of Mrs. Frank Wakefield," *Honolulu Star-Bulletin*, September 18, 1915, 9.

4. "What They Say of Mrs. Frank Wakefield." Edith would soon return to the papers, however, when she sued Wakefield for divorce on the ground of desertion.

5. Veil, *Adventure's a Wench*.

6. In the filing at Reno, she changed her first name from Sadie to Syida, and later to Sydi, both times generating considerable publicity. Veil referred to her as "Sidia."

7. Veil, *Adventure's a Wench*, 185–87.

8. "J. D. Spreckels, Jr., Killed When His Auto Is Wrecked," *Sacramento Union*, August 9, 1921.

9. "Spreckels' Son in Jail for Failure to Dim His Headlights," *Sacramento Union*, January 15, 1916.

10. "Spreckels Sends for Blankets to Soften His Couch in Jail," *Riverside (CA) Daily Press*, January 15, 1916.

11. "Seely for Governor," *The Day Book* (Chicago), January 22, 1916.

12. "Devil's Den," *Pacific Oil Reporter* (San Francisco), 1900, 7.

13. "The Spectator," *Town Talk*, 1910, 13.

14. Veil, *Adventure's a Wench*, 206.

15. Veil, *Adventure's a Wench*, 207.

16. Up to this point in the book, "Claus Jr." has referred to John's youngest son, who was born in 1888. From now on, however, that person will be referred to simply as "Claus," whereas *his* son, born in 1911, will be referred to as "Claus Jr.," or simply "Junior."

17. "Deals Handsomely with Son's Wives," *Santa Cruz (CA) Evening News*, March 14, 1922.

18. "Spreckels May Take Hand in the Triangle," *Riverside (CA) Daily Press*, August 23, 1922.

19. "Mrs. Edith Spreckels Wakefield," *Daily Capital Journal* (Salem OR), September 4, 1922; "John D. Spreckels v. Edith H. Wakefield," 696.

20. "Mrs. Edith Spreckels Wakefield."

21. *Music Magazine–Musical Courier* 75, September 6, 1917, 36.

22. Spreckels Companies Folder, September 27, 1918, CHA.

23. Spreckels Companies Folder, September 15, 1921, CHA.

24. "Claus Spreckels Gets Job Working for His Papa; He Says He'll Do His Best," *Coronado Eagle and Journal*, February 25, 1922.

25. *San Diego Sun* article quoted in "Claus Spreckels Gets Job Working for His Papa."

26. "About People," *Electric Traction* 18, March 1922, 260.

27. Spreckels Companies Folder, June 13, 1924, CHA.

28. "Claus Spreckels' Play-Toy," *AERA* 13 (October 1925): 350–51.

29. "Claus Spreckels' Play-Toy," 350.

30. "Claus Spreckels' Play-Toy."

31. Mengers, *San Diego Trolleys*, 84.

32. Peters, "Mission Beach: San Diego's Coney Island," 2.

33. Peters, "Mission Beach," 38.

34. Peters, "Mission Beach," 44. Today it is known as Belmont Amusement Park.

35. Adams, *The Man, John D. Spreckels*, 91.

36. Peters, "Mission Beach," 42.

37. Peters, "Mission Beach," 38.

38. Adams, *The Man, John D. Spreckels*, 285–308.

39. Quoted in "Spreckels, John," MSS 81, Box 27, Folder 8, General Correspondence, in Ed Fletcher Papers, 1870–1955, University of California, San Diego, Libraries.

40. Family archives, VW.

41. Quoted in Pourade, *The Rising Tide*, 24.

42. Fletcher, *Memoirs of Ed Fletcher*, 170–71.

43. "The Dinner," *Coronado Eagle and Journal*, June 16, 1923.

44. "The Dinner."
45. Pourade, *The Rising Tide*, 24.
46. "Hotel del Coronado," *The Wasp*, August 2, 1913, 11.
47. "Hotel del Coronado."
48. "Taking the Cure," *Bismarck (ND) Tribune*, November 2, 1911.
49. Guidry, "Mother Stork's Baby Book."
50. Guidry, "Mother Stork's Baby Book."
51. Guidry, "Mother Stork's Baby Book."
52. "Mrs. J. D. Spreckels Called by Death," *Coronado Eagle and Journal* 36, January 12, 1924.
53. Reproduced in Pourade, *The Rising Tide*, 77.
54. Pourade, *The Rising Tide*.
55. "C. Spreckels Dies in North of Pneumonia," unnamed, unnumbered, undated newspaper clipping, VW.
56. "J. D. Spreckels' Dog Victim of Poisoner," *Coronado Eagle and Journal*, December 15, 1923.
57. That is, every month for the rest of his life.
58. Adams died in 1931, five years after John, but toward the end, he requested the payments to stop. He had had enough.
59. "J. D. Spreckels' Biography Is Basis of Claim: Austin Adams, Local Writer, Files Letter Promising Compensation," *Coronado Eagle and Journal*, September 28, 1926.
60. Typed family essay by Harriet Hamilton, VW.
61. "Pleasure's Wand," *San Francisco News Letter*, January 17, 1925, 12.

18. THE DEPARTED SKIPPER

1. Hamilton and Hamilton, *Villa Calafia*, 1:38.
2. "Bulletin Issued from His Bedside on Sunday, May 23, Encouraging," *Coronado Eagle and Journal*, June 1, 1926.
3. Hamilton and Hamilton, *Villa Calafia*, 1:38.
4. Hamilton and Hamilton, *Villa Calafia*, 1:38.
5. MacTaggart, *Millionaires, Mansions, and Motor Yachts*, 95.
6. "Spreckels Are Reunited," *Coronado Eagle and Journal*, January 21, 1922.
7. Gus went back and forth over the years to New York to run the Federal Sugar Company, but he retired in the 1920s to enjoy a more relaxed European lifestyle. He lived part time in his Villa Baratier on the French Riviera with his wife, Orey, and daughter, Lurline. In the early 1930s, when Orey's health declined, they downsized and moved to Paris; she died in 1936. Gus stayed in Paris throughout World War II, cared for by Lurline. The European lifestyle

was apparently good for him because there is no record of any serious diseases until his death in 1946; his Paris death certificate listed the cause of death at the at the at the age of eighty-eight as "old age."

Rudolph was a controversial character in his era. He was called everything from a "robber baron" to a "fighter against corruption." He made millions from his long list of investments, including sugar, real estate, utilities, and banking, but he was seemingly relieved when he lost it all in the Great Depression. Many years later, he told a reporter, "Some financiers jumped out of windows when they found themselves bankrupt. I never lost a night's sleep over it." He and his wife, Nellie, had four children: Rudolph (1897), Howard (1898), Eleanor (1902), and Claudine (1906). Rudolph and Nellie lived for years in an opulent estate in San Mateo County's Hillsborough until she died in 1949. For a while, he moved back to San Francisco but then returned to San Mateo County. He died in 1958 at the age of eighty-six.

8. "John D. Spreckels Passes Away at Coronado Home on Monday Afternoon," *Coronado Eagle and Journal,* June 8, 1926.
9. "Services for J. D. Spreckels Held on Wed.: The Friends and Employees Gather at Bay Side Home to Pay Last Respects," *Coronado Eagle and Journal,* June 15, 1926.
10. "Tribute Paid Spreckels," *Los Angeles Times,* June 10, 1926.
11. "Services for J. D. Spreckels Held on Wed."
12. "Services for J. D. Spreckels Held on Wed."
13. "Tribute Paid Spreckels."
14. "Friends Are to Pay Final Tribute Today to John D. Spreckels," unnamed, undated newspaper clipping, vw.
15. "Friends Are to Pay Final Tribute Today to John D. Spreckels."
16. "Friends Are to Pay Final Tribute Today to John D. Spreckels."
17. "Friends Are to Pay Final Tribute Today to John D. Spreckels."

EPILOGUE

1. Anderson Borthwick, interview by Robert Wright, San Diego Historical Society Oral History Program, February 28, 1979, https://library.ucsd.edu/dc/object/bb2902188s/_1.html (site discontinued).
2. Borthwick, interview by Wright.
3. "Some Methods in City Travel Are Reviewed: East and West Trolley Folks Say Finance Ends Don't Meet," *Coronado Eagle and Journal,* May 28, 1930.
4. Starr, *The Dream Endures,* 154.
5. Scharlach, *Big Alma.*

6. Under the terms of Adolph's will, Alma was entitled to income from one half of the estate, with the rest to be shared by their children: Alma Emma ("Little Alma"), Adolph Bernard Jr., and Dorothy Constance. Even with just that one half from the will, Alma was left with the modern equivalent of more than $100 million, making her the richest woman in the West. She wanted more.

7. *Coronado Eagle and Journal,* May 28, 1930.

8. Matt Potter, "The Rise and Fall of the Copley Press," *San Diego Reader,* February 28, 2008.

9. "Large Deposit Gains Made by Bank of Italy Also a Remarkable Record of Total Resources Is Shown," *Coronado Eagle and Journal,* July 10, 1929.

10. "S. D. & A. May Be Bought by Espee Lines," *Calexico Chronicle,* September 5, 1931.

11. "Locomotives of the San Diego & Arizona Eastern Ry," 88.

12. "Locomotives of the San Diego & Arizona Eastern Ry."

13. On the West Coast, anyway. John's alienated brother Gus had retired from his Federal Sugar Refining Company on the East Coast in the early 1920s, but the other alienated brother, Rudolph, continued his involvement with Federal until the Great Depression of the 1930s.

14. Hamilton and Hamilton, *Villa Calafia,* 2:150–51.

15. Hamilton and Hamilton, *Villa Calafia,* 2:150–51.

16. "Spreckels Sugar History," Spreckels Sugar Company and Southern Minnesota Beet Sugar Corporation, Brawley CA, http://www.spreckelssugar.com/history.aspx, accessed November 11, 2019.

17. Hamilton and Hamilton, *Villa Calafia,* 1:151.

18. Hamilton and Hamilton, *Villa Calafia,* 2:142.

19. "Coronado 1920–40: A Paradoxical Era," *Coronado Eagle and Journal,* August 23, 1979.

20. "E. R. Tiedemann, Twice Councilman, Hotel Man, Dies," *Coronado Eagle and Journal,* December 24, 1964.

21. "New Troubles For San Diego Alessio Family," *Santa Cruz Sentinel,* December 13, 1972.

22. Langmead, *Icons of American Architecture,* 245.

23. "New Troubles For San Diego Alessio Family."

24. Langmead, *Icons of American Architecture,* 245.

25. Langmead, *Icons of American Architecture,* 245.

26. Langmead, *Icons of American Architecture,* 245.

27. "The Hotel an Ageless Beauty—The Eternal Woman," *Coronado Eagle and Journal,* July 31, 1969.

28. Dodge, *Rails of the Silver Gate*, 110.
29. "Absolutely Not!" *San Diego Independent*, July 3, 1926.
30. "Absolutely Not!"
31. "Organists Pay Problem Faced by San Diego," *San Diego Sun*, July 3, 1926.
32. Ross Porter, personal communication with author, August 2019.
33. "Colonel Copley Purchases J. D. Spreckels Home: Prominent Newspaper Publisher Acquires Fine Coronado Mansion," *Coronado Eagle and Journal*, May 22, 1929.
34. "Local Man Found Dead in Bathroom," *Coronado Eagle and Journal*, August 28, 1952.
35. Kathy Connor, personal communication with author, July 1, 2019.
36. "Spreckels Yacht Venetia Sold to Rich Canadian," handwritten notation on an unnamed, undated newspaper clipping, VW.
37. MacTaggart, *Millionaires, Mansions, and Motor Yachts*, 95.
38. "Spreckels et al., Executors, v. U.S.," 78–79.
39. "Spreckels Heirs Get Over $7,000,000 from His Estate," *Coronado Eagle and Journal*, April 16,1930.
40. Document that Virginia Wilson shared with author on September 7, 2019, VW.
41. "Mann Act" (Wikipedia), https://en.wikipedia.org/wiki/Mann_Act, accessed November 12, 2019.
42. "Mrs. Spreckels Asks Payment of $400,000," *Oakland Tribune*, June 30, 1932.
43. "Mrs. Spreckels Asks Payment of $400,000."
44. "Mrs. Spreckels Asks Payment of $400,000."
45. David Lewis, conversation with author, October 18, 2018.
46. "Spreckels Kin Dies of Heart Attack in San Francisco," *Coronado Eagle and Journal*, January 28, 1937.
47. Garry Belcher, conversation author, August 1, 2018.
48. "Mrs. Wegeforth Dies in S.F. Area," *San Diego Union*, April 24, 1965.
49. Garry Belcher, conversation with author, August 1, 2018; and Mike Belcher, conversation with author, April 19, 2020.
50. Mike Belcher, conversation with author, April 19, 2020.
51. "An Empire Builder Passes," unnamed, undated newspaper clipping, VW.

BIBLIOGRAPHY

"1915 San Diego Panama–California Exposition Centennial 2015." *Toldot San Diego: Newsletter of the Jewish Historical Society of San Diego* 24, no. 1 (May 2015). http://cbisd.org/wp-content/uploads/2015/06/JHSSD-May-2015-Newsletter -Special-Edition.pdf. Accessed November 10, 2019.

Adams, H. Austin. *The Man, John D. Spreckels.* San Diego: Press of Frye & Smith, 1924.

Adler, Jacob. "Claus Spreckels' Rise and Fall in Hawai'i with Emphasis on London Loan of 1886." In *Sixty-Seventh Annual Report of the Hawaiian Historical Society for the Year 1958*, 7–21. Honolulu: Advertiser Publishing, 1959.

Adler, Jacob, and Robert M. Kamins. "The Political Debut of Walter Murray Gibson." *Hawaiian Journal of History* 18 (1984): 96–115.

Albright, Harrison. "Reinforced Concrete Construction in Southern California." *Western Architect and Engineer* 7, no. 3 (January 1907): 37–43.

Alexander, Geoff. *America Goes Hawaiian: The Influence of Pacific Island Culture on the Mainland.* Jefferson NC: McFarland, 2018.

All about Hawaii: The Recognized Book of Authentic Information on Hawaii, Combined with Thrum's Hawaiian Annual and Standard Guide. Honolulu: Honolulu Star-Bulletin, 1886.

Ambrose, Stephen E. *Nothing Like It in the World: The Men Who Built the Transcontinental Railroad 1863–1869.* New York: Simon & Schuster, 2000.

American Sugar Refining Company, and Others: Hearings Held before the Special Committee to Investigate the American Sugar Refining Company. 62nd Cong. Washington DC: U.S. Government Printing Office, 1911.

Amero, Richard. *Balboa Park and the 1915 Exposition.* San Diego: History Press, 2013. Accessed via http://balboaparkhistory.net/, November 10, 2019.

Banks, Charles Eugene, and Opie Percival Read. *The History of the San Francisco Disaster and Mount Vesuvius Horror.* San Francisco: C. E. Thomas, 1906.

Barr, Edward S. "The Historians Corner." *StopTab.* San Diego, Spreckels Organ Society, Summer 1999, 5.

Basney, Dana Alan. "The Role of the Spreckels Business Interests in the Development of San Diego." Master's thesis, San Diego State University, 1975.

Bauer, Linda, and Steve Bauer. *Recipes from Historic California: A Restaurant Guide and Cookbook.* Lanham MD: Taylor Trade Publishing, 2008.

Bean, Walton. *Boss Ruef's San Francisco: The Story of the Union Labor Party, Big Business, and the Graft Prosecution.* Berkeley: University of California Press, 1952.

Bernhard, Jim. *Porcupine, Picayune, and Post: How Newspapers Get Their Names.* Columbia: University of Missouri Press, 2007.

Birmingham, Stephen. *California Rich: The Lives, the Times, the Scandals and the Fortunes of the Men and Women Who Made and Kept California's Wealth.* New York: Open Road Integrated Media, 2016.

Black, Samuel T. *San Diego County, California; A Record of Settlement, Organization, Progress and Achievement.* Chicago: S. J. Clarke Publishing, 1913.

Bonura, Sandra E. *Light in the Queen's Garden: Ida May Pope, Pioneer for Hawai'i's Daughters.* Honolulu: University of Hawai'i Press, 2017.

———. "Queen Lili'uokalani's Beloved Kawaiaha'o Seminary." *Hawaiian Journal of History* 51 (2017): 31–68.

Bonura, Sandra E., and Deborah Day, eds. *An American Girl in the Hawaiian Islands: Letters of Carrie Prudence Winter, 1890–1893.* Honolulu: University of Hawai'i Press, 2012.

Bradlee, Ben, Jr. *The Kid: The Immortal Life of Ted Williams.* New York: Little, Brown and Company, 2013.

Brainerd, Erastus. "A Man of Millions." *Hearst's Magazine* 26, July–December 1914, 716–17.

Brégent-Heald, Dominique. *Borderland Films: American Cinema, Mexico, and Canada during the Progressive Era.* Lincoln: University of Nebraska Press, 2015.

Bridges, Amy. *Morning Glories: Municipal Reform in the Southwest.* Princeton NJ: Princeton University Press, 1997.

Brigandi, Phil. "'What I Sought Is That Which I Have Found': The Origins of the Ramona Myth, 1885–1890." *Los Angeles Corral,* Winter 2005, 7.

Brissenden, Paul Frederick. *The I. W. W.: A Study of American Syndicalism.* New York: Columbia University Press, 1919.

Carlin, Katherine Eitzen, and Ray Brandes. *Coronado: The Enchanted Island.* 2nd ed. Coronado CA: Coronado Historical Association, 1988.

Chacón, Justin Akers, and Mike Davis. *No One Is Illegal: Fighting Racism and State Violence on the U.S.-Mexico Border.* Chicago: Haymarket Books, 2006.

Clarsen, Georgine. *Eat My Dust: Early Women Motorists.* Studies in Historical and Political Science. Baltimore MD: Johns Hopkins University Press, 2008.

"Claus Spreckels' Play-toy." *AERA* 13 (October 1924): 350–51.

Coffman, Tom. *Nation Within: The History of the American Occupation of Hawai'i.* Durham NC: Duke University Press, 2016.

"Construction and Improvements." *Railway Journal* 14, no. 5 (May 1908): 15.

Conway, Jimmie Don. "Spreckels Sugar Company: The First Fifty Years." Master's thesis, San Jose State University, 1999.

Cordray, William W. "Claus Spreckels of California." PhD diss., University of Southern California, 1955.

Coronado Beach, San Diego County, California: The Coronado Beach Company Has Been Organized with a Capital of One Million Dollars. Chicago: Rand, McNally, 1888.

Dearborn, R. F. *Saratoga, and How to See It: Containing a Description of the Watering Place.* Albany NY: Week, Parsons, 1873.

Deutsch, Reena. *San Diego and Arizona Railway: The Impossible Railroad.* Charleston SC: Arcadia Publishing, 2011.

Dice, Mark. *The Bohemian Grove: Facts & Fiction.* San Diego: The Resistance, 2015.

Dicks, Vincent J. "J. D. Spreckels and His Influence on San Diego City Politics: 1890–1909." Unpublished paper, 2019.

———. "J. D. Spreckels and the Reform Movement in California." Unpublished paper, 2019.

Dodge, John Mason. *"Jack" Dodge (John Mason Dodge): The Friend of Everyman; His Life and Times as Told to William H. Holcomb.* Los Angeles: S. Danby, 1937.

Dodge, Richard V. *Rails of the Silver Gate: The Spreckels San Diego Empire.* San Marino CA: Golden West Books, 1960.

Dubofsky, Melvyn. *We Shall Be All: A History of the Industrial Workers of the World.* Edited by Joseph A. McCartin. Urbana: University of Illinois Press, 2000. Originally published 1969.

"The Duchess of Windsor and the Coronado Legend, Part 1." *Journal of San Diego History* 11, no. 4 (Fall 1987). https://sandiegohistory.org/journal/1987/october/duchess/. Accessed November 9, 2019.

Ed Fletcher Papers, 1870–1955. University of California, San Diego, Libraries.

Electric Traction 18, January 1922, 260.

Ellen Browning Scripps Collection. Denison Library, Scripps College, Claremont CA.

Elson, Louis C., ed. *The Musical Herald.* Boston: Musical Herald Company, 1884.

Emmet, Boris. *The California and Hawaiian Sugar Refining Corporation of San Francisco: A Study of the Origin, Business Policies, and Management of a Co-operative Refining and Distributing Organization.* Palo Alto CA: Stanford University Press, 1928.

E. W. Scripps Papers. Mahn Center for Archives & Special Collections, Ohio University Libraries.

Faulconer, T. N. "The Zoo's Pioneer Expedition." *Zoonooz,* August 1943, 3–7.

Fletcher, Ed. *Memoirs of Ed Fletcher.* San Diego: Pioneer Printers, 1952.

Foner, Philip S., ed. *The AFL in the Progressive Era, 1910–1915.* Vol. 5 of *History of the Labor Movement in the United States.* New York: International Publishers, 1980.

———, ed. *Fellow Workers and Friends: I.W.W. Free-Speech Fights as Told by Participants.* Westport CT: Praeger, 1981.

Frizell, Robert W. *Independent Immigrants: A Settlement of Hanoverian Germans in Western Missouri.* Columbia: University of Missouri Press, 2007.

"Getting Respect from the San Diego Press." *NAACP (San Diego Branch) History News,* no. 2 (January 2012): 1–4.

Goldberg, Charlotte K. "A Cauldron of Anger: The Spreckels Family and Reform of California Community Property Law." *Western Legal History: The Journal of the Ninth Judicial Circuit Historical Society* 12, no. 2 (Summer/Fall 1999): 241–79.

———. *Community Property.* Aspen Casebook Series. New York: Wolters Kluwer Law & Business, 2008.

"A Good Story." *Land and Freedom* 16, no. 1 (January–February 1916): 59.

Gonzalez, Antonio. *Architects Who Built Southern California.* Charleston SC: The History Press, 2019.

Greene, Clay Meredith. *Venetia, Avenger of the Lusitania: Being the Narrative of the Adventures and Career of the Yacht "Venetia" during the World War as an Auxiliary Cruiser, Including Such Proof as Exists of Her Connection with the Expiation of Its Most Unforgivable Tragedy, Based upon the Cruiser's Official Log and the Diaries of Some of Her Officers.* San Diego: Privately printed, 1919.

Gregory, Mike. "1915–1916 San Diego Panama California Exposition." In *Expo Legacies: Names, Numbers, Facts & Figures,* 177–84. Bloomington IN: Author-House, 2009.

Guidry, Laurie. "Mother Stork's Baby Book." Personal collection, photo album and scrapbook.

Hackler, Rhoda E. A. "Princeville Plantation Papers." *Hawaiian Journal of History* 16 (1982): 65–86.

Hall, Henry, ed. *America's Successful Men of Affairs: An Encyclopedia of Contemporaneous Biography.* Vol. 2. New York: Tribune Association, 1896.

Hamilton, Edward Morse, and Harriet Holbrook Hamilton. *Villa Calafia.* 2 vols. Privately printed, 1961.

Hanft, Robert M. *San Diego and Arizona: The Impossible Railroad.* Glendale CA: Interurban Press, Trans-Anglo Books, 1985.

Harris, Iverson L., Jr. "John D. Spreckels and the San Diego and Arizona Railway." *Theosophical Path* 25 no. 2 (August 1923): 159–69.

Hill, Thomas Edie. *Hill's Album of Biography and Art: Containing Portraits and Pen-Sketches of Many Persons Who Have Been and Are Prominent as Religionists, Military Heroes, Inventors, Financiers, Scientists, Explorers, Writers, Physicians, Actors, Lawyers, Musicians, Artists, Poets, Sovereigns, Humorists, Orators and Statesmen, Together with Chapters Relating to History, Science, and Important Works in Which Prominent People Have Been Engaged at Various Periods of Time.* Chicago: Danks & Company, 1890.

Hobbs, Ewart W., ed. *Cases Decided in the Court of Claims of the United States, February 1, 1927, to June 30, 1927, with Abstract of Decisions of the Supreme Court.* Vol. 63. Washington DC: Government Printing Office, 1928.

Hofsommer, Donovan L. *The Southern Pacific, 1901–1985.* College Station: Texas A&M University Press, 1986.

Hoitt, Ira G. "Education in California." *The Sunset*, May 3, 1899.

Hotel del Coronado. Washington DC: National Park Service Office of Archeology and Historic Preservation: Historic American Buildings Survey, 1958.

"The Hotel Del Grew Up with the Film Industry." In *Hotel del Coronado: 1888–1988, Centennial Souvenir Edition*, edited by Aislinn Catherine Sotelo, 6–7. San Diego: Coronado Journal Publishing, 1988.

Innis, Jack Scheffler. *San Diego Legends: The Events, People, and Places that Made History.* San Diego: Sunbelt Publications, 2004.

"John D. Spreckels v. Edith H. Wakefield." *United States Circuit Court of Appeals for the Ninth Circuit*, no. 3832, March 10, 1922. https://archive.org/details/govuscourtsca9briefs1311/page/n695?q=spreckels+coronado+california. Accessed November 11, 2019.

"John Spreckels an Enthusiast." *The Automobile* 13, July 6, 1905, 375.

Johnston, Andrew K., Roger D. Connor, Carlene E. Stephens, and Paul E. Ceruzzi. *Time and Navigation: The Untold Story of Getting from Here to There.* Washington DC: Smithsonian Books, 2015.

"Julius Wangenheim: An Autobiography." *California Historical Society Quarterly* 35 no. 4 (December 1956): 345–66.

Kanahele, George S. *Emma: Hawai'i's Remarkable Queen: A Biography.* Honolulu: Queen Emma Foundation, 1999.

Kent, Harold W. *Charles Reed Bishop, Man of Hawai'i.* Palo Alto CA: Pacific Books, 1965.

Kettner, William. *Why It Was Done and How.* Edited by Mary B. Steyle. San Diego: Frye & Smith, 1923.

Kipling, Rudyard. *American Notes.* Boston: Brown and Co., 1899.

Kiyosaki, Wayne. *Talk Pidgin; Speak English; Go Local; Go American: The Japanese Immigrant Experience in Spreckelsville, Maui.* Bloomington IN: AuthorHouse, 2014.

Knight, Robert Edward Lee. *Industrial Relations in the San Francisco Bay Area, 1900–1918*. Berkeley: University of California Press, 1960.

Krauss, Bob. *Johnny Wilson: First Hawaiian Democrat*. Honolulu: University of Hawai'i Press, 1994.

Kropp, Phoebe S. *California Vieja: Culture and Memory in a Modern American Place*. Berkeley: University of California Press, 2006.

Laffaye, Horace A. *Polo in the United States: A History*. Jefferson NC: McFarland, 2014.

Lane, Rose Wilder. "Life and Jack London." *Sunset, the Pacific Monthly* 40, no. 4 February 1918, 30–34.

Langmead, Donald. *Icons of American Architecture: From the Alamo to the World Trade Center*. Vol. 1. Westport CT: Greenwood Press, 2009.

Laut, A. C. "San Diego: First Port of Call." *Sunset, the Pacific Monthly* 30, no. 2, February 1913, 110–20.

Leake, William Samuel. *The Healing of "Sam" Leake*. Los Angeles: Rob-Mar Press, 1920.

Leather, Fitzherbert. *The One-Story Schoolhouse Idea with Plans of Model Schools*. Chicago: National Lumber Manufacturers Association, Trade Extension Department, 1917.

LeRoux, Kelly, and Mary K. Feeney. *Nonprofit Organizations and Civil Society in the United States*. New York: Routledge, Taylor & Francis, 2015.

Levere, William Collin. *The History of the Sigma Alpha Epsilon Fraternity*. Vol. 2. Chicago: Lakeside Press, 1911.

Lili'uokalani. *Hawai'i's Story by Hawai'i's Queen Lili'uokalani*. Boston: Lee and Shepard, 1898.

Linder, Bruce. *The Navy in San Diego*. Mount Pleasant SC: Arcadia Publishing, 2007.

Lockwood, Herbert. *San Diego's Hilarious History: From the Skeleton's Closet Revisited*. Edited by William Carroll. Raton NM: Coda Publications, 2004.

"Locomotives of the San Diego & Arizona Eastern Ry." *Railroad Stories* 17, no. 4 (July 1935): 88–89.

MacLennan, Carol. "Kilauea Sugar Plantation in 1912: A Snapshot." *Hawaiian Journal of History* 41, no. 1 (2007): 1–34.

MacPhail, Elizabeth C. "A Little Gem of a Park." *Journal of San Diego History: San Diego Historical Society Quarterly* 29, no. 4 (Fall 1983), https://sandiegohistory.org/journal/1983/october/gem/.

———. *The Story of New San Diego and of Its Founder, Alonzo E. Horton*. 2nd ed. San Diego: San Diego Historical Society, 1979.

MacTaggart, Ross. *Millionaires, Mansions, and Motor Yachts: An Era of Opulence*. New York: W. W. Norton, 2004.

Magnuson, Torsten A. "History of the Beet Sugar Industry in California." *Annual Publication of the Historical Society of Southern California* 11, no. 1 (1918): 68–79.

Marston, Mary Gilman. *George White Marston: A Family Chronicle*. Vol. 2. Los Angeles: Ward Ritchie Press, 1956.

Marx, Karl. *Value, Price and Profit*. Beijing: Foreign Languages Press, 1973. Originally published as *Lohn, Preis und Profit*, 1865/1898.

Maulhardt, Jeffrey W. *Oxnard Sugar Beets: Ventura County's Lost Cash Crop*. San Francisco: Arcadia Publishing, 2016.

McClain, Molly. *Ellen Browning Scripps: New Money and American Philanthropy*. Lincoln: University of Nebraska Press, 2017.

McGrew, Clarence Alan. *The City of San Diego and San Diego County: The Birthplace of California*. Chicago: American Historical Society, 1922.

Mengers, Douglas W. *San Diego Trolleys*. Charleston SC: Arcadia Publishing, 2017.

Miller, Grace L. "The Origins of the San Diego Lincoln-Roosevelt League, 1905–1909." *Southern California Quarterly* 60, no. 4 (Winter 1978): 421–43. doi:10.2307/41170803.

Nolan, John. *San Diego: A Comprehensive Plan for Its Improvement*. Boston: Geo. H. Ellis, 1908.

O'Brien, Victor H. "Claus Spreckels, the Sugar King." *Ainslee's Magazine*, February 1901, 516–23.

"Oceanic Shipping Company." *Illustrated American* 13, April 1, 1893, 353.

O'Connell, Daniel. *The Inner Man: Good Things to Eat and Drink and Where to Get Them*. San Francisco: The Bancroft Company, 1891.

O'Day, James. "The Role of the Olmsted Firm in the Development and Design of Boston's Small Parks, Playgrounds, and Public Squares, 1897–1915." Prepared for the Massachusetts Association for Olmsted Parks, Boston Redevelopment Authority Environmental Intern Program, Northeast, March 1985.

"The Oil-Burning Ferryboat Ramona." *Marine Engineering* (1903): 625.

Our Navy. Vol. 12. San Francisco: Navy Publishing, 1919.

Panama–California Exposition, the Chamber of Commerce and the Citizens of San Diego. *Makers of San Diego 1915 Panama–California Exposition*. San Diego: Author, 1912.

Papers of the California Historical Society. San Francisco, California.

Pennsylvania State Board of Agriculture. *Agriculture of Pennsylvania, Containing Reports, etc., for 1882*. Vol. 6. Harrisburg PA: State Printer, 1883.

Pescador, Katrina, and Mark Aldrich. *San Diego's North Island, 1911–1941*. Charleston SC: Arcadia Publishing, 2007.

Peters, Gregory. "Mission Beach: San Diego's Coney Island." Master's thesis, California State University, San Marcos, 2013.

Peterson, J. Harold. *The Coronado Story*. 2nd ed. Coronado CA: Coronado Federal Savings and Loan Association, 1959. First published 1954.

Phelps, Alonzo. *Contemporary Biography of California's Representative Men: With Contributions from Distinguished Scholars and Scientists.* San Francisco: A. L. Bancroft, 1881.

Pontius, D. W. "San Diego & Arizona Railway." *Rock Island Employees' Magazine* 15, no. 7, July 1920, 4–5.

Pourade, Richard F. *The Glory Years.* Vol. 4 of *The History of San Diego.* San Diego: Union Publishing, 1964.

———. *Gold in the Sun.* Vol. 5 of *The History of San Diego.* San Diego: Union Publishing, 1965.

———. *The Rising Tide.* Vol. 6 of *The History of San Diego.* San Diego: Union Publishing, 1967.

"The Proposed Working Men's Hotel at San Diego." *Southwest Contractor and Manufacturer,* vol. 11, 1913, 8.

Purdy, Helen Throop. *San Francisco: As It Was, As It Is, and How to See It.* San Francisco: Paul Elder, 1912.

Rayback, Joseph G. *History of American Labor.* New York: Macmillan Free Press, 1959.

Retan, Iretta Hight. *The Iretta Hight Retan Collection.* Honolulu: Kamehameha Schools, 1988.

Richard Amero Balboa Park Collections. San Diego History Center, San Diego, California.

"Robert M. Hamilton." *The Iron Age* 51 (1893): 1129.

"San Diego Water Works." *San Diego Tourist* 9, no. 2 (1916): 52.

"Santa Fe and Southern Pacific Arrangements." *Railway Journal* 16, no. 7 (July 1910): 8–9.

Scharlach, Bernice. *Big Alma: San Francisco's Alma Spreckels.* 2nd ed. Berkeley CA: Heyday Books, 2015. Originally published 1990.

Scott, Edward B. *The Saga of the Sandwich Islands.* Lake Tahoe NV: Sierra-Tahoe Publishing, 1968.

Sea Letter of the National Maritime Museum. San Francisco: National Maritime Museum Association, 1988.

Showley, Roger M. *San Diego: Perfecting Paradise.* Carlsbad CA: Heritage Media Corp, 1999.

Simonds, William A. *Kama'aina: A Century in Hawai'i.* Honolulu: American Factors, 1949.

Simpson, Ernest S. "John D., Miracle-Maker." *Sunset, the Pacific Monthly* 30, no. 2 (February 1913): 201–3.

Smythe, William Ellsworth. *History of San Diego, 1542–1908: An Account of the Rise and Progress of the Pioneer Settlement on the Pacific Coast of the United States.* Vol. 2. San Diego: The History Company, 1908.

Sotelo, Aislinn Catherine, ed. *Hotel del Coronado: 1888–1988, Centennial Souvenir Edition*. San Diego: Coronado Journal Publishing, 1988.

Spiekermann, Uwe. "Claus Spreckels: A Biographical Case Study of Nineteenth-Century American Immigrant Entrepreneurship." *Business and Economic History On-Line* 8 (2010): 1–21. http://thebhc.org/sites/default/files/spiekermann.pdf. Accessed November 9, 2019.

———. "Expanding the Frontier(s): The Spreckels Family and the German-American Penetration of the Pacific, 1870–1920." In *Explorations and Entanglements: Germans in Pacific Worlds from the Early Modern Period to World War I*, edited by Hartmut Berghoff, Frank Biess, and Ulrike Strasser, 171–94. New York: Berghahn Books, 2019.

———. "An Ordinary Man among Titans: The Life of Walter P. Spreckels." In *Immigrant Entrepreneurship: The German-American Experience since 1700*, edited by Hartmut Berghoff and Uwe Spiekermann, 263–84. Washington DC: German Historical Institute, 2016.

Spofford, A. R., and Charles Annandale, eds. *XX Century Cyclopædia and Atlas: Biography, History, Art, Science and Gazetteer of the World*. Vol. 7. New York: Gebbie & Co., 1901.

Spreckels, John D. "Hawaii for Tourists." *Paradise of the Pacific Monthly* 8, no. 9 (September 1895): 661–62.

"Spreckels et al., Executors, v. U.S." In *Cases Decided in the Court of Claims of the United States, February 1, 1927, to June 30, 1927, with Abstract of Decisions of the Supreme Court*, vol. 63, edited by Ewart W. Hobbs, 64–79. Washington DC: Government Printing Office, 1928.

"Spreckels v. Spreckels et al." *California Appellate Divisions*. Vol. 22. California District Courts of Appeal, January–June 1916. San Francisco: Recorder Printing and Publishing Company, 1916.

Starr, Kevin. *The Dream Endures: California Enters the 1940s*. New York: Oxford University Press, 2002.

———. *Inventing the Dream: California through the Progressive Era*. New York: Oxford University Press, 1985.

Steffens, Lincoln. "Rudolph Spreckels: A Business Man Fighting for His City." *The American Magazine* 65 (November 1907–April 1908): 390–402.

———. *Upbuilders*. Seattle: University of Washington Press, 1968. Originally published 1909.

Stephenson, Lynda Rutledge. *The San Diego Zoo: The First Century, 1916–2016*. San Diego: Zoological Society of San Diego, 2015.

Strathman, Theodore. "Land, Water, and Real Estate: Ed Fletcher and the Cuyamaca Water Company, 1910–1926." *Journal of San Diego History* 50, no. 3 (Summer/Fall 2004): 124–44.

Street, Richard Steven. *Beasts of the Field: A Narrative History of California Farmworkers, 1769–1913.* Palo Alto CA: Stanford University Press, 2004.

Strickland, Jeffery G. "Ethnicity and Race in the Urban South: German Immigrants and African-Americans in Charleston, South Carolina, during Reconstruction." PhD diss., Florida State University, 2003.

Tate, E. Mowbray. *Transpacific Steam: The Story of Steam Navigation from the Pacific Coast of North America to the Far East and the Antipodes, 1867–1941.* New York: Cornwall Books, 1986.

Taylor, Albert Pierce. *Under Hawaiian Skies: A Narrative of the Romance, Adventure and History of the Hawaiian Islands.* Honolulu: Advertiser Publishing, 1922.

Teel, Leonard Ray. *The Public Press, 1900–1945: The History of American Journalism.* Westport CT: Praeger Publishers, 2006.

Trimble, William F. *Hero of the Air: Glenn Curtiss and the Birth of Naval Aviation.* Annapolis MD: Naval Institute Press, 2010.

Tucker, Alfred. "San Diego Free Speech Fight." In *Fellow Workers and Friends: I.W.W. Free-Speech Fights as Told by Participants,* edited by Philip S. Foner, 128–41. Westport CT: Praeger, 1981.

Vandegrift, Rolland A., and Lloyd Mecham. "San Diego City: History of Meeting Place of 1920 Grand Parlor, N.S.G.W." *The Grizzly Bear* 26, no. 6 (April 1920): 1–3, 42.

Veil, Charles. *Adventure's a Wench: The Autobiography of Charles Veil, As Told to Howard Marsh.* New York: W. Morrow and Company, 1934.

Walshok, Mary Lindenstein, and Abraham J. Shragge. *Invention and Reinvention: The Evolution of San Diego's Innovation Economy (Innovation and Technology in the World Economy).* Stanford CA: Stanford University Press, 2014.

Whitney, Craig R. *All the Stops: The Glorious Pipe Organ and Its American Masters.* New York: Public Affairs, 2004.

William Clayton Papers (Collection 256). Library Special Collections, Charles E. Young Research Library, UCLA.

Wright, John Lloyd. *My Father, Frank Lloyd Wright.* New York: Dover Publications, 2012.

Yenne, Bill. *San Francisco Beer: A History of Brewing by the Bay.* Charleston SC: American Palate, 2016.

Zinn, Howard. *A People's History of the United States, 1492–Present.* New York: HarperCollins, 2003.

INDEX

Page numbers in italics indicate illustrations.

Ach, Henry, 63

Active (tugboat), 103

Adams, Austin, 105, 312

Adams, Henry Austin, xxv, 151, 311

African Americans, 3, 140

Agua Caliente racetrack (Tijuana), 331

Alameda (ship), 34, 40, 73

Albany Brewery (San Francisco), 5–7

Albany Malt House (San Francisco), 6

Albright, Harrison, 149–50, 194, 209,
    230, 233, 236–37, 259

Alert (tugboat), 103

Alessio, John Salvatore, 331–32

Alexander & Baldwin, 65

Allen, Frank P., 257

Allen, William, 28

"Aloha 'Oe" (song), 75

American Board of Commissioners
    for Foreign Missions, 23

American Congregationalists, 22–23

American Electric Railway Associa-
    tion, 296

American Federation of Labor (AFL),
    248, 250

American flag, 34, 36, 126, 156

American Guild of Organists, 151

American National Bank, 237

American Sugar Refining Company,
    55, 329

Amstar Corporation, 329–30

Anbang Insurance Group, 333

Anthony, Susan B., 118

anti-German sentiment, 211–12

Anti-Saloon League, 180

Aptos resort (Aptos CA), 15–16, 127

Arlington National Cemetery (Arling-
    ton VA), 333

Asher, Josephus Marion, 297

Atchison, Topeka and Santa Fe Rail-
    way, 41

Austin, Basil, 260

Austin, John, 260

Austin Organ Company, 260

Australia, 35–36, 270–72

Australia (ship), 35–36, 210

Babcock, Arnold Edgar, 43, 137

Babcock, Elisha Spurr, Jr., 42–44, *46*, 47–48, 50–53, 122, 127–29, 134–37, 180, 204, 275

Babcock, Graham Elisha, 43, 129, 136–38

Babcock, Isabella Graham, 43, 48, 137, 205

Bacon, John, 320–21

Bailey, Ida, 232

Baker, Livingston, 94

Baker & Hamilton, 94

de Balboa, Vasco Núñez, 256

Balboa Park, xx, xxvi, 256–59, 263, 265, 267–68, 279, 298, 320, 324

Bank of America, 326

Bank of Coronado, 190

Barnes, Charles, 306

Barnes, W. H. L., 259

Barnum, P. T., 269

Barrymore, John, 234

Barrymore, Lionel, 234

Baum, L. Frank, 204

Bayonet Constitution (Hawai'i), 32, 70–71

Bay Sugar Refinery Company (San Francisco), 7, 9–10

Beam, Willard Metcalf, 167

"Bear" (dog), 203

Beaton, Welford, 212–14

Belcher, David Holbrook (great-grandson), 342

Belcher, Frank Garrettson, 237, 341–42

Belcher, Frank J., Jr., 237, 259, 303

Belcher, Frank "Mike" Garrettson, Jr. (great-grandson), 342

Belcher, Harriet Spreckels (grand-daughter), *193*, *195*; Adolph and, 312; birth of, 93; in Coronado, 291; death of John and, 316–17;

education of, 197; John and, 194, 196, 200–201; later life of, 341–42; marriage of, 237, 269–70; memo-rial to John and, 320; on selling off of sugar refining interests, 329–30

Belcher, John Garrettson, 201

Belcher, John "Garry" (great-grandson), 341–42

Belcher, Lyn (great-granddaughter), 330

Belcher, Virginia Caroline (great-granddaughter), 342

Bellomo, Lorenzo, 241–42

Belmont Amusement Park, 323, 335

Belmont School for Boys (San Fran-cisco), 95, 163, 168

Benedict, Julius, 24

Bennington (warship), 104, 192, 278

Berger, Henry, 24

Bierce, Ambrose, 106

"Big Four," 90, 173–74

Bishop, Bernice Pauahi Pākī (Hawai-ian Princess), 31

Bishop, Charles Reed, 31

Bishop Bank (Hawai'i), 31

Bishop Estate (Hawai'i), 31

Bishop Hall (Hawai'i), 31

Bishop Museum (Hawai'i), 31

Bishop Street (Hawai'i), 31

Bishop Trust (Hawai'i), 31

Blackstone Group LP, 333–34

Blue, Victor, 284

Bohemian Club, 106–7, 151

boom, 42–44

Borthwick, Anderson, 240, 259, 324

Boyer, Fred, 197

Boy Scouts, 212

Brainerd, Erastus, 239, 243

Breakwater (ship), 148

brewery business, 5–6

Broadway Amusement Company, 190

Brobeck, George, 202

Brommer, Anna, 157

Brooklyn Navy Yard (New York), 282

Brown, Joe E., 234

Brunn, Harold, 340

Brunton, George, 294–95

Bryan, William Jennings, 110

bull terrier, 85

Burge, James, 206

Burge's Barber Shop (Coronado), 206

bust, 50–52

Cabrillo, Juan Rodríguez, 264

Cahill, Arthur James, 140, 202

California (warship), 279

California Building, 264

California Palace of the Legion of
    Honor, 312–13

California Railroad Commission, 137

California Sugar Refinery (San Fran-
    cisco), 10–11, *11*, 14–15, 21, 33

California Tower, 264

Call Building (San Francisco), *98*,
    100–101, 146, 148, 151, 210, 230

Campbell, Roy, 319–20

Camp Coronado, 128

Camp Kearny Army Base, 285

Carnegie, Andrew, 79, 242–43, 260

"Carnegieism," 243

Carrizo Gorge, 222, 328

Carter, John Oliver, 74

Caruso, Enrico, 234

Casa de Estudillo, 126–27, 258

Case, Mary Adele, 165–67, 294

Central Pacific Railroad, 90

Chaplin, Charlie, 208

Charleston SC, 1–3

Chase, Levi, 48

"Chicago style," 236, 326

Chicago Union Club, 49

Chief's Children's School (Hawai'i), 22

"Chinatown," 246

C&H Sugar, 329

Church, Frederick A., 298

cigars, 63, 79, 104–5, 108, 141

Cincinnati (ship), 166

Citizens Traction Company, 123

City Park, 256

Civil War, 5–6, 20–21, 85

Clark, Frank King, 165

Claus Spreckels (ship), 33

Claus Spreckels Building (San Fran-
    cisco), 101. *See also* Call Building
    (San Francisco)

Clayton, Augusta Dohrmann, 130

Clayton, Emily, 130, 241

Clayton, William "Bill," 130–31, 136,
    216, 241–42, 277, 295, 328

Cleveland, Grover, 104

Clinton, Bill, 332–33

CNL Hospitality Properties Inc., 333

coal wharf, 43, 45, 228

Coffee, James V., 161

College of California (Oakland), 9

Collett, Josephus, 47

Collier, David "Charlie," 254, 257

Committee on Foreign Investment in
    the United States, 333

commodore, 104, 109

Compagnon, Frederick, 49–50

Condemnation Act, 283

Coney Island, 298

Congregationalists, 9, 23

Connor, Kathy, 337

Consmiller, Adele Siebein, 82

Continental Illinois Bank, 259

Cook, James (captain), 20

Cooke, Amos Starr, 22
Coolidge, Calvin, 310
Coos County OR, 148
Copley, Ira Clifton, 325, 336
Corbett, James John, 108
Corona (ship), 104
Coronado CA, *182*; ferries to, 191–93, *193*; Glorietta Bay, 149–51, *150*; incorporation of, 179–82; liquor and, 180, 182–89; liquor license controversy, 182–89; motion pictures in, 210–11; North Island, 275–78, *276*, 280, 282–83, 286, 323; Spreckels development in, 47–53, 148–51; Tent City, 127–31, 133, 148, 184–86, 188, 193, 209–10. *See also specific location or topic*
Coronado Bank Building, 190
Coronado Beach Company, 45, 47, 51–53, 179–81, 183, 189, 192, 230, 277, 282
Coronado Belt Line, 53
Coronado Country Club, 207–8
Coronado Eagle and Journal, 185–87, 209, 316
Coronado Ferry Company, 47, 192, 231, 335
Coronado Hotel Company, 231
Coronado Library, 209–10
Coronado Mercury, 180
Coronado National Horse Show, 341
Coronado Railroad Company, 47, 135, 230, 335
Coronado Strand, 185, 189, 277
Coronado Water Company, 47, 135, 231, 323, 335
Cost Plus World Market, 327
COVID-19 pandemic, 334
Cowan, Arthur S., 277

Crocker, Charles, 173
"Cuddle Pie" (koala bear), 272
Cummins, John Adams, 73
Curry, Charles Forrest, 174
Curtiss, Glenn, 275–77
Cuyamaca Club, 231
Cuyamaca Lake, 134
Cuyamaca Water Company (CWC), 137–38
Cypress Lawn Memorial Park (San Francisco), 306, 320, 340

Daniels, Josephus, 279–82
Dante Sanitarium (San Francisco), 340
Darroch, William, 275, 284, 317
Davidson, Ed, 241
Davidson, Gilbert "G." Aubrey, 254
Del Monte Hotel (Monterey CA), 129
Dewey, George, 162
de Young, Charles, 30
de Young, Michael, 30, 100, 229
Diamond Carriage Company, 232
Dilworth, Etta Elise Siebein, 82, 306
Dilworth, Read G., 328
Dixon, Maynard, 140
Dodge, John "Jack" Mason, 233
Domino Sugar, 329
Dore, Susan Oroville Spreckels "Orey" (sister-in-law), 56, 72, 156
Dow Jones Average, 55
Dowling, M. J., 112
Drewisch, Miss (teacher), 197
Dulzura Conduit, 323
Dwan, Allan, 210

earthquake in San Francisco (1906), 145–46, *147*, 148
Edison, Thomas, 204–5, 210, 263
Edison Company, 210

Edward (Prince of Wales), 198, 200
Eighteenth Amendment, 188
El Cortez Hotel, 238, 326
electrification, 205
Elettra (yacht), 200
Ellyson, Theodore, 277
El Patio, 212–14
"Emma Spreckels Building" (San Francisco), 66–67
Estudillo, José María, 126–27
Eucalyptus Reservoir, 134
European spas, 141–42, 303–4

Fairbanks, Douglas, 208
family disputes, 58–64, 155–61
Faulconer, Tom, 270–72
Fearless (tugboat), 103–4
Federal Sugar Refining, 65
feminism, 119, 252, 310
ferries, 191–93, *193*
Ferris, Jean, 157, 311
Ferris, John, 157
Firestone, Harvey, 204
First Congregational Church of San Diego, 319
First National Bank, 237, 259
First National Bank Building, 230, 237
Fletcher, Ed, 135–38, 169, 171, 301, 303
Flood, James Clair, 108
Foltz, Clara, 118
Ford, Henry, 204, 263
Fort Rosecrans, 104, 263, 278
Forward, John, 217, 262
"Foster Father of San Diego," 227–30

Gage, Henry Tifft, 115–17
Gandy, Newton S., 184–85
Gaslamp Quarter, 228
General Petroleum, 290

George Eastman Museum (Rochester), 337
George V (United Kingdom), 198
German Friendly Society, 2
Giant Dipper (roller coaster), 298
Gibson, Emily Augusta Siebein, 82
Gibson, Walter D. K., 107, 338
Giffard, Walter M., 225
Gill, Irving J., 257–58
Glorietta Bay (Coronado), 149–51, *150*
Glorietta Bay Inn (Coronado), *193*, 336
Golden Construction Company, 336
Golden Gate Park (San Francisco), 259, 261
Golden West Hotel, 230, 236–37, 323
Gold Rush, 4–5, 246
golf, 208–9
Goodhue, Bertram Grosvenor, 256–58, 264, 267, 298
Goodman, Barney, 331
Grande Hall Convention Center (Coronado), 332
Grant, Ulysses S., 235
Grant, Ulysses Simpson "Buck," Jr., 215, 235–36, 254
Great White Fleet, 278–79
Greenwood Cemetery, 320
Griffis, Townsend "Tim," 182
Griffis, Wilmot, 182–83, 185–86, 188
grocery business, 5–6
Grossmont Reservoir, 137
Gruendike, Jacob, 45, 47

Hackfeld, Heinrich, 15–16
Hackfeld and Company, 15
Hagenbeck, Carl, 268
Hall, Henry, 101
Halliday, Eliza, 44
Halstead, A. S., 281

Hamilton, Alexander "Alec," 94–95, *147*, 148, 168, 194, 330, 336, 338, 341

Hamilton, Grace Alexandria Spreckels (daughter), *25*, 148, 163, *207*, *305*, 330; birth of, 24; childhood of, 81; Claus Jr. and, 168; in Coronado, 194, 206; Glorietta Inn and, 336; in Hawai'i, 32; illness of John and, 145; inheritance of, 338; later life of, 340–41; marriage of, 92–96; social life of, 85–89; women's suffrage and, 119; yachts and, 34

Hamilton, Robert M., 94

Hamlin-Evans, Katharine, 182

Hanna, Marcus "Mark" Alonzo, 111

Hannam, William H., 225–26, 339

Hanover (Kingdom), xi–xii, 1–2, 12, 17, 22

Hardy, Charles S., 171–72

Hardy, George L., 171

Harland, Wilfred Charles, 183–84, 190

Harriman, Edward Henry, 173, 216–19

Hartupee, Joseph, 180–81

Haugh, Jesse L., 334

Havemeyer, Henry Osborne "H. O.," 55–58

Hawai'i: annexation of, 73–74; Bayonet Constitution, 32, 70–71; electrification in, 205; *haole*, 21; John in, xxiii, xxv, 15, 20–24, 26–29, 32; missionaries in, 22–23, 70–71; ouster of Spreckels family from, 71–72; overthrow of monarchy in, 70–71; Pearl Harbor, 21; polo in, 208; purchase of lands in, 26–27; Reciprocity Treaty of 1875, 21; Royal Hawaiian Orchestra, 24; sale of Spreckels holdings in, 61; shipping lines and, 33–34; Spanish-American War and, 73–74; sugar refining in, 20–22, 27–30, 33, 61–62, 64–65, 225

Hawaiian Commercial & Sugar Company, 27, 33, 61–62, 65

Hawaiian Gazette, 32

Hawaiian League, 32

Hawai'i Polo Club, 208

Hayward, Harry, 233

Hearst, William Randolph, 229, 263

Hearst's Magazine, 239, 243

Henderson, Dick, 185

Hennige, Jacob, 10

Hight, Iretta, 66

Hilton Hotels and Resorts, 333–34

Hinde, Charles T., 44

Hoboken NJ, 17, 20

Holbrook, Charles, 92

Holbrook, Henry "Harry," 92–93, 148, 269

Holbrook, Merrill & Stetson, 92

Holly Sugar Corporation, 330

Holmes, George, 182–83, 295

Home Federal Savings, 326

Homestead Steel Strike (Pennsylvania 1892), 242–43

Honolulu HI, 21, 23

Honolulu Music Hall, 38

Honolulu Opera House, 165

Hopkins, Mark, 173

Horton, Alonzo Erastus, 42, 126, 217, 226–27, 230

Hotel del Coronado (Coronado), xxii, *49*, 130, 275, 279, 297, 317; amenities of, 203–7; building of, 48–53, 135; celebrations at, 189–90, 202–3; Claus Jr. and, 294; COVID-19 pandemic, closure due to, 334; David Kalākaua at, 69–70; distinction of, 127–28; following

San Francisco earthquake, 148;
Lillian and, 285; liquor at, 180;
motion pictures and, 210; motor
cars at, 87; Prince of Wales at, 198;
sale of, 330–34; speech of John at,
299, 306; streetcars to, 193
Hotel Metropole, xx
Hotel San Diego, 230, 235–36, 240,
323, 326
Hotel Wolcott (New York), 166
Huntington, Collis P., 90, 173, 287
Huntington, Willard B., 287
Hutton, Arthur, 311
Hutton, Emma Claudine Spreckels
(sister): 155; Anna and, 157; birth
of, 14; death of, 311; elopement of,
66–67; family disputes and, 64; in
Hawai'i, 142; illness of John and,
72; inheritance of, 160–61; reconciliation with family, 152–53; social
life of, 86; yachts and, 34

Imperial Sugar Company, 330
"Impossible Railroad," 218–19, 328
Industrial Revolution, 13
Industrial Workers of the World
(IWW) ("Wobblies"), 245–52
Ingle, Heber, 47
'Iolani Palace (Honolulu), 23, 31, 38,
72, 77, 205
Irwin, William G., 225
Isthmus of Panama, 253

Jackson, Helen Hunt, 127, 258
James, Henry, 100
J. D. and A. B. Spreckels Securities
Company, 102, 324–25, 330, 334
J. D. Spreckels and Brothers Com-
pany, 33, 43, 101, 239

"Jiggs" (dog), 194
John "Demented" Spreckels, xxvi, 213
John D. Spreckels Building, 230, 237–
38, 316, 326
John D. Spreckels Cup, 208
John L. Stephens (ship), 5
Johnson, Hiram W., 174
Johnson, William Templeton, 183, 189
"John Sugarcane," 29
Jolson, Al, 234

Kalākaua, David (Hawaiian King):
Bayonet Constitution and, 32, 70–
71; in California, 15, 69–70, 108;
Claus and, 29–32, 175; concerts
and, 24; gambling of, 31; 'Iolani
Palace and, 23–24; John and, 75;
raising of, 22, 29–32; Spreckels
family and, 34
Kalloch, Isaac Milton, 30
Kalloch, Isaac Smith, 30
Kamehameha IV (Hawaiian King), 28
Kapi'olani (Hawaiian Queen), 24, 32
Karlsbad (spa), 303–4
Karl Weinhold Library (Berkeley),
83, 209
Kaths, Hertha "Babe," 339
Kearny, Dennis, 246
Ke'elikōlani, Ruth (Hawaiian Prin-
cess), 26–27
Kelham, Grace Alexandria Spreckels
Hamilton (granddaughter), 95,
193, 194, *305*
Kendrick, Rodney, 292
Kettner, William "Bill," 266–67, 279, 283
Kimball, Frederick, 140
Kipling, Rudyard, 105
Kipp, Sylvester, 187
koala bears, 271–72

Kofoid, Charles Atwood, xxii, 39
KSL Recreation Corporation, 333
KSL Resorts, 333
Kücken, Friedrich Wilhelm, 24

Lamb Players, 191
Lamstedt, Hanover, 1, 4
Lawrence, Maurice "Larry," 332–33
League Island Navy Yard (Philadelphia), 282
Leake, Sam, 115–17
Légion d'Honneur (Paris), 312
Lewis, David (great-grandson), 341
Lewis, Mary Leila "Happy" Hamilton (granddaughter), 95, 194, 305, 330
Lewis, Peter DeLancy, 330
Lili'uokalani (Hawaiian Queen), xxiii, 26, 32, 39, 70–75, 142–43, 321
Lincoln-Roosevelt League, 170, 173
Lindbergh, Anne Morrow, 201
Lindbergh, Charles, 201
Lindbergh, Charles Augustus, 201
Lipton Tea Company, 264
liquor, 180, 182–89, 223
liquor license controversy, 182–89
Littlefield, Jacquelyn Mae, 235, 326
Livermore, Mary, 85
London, Jack, 95, 106
Lorini, Raffaele, 205–6, 316, 319
Los Angeles Times Building (Los Angeles), 248
Lowe Enterprises, 333
Lower Otay Dam, 134–35, 323
Lubin, Sigmund "Pop," 211
Luce, Edgar A., 170–71
Lugosi, Bela, 234
Lurline (yacht), 42, 84, 273
Lusitania (ship), 280, 285

MacArthur, Arthur, 279
MacTaggart, Ross, 337
Maharaja of Kapurthala, 263
mail transport, 35–37
Maine (warship), 73, 210
Mangels, Claus, 2, 4–5, 10
Mann Act, 339
Marconi, Guglielmo, 200
Marconi Company, 200
Marine Firemen's Union, 246
Marine Ways & Drydock Company, 135
Mariposa (ship), 34, 36
Marston, George White, 125, 171–72, 215, 217–18
Marx, Karl, 245
Mason, Samuel E., 308
Matson Navigation Company, 327
McKinley, William, 73–74, 89, 110–12, 114–15, 156
McNab, James, 255
McNamara, James, 248
McNamara, John, 248
Menlo Circus Club (Menlo Park CA), 341
Mercy Hospital, 308, 339
Messner, Arthur, 206
Metzger, Louis B., 326
Mexican-American War, 126
Mexican Revolution, 219, 249–50
Misener, Robert Scott, 337
Miss Head's School (Berkeley), 168
Mission Beach, 296–99, 308
Mission Beach Amusement Center, 297–99, 323, 335
Mission Beach Company, 296, 308
Mission Beach Orchestra, 298
Mission Cliff Gardens, 125–26, 256, 259
Miss Mason's School (Tarrytown NY), 168

Moon, Delos, 168
Moon, Frank, 168
Moore, Edward Clarence, 340
Morena Dam, 135, 138, 323
Morgan, J. P., 79
Morning Call, 99–100, 112, 114
Morvich (race horse), 102
motion pictures, 210–11
motor cars, 87–88
Mountbatten, Louis (Lord), 198
Murray, James, 137
music, 24, 259–62, 312, 335–37

Napa Stock Farm (Napa), 102, 163
National City and Otay Railroad
    Company, 231
Native Sons of the Golden West
    Building (San Francisco), 88
Naval Board of Appraisal, 281
Naval Training Station, 279–80
Navy, 73, 103–4, 266, 273, 276–85, 297
Navy SEALS, 333
Neill, Phillip, 330
New Jersey, 17, 20
newspapers, 139–40, 324–25
New Zealand, 35–36
Nicolini, David, 275
Nineteenth Amendment, 119, 310
Norbloom, Robert A., 330–31
Northcutt, Jonde, 188

Oceanic Steamship Company, xxiv,
    34–36, *35*, 56, 60, 62, 84, 91, 144–
    45, 226, 239, 246, 323, 326–27
Ocean Towers (Hotel del Coro-
    nado), 332
Ohio (battleship), 89
Ohio (yacht), 140
Ohlmeyer, Henry, 130–31

oil industry, 290
"Old Guard" Republicans, 169, 171
Old Town, 126–27
Olmsted, John Charles, 256
Olmsted Brothers, 256–58
Olympic Club, 108–9
Otay Water Company, 135
Otis, Harrison Gray, 250

Pa'auhau Plantation (Hawai'i),
    61–62, 64
Pacific Advertiser, 71
Pacific Club, 107–8
Pacific Commercial Advertiser, 26, 139, 145
Pacific Heights (San Francisco), 78–
    81, *80*
Pacific Mail Steamship Company,
    15–16, 35
Pacific-Union Club, 106–8, 231
Pajaro Valley Consolidated Railroad
    Company, 239, 323
Pajaro Valley Railroad, 217
Palace Hotel (San Francisco), 91, 129
Palace of the Legion of Honor (San
    Francisco), 341
Panama–California Exposition (1914–
    1915), 184, 233, 236, 248–49, 255–58,
    261–67, 273, 279–80, 298, 324
Panama–California Exposition Com-
    pany, 254
Panama Canal, 233, 249, 253–55, 263–
    65, 282, 310–11
Panama–Pacific International Expo-
    sition (San Francisco 1915), 255,
    263, 267
Paris, France, 83
Parkinson, Donald, 238
Parkinson, John, 238
Pavlova, Anna, 234

Pearl Harbor (Hawai'i), 21
Pendleton, Joseph H., 266
Pennell, Robert, 48
Perkins, George Clement, 112, 114
Peterson, J. Harold, xx
philanthropy, 242–44
Philippines, annexation of, 114–15
piano, 75, 151
Pickford, Mary, 210, 234, 275
pipe organs, 259–61, 312, 335–37
Playfair, James, 337
Plaza de Panama, 263
Point Loma Railroad, 295
polo, 182–83, 207–8
Polytechnic High School (San Francisco), 84
Polytechnic Institute (Hanover), 12–14
Pope, Ida May, xxiii
Porter, Ross, 335–36
Powell, William, 234
Preparedness Movement, 212
Prieto Quemper, Juan, 221
Princeville Plantation Company, 28
Prior, Frank, 298
"progressives," 169–71, 174
Prohibition, 188–89, 211, 223
railways, 122–23, 125, 133, 215–23, 327–29. *See also specific railway*
Ramona (ferryboat), 320
Ramona (novel, Jackson), 127, 258
Ramona (yacht), 192
"Ramona's Marriage Place," 127, 258
Red Cross, 148, 191
Reichter, C. M., 157
Reid, James, 48–49, 79–80, 99, 261
Reid, Merritt, 48–49, 79–80, 99, 261
Reid, Watson, 48–49, 79–80, 99
Reliance (tugboat), 103
Relief (tugboat), 103, 192

Renown (yacht), 198, 200
Republican Party, 100, 109–15, 117, 139–40, 144, 169–71, 174, 236, 310
Riordan, Patrick, 91
Risdon Iron Works, 192
Ritter, William Emerson, xxii
Robinson, William E., 134
Rockefeller, John D., 55, 79, 216, 243, 285
Rogers, Will, 234
Rooke, Emma Kalanikaumaka'amano (Hawaiian Queen Consort), 28–29
Roosevelt, Franklin Delano, 266, 279
Roosevelt, Theodore, 115, 175, 186, 212, 216, 263, 265–66, 278–79
Rosario (ship), 33
Ross, Charlie, 201
Royal Hawaiian Orchestra, 24
Royal Inn (Coronado), 184–85
Royal School (Hawai'i), 22

sailing. *See* yachts
St. John, Vincent, 251
St. Markus Kirche (San Francisco), 81, 155–56
Salinas Valley, 97, 99
Salvation Army, 244
Samuels, Fred S., 327
San Diego CA: African Americans in, 140; as "bankrupt village," 121–22; boom in, 42–44; Broadway, 229, 229–30; bust in, 50–52; Chamber of Commerce, 215, 254; collapse of land boom in, 50–52; D Street, 228–29; Eastern Railroad Committee, 215, 217; infrastructure in, 121–22; land boom in, 41–42; Metropolitan Transit Development Board, 328; as part of Mexico, 126; railways in, 122–23, 125, 133;

Save Our Heritage Organization (SOHO), 325; water in, 134–39. *See also specific location or topic*

San Diego Advertising Club, 241

San Diego and Coronado Ferry Company, 53, 135, 295, 308, 323

San Diego and Coronado Transfer Company, 135, 323

San Diego & Arizona Eastern, 328

San Diego & Arizona Railroad Company, 239

San Diego & Arizona Railway (SD&A), 173, 215–23, 222, 249, 297, 323, 327–29

San Diego–Coronado Bay Bridge, 332

San Diego Electric Railway Company (SDERy), 122–23, *124*, 125, 135, 239, 295–96, 308, 323, 334

San Diego Evening Tribune, 139–40, 229–30, 248, 251, 324–25

San Diego Flume Company, 134, 137

San Diego Land and Town Company, 52

San Diego Light & Fuel Company, 239

San Diego Pipe Organ Company, 336

San Diego & Southeastern Railway Company, 239

San Diego Street Car Company, 122–23

San Diego Sun, 133, 139–40, 170, 176–77, 248, 250–51, 266, 325

San Diego Transit System, 334

San Diego Union, 69, 135, 139–40, 176–77, 229–30, 248–49, 251–52, 258, 302–3, 324–25

San Diego Zoo, xxvi, 268–72, 280

San Francisco CA: earthquake (1906), 145–46, *147*, 148; Golden Gate Park, 259, 261; Howard Street, 77–78, 146, 156; John in, xxv, 5–7; Mission District, 77–79, 99,

146; Pacific Heights, 78–81, *80*; Panama–Pacific International Exposition (1915), 255, 263, 267; Spreckels Temple of Music, 259, 261; Union Square, 162

San Francisco and San Joaquin Valley Railway, 217

San Francisco Call, 64, 71, 79, 99–102, 110–11, 115–19, 139–40, 145, 202, 229–30, 235, 247

San Francisco Chronicle, 30, 63–64, 99–100, 118–19, 162

San Francisco Republican Club, 109–15

San Francisco Sugar Refinery, 6

San Francisco Yacht Club, 42

San Mateo Electric Railway Company, 130

Santa Cruz Railroad, 16, 217

Santa Fe (tugboat), 104, 192

Santa Fe Railway, 43–44, 52, 215

Schoberg, Wendell, 336

Schonewald, George, 129–30

Schumann-Heink, Ernestine, 191, 306

Scott Misener Steamships, 337

Scripps, Edward Willis, *132*; death of, 325; newspapers and, 133, 139, 189; politics and, 266–67; rivalry with John, 170, 176–77, 242, 254–55, 257, 295, 303; "Wobblies" and, 248, 250

Scripps, Ellen Browning, 242–43, 252, 254, 256, 268

Scripps Institution of Oceanography, xxii

Security Savings Bank and Trust Company, 232

Seeley, George, 289

Seghers, John B., 49

Sehon, John L., 170–73

Serra, Junipero, 126

Shaw, Victor, 117

Sherman Silver Purchase Act, 109–10

Ship Owners' Protective Association, 247

shipping lines, 15–16, 33–40, 42–43, 326–27. *See also specific ship*

Shortridge, Charles Morris, 99–100, 112–14, *113*, 118

Shortridge, Samuel, 118, 188–91, 262, 287

show dogs, 85

Siebein, Caroline, 20, 82

Siebein, John, 20

Siebein, Louis J., 82

Siebein, Minnie, 82

Sierra (ship), 270–71, 327

Sigma Alpha Epsilon (fraternity), 89

Silver Strand Road (Coronado), 188

Silver Strand Theatre (Coronado), 190–91

Skinner, Ernest M., 312

Skinner Organ, 312

slavery, 3

Smythe, William, 171

"Snuggle Pot" (koala bear), 272

social clubs, 103–9, *106*

Sonoma (ship), 271, 327

Southern California Mountain Water Company, 134–37, 172, 249, 323

Southern Minnesota Beet Sugar Cooperative, 330

Southern Pacific Railroad, 41, 115, 170, 173–74, 216–18

Southern Pacific Transportation Company, 328

Spalding, Albert, 254

Spanish-American War, 73–74, 114, 281

Spencer, Wallis Warfield, 200

Spreckels, Adolph Bernard (brother), 7, *8*, 14, 133, 246, 324, 329; in business, 33,

43, 52, 102–3, 122, 142, 225–26; Claus Jr. and, 168; in Coronado, 129–30; David Kalākaua and, 69; death of, 312–13, 315; family disputes and, 59–64, 155–58, 160–61; in Hawai'i, 27; illness of John and, 144; marriage of, 161–63; railways and, 216; reconciliation with family, 152–53; Rudolph and, 317

Spreckels, Adolph Bernard, II (grandson), 91, *193*, 194, 287, 291, 338

Spreckels, Adolph Bernard, Jr. (nephew), 162

Spreckels, Adolphus "Claus" Johann (father), xxiv, *8*, 91, 129, *143*; death of, 155–56; early life and career of, 1–7, 9–11; in Hawai'i, 21–24, 26–27, 31–32, 69–72, 142–43; Jack and, 84–85, 290; John and, 12–13; Lillie and, 93; nervous breakdown of, 14–16; newspapers and, 139; politics and, 112–14, 174; reconciliation with family, 151–55; retirement of, 144; in San Francisco, 78–79, 97, 99–100; San Francisco earthquake and, 146; on Southern California, 53; strokes, 141–43; as "Sugar King," xi, xxiv, 26–27, 55–58, 142, 151, 156; sugar refining and, 55–67; trial of, 30–31; will of, 154–58, 160–61; yachts and, 34

Spreckels, Alma de Bretteville, 161–63, 168, 312, 324–25, 329

Spreckels, Alma Emma (niece), 162–63

Spreckels, Anna Christina Mangels (mother), 7, *159*; David Kalākaua and, 69; death of, 158; early life of, 2–4; family disputes and, 64; in Hawai'i, 22, 24, 142–43; Lili'uokalani and, 72; Lillian and, 304; loss of children, 57; reconciliation with family,

152–55; in San Francisco, 78–79; San Francisco earthquake and, 146; will of, 160–61; yachts and, 34

Spreckels, Anna Gesina (sister), 14

Spreckels, Barbara Ellis "Tookie" (granddaughter), 194, *196*, 198, 291, 321, 340

Spreckels CA (company town), 97, 99

Spreckels, Carol Ellis (great-granddaughter), 340

Spreckels, Claire (granddaughter), 194, *196*, 206, 340

Spreckels, Claudine (niece), 152, *153*

Spreckels, Claus Augustus "Gus" (brother), 14, 27, 33, 56–65, 72, 152–58, 160–61, 318

Spreckels, Claus, Jr. (son), 25, *207*, 270, 291–92, *293*, 299; birth of, 26; childhood of, 81; in Coronado, 194, 206; disappointment of John in, 316; divesting of power, 308–10; illness of John and, 148; inheritance of, 338; John on, 301; later life of, 339–40; Lillian and, 303–4; marriage of, 167–68; memorial to John and, 320; mischief and, 95–96; pipe organ and, 259, 335–36; Prince of Wales and, 198; problems of, 292, 294–96; romantic involvement of, 163, *164*, 165–67; social clubs and, 107; social life of, 87; speech by, 240

Spreckels, Claus "Junior," Jr. (grand-son), 194, *196*, 197, 270, 291, 304, 306, 340

Spreckels, Dorothy Constance (niece), 162

Spreckels, Edith Marie Huntington (daughter-in-law), 90–92, 173, 194, 287–88, 290–92, 311

Spreckels, Edward H. (brother), 14

Spreckels, Eleanor (niece), 152, *153*

Spreckels, Eleanor "Nellie" Jolliffe (sister-in-law), 65, 152, *153*

Spreckels, Ellis Ethel Moon (daughter-in-law), 198, *199*, 206, 270, 294, 304; children of, 194; in Coronado, 188; inheritance of, 339–40; marriage of, 167–68; memorial to John and, 320; Prince of Wales and, 197, 200; show dogs and, 203

Spreckels, Frank "Frankie" Leslie (grandson), 194, *196*, 197, 206, 270, 291, 304, 340

Spreckels, Geraldine Anne (grand-daughter), 194, 288, 291–92, 338

Spreckels, Henry (brother), 4, 7, 14

Spreckels, Howard (nephew), 152, *153*

Spreckels, Jack (grandnephew), 197

Spreckels, John Diedrich, *xxi, 8, 18, 83, 193, 314*; Adolph and, 102–3, 162–63; Balboa Park and, 256–58; biography of, xxv, 311–12; birth of, 3; children of, 24, 25, 26, 81–96; Claus Jr. and, 165–67; on collapse of land boom, 50–51; in Coronado, 45, 47–53, 148–51; Coronado Beach Company and, 45, 47; criticisms of, xxiv–xxvi; David Kalākaua and, 69; death of, 318–20; death of father and, 155–56; decline of, 315–18; development along Broadway and, 227–38; disinheritance of, 154–55, 160–61; dismantling of empire, 323–38; education of, 7, 9, 12–13; Emma and, 66; as employer, 238–41; family disputes and, 61–64, 155–61; as "Foster Father of San Diego," 227–30; in Germany, 12–13; golf and, 208–9; grandchildren of, 200–203; in Hawai'i, xxiii, xxv, 15,

Spreckels, John Diedrich (*cont.*)
20–24, 26–29, 32; in Hoboken, 17, 20;
Hotel del Coronado and, 49, 203–7;
illness of, 144–45; Jack and, 288–91;
as John "Demented" Spreckels, xxvi,
213; as "John Sugarcane," 29; legacy
of, 342–43; libel charges against,
115–17; Lili'uokalani and, 72–75; loss
of siblings, 14; loyalty of, 241–42; mail
transport and, 35–37; marriage of, 20;
memorial for, 320–21; Mission Beach
and, 296–99; motor cars and, 87–88;
newspapers and, 139–40; in New York,
4, 7, 17; North Island and, 275–78,
286; as "Opa," *193*, 194, 196; Panama–
California Exposition and, 261–67;
philanthropy and, 242–44; politics
and, 169–77; polo and, 182–83, 207–8;
pranks and, 201–3; Prince of Wales
and, 198, 200; railways and, 215–23;
recuperation of, 148–51; relocation
to California, 4–5; Republican Party
and, 109–15, 169–71, 174; rivalry with
Scripps, 170, 176–77, 242, 254–55,
257, 295, 303; sailing and, 83–84; San
Diego Zoo and, 268–70; in San Francisco, xxv, 5–7, 77–83, *80*; *San Francisco
Call* and, 99–102; San Francisco earthquake and, 145–46, 148; shipping
lines and, 15–16, 33–40, 42–43; show
dogs and, 85; social clubs and, 103–9;
speech by, 299–303; Spreckels Organ
Pavilion and, 259–61; strikes and,
245–52; "sugar daddy," 162; as "Sugar
Prince," 11, 42; sugar refining and, 7,
11, 14–15, 17, 27–29; tugboats and, 103–
5; as "Uncle John," 189–92; wartime
appropriation of property of, 280–83;
water and, 134–39; wharves and,
43–45; will of, 338–39; "Wobblies"
and, 245–52; women's clubs and, 117–
19; yachts and, 273–75, 283–85

Spreckels, John Diedrich, III (grandson), 91–92, *193*, 194, 287, 291, 338

Spreckels, John Diedrich "Jack," Jr.
(son), 25, 96, 136, *207*, 311, 320;
birth of, 26; in business, 91–92;
childhood of, 81; Claus Jr. and,
168; in Coronado, 194, 206; death
of, 287–92, 294; education of,
84–85; inheritance of, 338; Lillian
and, 306; marriage of, 89–91, *90*;
railways and, 216; social clubs and,
107; social life of, 87

Spreckels, Lillian Caroline Siebein
(wife), *19*, 65, 93, *307*, 320; children of, 81–82, 96; Claus Jr. and,
165–67, 294; in Coronado, 148–50,
194, 270; courtship of, 17; death
of, 303–4, 306, 308, 310, 315, 318;
ferries and, 191; generosity of, 285–
86; in Hawai'i, 23–24, 143; illness
of John and, 144–46; Lili'uokalani and, 72, 75; marriage of, 20;
memoriam to, 339; Prince of Wales
and, 198; in San Francisco, 77, 80;
social life of, 86–88; speech by, 241;
tugboats and, 103; yachts and, 84

Spreckels, Louis Peter (brother), 14

Spreckels, Marie (granddaughter),
91, *193*, 194, 198, 287, 291, 311, 338

Spreckels, Peter (uncle), 4–5, 10

Spreckels, Rudolph (brother), 14,
34, 57, 61–65, 73, 146, 152–58, *153*,
160–61, 317–18

Spreckels, Rudolph, Jr. (nephew), 152

Spreckels, Syida Wirt (daughter-in-
law), 194, 288–92

Spreckels Bank (Honolulu), 71, 75
Spreckels Beet Sugar Company, 239
Spreckels Brothers Commercial Company, 43–45, 135, 239
Spreckels Oil Company, 290
Spreckels Organ Pavilion, xx, 259–62, 262, 264, 266–67, 320, 324, 335–36
Spreckels Organ Society (SOS), 335–36
Spreckels Security Company Building, 190
Spreckels Sugar Company, 144, 225, 329–30
Spreckels Sugar Company, Incorporated, 330
Spreckels Theatre, xx, 230–36, 231, 252, 323, 326
"Spreckelsville," 27, 33, 97
Spreckels Wharf, 44, 52, 327
"Square Deal," 186–87
Standard Oil, 290
Stanford, Leland, 173
Stanford Convalescent Home for Children, 341
Stanford University, 84–85, 89–90, 92
Stanton, Elizabeth Cady, 118
Steffens, Lincoln, 97, 154
Steinbeck, John, 99
Stetson, James, 146
Stevenson, Adlai, 104
Stevenson, Robert Louis, 106
Stewart, Humphrey John, 151, 260, 263, 270, 320–21, 335
Stingaree District, 228
Story, Addie, 47
Story, Adella B. Ellis, 45, 48
Story, Edward, 47
Story, Frank, 47
Story, Hampton Lovegrove, 45, 47, 50–52, 122, 127, 180, 204

Story, James, 47
Story, Marion Lydia Fuller, 45
Story, Robert, 47
Strategic Hotels & Resorts Inc., 333
strikes, 245–52
strokes, 141–44, 163, 312
sugar beets, 10
"sugar daddy," 162
"Sugar King," xi, xxiv, 26–27, 55–58, 142, 151, 156
"Sugar Prince," 11, 42
sugar refining: 9–11; in Hawai'i, 20–22, 27–30, 33, 61–62, 64–65, 225; John and, 6–7, 11, 14–15, 17; selling off interests in, 329–30; Sugar Trust, battle with, 55–58. See also specific company
Sugar Trust, 55–58, 60, 63–64, 246
Sullivan, John L., 108
Sultan's Harem, 264
Swanson, Gloria, 208
syphilis, 103, 162–63, 312, 324

Taft, William Howard, 209, 255, 263
Taylor, William Desmond, 211
Temple of Mirth, 264
Tent City (Coronado), 127–31, 133, 148, 184–86, 188, 193, 209–10
Tent City Café, 129
Texas Pacific Railway, 227
Tiedemann, Ernest R., 331
Tiedemann, Hans, 318, 331, 336
Tijuana, Mexico, 188, 211, 331
Tijuana & Tecate Railway, 328
Tingley, Katherine, 150
Titus, Harry Lewis, 136, 216
Townsend, Eveline "Kitty," 39
Travelers Insurance Company, 333
Triad Amphibian (plane), 276

Tucker, Albert, 252
tugboats, 103–5
Twain, Mark, 106

Union Building, 192, 230–31, 236, 238, 241, 250, 323, 325
Union Club, 107–8
Union Iron Works, 104–5
Union Pacific Railroad, 216
Union Station, 221
Union-Tribune Publishing Company, 323
United States Navy, 278–80
United States Polo Association, 208
United States Refinery (New York), 7
University of California, Berkeley, 9, 83, 92, 209
University of California, San Diego, xxii
Upper Otay Dam, 323
U.S. Grant Hotel, 236, 303, 326
U.S. Steel Company, 245

Valentino, Rudolph, 208
Vanderbilt, Cornelius, 216
Vanderwort, Charles T., 197
Van Dyke, Theodore S., 134
Van Ness, James, 78–79
Veil, Charles Herbert, 288–89, 291
Venetia (yacht), 188–89, 200–201, 210, 253, 273–75, 274, 278–81, 283–85, 292, 310–11, 315–17, 319–20, 337–38
Ventura (ship), 327
Vigilant (tugboat), 103
von Tesmar, Frank, 190
voting rights, 119, 310

Wadham, James E., 251
Wakefield, Franklin W., 287, 291
Wangenheim, Julius, 183, 234, 257, 265
Ward, Martin Luther, 243, 321

Warfield, Richard Henry, 89
wartime appropriation of property, 280–83
Washburn Preparatory School (San Jose), 168
The Wasp, 90, 94
water, 134–39
Watson, Thomas Palmer, 66–67, 86
Wegeforth, Harry, 268–70
Wegeforth, Lillian "Lillie" Caroline Spreckels (daughter), 25, 96, 207, 291, 329; birth of, 24; childhood of, 81; Claus Jr. and, 168; in Coronado, 194, 206; illness of John and, 148; inheritance of, 338; later life of, 341–42; marriage of, 92–93, 269–70; memorial to John and, 320; pipe organ and, 336; social life of, 84–89; yachts and, 200
Wegeforth, Paul, 194, 268–70
Weinhold, Karl, 82–83
Western Beet Sugar Factory (Watsonville), 10, 97
Western Sugar Refinery Company (San Francisco), 27, 239, 323, 329
wharves, 43–45, 327
White Motor Company, 87
Wilde, Louis J., 125
Wilde, Oscar, 106
Wilhelm II (German Kaiser), 79
Williams, May, 244
Williams, Ted, xxvi, 243–44
William Warren School (Menlo Park CA), 197
Wilson, Charles Burnett, 39–40
Wilson, Johnny, 39–40
Wilson, Virginia "Lyn," 201, 330
Wilson, Woodrow, 219–20, 263, 266, 280, 282–83

Winslow, Carleton, 258, 261
Winter, Carrie, xxii–xxiii, 38–39, 86
"Wobblies," 245–52
women's clubs, 117–19
women's suffrage, 119, 310
Wooley, H. M., 62
World War I, 175, 211–12, 219, 259, 280–83
Wright, Frank Lloyd, 237
Wright, John Lloyd, 237

yacht clubs, 109
yachts, *83*, 83–84, 273–75, 283–85, 337–38. *See also specific yacht*

Zealandia (ship), xxii, 35, 37
Zimmerman, Arthur, 280
Zimmerman Telegram, 280
Zipf, Richard F., 336–37
zoo, xxvi, 268–69, 271–72, 280
Zoological Society, 268